Frommer's®

5th Edition

Seattle & Portland

by Karl Samson with Jane Aukshunas

Eileen + Greg
Best Wishes for the
Great Pacific NW!

Steve Smith
Jan 2005

Macmillan • USA

For my wife, Jane, who followed me down the Oregon trail.

ABOUT THE AUTHORS

Karl Samson and **Jane Aukshunas,** husband and wife travel-writing team, make their home in the Northwest, where they've never been able to decide which city they like best, Seattle or Portland. Together they also cover the rest of Washington and Oregon for Frommer's, and Karl is also the author of *Outside Magazine's Adventure Guide to the Pacific Northwest* (which is published by Frommer's).

MACMILLAN TRAVEL

A Simon & Schuster Macmillan Company
1633 Broadway
New York, NY 10019

Find us online at **www.frommers.com**

ISBN 0-02861670-7
ISSN 1045-9308

Editor: Dan Glover
Production Editor: Jessica Ford
Design by Michele Laseau
Digital Cartography by Peter Bogaty

SPECIAL SALES

Bulk purchases (10+ copies) of Frommer's and selected Macmillan travel guides are available to corporations, organizations, mail-order catalogs, institutions, and charities at special discounts, and can be customized to suit individual needs. For more information write to Special Sales, Macmillan General Reference, 1633 Broadway, New York, New York 10019.

Manufactured in the United States of America

Contents

List of Maps

AN INVITATION TO THE READER

In researching this book, we discovered many wonderful places—hotels, restaurants, shops, and more. We're sure you'll find others. Please tell us about them, so we can share the information with your fellow travelers in upcoming editions. If you were disappointed with a recommendation, we'd love to know that, too. Please write to:

Frommer's Seattle & Portland, 5th Edition
Macmillan Travel
1633 Broadway
New York, NY 10019

AN ADDITIONAL NOTE

Please be advised that travel information is subject to change at any time—and this is especially true of prices. We therefore suggest that you write or call ahead for confirmation when making your travel plans. The authors, editors, and publisher cannot be held responsible for the experiences of readers while traveling. Your safety is important to us, however, so we encourage you to stay alert and be aware of your surroundings. Keep a close eye on cameras, purses, and wallets, all favorite targets of thieves and pickpockets.

WHAT THE SYMBOLS MEAN

✪ Frommer's Favorites

Our favorite places and experiences—outstanding for quality, value, or both.

The following abbreviations are used for credit cards:

AE	American Express	EURO	Eurocard
CB	Carte Blanche	JCB	Japan Credit Bank
DC	Diners Club	MC	MasterCard
DISC	Discover	V	Visa
ER	enRoute		

FIND FROMMER'S ONLINE

Arthur Frommer's Outspoken Encyclopedia of Travel (www.frommers.com) offers more than 6,000 pages of up-to-the-minute travel information—including the latest bargains and candid, personal articles updated daily by Arthur Frommer himself. No other Web site offers such comprehensive and timely coverage of the world of travel.

Greater Seattle Orientation

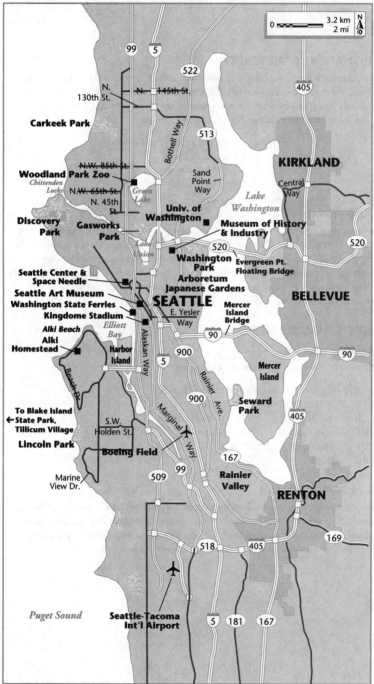

0 — 3.2 km / 2 mi

N

99 **5**

522

405

N. 130th St. — N. 145th St.

Carkeek Park

Bothell Way

513

KIRKLAND

N.W. 85th St.

Woodland Park Zoo

Chittenden Locks

N.W. 65th St.

N. 45th St.

Sand Point Way

Central Way

Lake Washington

Green Lake

Univ. of Washington

Discovery Park

Gasworks Park

Museum of History & Industry

Lake Union

520

520

Washington Park

Evergreen Pt. Floating Bridge

Seattle Center & Space Needle

Seattle Art Museum

Arboretum

Japanese Gardens

BELLEVUE

Washington State Ferries

Kingdome Stadium

SEATTLE

E. Yesler Way

Mercer Island Bridge

Alki Beach

Alki Homestead

Elliott Bay

90

Alaskan Way

5

Harbor Island

900

Mercer Island

90

To Blake Island State Park, Tillicum Village

Beach Dr.

Marginal Way

Rainier Ave.

Seward Park

405

S.W. Holden St.

Lincoln Park

Boeing Field

509

99

167

Rainier Valley

RENTON

169

Marine View Dr.

518

405

Puget Sound

5 **181** **167**

Seattle-Tacoma Int'l Airport

1-0877

Introducing Seattle

Y ou can get a latte almost anywhere in the country these days, and it's been years since Tom Hanks was sleepless in Seattle. Grunge music has lost its preeminence and Seattle's fringe theater is looking a bit frayed around the edges. Martinis are replacing the Northwest microbrews that helped reacquaint the nation with the flavor of real beer, and the flavors of Asia have replaced those of the Northwest on restaurant menus all over the city.

Could it be that the shine has worn off the Emerald City? Don't bet on it. Seattle may have stepped out of the national limelight for the moment, but in 1996, *Conde Naste Traveler, Travel and Leisure, Money, Fortune,* and the American Society of Travel Agents all ranked this city among the top 10 cities in the U.S. to live in or visit. Seattle-ites would love it if companies would quit publishing such polls, but the accolades continue to roll in year after year. Sure the city has its problems—high housing costs, traffic congestion to rival San Francisco's, and a penchant for spending tax dollars on sports arenas rather than on education or street repairs—but when the sun is setting across Puget Sound and the great snowy bulk of Mount Rainier is glowing salmon pink in the waning light, it's almost impossible not to order up a double tall skinny latte and enjoy the show.

1 Frommer's Favorite Seattle Experiences

- **Taking in the Sunset from the Waterfront.** On a clear summer day, the setting sun silhouettes the Olympic Mountains on the far side of Puget Sound and makes the view from the Seattle waterfront truly memorable. Try the rooftop park at the Bell Street Pier or Myrtle Edwards Park at the north end of the waterfront.
- **Riding a Ferry Across Puget Sound.** Sure you can spend $20 for a narrated tour of the Seattle waterfront, but for a fraction of that you can take a ferry to Bremmerton or Bainbridge Island and see not just Elliott Bay but plenty more of the Sound. Keep an eye out for porpoises, orca whales, and bald eagles.
- **A Day at Pike Place Market.** Breakfast at Le Panier, espresso at the original Starbucks, lunch at Cafe Campagne, a martini at the Pink Door, dinner at Chez Shea, live jazz at the Patti Summers Cabaret or Celtic music at Kells, and a nightcap at Il Bistro. Between stops on this rigorous itinerary you can people-watch, listen to street musicians, and shop for everything from fresh salmon to tropical fruits to magic tricks to art glass to live parrots.

- **Relaxing Over a Latte in a Cafe.** When the rain and gray skies finally get to you, there is no better prescription (short of a ticket to the tropics) than a frothy latte in a cozy cafe. Grab a magazine and just hang out until the rain stops (maybe sometime in June).

- **Wandering Around Fremont.** This quirky neighborhood considers itself the center of the universe; it's really just a bit off center. Retro clothing and vintage furniture stores, cafes, a brewery, a great flea market, and the city's best public art make this the most eccentric neighborhood in Seattle.

- **Attending a Show at the Fifth Avenue Theatre.** This historic theater was designed to resemble the imperial throne room in Beijing's Forbidden City. Can you say ornate? Nothing else in Seattle compares, including the show on stage.

- **Going to the Spring Flower and Garden Show.** Each spring gardening madness descends on the Washington State Convention and Trade Center during the nation's third largest flower-and-garden show. There are more than five acres of garden displays and hundreds of vendors.

- **Trying to Decide Which Performances to Attend at Bumbershoot.** It isn't often that you can agonize about picking one great music performance over another, but that's just what you have to do at the annual Labor Day music and arts extravaganza known as Bumbershoot. Whether your tastes run to Grieg or grunge you'll have plenty of choices.

- **Riding the Monorail.** Though the ride is short, covering a distance that could easily be walked in about a half hour, the monorail provides a different perspective on the city. The retro-futurist transport, built for the Seattle world's fair in 1962, ends at the foot of the Space Needle.

- **A Morning at Volunteer Park.** Whether the day is sunny or not, this park on Capitol Hill is a great spot to spend a morning. You can relax in the grass, study Chinese snuff bottles in the Seattle Asian Art Museum, marvel at the orchids in the park's conservatory, or simply enjoy the great view of the city from the top of the park's water tower.

- **A Day at the Zoo.** The cages are almost completely gone from this big zoo, replaced by spacious animal habitats that give the residents the feeling of being back at home in the wilds. Zebras gallop, brown bears romp, river otters cavort, elephants stomp, orangutans swing. The levels of activity here make it clear that the animals are happy with their surroundings.

- **Strolling Through the Arboretum in Spring.** Winters in Seattle may not be long but they do lack color. So, when spring hits, the sudden bursts of brightness it brings are reverently appreciated. There's no better place in the city to appreciate the spring floral displays than at the Washington Park Arboretum.

- **Walking, Jogging, Biking, or Skating a Seattle Path.** There are several paved trails around Seattle that are ideal for pursuing any of these sports. The trail around Green Lake is the all-time favorite, but the Burke-Gilman Trail, the trail along the western shore of Lake Washington, the trail along Alki Beach, and the trail through Myrtle Edwards Park at the north end of the Seattle waterfront are all equally good choices.

- **Sea Kayaking on Lake Union.** Lake Union is a very urban body of water, but it has a great view of the Seattle skyline, and you can paddle right up to several waterfront restaurants. For more natural surroundings, you can paddle to the marshes at the north end of the Washington Park Arboretum.

- **A Walk at a Waterfront Park.** Seattle abounds in waterfront parks where you can gaze out at distant shores, wiggle your toes in the sand, or walk through a remnant patch of old-growth forest. Some of our favorites include Discovery Park, Seward Park, Lincoln Park, and Golden Gardens Park.

2 The City Today

Once a sleepy backwoods town run by Boeing and big timber companies, Seattle has in recent years become one of the gateway cities of the Pacific Rim, forging new trading links with Japan and the rest of Asia. As trade with Asia has grown in national importance, so have the fortunes of this city in the upper left corner of the nation. With its newfound role as an international trading center, Seattle has made the leap from a city of regional importance to one of international stature.

Though Seattle's fortunes once rode on the wings of Boeing passenger jets, today the city has managed to diversify its economy enough so that it no longer must suffer the economic pendulum swings of the airline and aerospace industries. Once layoffs at Boeing could cripple the city, but today Boeing's importance has been diluted by software giant Microsoft, which is headquartered just east of Seattle on the far shore of Lake Washington. Computer whiz kid Bill Gates, the richest man in America, and his Microsoft Corporation, which with its Windows software has become the most important software manufacturer in the world, have given the Seattle area a new economic diversity.

In its newfound role as international trading center, Seattle has been rapidly adopting all the trappings of a major metropolitan area. New construction is going on all over the city. The waterfront and the Belltown area have for several years been in the throes of extensive development as new piers and new high-rise condominiums have transformed these downtown neighborhoods from run-down industrial districts into the hottest urban residential areas in the city. With more and more people moving into downtown Seattle, it is not surprising that stores and restaurants have been springing up to meet the needs of these new residents. Big-name national stores and restaurants such as Banana Republic, NIKETOWN, Planet Hollywood, and two restaurants by famed chef Wolfgang Puck have moved into town, and in 1998, the new Nordstrom flagship store should be opening in the former Frederick and Nelson department store building.

However, it is not just in the sphere of retail and culinary consumption that the city has been expanding. In 1997, three Seattle museums—the Henry, the Frye, and the Burke—underwent extensive renovations and expansions. Ground was also broken for the Music Experience museum of rock 'n' roll, which was inspired by Seattle resident and Microsoft cofounder Paul Allen's obsession with Jimi Hendrix, who was also from Seattle. By 1998 there will also be a new symphony hall, Benaroya Hall, located adjacent to the Seattle Art Museum. Plans are also on the drawing board to build a new and much larger Seattle Aquarium.

Despite the controversies surrounding public tax dollars being spent to construct new stadiums for both the Seattle Seahawks football team and the Seattle Mariners baseball team, most Seattleites are happy that their teams will be staying put for a while. The Seattle Supersonics NBA basketball team also got a new arena this past year (without controversies), and women's professional basketball arrived in the form of the American Basketball League's Seattle Reign.

While Seattle is growing more cosmopolitan by the minute, it is the wildness of the Northwest that has attracted many of the city's residents. The sparkling waters of Elliott Bay, Lake Union, and Lake Washington surround this city of shimmering skyscrapers, and forests of evergreens crowd the city limits. Everywhere you look, another breathtaking vista unfolds. With endless boating opportunities and beaches and mountains within a few hours' drive, Seattle is ideally situated for the active lifestyle that is so much a part of life in the Northwest.

Few other cities in the United States are as immersed in the outdoors aesthetic as Seattle. The Cascade Range lies less than 50 miles to the east of downtown Seattle, and across Puget Sound stand the Olympic Mountains. It is to these lands that Seattleites head throughout the year. In the spring, summer, and fall, the forests and mountains attract hikers, mountain bikers, anglers, and campers, and in winter the ski areas of Snoqualmie Pass and Stephens Pass attract downhill and cross-country skiers.

Though impressive mountains line both the city's eastern and western horizons, a glance to the southeast on a sunny day will reveal the city's most treasured sight. Mount Rainier, a 14,410-foot-tall dormant volcano, looms so large and unexpected that it demands attention. When "The Mountain is out," as they say here in Seattle, Seattleites head for the hills.

However, as important as The Mountain is to Seattle, it is water that truly defines the city's character. To the west lies Elliott Bay, an arm of Puget Sound; to the east is Lake Washington; and right in the middle of the city there is Lake Union. Seattle claims the highest per capita private boat ownership of any city in America. These pleasure craft range in size from regally appointed yachts to slender sea kayaks. So popular is boating in this city that the opening day of boating season is one of Seattle's most popular annual festivals.

However, despite the city's affinity for its nearby natural environment, Seattle is best known as the coffee capital of America. To understand Seattle's coffee addiction, it is necessary to study the city's geography and climate. Seattle lies at a latitude of almost 50° north, which means that winter days are short. The sun comes up around 7:30am and goes down as early as 4:30pm and is frequently hidden behind leaden skies. A strong stimulant is almost a necessity to get people out of bed and through the gray days of winter. Seattleites love to argue over which cafe in town serves the best coffee (and the answer isn't always Starbucks, despite this company's massive expansion across the country).

Seattle's popularity and rapid growth, though it has brought fine restaurants, a new art museum, rock-music fame, and national recognition of the city's arts scene, has not been entirely smooth. The streets and highways have been unable to handle the increased traffic load and commuting has become almost as nightmarish as in California, from whence so many of the city's recent transplants fled (partly due to the traffic congestion). With roads growing ever more crowded and the cost of living continuing to rise, Seattle may not be the Emerald City it once was, but it remains a city of singularly spectacular setting. To stand in a park on Queen Anne Hill at sunset and gaze out at the city skyline, Puget Sound, and Mount Rainier in the distance is to understand why Seattleites love their city despite its flaws.

3 A Look at the Past

Dateline

- 1792 Capt. George Vancouver of the British Royal Navy explores Puget Sound.
- 1841 Lt. Charles Wilkes surveys Puget Sound and names Elliott Bay.

continues

Seattle got a late start in U.S. history. Although explorers had visited the region as early as the late 18th century, the first settlers didn't arrive until 1851. Capt. George Vancouver of the British Royal Navy—who lent his name to both Vancouver, British Columbia, and Vancouver, Washington—had explored Puget Sound as early as 1792. However, there was little to attract anyone permanently to this remote region. Unlike Oregon to the south, Washington had little rich farmland, only acres and acres of forest. It was this seemingly endless supply of wood that finally enticed the first settlers.

The first settlement was on Alki Point, in the area now known as West Seattle. Because this location was exposed to storms, within a few years the settlers moved across Elliott Bay to a more protected spot, the present downtown Seattle. The new location for the village was a tiny island surrounded by mud flats. Although some early settlers wanted to name the town New York—even then Seattle had grand aspirations—the name Seattle was chosen as a tribute to Chief Sealth, a local Native American who had befriended the newcomers.

In the middle of town, on the waterfront, the first steam-powered lumber mill on Puget Sound was built by Henry Yesler. It stood at the foot of what is now Yesler Way, but what for many years was simply referred to as Skid Road, a reference to the way logs were skidded down from the slopes behind town to the sawmill. Over the years Skid Road developed a reputation for its bars and brothels. Some say that after an East Coast journalist incorrectly referred to it as Skid Row in his newspaper, the name stuck and was subsequently applied to derelict neighborhoods all over the country. To this day, despite attempts to revamp the neighborhood, Yesler Way attracts the sort of visitors one would expect, but it is also in the center of the Pioneer Historic District, one of Seattle's main tourist attractions.

By 1889 the city had more than 25,000 inhabitants and was well on its way to becoming the most important city in the Northwest. On June 6 of that year, however, 25 blocks in the center of town burned to the ground. By that time the city, which had spread out to low-lying land reclaimed from the mud flats, had begun experiencing problems with mud and sewage disposal. The fire gave citizens the opportunity they needed to rebuild Seattle. The solution to the drainage and sewage problems was to regrade the steep slopes to the east of the town and raise the streets above their previous levels. Because the regrading lagged behind the rebuilding, the ground floor of many new buildings wound up below street level. Eventually these lower-level shops and entrances were abandoned when elevated sidewalks bridged the space between roadways and buildings. Today sections of several abandoned streets that are now underground can be toured (see "Good Times in Bad Taste" in chapter 6 for details).

- **1851** The first white settlers arrive in what will become West Seattle's Alki Point.
- **1852** These same settlers move to the east side of Elliott Bay from Alki Point, which is subject to storms.
- **1853** Washington Territory is formed.
- **1864** The transcontinental telegraph reaches Seattle, connecting it with the rest of the country.
- **1866** Chief Sealth, for whom Seattle is named, dies and is buried across Puget Sound at Suquamish.
- **1875** Regular steamship service begins between Seattle and San Francisco.
- **1889** The Great Seattle Fire levels most of downtown.
- **1893** The railroad reaches Seattle.
- **1897** The steamer Portland arrives from Alaska carrying more than a ton of gold, thus starting the Yukon gold rush.
- **1907** Pike Place Market is founded.
- **1916** William Boeing launches his first airplane from Lake Union, beginning an industry that will become Seattle's lifeblood.
- **1940** The Mercer Island Floating Bridge opens.
- **1962** The Century 21 exposition is held in Seattle and the famous Space Needle is erected.
- **1971** Starbucks Coffee is founded in Seattle.
- **1977** Seattle is called the most livable city in America.
- **1982** Seattle ranked as the number-one recreational city.
- **1990** Metro bus tunnel, a sort of subway for buses, opens beneath downtown Seattle.
- **1992** Seattle Art Museum moves from Volunteer Park to a controversial new downtown building.

continues

■ 1995 Seattle citizens vote not to tax themselves to build a new baseball stadium for the Seattle Mariners (the state legislature overrides Seattle voters and comes up with tax dollars for stadium construction).

■ 1997 Seattle citizens vote in favor of building a new football stadium to replace the Kingdome.

One of the most amazing engineering feats that took place after the fire was the regrading of Denny Hill. Seattle once had seven hills, but now has only six—nothing is left of Denny Hill. Hydraulic mining techniques, with high-powered water jets digging into hillsides, were used to level the hill, of which only a name remains—Denny Regrade, a neighborhood just south of Seattle Center.

The new buildings went up quickly after the fire, and 8 years later, on July 17, 1897, another event occurred that changed the city almost as much. On that date, the steamship *Portland* arrived in Seattle from Alaska carrying a ton of gold from the recently discovered Klondike goldfields. Within the year Seattle's population swelled with prospectors ultimately heading north. Few of them ever struck it rich, but they all stopped in Seattle to purchase supplies and equipment, thus lining the pockets of Seattle merchants and spreading far and wide the name of this obscure Northwest city. When the prospectors came south again with their hard-earned gold, much of it never left Seattle, sidetracked by beer halls and brothels.

In 1916, not many years after the Wright brothers made their first flight, Seattle residents William Boeing and Clyde Esterveld launched their first airplane, a floatplane, from the waters of Lake Union with the intention of operating an airmail service to Canada. Their enterprise eventually became the Boeing Company, which has since grown to become the single largest employer in the area. Unfortunately, until recently Seattle's fortunes were so inextricably bound to those of Boeing that hard times for the aircraft manufacturer meant hard times for the whole city. In recent years, however, industry in the Seattle region has become much more diversified. Leading the region in its role as high-tech development center is software giant Microsoft, the presence of which has attracted many other computer-related companies. Floatplanes still call Lake Union home, and if you should venture out on the lake by kayak, sailboard, or boat, be sure to watch out for air traffic.

The single most recognizable structure on the Seattle skyline is, of course, the Space Needle. Built in 1962 for Century 21, the Seattle World's Fair, the Space Needle was, and still is, a futuristic-looking observation tower. Situated just north of downtown in the Seattle Center complex that was the site of the World's Fair, the Space Needle provides stupendous views of the city and all its surrounding natural beauty. Over the nearly 40 years since the Space Needle was erected, the skyline it overlooks has changed radically. As the city approaches the 21st century for which the Space Needle was built, its skyline is becoming more and more dominated by towering skyscrapers, symbols of Seattle's ever-growing importance as a gateway to the Pacific Rim.

The 1962 World's Fair was far more than a fanciful vision of the future—it was truly prophetic for Seattle. The emergence of the Emerald City as an important Pacific Rim trading center is a step toward a bright 21st century. The Seattle area has witnessed extraordinary growth in recent years, with the migration of thousands of people in search of jobs, a higher quality of life, and a mild climate. To keep pace with its sudden prominence on the Pacific Rim, Seattle has also been rushing to transform itself from a sleepy Northwest city into a cosmopolitan metropolis. New restaurants, theaters, and museums are cropping up all over the city as new residents demand more cultural attractions. Visitors to Seattle will immediately sense the quickening pulse of this awakening city.

Planning a Trip to Seattle 2

Seattle has in recent years become one of the West Coast's most popular vacation destinations and as its popularity has grown, so too has the need for previsit planning. Before leaving home, you should try to make hotel and car reservations. Not only will these reservations save you money, but you won't have to struggle to find accommodations after you arrive. Summer is the peak tourist season in Seattle, and from June through September downtown hotels are often fully booked for days or even weeks at a time. Consequently, reservations—for hotel rooms, rental cars, or a table at a restaurant—are imperative. If you plan to visit during the city's annual Seafair summer festival in late July and early August, when every hotel in town can be booked up, reservations are especially important.

Oh, yeah, and about that rain. Seattle's rainy weather may be infamous, but Seattleites have ways of dealing with the dreary days. They either put on their rain gear and head outdoors just as if the sun were shining or retreat to the city's hundreds of excellent restaurants and cafes, its dozens of theaters and performance halls, its outstanding museums, its many movie theaters, and its excellent bookstores. They rarely let the weather stand in the way of having a good time, and neither should you.

Although summer is the best time to visit, Seattle offers year-round diversions and entertainment, and because it is still a seasonal destination, hotel rooms here are a real bargain during the rainy months between October and April.

1 Visitor Information

The sources of information listed here can provide you with plenty of free brochures on Seattle, many with colorful photos to further tempt you into a visit.

If you still have questions about Seattle after reading this book, contact the **Seattle–King County Convention and Visitors Bureau,** 520 Pike St., Suite 1300, Seattle, WA 98101-9927 (☎ 206/461-5840; Web site www.seeseattle.org), which operates a Visitor Information Center inside the Washington State Convention and Trade Center, 800 Convention Place, Galleria Level. To find this information center, which is open Monday through Friday from 8:30am to 5pm, walk up Union Street until it goes into a tunnel under the Washington State Convention and Trade Center. You'll see the information center on your left as you enter the tunnel.

Alternatively, you can access the information center from the galleria's main entrance at 725 Pike St.

The convention and visitors bureau also operates a Visitor Information Center at Seattle-Tacoma (Sea-Tac) International Airport (☎ **206/433-5218**). You can't miss it—it's right beside the baggage-claim area (by carousel no. 8). They have brochures on many area attractions and can answer any last-minute questions.

For information on other parts of Washington, contact the **Washington State Tourism Office,** P.O. Box 42500, Olympia, WA 98504-2500 (☎ **800/544-1800 ext. 014,** 206/586-2088, or 360/586-2102).

2 When to Go

CLIMATE

I'm sure you've heard about the climate in Seattle. Let's face it, the city's weather has a bad reputation. As they say out here, "The rain in Spain stays mainly in Seattle." I wish I could tell you that it just ain't so, but I can't. It rains in Seattle—and rains and rains and rains. However, when December 31 rolls around each year, a funny thing happens: They total up the year's precipitation, and Seattle almost always comes out behind such cities as Washington, D.C., Boston, New York, and Atlanta. Most of the rain falls between September and April, so if you visit during the summer, you might not see a drop of rain the entire time. If July in Seattle is just too sunny for you, take a trip out to the Hoh Valley on the Olympic Peninsula. With more than 150 inches of rain a year, this is the wettest spot in the continental United States.

No matter what time of year you plan to visit Seattle, be sure to bring at least a sweater or light jacket. Summer nights can be quite cool, and daytime temperatures rarely climb above the low 80s. Winters are not as cold as in the East, but snow does fall in Seattle.

To make things perfectly clear, here's an annual weather chart:

Seattle's Average Temperature & Days of Rain

	Jan	Feb	Mar	Apr	May	June	July	Aug	Sept	Oct	Nov	Dec
Temp. (°F)	46	50	53	58	65	69	75	74	69	60	52	47
Temp. (°C)	8	10	12	14	18	21	24	23	21	16	11	8
Rain (days)	19	16	17	14	10	9	5	7	9	14	18	20

THE FESTIVAL CITY

Seattleites will hold a festival at the drop of a rain hat and summers here seem to revolve around the city's myriad festivals. To find out what special events will be taking place while you're in town, check the "Tempo" arts-and-entertainment section of the Friday *Seattle Times* or pick up a copy of *Seattle Weekly*. Remember, festivals here take place rain or shine.

SEATTLE CALENDAR OF EVENTS

February

- **Chinese New Year,** International District. Date depends on lunar calendar (may be in January). (☎ **206/382-1197**).
- **Northwest Flower and Garden Show,** Washington State Convention and Trade Center. Massive show for avid gardeners. Mid- to late February (☎ **800/229-6311** or 206/224-1700).

Impressions

. . . on a famous ferry going into famous Seattle, dusk on a November night, the sky, the water, the mountains are all the same color: lead in a closet. Suicide weather. The only thing wrong with this picture is that you feel so happy.

—Esquire magazine

- **Fat Tuesday,** Pioneer Square. Fat Tuesday is Seattle's Mardi Gras festival, which takes place in the streets and bars of the Pioneer Square area. (☎ **888/608-6337** or 206/682-4649). The Tuesday before Ash Wednesday (roughly 6 weeks before Easter).

March

- **Seattle Fringe Festival,** various venues. Avant-garde, experimental, and otherwise uncategorizable plays and theater performances from a wide variety of companies (☎ **206/325-5446**). Early March.

April

- **Cherry Blossom and Japanese Cultural Festival,** Seattle Center. Traditional Japanese spring festival. Late April (☎ **206/684-7200**).

May

- **Opening Day of Boating Season,** Lake Union and Lake Washington. A parade of boats and much fanfare as Seattle boaters bring out everything from kayaks to yachts. First Saturday in May (☎ **206/325-1000**).
- **Seattle International Film Festival,** theaters around town. New foreign and independent films are screened for several weeks. Mid-May to mid-June (☎ **206/ 324-9996**).
- ✪ **Northwest Folklife Festival.** This is the largest folklife festival in the country, with dozens of national and regional folk musicians performing on numerous stages. In addition, craftspeople from all over the Northwest show and sell. There's lots of good food and dancing too. The festival takes place Memorial Day weekend at the Seattle Center. All performances are free (☎ **206/684-7300**).
- **Pike Place Market Festival,** Pike Place Market. A celebration of the market, with lots of free entertainment. Memorial Day weekend (☎ **206/682-7453**).

June

- **Seattle International Music Festival,** Meany Hall, University of Washington and other locations. This is the city's biggest chamber music event of the year. Mid-June (☎ **206/233-0993**).
- **Fremont Street Fair,** Fremont neighborhood. A celebration of the summer solstice with a wacky parade, food, arts and crafts, and entertainment in one of Seattle's favorite neighborhoods. Third weekend in June (☎ **206/633-4409** or 206/547-7440).
- **Out to Lunch,** locations throughout Seattle. Free lunchtime music concerts. Mid-June through early September (☎ **206/623-0340**).

July

- **Fourth of July fireworks,** Elliott Bay and Seattle waterfront. July 4.
- **Wooden Boat Festival,** Lake Union. Wooden boats, both old and new, from all over the Northwest. Races, demonstrations, food, and entertainment. First weekend in July (☎ **206/382-BOAT**).
- **Chinatown/International District Summer Festival,** International District. Features the music, dancing, arts, and food of Seattle's Asian district. Second weekend in July.

What Things Cost in Seattle	U.S. $
Taxi from the airport to the city center	28.00
Bus ride between any two downtown points	Free
Local telephone call	.25
Double at Alexis Hotel (very expensive)	195.00–210.00
Double at Pacific Plaza Hotel (moderate)	80.00–125.00
Double at Seattle City Center Travelodge (inexpensive)	59.00–70.00
Lunch for one at Salty's on Alki (expensive)	25.00
Lunch for one at Queen City Grill (moderate)	12.00
Lunch for one at Emmett Watson's Oyster Bar (inexpensive)	8.00–12.00
Dinner for one, without wine, at Fuller's (expensive)	50.00
Dinner for one, without wine, at Etta's (moderate)	35.00
Dinner for one, without wine, at Belltown Pub (inexpensive)	12.00–20.00
Pint of beer	3.50
Coca-Cola	1.00
Cup of coffee (latte)	1.90
Roll of ASA 100 Kodacolor film, 36 exposures	5.50
Movie ticket	7.00
Theater ticket to Seattle Repertory Theater	10.00–40.00

- **Bite of Seattle,** Seattle Center. Sample offerings from Seattle's best restaurants. Third weekend in July (☎ 206/232-2982).
- ✪ **Seafair.** This is the biggest Seattle event of the year, during which festivities occur every day—parades, hydroplane boat races, performances by the Navy's Blue Angels, a Torchlight Parade, ethnic festivals, sporting events, and open house on naval ships. This one really packs in the out-of-towners and sends Seattleites fleeing on summer vacations. Events take place all over Seattle. Third weekend in July to first weekend in August. Call ☎ 206/728-0123 for details on events and tickets.
- **Pacific Northwest Arts and Crafts Fair,** Bellevue Square shopping mall, Bellevue. This is the largest arts and crafts fair in the Northwest. Last weekend in July (☎ 425/454-4900).

August
- **Chief Seattle Days,** Suquamish. Celebration of Northwest Native American culture across Puget Sound from Seattle. Third weekend in August (☎ 360/598-3311).

September
- ✪ **Bumbershoot, the Seattle Arts Festival.** Seattle's second most popular festival derives its peculiar name from a British term for umbrella—an obvious reference to the rainy weather. Lots of rock music and other events pack Seattle's youthful set into Seattle Center and other venues. You'll find plenty of arts and crafts on display too. Labor Day weekend (☎ 206/281-8111 for the schedule).

October
- **Salmon Days Festival,** Issaquah. This festival in the nearby town of Issaquah (15 miles east of Seattle), celebrates the annual return of salmon that spawn within the city limits. First full weekend in October (☎ 425/392-0661).

December
- **Seattle Christmas Ships,** various locations. Boats decked out with imaginative Christmas lights parade past various waterfront locations. Argosy Cruises offers tours. Throughout December (☎ **206/623-1445**).

3 Tips for Travelers with Special Needs

FOR TRAVELERS WITH DISABILITIES

When making airline reservations, always mention your disability. Airline policies differ regarding wheelchairs and Seeing Eye dogs. Most hotels now offer wheelchair-accessible accommodations, and some of the larger and more expensive hotels also offer TDD telephones and other amenities for the hearing and sight impaired.

The greatest difficulty of a visit to Seattle for anyone who is restricted to a wheelchair is dealing with the city's many steep hills, which rival those of San Francisco. One solution for dealing with downtown hills is to use the elevator at the Pike Place Market for getting between the waterfront and First Avenue. Also, by staying at The Edgewater hotel, right on the waterfront, you will have easy access to all of the city's waterfront attractions and can use the Waterfront Streetcar for getting between the Pike Place Market and Pioneer Square area. Also keep in mind that the downtown bus tunnel, which connects the International District to Westlake Center shopping mall and is wheelchair accessible, can make traveling across downtown somewhat less strenuous.

If you plan to visit Mount Rainier or Olympic National Park, you can avail yourself of the **Golden Access Passport.** This lifetime pass is issued free to any U.S. citizen or permanent resident who has been medically certified as disabled or blind. The pass permits free entry into national parks and monuments.

Rick Crowder of the **Travelin' Talk Network,** P.O. Box 3534, Clarksville, TN 37043-3534 (☎ **615/552-6670** Monday through Friday between noon and 5pm central time), organizes a network for travelers with disabilities. They charge $35 for a directory of people and organizations around the world who can provide firsthand information about chosen destinations.

FOR GAY & LESBIAN TRAVELERS

Seattle is well known as one of the most gay-friendly cities in the country and has a large gay and lesbian community centered around the Capitol Hill neighborhood, just east of downtown. It is here that you will find numerous bars, nightclubs, stores, and bed-and-breakfast inns catering to the gay community. Broadway Avenue, Capitol Hill's main drag, is also the site of the annual Gay Pride March held each year in late June.

The *Seattle Gay News* (☎ **206/324-4297**) is the community's newspaper and is available at gay bars and nightclubs. For a guide to Seattle's gay community, get a copy of the *Greater Seattle Business Association (GSBA) Guide Directory.* It's available at the GSBA's office at 2033 Sixth Ave., Suite 804 (☎ **206/443-4722**). The *Pink Pages,* a free directory to gay- and lesbian-friendly businesses, available at 1122 E. Pike St., Suite 1226 (☎ **206/328-5850**), is another good resource. Both of these publications are available at the **Pink Zone,** 211 Broadway Ave. E. (☎ **206/ 325-0050**), a gay-oriented shop on Capitol Hill.

Beyond the Closet, 518 E. Pike St. (☎ **206/322-4609**), and **Bailey Coy Books,** 414 Broadway Ave. E. (☎ **206/323-8842**), are the gay community's two main bookstores and are good sources of information on what's going on within the community.

❓ Did You Know?

- Woody Guthrie was once arrested for singing on the street in Pike Place Market.
- UPS (United Parcel Service) got its start in the seamy red-light district of Seattle's Pioneer Square area. Where they lost their first parcel is open to speculation.
- The Kingdome is so large that you could turn the Space Needle on its side inside the dome and spin it around like the pointer on a gargantuan game of Twister.
- Rumor has it that Seattleites buy more sunglasses per capita than the citizens of any other American city. Whether this is because people forget where they left their shades the last time the sun was out or because Seattle commuter routes are primarily from east to west and cloudy skies cause more glare than clear skies is open to speculation.
- The only NBA basketball game ever called off on account of rain was scheduled for January 5, 1986, in Seattle.
- The Seattle Public Library loans more books per capita than any other city library in the country.
- Seattle has the highest percentage of bicycle commuters in the nation, with 4,000 to 8,000 people commuting to and from work on bicycles each day. The number, of course, depends on the weather conditions.
- There are more than 200 licensed espresso carts in Seattle/King County.

The **Lesbian Resource Center,** 1808 Bellevue Ave., Suite 204 (☎ **206/322-3953**), is a community resource center providing housing and job information, therapy, and business referrals.

For information on gay and lesbian bars and nightclubs, see "The Bar Scene" in chapter 9. **The Gaslight Inn** is a gay-friendly bed-and-breakfast in the Capitol Hill area; see chapter 4 for details.

FOR SENIORS

When making airline and hotel reservations, always mention that you are a senior citizen. Many airlines and hotels offer discounts. Also be sure to carry some form of photo ID with you when touring Seattle. Most attractions, some theaters and concert halls, tour companies, and the Washington State Ferries all offer senior-citizen discounts. These can add up to substantial savings, but you have to remember to ask for the discount.

If you are planning on visiting either Mount Rainier National Park or Olympic National Park while in the Seattle area, you can save on park admissions by getting a **Golden Age Passport,** which is available for $10 to U.S. citizens and permanent residents age 62 and older. This federal government pass allows lifetime entrance privileges. You can apply in person for this passport at a national park, national forest, or other location where it's honored, and you must show reasonable proof of age.

Also, if you aren't already a member of the **American Association of Retired Persons (AARP),** 601 E. St. NW, Washington, DC 20077-1214 (☎ **800/424-3410**), you should consider joining. This association provides discounts at many lodgings and attractions throughout the Seattle area, although you can sometimes get a similar discount simply by showing your ID.

FOR FAMILIES

Many of the city's hotels allow kids to stay free in their parents' room. Be sure to ask when you contact a hotel. Also, note that most downtown hotels cater almost exclusively to business travelers and don't offer the sort of amenities that will appeal to families—a swimming pool, game room, or inexpensive restaurant. At mealtimes, keep in mind that many of the larger restaurants, especially along the waterfront, offer children's menus. You'll also find plenty of variety and low prices at the Pike Place Market's many food vendors stalls. There's also a food court in Westlake Center shopping mall.

4 Getting There

BY PLANE

The Major Airlines   Sea-Tac Airport is served by about 30 airlines. The major carriers include **Alaska Airlines** (☎ 800/426-0333); **American Airlines** (☎ 800/433-7300); **America West** (☎ 800/235-9292); **Continental** (☎ 800/523-3273); **Delta** (☎ 800/221-1212); **Horizon Air** (☎ 800/547-9308); **Northwest** (☎ 800/225-2525); **Reno Air** (☎ 800/736-6247); **Southwest** (☎ 800/435-9792); **TWA** (☎ 800/221-2000); **United** (☎ 800/241-6522 or 206/441-3700); and **US Airways** (☎ 800/428-4322).

Seaplane service between Seattle and the San Juan Islands and Vancouver and Victoria, British Columbia, is offered by **Kenmore Air** (☎ **800/543-9595** or 206/486-1257), which has its Seattle terminals at the south end of Lake Union and at the north end of Lake Washington.

There is also now helicopter service to Seattle's Boeing Field from Victoria and Vancouver, British Columbia on **Helijet Airways** (☎ **800/665-4354**). The flights, of which there are three a day, take only 35 minutes from Victoria and 90 minutes from Vancouver. The round-trip airfare is $170 between Victoria and Seattle and $299 between Vancouver and Seattle.

Finding the Best Airfare   The way airline ticketing is going these days, finding the best fare on a flight to Seattle is mostly about paying attention to special sales on tickets. If you are flexible about when you fly and start checking with a travel agent or watching the newspapers for sale ads, you may be able to get a bargain on a flight. Any time of year you may be able to save some money on your ticket by shopping the discount ticket brokers that advertise in major newspapers. Also, don't forget to ask for a student or senior discount if either of these happens to apply to you.

If you happen to be flying from another city on the West Coast or somewhere else in the West, check with Shuttle by United, Alaska Airlines, Horizon Airlines, Reno Air, or Southwest. These airlines often have the best fares between western cities.

Also try surfing the Internet for bargains on tickets. Services like America Online list ticket discounts in their travel sections, and airlines are beginning to auction seats that they can't unload otherwise. You can be the beneficiary at greatly reduced fares. Use electronic reservation and tracking services, like Travelocity and EasySabre, to keep abreast of fare changes and give your travel agent and dialing finger a break.

Seattle-Tacoma International Airport   Also known as Sea-Tac, Seattle-Tacoma International Airport (☎ **800/544-1965** or 206/431-4444) is located about 14 miles south of Seattle. It's connected to the city by I-5. Generally, allow 30 minutes for the trip between the airport and downtown, and more during rush hour. When leaving the arrivals loading/unloading area, take the first exit if you are staying near the airport or the second exit if you are headed to downtown Seattle.

Gray Line Airport Express (☎ 206/626-6088) provides service between the airport and downtown Seattle daily from about 4:40am to 10:40pm. This shuttle van stops at the Madison Hotel, Crowne Plaza, Four Seasons Olympic, Sheraton Seattle, Westin Hotel, and the Warwick Hotel. Rates are $7.50 one way and $13 round trip.

Shuttle Express (☎ 800/487-RIDE or 206/622-1424) provides 24-hour service between Sea-Tac and the Seattle, North Seattle, and Bellevue areas. Their rates vary from $13 to $19. You need to make a reservation to get to the airport, but to leave the airport, just give them a call when you arrive. Push 48 on one of the courtesy phones outside the baggage-claim area.

Metro Transit (☎ 800/542-7876 or 206/553-3000) operates three buses between the airport and downtown. It's a good idea to call for the current schedule when you arrive in town. At this writing, **no. 194** operates (to Third Avenue and Union Street or the bus tunnel, depending on the time of day) every 30 minutes weekdays from about 5:30am to 8:30pm and weekends from about 6:30am to 6:30pm. **No. 174** operates (to Second Avenue and Union Street) every 30 minutes weekdays from about 5:30am to 1:20am and weekends from about 6:30am to 1:20am. **No. 184** has two runs from the airport (to Second Avenue and Union Street) in the early morning 7 nights a week. The first bus leaves for the airport at 2:15am and the second leaves at 3:30am. Bus trips takes 30 to 40 minutes depending on conditions. The fare is $1.10 during off-peak hours and $1.60 during peak hours.

A **taxi** into downtown Seattle will cost you about $28. There are usually plenty of taxis around, but if not, call **Yellow Cab** (☎ 206/622-6500) or **Farwest Taxi** (☎ 206/622-1717). The flag-drop charge is $1.80; after that, it's $1.80 per mile.

Flying with Film, Camcorders & Laptops   Traveling with electronic devices and film (exposed or not) can take a little extra time in this age of heightened security. X-ray machines won't affect film up to ASA 400, but you might want to request a visual check (in which the camera is inspected by hand) anyway. A visual check for computers is standard practice in most airports—you'll probably be asked to switch it on, so be sure the batteries are charged. You may use your computer in flight, but not during take-off and landing because of possible interference with cockpit controls. In many cases, airport security guards will also ask you to turn on electronic devices (including camcorders and personal stereos) to prove that they are what they appear to be, so make sure batteries are charged and working for these items as well.

BY CAR

I-5 is the main north-south artery through Seattle, running south to Portland and north to the Canadian border. I-405 is Seattle's east-side bypass and accesses the cities of Bellevue, Redmond, and Kirkland on the east side of Lake Washington. I-90, which ends at I-5, connects Seattle to Spokane in the eastern part of Washington. Wash. 520 connects I-405 with Seattle just north of downtown and also ends at I-5. Wash. 99, the Alaskan Way Viaduct, is another major north-south highway through downtown Seattle; it passes through the waterfront section of the city.

Here are some driving distances from selected cities (in miles):

Los Angeles	1,190
Portland	175
Salt Lake City	835
San Francisco	810
Spokane	285
Vancouver, B.C.	110

BY FERRY

Seattle is served by the Washington State Ferries (☎ 800/84-FERRY in Washington State, or 206/464-6400 in Seattle), the most extensive ferry system in the United States. Car ferries travel between downtown Seattle and both Bainbridge Island and Bremerton (on the Kitsap Peninsula) from Pier 52. A passenger-only ferry to Vashon Island uses the adjacent Pier 50. Car ferries also sail between Fauntleroy in west Seattle and both Vashon Island and the Kitsap Peninsula at Southworth, between Tahlequah at the south end of Vashon Island and Pt. Defiance in Tacoma, between Edmonds and Kingston (on the Kitsap Peninsula), between Mukilteo and Whidbey Island, between Whidbey Island at Keystone and Port Townsend, and between Anacortes and the San Juan Islands and Sidney, British Columbia, on Vancouver Island near Victoria. See "Getting Around" in chapter 3 for fare information.

If you are traveling between Victoria, British Columbia, and Seattle, there are several options available from **Victoria Clipper,** Pier 69, 2701 Alaskan Way (☎ 800/888-2535, 206/448-5000, or 250/382-8100 in Victoria). Throughout the year, a catamaran passenger ferry taking 3 to 5 hours and a high-speed turbo-jet passenger ferry taking only 2 hours make the trip ($79 to $109 round-trip for adults). This latter ferry is the fastest passenger boat in the western hemisphere. The lower fare is for advance-purchase tickets. Some scheduled trips also stop in the San Juan Islands. During the summer months, this company also operates a car ferry, the *Princess Marguerite III,* from Pier 48 in Seattle ($49 one-way for car and drive, $29 for passengers).

BY TRAIN

There is **Amtrak** (☎ 800/872-7245) service to Seattle from Vancouver, British Columbia; Spokane and points east on the *Empire Builder;* and Portland and points south (including San Francisco and Los Angeles) on the *Coast Starlight.* The trains stop at King Street Station (☎ 206/382-4125), Third Avenue South and Jackson Street, near the Kingdome and the south entrance to the downtown bus tunnel. The Waterfront Streetcar also stops near King Street Station.

Several trains run daily between Seattle and both Portland, Oregon, and Vancouver, British Columbia. Portland to Seattle takes about four hours and fares range from $15.50 to $29 one way. Vancouver to Seattle takes about 4 hours and the fare is $19. This route includes a bus segment.

BY BUS

The **Greyhound bus station,** Eighth Avenue and Stewart Street (☎ 800/231-2222 or 206/628-5530), is located a few blocks northeast of downtown Seattle. **Greyhound** bus service provides connections to almost any city in the continental United States. From the bus station it is only a few blocks to several budget chain motels. It's a bit farther to the Hosteling International–Seattle hostel and the Seattle Downtown YMCA, walkable if you don't have much luggage or a free bus ride on a Metro bus.

Gray Line of Seattle (☎ 800/426-7505 or 206/624-5813) also offers scheduled shuttle service between Victoria and Seattle. The trip takes a little more than 8 hours (by way of the San Juan Islands ferry), and the one-way fare is $30 for adults and $15 for children. There is also continuing service to Seattle-Tacoma International Airport. **Quick Shuttle** (☎ 800/665-2111 or 604/244-3744) offers express bus service between Vancouver, British Columbia, and Seattle. The trip takes about 4 hours, and the one-way fare is $28 for adults, $26 for seniors, and $14 for children. It also offers continuing service to Sea-Tac Airport.

3

Getting to Know Seattle

Because it is surrounded on three sides by water, built on six hills, and divided into numerous neighborhoods, Seattle can be a very disorienting city. While most of the city's top attractions are located in the downtown area, there are enough other places of interest, including eclectic neighborhoods, that the city's charms aren't all right in your face. This chapter, which includes information on the city's layout, its neighborhoods, and the basics of how to get around town, should help you to get out and explore enough of the city that you can get a real feel for why Seattle is such a popular city to live in and visit.

1 Orientation

VISITOR INFORMATION

Visitor information on Seattle and the surrounding area is available by contacting the **Seattle-King County Convention and Visitors Bureau,** 520 Pike St., Suite 1300, Seattle, WA 98101 (☎ 206/461-5840; Web site www.seeseattle.org), which operates a **Visitor Information Center** in the Washington State Convention and Trade Center, 800 Convention Place, Level 1, Galleria, at the corner of Eighth Avenue and Pike Street. To find it, walk up Union Street until it goes into a tunnel under the Convention Center. You'll see the information center on your left. Alternatively, you can enter the building from Pike Street. There is also a **Visitor Information Center** in the baggage-claim area at Sea-Tac Airport. It's across from carousel no. 8 (open daily from 9:30am to 7:30pm; ☎ 206/433-5218).

CITY LAYOUT

Although downtown Seattle is fairly compact and can easily be navigated on foot, finding your way by car can be frustrating. The Seattle area has been experiencing phenomenal growth in the past few years, and this has created traffic-congestion problems that must be anticipated. Here are some guidelines to help you find your way around.

Main Arteries & Streets　There are three interstate highways serving Seattle. I-90 comes in from the east and ends downtown. I-405 bypasses the city completely, traveling up the east shore of Lake Washington through Bellevue, Redmond, and Kirkland. The main artery is I-5, which runs through the middle of Seattle. Take the

The Bridges of King County

Ever wish you had the perfect excuse for those mornings when you just can't get out the door soon enough to make it to work on time? Seattleites have got just the excuse: "The bridge was open." With water on three sides, Seattle is a collection of neighborhoods connected by bridges, many of which are drawbridges that open at particularly inconvenient times (such as when you're trying to get across town in a hurry). At times it seems as though the city has a love-hate relationship with its bridges, which are the object of derision, curses, humor, and affection.

"Welcome to the center of the universe," reads a sign on the Fremont Bridge as you drive from the north side of Queen Anne Hill across the Lake Washington Ship Canal and into the funky neighborhood of Fremont. You might just get plenty of time to contemplate this lighthearted sign; this is the busiest drawbridge in the United States. Two blocks away, under the Aurora Avenue Bridge, the Fremont Troll, a huge cement sculpture, attacks a real Volkswagen Beetle.

Seattle likes to boast that its Evergreen Point Bridge, which connects Seattle to Bellevue and Kirkland on the east side of Lake Washington and is one of two floating bridges in the city, is the longest floating bridge in the world. What Seattle doesn't like to tell visitors is that the I-90 Bridge across Lake Washington (the city's second floating bridge), sank in a storm less than a decade ago.

Further afield (and not actually in King County), there are the Hood Canal Bridge and the Tacoma Narrows Bridge, both of which have had their own problems over the years. The former, which connects the Kitsap Peninsula with the Olympic Peninsula, is another of the Northwest's floating bridges. It, too, once sank in a storm. The Tacoma Narrows Bridge spans a southern arm of Puget Sound and, at 2,800 feet long, is one of the largest suspension bridges in the world. Since it doesn't float it shouldn't have any problems, right? Wrong. The original bridge here bucked itself apart back in 1940, only 4 months and 7 days after it opened. It seems the suspension cables resonated in the high winds that blow through the narrows. This resonance caused the main suspension cables to sway up and down until the entire bridge collapsed. In souvenir shops around Seattle, you can even find film clips of "Galloping Gertie," as the bridge was dubbed.

James Street exit west if you're heading for the Pioneer Square area; take the Seneca Street exit for Pike Place Market; or the Olive Way exit for Capitol Hill.

Downtown is roughly defined as extending from the Kingdome on the south to Denny Way on the north and from Elliott Bay on the west to Broadway on the east. Within this area, avenues are numbered, whereas streets have names. The exceptions to this rule are the first two roads parallel to the waterfront. They are Alaskan Way and Western Avenue. Spring Street is one way eastbound, and Seneca Street one way westbound. Likewise, Pike Street is one way eastbound, and Pine Street, one way westbound. First Avenue and Third Avenue are both two-way streets, but Second and Fifth are one way southbound. Fourth Avenue and Sixth Avenue are one way northbound.

To get from downtown to Capitol Hill, take Pike Street or Olive Way. Yesler Way or South Jackson Street will get you over to Lake Washington on the east side of Seattle. If you are heading north across town, Westlake Avenue will take you to the Fremont neighborhood and Eastlake Avenue will take you to the University District. These two roads diverge at the south end of Lake Union.

There is an irreverent little mnemonic device locals use for remembering the names of Seattle's downtown streets, and since most visitors spend much of their time downtown, this little phrase could be useful to you as well. It goes like this: "Jesus Christ made Seattle under protest." What this stands for is all the downtown east-west streets north of Yesler Way and south of Olive Way/Stewart Street—Jefferson, James, Cherry, Columbia, Marion, Madison, Spring, Seneca, University, Union, Pike, Pine.

Finding an Address   After you become familiar with the streets and neighborhoods of Seattle, there is really only one important thing to remember to find an address: Pay attention to the compass point of the address. Downtown streets have no direc-tional designation attached to them, but when you cross I-5 going east, most streets and avenues are designated "East." South of Yesler Way, which runs through Pioneer Square, streets are designated "South." West of Queen Anne Avenue, streets are des-ignated "West." The University District is designated "NE" (Northeast); the Ballard neighborhood, "NW" (Northwest). Therefore, if you are looking for an address on First Avenue South, head south of Yesler Way.

Another helpful hint is that odd-numbered addresses are likely to be on the west and south sides of streets, whereas even-numbered addresses will be on the east and north sides of streets. Also, in the downtown area, address numbers increase by 100 with each block as you move away from Yesler Way going north or south, and as you go east from the waterfront.

Street Maps   Even if the streets of Seattle seem totally unfathomable to you, rest assured that even longtime residents sometimes have a hard time finding their way around. Don't be afraid to ask directions. You can obtain a free map of the city from one of the two Seattle-King County Convention and Visitors Bureau Visitor Infor-mation Centers (see above).

You can buy a decent map of Seattle in most convenience stores and gas stations around the area, or for a greater selection, stop in at **Metsker Maps,** 702 First Ave. (☎ **206/623-8747**).

If you happen to be a member of AAA, you can get free maps of Seattle and Wash-ington State from them, either at an office near you or at the Seattle office, 330 Sixth Ave. N. (☎ **206/448-5353**). They're open Monday through Friday from 8:30am to 5:30pm (Saturday 9am to 1pm in summer).

2 Getting Around

BY PUBLIC TRANSPORTATION

By Bus   The best thing about Seattle's **Metro** (☎ 206/553-3000) bus system is that as long as you stay within the downtown area, you can ride for free between 6am and 7pm. The Ride Free Area is between Alaskan Way (the waterfront) in the west, Sixth Avenue in the east, Battery Street in the north, and South Jackson Street in the south. Within this area are Pioneer Square, the waterfront attractions, Pike Place Market, and almost all the city's major hotels. Two blocks from South Jackson Street is the Kingdome, and 6 blocks from Battery Street is Seattle Center. Keeping this in mind, you can visit nearly every tourist attraction in Seattle without having to spend a dime on transportation.

The Ride Free Area also encompasses the Bus Tunnel, which allows buses to drive underneath downtown Seattle, thus avoiding traffic congestion. The tunnel extends from the International District in the south to the Convention Center in the north, with three stops in between. Commissioned artworks decorate each of the stations, making a trip through the tunnel more than just a way of getting from point A to point B. It's open Monday through Friday from 5am to 7pm, on Saturday from 10am to 6pm (closed on holidays). When the Bus Tunnel is closed, buses operate on surface streets. Because the tunnel is within the Ride Free Area, there is no charge for riding through it, unless you are traveling to or from outside of the Ride Free Area.

If you travel outside the Ride Free Area, fares range from 85¢ to $1.60, depending on the distance and time of day. Keep in mind when traveling out of the Ride Free Area that you pay when you get off the bus. When traveling into the Ride Free Area, you pay when you get on the bus. Exact change is required.

Discount Passes   On Saturday, Sunday, and holidays, you can purchase an All Day Pass for $1.70; it's available on any Metro bus or the Waterfront Streetcar.

By Ferry   Washington State Ferries (☎ **800/84-FERRY** within Washington state, or 206/464-6400) is the most extensive ferry system in the United States, and while these ferries won't help you get around Seattle itself, they do offer scenic options for getting out of town (and cheap cruises, too). From downtown Seattle, car ferries sail to Bremerton and Bainbridge Island. A passenger-only ferry goes to Vashon Island. From West Seattle, car ferries go to Vashon Island and Southworth, which is on the Kitsap Peninsula. One-way fares from Seattle to Bainbridge Island via car ferry (a 60-minute crossing) are $5.90 ($7.10 from mid-May to mid-October) for a car and driver one way, $3.50 for adult car passengers or walk-ons, and $1.75 for seniors and children ages 5 to 11. Car passengers and walk-ons only pay fares on westbound ferries. Fares to from Seattle to Bremerton, Seattle to Vashon Island, Edmonds to Kingston, and Fauntleroy to Southworth (a 35-minute crossing) are the same.

By Water Taxi   In the summer of 1997 a pilot water taxi service was operating on a fixed route between the downtown Seattle waterfront (with stops at Pier 66 and Pier 55) and Seacrest Park in West Seattle. This service was aimed at both commuters and visitors and provided access to the popular Alki Beach and adjacent bike/foot path in West Seattle. The water taxi was running between 6am and 8pm and the fare was $2 each way for adults and $1 for children ages 5 to 12. To see if the water taxi is running when you visit, call **Elliott Bay Water Taxi** (☎ **206/684-0224**).

By Monorail   If you are planning a visit to Seattle Center, there is no better way to get there from downtown than on the monorail. It leaves from Westlake Center shopping mall (Fifth Avenue and Pine Street). The once-futuristic elevated trains cover the 1.2 miles in 90 seconds and provide a few nice views along the way. The monorail leaves every 15 minutes daily from 9am to midnight during the summer; the rest of the year, Sunday through Thursday from 9am to 9pm, on Friday and Saturday until midnight. The one-way fare is $1 for adults, 50¢ for senior citizens and people with disabilities, and 75¢ for children 5 to 12.

By Waterfront Streetcar   Old-fashioned streetcars run along the waterfront from Pier 70 to the corner of Fifth Avenue South and South Jackson Street on the edge of the International District. These streetcars are more tourist attraction than commuter transportation, and actually are much more useful to visitors than are most of the city's buses. Tourist sites along the streetcar route include Pioneer Square, the Seattle Aquarium, Omnidome Film Experience, and Pike Place Market. In summer streetcars operate Monday through Friday from around 7am to around 11pm, departing every 20 to 30 minutes; on Saturday, Sunday, and holidays from around 9am to almost midnight (shorter hours in other months). One-way fare is 85¢ in off-peak hours and $1.10 in peak hours. If you plan to transfer to a Metro bus, you can get a transfer good for 70 minutes. Streetcars are wheelchair accessible.

BY CAR

Before you venture into downtown Seattle in a car, keep in mind that traffic congestion is bad, parking is limited (and expensive), and streets are almost all one way.

You'll avoid a lot of frustration and aggravation by leaving your car outside the downtown area.

Depending on what your plans are for your visit, you might not need a car at all. If you plan to spend your time in downtown Seattle, a car is a liability. With public buses free in the downtown area, the monorail from downtown to Seattle Center, and the Waterfront Streetcar connecting Pike Place Market and Pioneer Square by way of the waterfront, the city center is well serviced by public transport. You can even take the ferries over to Bainbridge Island or Bremerton for an excursion out of the city. Most Seattle neighborhoods of interest to visitors are also well served by public buses. However, if your plans include any excursions out of the city, say to Mount Rainier or the Olympic Peninsula, you'll definitely need a car.

Car Rentals It always pays to shop around for a rental car and call the same companies a few times over the course of a couple of weeks (rates change depending on demand). For the very best deal on a rental car, make your reservation at least one week in advance. If you decide on the spur of the moment that you want to rent a car, check to see whether there are weekend or special rates available. If you are a member of a frequent-flier program, be sure to mention it: You might get mileage credit for renting a car. In the summer of 1997, daily rates for a subcompact were between $36 and $54, with weekly rates running between $150 and $300. Expect lower rates between October and April.

All the major car-rental agencies have offices in Seattle and at or near Seattle-Tacoma International Airport. These include **Alamo** (☎ **800/327-9633,** 206/433-0812 or 206/292-9770), **Avis** (☎ **800/831-2847,** 206/433-5231, or 206/448-1700), **Budget** (☎ **800/527-0700** or 206/682-2277), **Dollar** (☎ **800/800-4000,** 206/433-6777, or 206/682-1316), **Enterprise** (☎ **800/325-8007,** 206/246-1953, or 206/382-1051), **Hertz** (☎ **800/654-3131,** 206/433-5275, or 206/682-5050), **National** (☎ **800/227-7368,** 206/433-5501, or 206/448-7368), and **Thrifty** (☎ **800/367-2277,** 206/246-7565, or 206/625-1133).

Parking On-street parking in downtown Seattle is expensive, extremely limited, and, worst of all, rarely available near your destination. Downtown parking decks (either above or below ground) charge from $7 to $16 per day. Many lots offer early-bird specials that, if you park before a certain time in the morning (usually around 9am), allow you to park all day for $6 to $7. With the purchase of $20 or more, many downtown merchants offer Easy Streets tokens that can be used toward parking fees in many downtown lots. Look for the black and yellow signs.

You'll also save money by parking near the Space Needle, where parking lots charge around $6 per day. The Pike Place Market parking garage, accessed from Western Avenue under the sky bridge, charges only $1 from 4 to 11pm, which makes this a good choice if you are headed downtown for dinner or a show. If you don't mind a bit of a walk, try the parking lot off Jackson Street between Eighth and Ninth avenues in the International District. This lot charges only $3 to park all day on weekdays and $1 on weekends. Also in the International District you'll find free 2-hour on-street parking.

Driving Rules A right turn at a red light is permitted after coming to a full stop. A left turn at a red light is permissible from a one-way street onto another one-way street. If you park your car on a sloping street, be sure to turn your wheels to the curb—you may be ticketed if you don't. When parking on the street, be sure to check the time limit on your parking meters. Some allow only as little as 15 minutes of parking, while others are good for up to 4 hours. Also be sure to check whether or not you can park in a parking space during rush hour.

BY TAXI

If you decide not to use the public-transit system, call **Yellow Cab** (☎ **206/ 622-6500**) or **Farwest Taxi** (☎ **206/622-1717**). Taxis can be difficult to hail on the street in Seattle, so it's best to call or wait at the taxi stands at major hotels. The flag-drop charge is $1.80; after that, it's $1.80 per mile. **Graytop Cab** (☎ **206/ 282-8222**), which operates only within the Seattle city limits, charges $1.20 for the flag-drop and $1.40 per mile.

BY BICYCLE

Downtown Seattle is congested with traffic and is very hilly. Unless you have experience with these sorts of conditions, I wouldn't recommend riding a bicycle downtown. However, there are many bike paths that are excellent for recreational bicycling, and some of these can be accessed from downtown by routes that avoid the steep hills and heavily trafficked streets. See "Outdoor Activities" in chapter 6 for details.

ON FOOT

Seattle is a surprisingly compact city. You can easily walk from Pioneer Square to Pike Place Market and take in most of downtown. Remember, though, that the city is also very hilly. When you head in from the waterfront, you will be climbing a very steep hill. If you get tired of walking around downtown Seattle, remember that between 6am and 7pm you can always catch a bus for free as long as you plan to stay within the Ride Free Area. Cross streets only at corners and only with the lights in your favor. Jaywalking, especially in the downtown area, is a ticketable offense.

NEIGHBORHOODS IN BRIEF

Partly because it is divided by bodies of water, Seattle is a city of neighborhoods.

International District The most immediately recognizable of Seattle's neighborhoods, the International District is home to a large Asian population. Here you'll find the Wing Luke Museum, Nippon Kan Theatre, Hing Hay Park (with an ornate pagoda), Uwajimaya (an Asian supermarket), and many other small shops and restaurants. The International District begins around Fifth Avenue South and South Jackson Street. While this neighborhood is interesting for a stroll, there really isn't a lot to do here.

Pioneer Square The Pioneer Square Historic District, known for its restored 1890s buildings is centered around the corner of First Avenue and Yesler Way. The tree-lined streets and cobblestoned plazas make this one of the prettiest downtown neighborhoods. Pioneer Square, which refers to the neighborhood and not a specific square, is full of antiques shops, art galleries, restaurants, and bars, but is also home to a large population of street people. After dark, this is the most unsafe neighborhood in which Seattle visitors are likely to find themselves.

Downtown This is Seattle's main business district and can roughly be defined as the area from Pioneer Square in the south to around Pike Place Market in the north and from First Avenue to Eighth Avenue. It's characterized by high-rise office buildings, luxury hotels, and the city's greatest diversity of retail shops, and steep streets. This is also where you'll find the Seattle Art Museum and the new Benaroya Hall, which, when completed, will be the home of the Seattle Symphony. Because hotels in this area are convenient to both Pioneer Square and Pike Place Market, this is a good neighborhood to stay in.

Belltown   Located in the blocks north of Pike Place Market between Western and Third or Fourth avenues, this area once held mostly warehouses, but now is rapidly gentrifying and contains lots of restaurants, nightclubs, and high-rise condominiums. The area is popular with a young, hip crowd, and is becoming another art gallery district.

First Hill   Known as Pill Hill by Seattleites, this hilly neighborhood, just east of downtown across I-5, is home to several hospitals as well as the Frye Art Museum. There are a couple of hotels in this neighborhood, and the blocks along Pike and Pine streets are becoming known for their nightclubs and stores selling mid-century collectibles.

Capitol Hill   To the northeast of downtown, centered along Broadway near Volunteer Park, Capitol Hill is Seattle's cutting-edge shopping district and gay community. Broadway sidewalks are always crowded and it is nearly impossible to find a parking place in the neighborhood. While there are lots of inexpensive restaurants in the area, few are really worth recommending. However, the city's two best dessert spots are here. This is also the city's main hangout for runaways and street kids, many of whom have gotten involved in the city's infamous heroin scene.

Queen Anne Hill   Queen Anne is located just northwest of Seattle Center and offers great views of the city. This affluent neighborhood, one of the most prestigious in Seattle proper, is where you'll find some of Seattle's oldest homes, several of which are now bed-and-breakfast inns. Today the neighborhood is divided into the Upper Queen Anne and Lower Queen Anne neighborhoods, with the lower area, adjacent to Seattle Center, having a more urban feel and the upper area having a more neighborhood feel. There are several excellent restaurants in the neighborhood.

Magnolia   This affluent residential neighborhood lies to the west of Queen Anne Hill. Although the neighborhood has a few cafes, restaurants, and bars, these are frequented primarily by area residents. Magnolia is, however, home to Palisade, one of Seattle's best waterfront restaurants. The west side of Magnolia borders the sprawling Discovery Park.

Ballard   In northwest Seattle, bordering the Lake Washington Ship Canal and Puget Sound, you'll find Ballard, a former Scandinavian community now known for its busy nightlife, but with remnants of its past still visible. While Ballard does have a bustling business district, it is mostly geared toward the needs of area residents.

University District   As the name implies, this neighborhood surrounds the University of Washington in the northeast section of the city. The U District, as it's known to locals, provides all the amenities of a college neighborhood: cheap ethnic restaurants, bars and pubs, and music stores.

Wallingford   This neighborhood is one of Seattle's up-and-comers. Located just west of the University District and adjacent to Lake Union, it's filled with small, inexpensive but good restaurants. There are also interesting little shops and an old school that has been renovated and is now filled with boutiques and restaurants.

Fremont   Located north of the Lake Washington Ship Canal between Wallingford and Ballard, Fremont is home to Seattle's best-loved piece of public art— *Waiting for the Interurban*—as well as the famous *Fremont Troll* sculpture. This is Seattle's wackiest neighborhood and is filled with eclectic shops, ethnic restaurants, and artists' studios. During the summer, there's a Sunday flea market and almost-free Saturday night outdoor movies. If you have time to visit only one neighborhood outside of downtown, make it Fremont.

Madison Park   One of Seattle's more affluent neighborhoods, Madison Park fronts the western shore of Lake Washington, northeast of downtown. Its center-piece is the University of Washington Arboretum, including the Japanese Gardens. There are several excellent restaurants here, at the end of East Madison Street.

The Eastside   Home to Bill Gates, Microsoft, countless high-tech spin-off companies, and seemingly endless suburbs, the Eastside lies across Lake Washington from Seattle proper and is comprised of the fast-growing cities of Kirkland, Bellevue, Redmond, Bothell, and a few other smaller communities. As the presence of Bill Gates's media-hyped mansion attests, there are some pretty wealthy neighborhoods here, but wealth doesn't necessarily equal respect, and the Eastside is still much derided by Seattle citizens as uncultured and nothing more than a bedroom community.

FAST FACTS: Seattle

Airport   See "Getting There" in chapter 2.

American Express   In Seattle, the Amex office is in the Plaza 600 building at 600 Stewart St. (☎ **206/441-8622**). The office is open Monday through Friday from 9am to 5pm.

Area Code   The telephone area code in Seattle is **206.** The area code for the Eastside (including Kirkland and Bellevue) is **425.**

Baby-Sitters   Check at your hotel first if you need a sitter. If they don't have one available, contact **Best Sitters** (☎ **206/682-2556**).

Business Hours   Banks are generally open weekdays from 9am to 5pm, with later hours on Friday; some have Saturday morning hours. Offices are generally open weekdays from 9am to 5pm. Stores typically open Monday through Saturday between 9 and 10am and close between 5 and 6pm. Some department stores have later hours on Thursday and Friday evenings until 9pm and are open on Sunday from 11am to 5 or 6pm, and stores in malls are usually open until 9pm. Bars stay open until 1 or 2am; dance clubs often stay open much later.

Car Rentals   See "Getting Around" earlier in this chapter.

Climate   See "When to Go" in chapter 2.

Dentist   If you need a dentist while you're in Seattle, contact the **Dentist Referral Service,** the Medical Dental Building, 509 Olive Way (☎ **206/448-CARE**).

Doctor   To find a physician in Seattle, check at your hotel for a reference, or call the **Medical Dental Building** line (☎ **206/448-CARE**).

Embassies/Consulates   See the appendix, "For Foreign Visitors."

Emergencies   For police, fire, or medical emergencies, phone **911.**

Hospitals   Virginia Mason Hospital and Clinic, 925 Seneca St. (☎ **206/583-6433** for emergencies, or 206/624-1144 for information) is on First Hill just outside downtown Seattle. There's also the **Virginia Mason Fourth Avenue Clinic,** 1221 Fourth Ave. (☎ **206/223-6490**), open Monday through Friday from 7am to 4:30pm, Saturday from 10am to 1:30pm, which provides medical treatment for minor ailments without an appointment.

Hot lines   The local rape hot line is ☎ **206/632-7273.**

Information   See "Visitor Information" earlier in this chapter.

Liquor Laws   The legal minimum drinking age in Washington is 21.

Luggage Storage/Lockers   Most hotels will let you store your bags if you arrive before check-in or won't be departing until late in the day that you check out. Some will also store extra bags if you are going off on an overnight excursion but plan to return to the hotel. **Ken's Baggage,** Room MT3080B, Sea-Tac Airport (☎ **206/433-5333**), will store your extra bags at the airport. There is also a luggage-storage facility at Amtrak's King Street Station, as well as lockers at the Greyhound bus station, 811 Stewart St.

Newspapers/Magazines   The *Seattle Post-Intelligencer* is Seattle's morning daily, and the *Seattle Times* is the evening daily. *Seattle Weekly* is the city's free arts-and-entertainment weekly.

Photographic Needs   **Cameras West,** 1908 Fourth Ave. (☎ **206/622-0066**), is the largest-volume camera and video dealer in the Northwest. Best of all, it's right downtown and also offers 1-hour film processing. It's open Monday through Saturday from 10am to 6pm, and on Sunday from noon to 5pm.

Police   For police emergencies, phone **911.**

Post Office   Besides the main post office, 301 Union St., there are also convenient postal stations in Pioneer Square at 91 Jackson St. S., and on Broadway at 101 Broadway E. All stations are open Monday through Friday with varying hours; the Broadway station is open Saturday from 9am to 1pm as well. For more information, call the Postal Service's toll-free phone number (☎ **800/275-8777**).

Rest Rooms   There are public rest rooms in Pike Place Market, Westlake Center, Seattle Center, and the Washington State Convention and Trade Center. You'll also find rest rooms in most hotel lobbies in downtown Seattle.

Safety   Although Seattle is rated as one of the safest cities in the United States, it has its share of crime. The least safe neighborhood you're likely to be in is the Pioneer Square area, which is home to more than a dozen bars and nightclubs. By day this area is quite safe, but late at night, when the bars are closing, extra precaution should be taken. Also take extra precaution with your wallet or purse when you're in the crush of people at Pike Place Market—this is a favorite spot of pickpockets. Whenever possible try to park your car in a garage, not on the street, at night.

Taxes   The state of Washington makes up for its lack of an income tax with its heavy sales tax of 6.5%; King County adds another 1.7% for an 8.2% total. Hotel-room tax is 15.2% in Seattle.

Taxis   See "Getting Around" earlier in this chapter.

Time   Seattle is on Pacific time (PT), and daylight saving time, depending on the time of year, making it 3 hours behind the East Coast.

Transit Information   For 24-hour information on Seattle's Metro bus system, call ☎ **206/553-3000.** For information on the Washington State Ferries, call ☎ **800/84-FERRY** or 206/464-6400. For Amtrak information, call ☎ **800/872-7245.** To contact the King Street Station (trains), call ☎ **206/382-4125.** To contact the Greyhound bus station, call ☎ **206/628-5530.**

Useful Telephone Numbers   For a wide variety of local information on topics that range from personal health to business news, from entertainment listings to the weather report and marine forecast, call the *Seattle Times* Info Line at ☎ **206/464-2000.**

Weather   If you can't tell what the weather is by looking out the window, or you want to be absolutely sure that it's going to rain the next day, call the *Seattle Times* Info Line at ☎ **206/464-2000,** ext. 9900.

Seattle Accommodations

4

Seattle has become such a hot summer destination in the past few years, that the city has been unable to keep up with the demand for hotel rooms. As of the summer of 1997, most downtown hotels were staying completely full, and were in fact often overbooking reservations and having to send guests as far away as the airport or even Tacoma when they showed up to check in. To handle the crowds that continue to descend on Seattle each summer, several new luxury hotels have recently opened downtown and others are either under construction or in the planning stages. Still other hotels are busy expanding.

What all this means is that visitors now have a broader spectrum of choices here in Seattle, but concurrent with new construction has been an escalation in room rates that has brought Seattle hotels up to pricing par with hotels in major cities throughout the nation. However, Seattle is still a seasonal destination and in the winter months hotel rooms here are a real bargain.

Seattle's largest concentrations of hotels are in downtown and near the airport, with a few good hotels in the University District and also over in the Bellevue/Kirkland area. If you don't mind high prices, downtown hotels are the most convenient. However, if your budget won't allow for a first-class business hotel, you'll have to stay near the airport or elsewhere on the outskirts of the city. Also, be sure to make reservations as far in advance as possible, especially if you plan a visit during Seafair or another major Seattle festival (see "Seattle Calendar of Events" in chapter 2 for dates of festivals).

In the following listings, price categories are based on the rate for a double room (most hotels charge the same for a single or double room) in high season and are as follows: **very expensive,** more than $175 per night; **expensive,** $126 to $175 per night; **moderate,** $75 to $125 per night; and **inexpensive,** under $75 per night. Keep in mind that these rates do not include taxes, which add up to 15.2% in Seattle.

Keep in mind that we list what hotels call "rack rates," or walk-in rates. Various discounts are often available that will reduce these rates, so be sure to ask if there are any specials or discounted rates available. At inexpensive chain motels, there are almost always discounted rates for AAA members and senior citizens. You'll also find that room rates are almost always considerably lower from October through April (the rainy season), and downtown hotels often offer substantially reduced prices on weekends throughout the year. A few hotels include breakfast in their rates; others offer complimentary breakfast only on certain deluxe floors. Most all hotels in the Seattle area now offer nonsmoking rooms, and, in fact, most bed-and-breakfast inns are exclusively nonsmoking establishments. Most hotels also offer wheelchair-accessible rooms.

There are plenty of fine B&Bs in Seattle, and we have listed a few of our favorites. To find out about other good B&Bs in Seattle, contact the **Bed and Breakfast Association of Seattle,** P.O. Box 31772, Seattle, WA 98103-1772 (☎ **206/547-1020**). Alternatively, you can contact **A Pacific Reservation Service,** P.O. Box 46894, Seattle, WA 98146 (☎ **206/439-7677;** fax 206/431-0932), which offers many accommodations, mostly in bed-and-breakfast homes, in the Seattle area. Rates range from $45 to $200 for a double and a small booking fee may be charged. They charge $5 for a directory of members.

1 Best Bets

- **Best Historic Hotel:** Built in 1909 atop First Hill and now just a few blocks from downtown Seattle, the **Sorrento Hotel,** 900 Madison St. (☎ **800/426-1265** or 206/622-6400), is the city's oldest hotel. A brick and terra-cotta facade and a circular entry drive flanked by palm trees lend this hotel an old-world, Mediterranean charm.
- **Best for Business Travelers:** Maybe you're in Seattle to get serious about your work, but why not do it with a view? At the **Westin Hotel Seattle,** 1900 Fifth Ave. (☎ **800/228-3000** or 206/728-1000), work desks in deluxe rooms face out to views. If you're here on Microsoft business, insist on staying at the **Woodmark Hotel on Lake Washington,** 1200 Carillon Point, Kirkland, WA (☎ **800/822-3700** or 425/822-3700). Rooms have two phones, computer hookups, and most have water views.
- **Best for a Romantic Getaway:** Though Seattle has quite a few hotels that do well for a romantic weekend, the **Inn at the Market,** 86 Pine St. (☎ **800/446-4484** or 206/443-3600), gets my vote for its Elliott Bay views, European atmosphere, and proximity to many great and romantic restaurants.
- **Best Trendy Hotel:** Although it was yet to open at press time, the **Hotel Monaco,** 1101 Fourth Ave. (☎ **800/945-2240** or 206/621-1770), was already billing itself as the coolest hotel in town, and with its roots in a similarly named San Francisco hotel, it's likely the Monaco will live up to its claims. Its logo alone, a reproduction of an old luggage stamp, was enough to give this hotel our hip seal of approval.
- **Best Hotel Lobby for Pretending You're Rich:** So you've got a Napoleon complex and have always dreamed of subletting Versailles; if things haven't yet worked out for you, spend the day lounging in the lobby of the **Four Seasons Olympic Hotel,** 411 University St. (☎ **800/332-3442** or 206/621-1700). This place has all the same architectural ingredients as any old palace.
- **Best for Families:** The **Seattle Sea-Tac Marriott,** 3201 S. 176th St. (☎ **800/228-9290** or 206/241-2000), down by the airport, is your best bet if you have the family along. In addition to the huge atrium with a pool, waterfall, and model train going round in circles, there's a game room. Turn the kids loose and relax.
- **Best Moderately Priced Hotel:** The **Sixth Avenue Inn,** 2000 Sixth Ave. (☎ **800/648-6440** or 206/441-8300), is a low-rise motel just a few blocks from Pike Place Market and the heart of Seattle's shopping district. For these reasons, it's a good deal.

- **Best Budget Hotel:** Situated in the University District in a building almost a century old, the **College Inn,** 4000 University Way NE (☎ **206/633-4441**), is a casual bed-and-breakfast. However, it is also one of the best values in the city. Although you won't get a private bathroom, you will get a room and breakfast for under $75.
- **Best B&B:** Set in the Capitol Hill neighborhood, the **Gaslight Inn,** 1727 15th Ave. (☎ **206/325-3654**), is a lovingly restored and maintained Craftsman bungalow filled with original Stickley furniture. Lots of public spaces, very tasteful decor, and a swimming pool in the backyard all add up to unexpected luxury for a Seattle B&B.
- **Best Service:** The **Alexis Hotel,** 1007 First Ave. (☎ **800/426-7033** or 206/624-4844), a boutique hotel in downtown Seattle, is small enough that guests manage to get very personal service. You also won't have to think about tipping since it is included in room rates.
- **Best Location:** Located on a pier right on the Seattle waterfront, **The Edgewater,** Pier 67, 2411 Alaskan Way (☎ **800/624-0670** or 206/728-7000), is only 5 blocks from Pike Place Market and the Seattle Aquarium and 3 blocks from the clubs and restaurants of Belltown. The Waterfront Streetcar, which goes to Pioneer Square and the International District, stops right in front of the hotel, and ferries to Victoria, British Columbia, leave from the adjacent pier.
- **Best Health Club:** So, you're on the road again, but you don't want to give up your circuit training. Don't worry, bring your Lycra and book a room at the **Bellevue Club Hotel,** 11200 SE Sixth St., Bellevue, WA (☎ **800/579-1110** or 425/454-4424), where you'll have access to a huge private health club complete with indoor Olympic pool.
- **Best Hotel Pool:** Most city-center hotels stick their swimming pool (if they have one at all) down in the basement or on some hidden-away terrace, but at the **Sheraton Seattle Hotel and Towers,** 1400 Sixth Ave. (☎ **800/325-3535** or 206/621-9000), you can do laps up on the top floor with the lights of the city twinkling all around.
- **Best Views:** If you're not back in your room by sunset at **The Edgewater,** Pier 67, 2411 Alaskan Way (☎ **800/624-0670** or 206/728-7000), the hotel won't turn into a pumpkin, but you will miss the smashing sunsets over the Olympic Mountains on the far side of Puget Sound.
- **Best Eastside Hotel:** If you happen to be in the area on high-tech business, or you just want to stay outside the city, there is no better choice than the **Woodmark Hotel on Lake Washington,** 1200 Carillon Point, Kirkland, WA (☎ **800/822-3700** or 425/822-3700). This place has views, a waterfront location, and services and amenities that just don't quit.
- **Best Hotel Restaurant:** Despite changes in chefs over the years, **Fuller's,** in the **Sheraton Seattle Hotel and Towers,** 1400 Sixth Ave. (☎ **800/325-3535** or 206/621-9000), has continued to maintain its impeccable standards and perfectly prepared cuisine—all without pretense.
- **Best Hotel for Oenophiles:** Washington State is close on the heels of California when it comes to winemaking, and to introduce guests to the joys of Washington wines, the **Hotel Vintage Park,** 1100 Fifth Ave. (☎ **800/624-4433** or 206/624-8000), hosts complimentary evening wine tastings.
- **Best Room Decor:** If you plan to spend a lot of time in your room, then a room at the **Bellevue Club Hotel** in Bellevue, 11200 SE Sixth St. (☎ **800/579-1110** or 425/454-4424), is the place to be. The rooms here are plush enough to please the most demanding of hedonists.

2 Downtown, the Waterfront & Pioneer Square

VERY EXPENSIVE

✪ **Alexis Hotel.** 1007 First Ave. (at Madison St.), Seattle, WA 98104. ☎ **800/426-7033** or 206/624-4844. Fax 206/621-9009. 65 rms, 44 suites. A/C TV TEL. $195–$210 double; $240–$380 suite. Rates include continental breakfast. AE, CB, DC, MC, V. Valet parking $18.

Unbelievable as it sounds, this elegant boutique hotel was once a parking garage. Now listed in the National Register of Historic Places, the 90-year-old building is a sparkling gem. The hotel also has an enviable location halfway between Pike Place Market and Pioneer Square and only 2 blocks from the waterfront. Throughout the hotel there's a pleasant mix of old and new, contemporary and antique, giving the Alexis a very special atmosphere. The cheerful service—from doormen to chambermaids, none of whom you need to tip due to the hotel's no-tipping policy—will make you feel as if you are visiting old friends.

Classic styling prevails in the guest rooms, which have a very European flavor and even the occasional piece of antique furniture. Each room is a little different, but the nicest by far are the fireplace suites, which have raised king-size beds, whirlpool baths, and wet bars. In the black-tiled bath, you'll find a marble counter, luxurious terry-cloth robes, a shaving mirror, and a telephone. The only drawback is the lack of coffeemakers in the rooms. If you need that extra bit of space that only a suite can provide, there's a wide variety to choose from here, including spa suites and fireplace suites.

Dining/Entertainment: You'll enjoy highly creative meals at **The Painted Table,** which is the hotel's main dining room. This informal restaurant takes its name from the colorful, handmade ceramic plates that frame the meals (see listing in chapter 5 for details). Just off the lobby, the **Bookstore Bar** serves light lunches as well as drinks, and is filled with books, magazines, and newspapers for browsing.

Services: 24-hour room service, concierge, valet/laundry service, your choice of morning newspaper, complimentary evening sherry, shoeshine service, portable headsets available for joggers/walkers.

Facilities: Steam room, small fitness room (and privileges at two sports clubs), Aveda day spa, business center.

Four Seasons Olympic Hotel. 411 University St., Seattle, WA 98101. ☎ **800/332-3442,** 800/821-8106 (in Washington State), 800/268-6282 (in Canada), or 206/621-1700. Fax 206/682-9633. 240 rms, 210 suites. A/C MINIBAR TV TEL. $260–$290 double; $310–$1,250 suite. AE, CB, DC, ER, JCB, MC, V. Valet parking $20; self-parking $16.

If nothing will do for you but the poshest of surroundings, then there is no question of where to stay when in Seattle. The Four Seasons Olympic Hotel, an Italian Renaissance palace, is without a doubt the grandest hotel in the city. Gilt-and-crystal chandeliers hang from the arched ceiling, and ornate moldings grace the glowing hand-burnished oak walls and pillars.

Unfortunately, what you seem to be paying for here are the hotel's public areas and the service, not the guest rooms, some of which are a bit small and even a bit worn around the edges. While you will find hairdryers and plush bathrobes in all the rooms, you won't find irons and ironing boards or coffeemakers. In case you're considering an executive suite, you should know that these particular rooms aren't much bigger than the hotel's deluxe rooms.

Dining/Entertainment: In keeping with the overall character of the hotel, **The Georgian** is the most elegant (and most expensive) restaurant in Seattle. The menu combines creative Northwest and continental cuisines. (See listing in chapter 5 for details.) For much more economical meals, there is the casual **Garden Court,** and downstairs from the lobby, there is **Shuckers,** an English pub featuring fresh seafood.

Services: 24-hour room service, concierge, valet/laundry service, 1-hour pressing, complimentary shoeshine, massages available.

Facilities: Indoor pool, whirlpool spa, sauna, sundeck, health club, exclusive shopping arcade (Bally, Laura Ashley, and others), business center.

Hotel Monaco. 1101 Fourth Ave., Seattle, WA 98101. ☎ **800/945-2240** or 206/621-1770. Fax 206/621-7779. 144 rms, 45 suites. A/C TV TEL $210–$230 double; $250–$900 suite. AE, CB, DC, DISC, JCB, MC, V.

This hotel was scheduled to open shortly after this book had gone to press, but it promised to be a bright new addition to the Seattle hotel scene. Billing itself as the coolest hotel in town, and adopting a classic 1940s style for its logo, the hotel will be boldly styled throughout public areas and in guest rooms. Reproductions of ancient Greek murals are planned for the lobby. From the outside, however, it will be difficult to tell what is hidden within. The hotel building used to be a telephone company office building and switching center.

Expect wild color schemes and bold striped wallpaper in your room, and if you happen to opt for a Monte Carlo suite, your bed will be tucked behind heavy draperies. Some of the suites have whirlpool tubs. All the rooms and suites have fax machines and all the other requirements of modern business.

Dining/Entertainment: Sazerac, the hotel's restaurant, will serve upscale southern cuisine inspired by Cajun cooking styles. It's open for three meals a day, and also has a bar area.

Services: 24-hour room service, concierge, complimentary morning newspaper and coffee, complimentary evening wine receptions.

Facilities: Fitness center, business center.

✪ **Hotel Vintage Park.** 1100 Fifth Ave., Seattle, WA 98101. ☎ **800/624-4433** or 206/624-8000. Fax 206/623-0568. 126 rms, 1 suite. A/C MINIBAR TV TEL. $190–$220 double; $370 suite. AE, CB, DC, DISC, JCB, MC, V. Valet parking $17.

Small and classically elegant, the Vintage Park is a must for oenophiles interested in Washington wines. Every guest room is named for a Washington winery and each evening in the library-like lobby there is a complimentary wine tasting featuring Washington wines. Throughout the hotel, you'll likely also spot other homages to the grape, and even the minibars are stocked with Washington wines.

Rooms vary quite a bit here, but if you opt for a deluxe room, you'll likely want to spend your days luxuriating in the elegant canopied bed. Deluxe rooms also have the best views (including some views of Mount Rainier). The bathrooms, though small, feature attractive granite counters, hair dryers, and telephones. Standard rooms, though smaller and less luxuriously appointed, are still very comfortable, and surprisingly the bathrooms are larger than in the deluxe rooms. All rooms have hair dryers and irons and ironing boards.

Dining/Entertainment: The adjacent **Tulio Restaurant** serves good Tuscan Italian meals. A small bar adjoins the restaurant.

Services: Room service, concierge, access to health club, complimentary daily newspaper and morning coffee, valet/laundry service.

Facilities: Limited in-room fitness equipment is available.

The Westin Hotel Seattle. 1900 Fifth Ave., Seattle, WA 98101. ☎ **800/228-3000** or 206/728-1000. Fax 206/728-2259. 822 rms, 43 suites. A/C MINIBAR TV TEL. $240–$280 double ($169 weekends); $240–$1,100 suite. AE, CB, DC, DISC, JCB, MC, V. Valet parking $18; self-parking $15.

Seattle Accommodations—Downtown

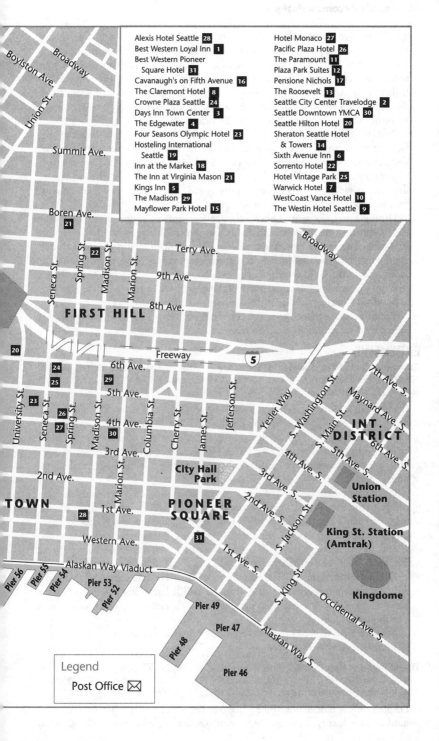

Alexis Hotel Seattle **28**
Best Western Loyal Inn **1**
Best Western Pioneer
  Square Hotel **31**
Cavanaugh's on Fifth Avenue **16**
The Claremont Hotel **8**
Crowne Plaza Seattle **24**
Days Inn Town Center **3**
The Edgewater **4**
Four Seasons Olympic Hotel **23**
Hosteling International
  Seattle **19**
Inn at the Market **18**
The Inn at Virginia Mason **21**
Kings Inn **5**
The Madison **29**
Mayflower Park Hotel **15**

Hotel Monaco **27**
Pacific Plaza Hotel **26**
The Paramount **11**
Plaza Park Suites **12**
Pensione Nichols **17**
The Roosevelt **13**
Seattle City Center Travelodge **2**
Seattle Downtown YMCA **30**
Seattle Hilton Hotel **20**
Sheraton Seattle Hotel
  & Towers **14**
Sixth Avenue Inn **6**
Sorrento Hotel **22**
Hotel Vintage Park **25**
Warwick Hotel **7**
WestCoast Vance Hotel **10**
The Westin Hotel Seattle **9**

Boylston Ave.
Broadway

Union St.

Summit Ave.

Boren Ave.
21

Terry Ave.
Broadway

Spring St.
Madison St.
Marion St.
Seneca St.
9th Ave.
22

8th Ave.

FIRST HILL

20

Freeway
5

24
25
6th Ave.

University St.
Seneca St.
Spring St.
Madison St.
5th Ave.
29

23
26
4th Ave.
30
27
3rd Ave.

Columbia St.
Cherry St.
James St.
Jefferson St.
Yesler Way
S. Washington St.
S. Main St.
Maynard Ave. S.
7th Ave. S.
6th Ave. S.
5th Ave. S.
INT.
DISTRICT

2nd Ave.

Marion St.
4th Ave. S.
City Hall
Park
3rd Ave. S.

Union
Station

TOWN
28
1st Ave.
PIONEER
SQUARE
2nd Ave. S.
S. Jackson St.

King St. Station
(Amtrak)

Western Ave.
31
1st Ave. S.

S. King St.

Kingdome
Occidental Ave. S.

Alaskan Way Viaduct
Pier 56
Pier 55
Pier 54
Pier 53
Pier 52

Pier 49

Pier 47
Alaskan Way S.
Pier 48

Pier 46

Legend
Post Office ⊠

The Westin caters primarily to conventions and tour groups and consequently can be crowded and impersonal, especially during the busy summer months. This said, it's still one of the better downtown choices, especially if you want a view from your room. The hotel's twin cylindrical towers provide interesting vistas from most of the higher floors. A wide variety of eating establishments also makes this a good choice if you don't have time in your schedule to go searching for food. Note, also, that this is one of the few downtown hotels with a swimming pool.

Primarily because of their unusual curved walls of glass and the fact that the beds face out to the views, guest rooms here are some of the nicest in town. Of course, some rooms have much better views than others (ask for a western view), and the higher up you get (there are 47 floors here), the better the views. All the rooms have irons and ironing boards, as well as hair dryers and coffeemakers (with Starbucks coffee). Bathrooms have plenty of counter space.

Dining/Entertainment: The Westin doesn't want you to forget that this is the Pacific Rim and offers two upscale Asian restaurants. The cuisine at **Roy's** can only be described as creative Euro-Asian, while at **Nikko** you'll find superb Japanese meals and high-tech decor. (See listings in chapter 5 for details.) For breakfast and quick meals, there's the **Gold Bagel,** which serves all foods hip—from espresso to bagels to wraps to foccacia sandwiches. Much of the lobby is set aside as a quiet lounge area.

Services: Concierge, 24-hour room service, valet/laundry service.

Facilities: Large indoor pool, exercise room with new equipment, whirlpool spa, sauna, sundeck, gift shops, business center.

EXPENSIVE

Cavanaugh's on Fifth Avenue. 1415 Fifth Ave., Seattle, WA 98101. ☎ **800/THE INNS** or 206/971-8000. Fax 206/971-8100. 300 rms, 10 suites. A/C MINIBAR TV TEL. $155–$185 double; $275–$950 suite. AE, DC, DISC, MC, V. Self-parking $14.

If when you arrive at this hotel, you think we've sent you to a bank and not a hotel, you're almost right. Until 1996, this building did house bank offices, but what with all the bank mergers, the building came up for sale and was converted into a hotel catering primarily to the business traveler. However, even if you aren't here on business, you may appreciate the location right in the middle of all the best upscale shopping in Seattle.

Guest rooms here are some of the largest in downtown, which for many travelers will be reason enough to choose this over other area choices. You'll also find comfortable easy chairs with hassocks, plenty of space in the bathrooms, and Nintendo games on the TV. Coffeemakers and hair dryers are standard, and most rooms have wet bars. Corner rooms, although they have more windows, are a bit smaller than other rooms. The views from the west-side rooms above about the 10th floor are excellent.

Dining/Entertainment: While the **Terrace Garden** doesn't serve food that you'll write home about, it does live up to its name with a large terrace dining area with views of Puget Sound. There's also live jazz here in the evenings. At press time, a pub was also being added.

Services: Concierge, 24-hour room service, valet/laundry service.

Facilities: Aerobic fitness room.

The Claremont Hotel. 2000 Fourth Ave., Seattle, WA 98121. ☎ **800/448-8601** or 206/448-8600. Fax 206/441-7140. 80 rms, 40 suites. TV TEL. $129–$149 double; $169–$295 suite. Rates include continental breakfast. AE, CB, DC, DISC, MC, V. Parking $12.

Located only 4 blocks from Pike Place Market, this renovated 1920s hotel tries hard to be a luxury, boutique hotel, but doesn't quite hit the mark. With no air-conditioning in the hotel (and a lot of west-facing rooms) a summer stay here can be a bit uncomfortable. Unfortunately, it is the west-side rooms on the upper floors that have the best views. If you don't mind paying extra, you can get a very spacious room or even a small suite for what you would pay for a small room at most downtown hotels. Bathrooms tend to be small. All things considered, this hotel seems overpriced for what you get.

Dining/Entertainment: Assaggio Ristorante, a northern Italian bistro, is one of Seattle's best and most popular restaurants (see chapter 5 for details).

Services: Room service, complimentary morning newspaper.

Facilities: Use of nearby health club ($7).

Crowne Plaza Seattle. 1113 Sixth Ave., Seattle, WA 98101 ☎ **800/521-2762**, 800/2CROWNE, or 206/464-1980. Fax 206/340-1617. 415 rms, 28 suites. A/C TV TEL. $109–$189 double; $209–$500 suite. AE, CB, DC, DISC, JCB, MC, V. Valet parking $17.

This 34-story tower in the heart of downtown is popular with people attending conventions at the nearby Washington State Trade and Convention Center. Don't look for a pool here, but you will find a few other recreational facilities. Almost all the rooms offer views of Puget Sound or the Cascade Mountains through large picture windows; ask for an even-numbered room on one of the higher floors for the best views. The oversized guest rooms all have spacious sitting areas, and come with two phones and an iron and ironing board. On the club-level floors, guests receive a complimentary breakfast and afternoon hors d'oeuvres, use of the concierge lounge, and upgraded room amenities.

Dining/Entertainment: The **City Views Restaurant** offers American and Northwest meals and informal dining in a mezzanine-level atrium. There's also a lounge area adjacent.

Services: Room service, concierge, valet/laundry service.

Facilities: Whirlpool spa, sauna, exercise facilities, gift shop.

✪ The Edgewater. Pier 67, 2411 Alaskan Way, Seattle, WA 98121. ☎ **800/624-0670** or 206/728-7000. Fax 206/441-4119. 230 rms, 3 suites. A/C TV TEL. $129–$250 double; $275–$750 suite. AE, CB, DC, DISC, MC, V. Valet parking $12; self-parking $10.

Built on a pier, The Edgewater, Seattle's only waterfront hotel, is incongruously designed to resemble a deluxe mountain lodge, but somehow it works and is one of our favorite downtown hotels. A vaulted open-beamed ceiling, deer-antler chandelier, a river-stone fireplace, and a wall of glass that looks out on busy Elliott Bay and gorgeous sunsets all combine to make the lobby a great place to hang out for a while. With such a lodgelike atmosphere, it's difficult to believe that the crowded streets of downtown Seattle are only steps away.

The mountain-lodge theme continues in the rooms, which feature rustic lodgepole pine furniture. Half the rooms have minibars and balconies over the water, and some have high ceilings. While the least expensive rooms here overlook the parking lot (and city), you really should opt for a water-view or partial water-view room if you choose to stay here. It makes all the difference. In fact, the rooms with balconies are our top choice.

Dining/Entertainment: Ernie's, the hotel's main restaurant, is a woodsy retreat that could have been designed by Eddie Bauer or Ralph Lauren. You'll find somewhat pricey Northwest cuisine featured on the menu but the restaurant's stunning view of Elliott Bay and the Olympic Mountains is the real main course here. In the pine-walled **Lobby Lounge,** there are more great views and a fireplace to warm your toes in winter.

Services: Room service, concierge, same-day laundry/valet service, courtesy shuttle to downtown locations.

Facilities: Gift shop, access to nearby athletic club.

Inn at the Market. 86 Pine St., Seattle, WA 98101. ☎ **800/446-4484** or 206/443-3600. 65 rms, 9 suites. A/C MINIBAR TV TEL. $130–$210 double; $225–$325 suite. AE, CB, DC, DISC, MC, V. Parking $15.

French country decor is the theme at this inconspicuous little hotel in the middle of Pike Place Market, which unfortunately has been looking quite threadbare of late. There's no grand entrance, no large sign—only a plaque on the wall to indicate that this simple brick building in fact houses a luxury hotel. A small lobby with a fireplace and a few pieces of antique furniture has been designed to give you the impression that you've stepped into the living room of a French country home and this theme continues in the guest rooms. A rooftop deck overlooking the harbor provides a tranquil spot to soak up the sun on summer afternoons.

In 18 of the guest rooms, wide bay windows overlook Puget Sound and can be opened to let in refreshing sea breezes. These water-view rooms are definitely the rooms to opt for if you can afford the $185 to $210 rates. Antique furniture, stocked minibars and refrigerators, coffeemakers with complimentary coffee, and well-lit writing desks are amenities that will make you feel right at home. The huge bathrooms are equipped with telephones and hair dryers. Don't look for any wine or cocktails in your minibar—the hotel doesn't have a liquor license. If you need more room than a standard hotel room offers, consider the two-floor town house suites.

Dining/Entertainment: Bacco, the hotel's little bistro, serves fresh juices, simple-but-tasty breakfasts, and lunches. **Café Campagne** offers French country-style meals, while the more formal **Campagne** serves excellent southern French fare (see chapter 5 for details).

Services: Limited room service, concierge, valet/laundry service, complimentary limousine service in downtown Seattle.

Facilities: Health spa, privileges at athletic club.

The Madison—A Renaissance Hotel. 515 Madison St., Seattle, WA 98104. ☎ **800/468-3571** or 206/583-0300. Fax 206/622-8635. 553 rms, 78 suites. A/C MINIBAR TV TEL. $129–$210 double; $250–$2,000 suite. AE, CB, DC, DISC, JCB, MC, V. Parking $13.

Despite its large size, The Madison manages to stay quieter and less hectic than most convention hotels, and with its rooftop restaurant and swimming pool with a view, it is a good choice for leisure travelers as well as those in town on business.

All rooms are larger than average and many have views of either Puget Sound or the Cascade Range. For the best views, ask for a room on the west side of the hotel. In the bath you'll find plenty of counter space. On the Club Floors, you'll find slightly more luxurious accommodations and a lounge in which complimentary continental breakfast and afternoon hors d'oeuvres are served.

Dining/Entertainment: Prego, way up on the 28th floor, serves northern Italian cuisine amid eye-catching views of Seattle. There's live jazz here several nights a week. Down on the second floor, **Maxwell's** serves American food in a casual cafe atmosphere; Sunday brunch here is very popular. **The Lobby Court** is a convivial place, and when the weather permits, tables spill out onto an outdoor terrace complete with waterfall.

Services: 24-hour room service, concierge, complimentary morning coffee and newspaper, valet/laundry service, complimentary shoeshine, massages available.

Facilities: The rooftop indoor pool is this hotel's best selling point. There's also a whirlpool tub, sauna, fitness room, and gift shop.

⊙ Mayflower Park Hotel. 405 Olive Way, Seattle, WA 98101. ☎ **800/426-5100,** 206/382-6990, or 206/623-8700. Fax 206/382-6997. 172 rms, 20 suites, A/C TV TEL. $150–$180 double; $190 suite. AE, CB, DC, DISC, MC, V. Valet parking $9.

If shopping or sipping martinis are among your favorite recreational activities, there's no question of where to stay in Seattle. The Mayflower Park Hotel, built in 1927 and completely renovated a few years back, is connected to the upscale shops of Westlake Center and is flanked by Nordstrom and The Bon Marché. In Oliver's Lounge, the hotel also serves up the best martinis in Seattle. So famous are the martinis here that the hotel holds an annual martini challenge. The martinis at the hotel's popular Andaluca restaurant aren't bad either.

Most rooms are furnished with an eclectic blend of contemporary Italian and traditional European furnishings. Some rooms have bathrooms that are old-fashioned, small, and lack counter space but have large old tubs that are great for soaking. If you crave space, ask for one of the large corner rooms or a suite. The smallest rooms here are very cramped.

Dining/Entertainment: Andaluca is currently one of Seattle's hottest restaurants (see chapter 5 for details). **Oliver's Lounge,** which was once a pharmacy, is martini central for Seattle and also serves light lunches and free hors d'oeuvres in the evening.

Services: 24-hour room service, valet/laundry service.

Facilities: There's a small state-of-the-art fitness room, but guests can also use a nearby health club.

The Paramount. 724 Pine St., Seattle, WA 98101. ☎ **800/426-0670** or 206/292-9500. Fax 206/292-8610. 146 rms, 1 suite. A/C TV TEL. $169–$189 double; from $325 suite. AE, DC, DISC, MC, V. Valet parking $13

This new 11-story hotel near the Paramount Theater and the Washington State Convention and Trade Center is designed to resemble a modern, French chateau-style hotel. The hotel is dwarfed by the surrounding skyscrapers so don't expect any views to speak of, and don't bother looking for a pool. Although the hotel was newly built in 1996, leisure travelers were obviously not a consideration in the hotel design. Business travelers and anyone in town to attend a convention will find the rooms quite acceptable and a bit larger than rooms at some of the other WestCoast Hotel chain hotels in downtown Seattle. You'll find hair dryers, coffeemakers, and irons and ironing boards in all the rooms. Shoppers take note: The new Nordstrom will be only 2 blocks away.

Dining/Entertainment: The hotel's **Blowfish** restaurant has an Asian menu and tries way too hard to be hip. Perhaps by the time you visit, they will have smoothed things out.

Services: Room service, valet/laundry service.

Facilities: Small fitness center with modern equipment.

Seattle Hilton Hotel. Sixth Ave. and University St., Seattle, WA 98101. ☎ **800/426-0535** or 206/624-0500. Fax 206/682-9029. 237 rms, 6 suites. A/C TV TEL. $160–$230 double; $250–$475 suite. AE, CB, DC, DISC, MC, V. Parking $16.

When you step into the street-level lobby of the Seattle Hilton, you won't find the check-in desk, no matter how hard you look. The main lobby is actually up on the 13th floor, though the elevator labels it the lobby floor or second floor. Unfortunately, you also won't find a swimming pool here, but you will find very comfortable rooms, all of which have been recently redecorated in a sort of plush Italianate style with contemporary accents. These are now some of the prettiest rooms downtown. All the rooms have irons and ironing boards and hair dryers and minibars were on the way at press time. The hotel caters primarily to convention crowds.

Dining/Entertainment: Up on the top floor at **Asgard Restaurant,** there is continental cuisine with a Northwest accent, as well as a piano bar. The views are superb. **Macaulay's Restaurant and Lounge** is a casual spot serving good old-fashioned American food, though without any views.

Services: 24-hour room service, concierge, valet/laundry service.

Facilities: Gift shop, small exercise room (plus access to nearby health club for $10).

✪ **Sheraton Seattle Hotel and Towers.** 1400 Sixth Ave., Seattle, WA 98101. ☎ **800/ 325-3535** or 206/621-9000. Fax 206/621-8441. 798 rms, 42 suites. A/C MINIBAR TV TEL. $165–$250 double; $250–$650 suite. AE, CB, DC, DISC, ER, JCB, MC, V. Valet parking $17; self-parking $14.

At 35 stories, this is the largest hotel in Seattle, and you'll almost always find the building buzzing with activity—tour groups, conventions, wedding parties, you name it. However, don't let the crowds put you off. There's a reason so many people want to stay here—the hotel does things right. From the collection of art glass in the lobby to the top-of-the-hotel health club and swimming pool, the Sheraton has figured out what travelers want.

Fresh from a complete remodeling, the rooms here are looking better than ever. The standard rooms have coffeemakers, hair dryers, irons and ironing boards, and plenty of bathroom counter space. King rooms are more spacious and are designed for business travelers. If you book a room on the Club or Tower Level, you'll get the kind of service you would expect only from a boutique hotel. The Tower Level offers the most luxurious upgrades (butler, champagne at check-in, executive work station, fax machines).

Dining/Entertainment: For nearly a decade, **Fuller's** has been one of Seattle's most talked about restaurants (see listing in chapter 5 for details). For casual meals, there's the **Pike Street Cafe,** which has an outrageous 27-foot dessert bar. **The Gallery Lounge** serves light meals and cocktails and features live jazz on weekends. There's also a tiny oyster bar, and for quick eats, there's **Andiamo Presto,** a tiny place just outside the front door. There's also an espresso stand and a nautical-theme sports bar.

Services: 24-hour room service, concierge, valet/laundry service, tour desk, American Airlines desk.

Facilities: The 35th-floor fitness center provides some of the best views in the city and includes an indoor pool, whirlpool spa, sauna, and exercise room. The hotel also has a business center, art-glass gallery, a gift shop, and a currency exchange desk.

Warwick Hotel. 401 Lenora St., Seattle, WA 98121. ☎ **800/426-9280** or 206/443-4300. Fax 206/448-1662. 229 rms, 4 suites. A/C MINIBAR TV TEL. $160–210 double ($119 weekends); $375–$475 suite. AE, CB, DC, DISC, MC, V. Parking $12.

Located in the heart of downtown Seattle, only 6 blocks from Pike Place Market and 2 blocks from the monorail terminal, the Warwick offers European charm and exceptional service. A small sunken lobby with a copper fireplace provides a quiet setting for relaxing conversation, while black mirrored walls, spotlighted bouquets of flowers, and Asian art offer just the right touch of sophistication.

The best rooms here are those on the north side of the hotel. These have views of the Space Needle and are particularly popular when there are fireworks at the Seattle Center. Corner rooms are a bit smaller than other rooms, many of which have king beds and sofa beds. Modern furnishings, a desk for working, and a couch or an easy chair for relaxing will help you settle in. All rooms have refrigerators, and rooms on the 10th floor and above have stocked minibars. At press time there were plans to get irons and ironing boards. An abundance of marble adds a touch of class to the bathrooms, which also have telephones.

Dining/Entertainment: Liaison is the hotel's distinctive dining room, serving Northwest-influenced Pacific Rim cuisine. There is live piano music several nights a week in the adjacent lounge.

Services: 24-hour room service, concierge, valet/laundry service, complimentary shuttle service in downtown Seattle.

Facilities: Indoor pool, whirlpool spa, sauna, fitness room.

MODERATE

Best Western Loyal Inn. 2301 Eighth Ave., Seattle, WA 98121. ☎ **800/528-1234** or 206/682-0200. Fax 206/467-8984. 91 rms, 12 suites. A/C TV TEL. $80–$102 double; $150–$200 suite. Rates include continental breakfast. AE, DC, DISC, MC, V. Free parking.

Located only a few blocks from Seattle Center and the Space Needle, this motel is a good city-center choice for anyone on a budget, especially families, who may want to spend the extra money for a suite with microwave and refrigerator. Deluxe rooms have wet bars, coffeemakers, remote-control TVs, king-size beds, and two sinks in the bathrooms. Facilities here include a 24-hour sauna and a whirlpool spa, but there is no pool or restaurant.

Best Western Pioneer Square Hotel. 77 Yesler Way, Seattle, WA 98104. ☎ **800/528-1234** or 206/340-1234. Fax 206/467-0707. 75 rms, 4 suites. A/C TV TEL. $99–$149 double; $169 suite. AE, CB, DC, DISC, MC, V. Parking $12.

Located right in the heart of the Pioneer Square historic district, this hotel was until fairly recently little more than a flophouse, and although it has now been completely renovated, we still recommend it only for urban dwellers accustomed to dealing with street people and noise. Pioneer Square is Seattle's nightlife district and gets especially rowdy on weekend nights. However, if you're in town to party (or to attend a game at the nearby Kingdome), there's no more convenient location in the city. Care should be taken if you are on the streets around here late at night; muggings are commonplace. Warnings aside, Pioneer Square is one of the prettiest corners of Seattle and the only downtown neighborhood with historic flavor. Guest rooms here are mostly fairly small (some are positively cramped) and are furnished in a classic style. Service can be slow here, so bring your patience.

Days Inn Town Center. 2205 Seventh Ave., Seattle, WA 98121. ☎ **800/329-7466** or 206/448-3434. Fax 206/441-6976. 91 rms. A/C TV TEL. $79–$135 double. AE, CB, DC, DISC, MC, V. Free parking.

Conveniently located close to Seattle Center and within walking distance (or a free bus ride) of the rest of downtown Seattle, this three-story hotel offers large, clean accommodations. There's a combination restaurant and bar on the premises if you don't feel like going out.

Pacific Plaza Hotel. 400 Spring St., Seattle, WA 98104. ☎ **800/426-1165** or 206/623-3900. Fax 206/623-2059. 160 rms. A/C TV TEL. $80–$104 double. Rates include continental breakfast. AE, DC, DISC, MC, V. Parking $9.

There aren't too many choices left for economical accommodations in downtown Seattle, but this fairly well maintained hotel, built in 1928, offers economical rooms and a prime location. You're halfway between Pike Place Market and Pioneer Square, and just about the same distance from the waterfront. Rooms are small and sometimes cramped, but overall they're fairly comfortable and generally clean. Bathrooms are small and dated. If you aren't too fussy, this is as good a choice as any of the chain motels near the Space Needle. A **Red Robin Restaurant** serves gourmet hamburgers on the lower level of the hotel. The hotel offers valet/laundry service to its guests.

Pensione Nichols. 1923 First Ave., Seattle, WA 98101. ☎ **800/440-7125** or 206/441-7125. 8 rms (none with private bath), 2 suites (both with private bath). $85 double; $160 suite. Two-night minimum on summer weekends. Rates include breakfast. AE, MC, V.

If you have ever traveled through Europe on a budget, you have probably stayed at bed-and-breakfast lodgings that started on the second or third floor of a building. This city-center bed-and-breakfast is just such a European-style lodging, and you'll find it up two flights of stairs. Located only a block from Pike Place Market, Pensione Nichols is a touch expensive for what you get (some of the furniture is getting quite worn), though it is hard to beat the location. Only two of the guest rooms have windows (the two rooms facing the street), but all the rest have skylights. High ceilings and white bedspreads brighten the rooms and make them feel spacious. The two suites on the other hand are huge and have full kitchens as well as large windows overlooking the bay. Suites have a few antiques here and there, as does the inn's living room, which also overlooks the water.

The Roosevelt. 1531 Seventh Ave., Seattle, WA 98101. ☎ **800/426-0670** or 206/621-1200. Fax 206/233-0335. 151 rms. A/C TV TEL. $95–$180 double. AE, DC, DISC, MC, V. Parking $13.

If you happen to be visiting Seattle in the rainy season, you'll find that this restored 1929 hotel is a good deal. However, during the summer, rooms here are considerably overpriced. The rooms do, however, have a classic elegance and plenty of modern amenities. The hotel's small lobby is decorated to look like a library in an old mansion, with bookshelves around the fireplace and a grand piano off to one side. Service here can be brusque.

The smallest rooms, known here as studios, have a single double bed and a tiny bathroom with a shower only (no tub) and are very cramped. For more space, you'll have to opt for a queen or king room. The queen rooms are still rather small, but the parlor rooms have good layouts. Most rooms, unfortunately, have small bathrooms with little counter space. The largest rooms verge on being suites and have double whirlpool tubs. The hotel offers room service, concierge, valet/laundry service and has an exercise room.

Just off the lobby is **Von's Grand City Café** and **Martini Manhattan Memorial** bar. The restaurant, which can trace its history back 80 years, dedicates itself to preparing juicy steaks, lamb, veal, chicken, and salmon cooked over apple wood. In the bar you'll be fascinated by the wild array of "objets d'junk" that hangs from the ceiling. Martinis are the specialty, and happy hour is a good deal.

✪ **Sixth Avenue Inn.** 2000 Sixth Ave., Seattle, WA 98121. ☎ **800/648-6440** or 206/441-8300. Fax 206/441-9903. 166 rms. A/C TV TEL. $80–$135 double. AE, CB, MC, V. Free parking.

Located close to Pike Place Market and the Westlake Center monorail station, this low-rise hotel is convenient and economically priced for downtown Seattle. This is more than your standard budget hotel. In the guest rooms you'll find a brass bed, old photos of Seattle, and a small wall shelf with a selection of old hardcover books and Readers Digest condensed books. And if you ever need to know what time it is, you can consult the huge railway clock behind the front desk. Guests may also take advantage of room service and valet/laundry service.

The **Sixth Avenue Bar and Grill** serves breakfast, lunch, and dinner looking out to a Japanese garden that makes dining a tranquil experience. Steak, pasta, and seafood are featured on the menu. There's also a quiet lounge.

WestCoast Vance Hotel. 620 Stewart St., Seattle, WA 98101. ☎ **800/426-0670** or 206/441-4200. Fax 206/441-8612. 165 rms. A/C TV TEL. $115–$149 double. AE, DC, DISC, MC, V. Parking $11.

Built in the 1920s by lumber baron Joseph Vance, this hotel has a very elegant little lobby with wood paneling, marble floors, Oriental carpets, and ornate plasterwork moldings. With neither a fitness room nor a swimming pool, it's obvious that this hotel caters to business travelers simply looking for a convenient place to sleep at night. With the convention center only a couple of blocks away, it isn't surprising that the hotel does a lot of convention business. Accommodations vary in size and style and some are quite small; corner rooms compensate with lots of windows. Furniture is in keeping with the style of the lobby, and for the most part is fairly elegant. Bathrooms are uniformly small. If you're here on business or don't care about exercise facilities, this hotel offers good value for a downtown business hotel.

Salute in Città Ristorante is a bright and popular Italian restaurant. The hotel also has valet/laundry service.

INEXPENSIVE

Hosteling International—Seattle (HI). 84 Union St., Seattle, WA 98101-2084. ☎ **206/ 622-5443.** Fax 206/682-2179. 195 beds. $15–$20 per person for members. AE, JCB, MC, V. Self-parking $9.

This conveniently located hostel is housed in the former Longshoreman's Hall, which was built in 1915, and is popular with young European and Japanese travelers. The hostel is located between Pike Place Market and Pioneer Square only 2 blocks away from the waterfront, which makes it very convenient for exploring downtown Seattle. There's a kitchen and a self-service laundry, and from some of the hostel's rooms there are views of Puget Sound. To find the hostel, walk down Post Alley, which runs through and under Pike Place Market, to the corner of Union Street.

Kings Inn. 2106 Fifth Ave., Seattle, WA 98121. ☎ **800/546-4760** or 206/441-8833. Fax 206/ 441-0730. 69 rms, 21 suites. A/C TV TEL. $55–$65 double; $65–$90 suite. AE, CB, DC, DISC, MC, V. Free parking.

You'll find this economical motel in the shadow of the monorail (midway between Westlake Center and the Space Needle). Rooms are a bit small and show their age. Suites have various sleeping arrangements that can fit several people. Best of all, there's no charge for local calls or parking. Although you won't find an acceptable room in downtown for less, I suggest that finicky travelers ask to see a room here before committing to one, however.

Seattle City Center Travelodge. 2213 Eighth Ave., Seattle, WA 98121. ☎ **800/578-7878** or 206/624-6300. Fax 206/233-0185. 73 rms. A/C TV TEL. $59–$99 double. AE, CB, DC, DISC, MC, V. Free parking.

This conveniently located and moderately priced downtown motel is located about midway between the Westlake Center shopping mall and Seattle Center, which makes it a fairly convenient choice if you don't mind doing a bit of walking. The rooms are attractive and some even have balconies and views of the Space Needle.

Seattle Downtown YMCA. 909 Fourth Ave., Seattle, WA 98104-1194. ☎ **800/474-YMCA** or 206/382-5000. Fax 206/382-4927. 185 rms (3 with private bath). $39–$52 double. DISC, MC, V. Self-parking $10.

This YMCA welcomes men, women, and families, and primarily has rooms with shared bathrooms. If you want, you can get a room with a TV or just walk down the hall to the TV lounge. The rooms are basic and fairly clean. The best part of staying here is that you get to use all of the athletic facilities, and you'd have to stay at the most expensive hotel in the city to find facilities like these (indoor pool, running track, exercise room with weights and aerobic machines, racquetball and squash courts).

3 Lake Union & Queen Anne Hill

EXPENSIVE

Seattle Downtown—Lake Union Marriott Residence Inn. 800 Fairview Ave. N., Seattle, WA 98109. ☎ **800/331-3131** or 206/624-6000. Fax 206/223-8160. 234 suites. A/C TV TEL. $110–$200 one-bedroom suite; $170–$300 two-bedroom suite. Rates include continental breakfast. AE, DC, DISC, JCB, MC, V. Parking $9.

Located at the north end of downtown Seattle and just across the street from Lake Union, this Marriott Residence Inn is within a block or two of several waterfront restaurants, which makes a stay here a quintessential Seattle experience. A seven-story atrium floods the hotel's plant-filled lobby court with light, while the sound of a waterfall soothes traffic-weary nerves. All accommodations here are suites, so you'll buy quite a bit more space for your money here. You'll also have use of a full kitchen, complete with dishes, so you can fix your own meals if you like, though the buffet breakfast down in the lobby shouldn't be missed.

Though the suites here are generally quite spacious, they don't have much in the way of character. However, they do have phones and televisions in bedrooms and living rooms and there are large desks as well.

Dining/Entertainment: Though the hotel has no restaurant of its own, there are several restaurants right across the street, and one of these provides the hotel's room service.

Services: Complimentary cookies and coffee, evening dessert, Wednesday night guest reception, grocery shopping service, complimentary morning newspaper, valet/laundry service, free downtown shuttle service.

Facilities: Indoor lap pool, children's pool, steam room, sauna, whirlpool spa, exercise room.

MODERATE

Houseboat Hideaways. Boat World Marina, 2144 Westlake Ave., Seattle, WA 98109 (mailing address: c/o Kent Davis, P.O. Box 782, Edmonds WA 98020). ☎ **206/323-5323.** 2 houseboats. TV. $105–$135 double. AE, MC, V.

🏠 Family-Friendly Hotels

Sheraton Seattle Hotel and Towers *(see p. 36)* With a 35th-floor swimming pool, a little snack shop selling pizza and pasta, and a 27-foot-long dessert bar in another of the hotel's restaurants, this downtown convention hotel is a good choice for families.

Seattle Sea-Tac Marriott *(see p. 47)* With a huge jungly atrium containing a swimming pool and whirlpool spas, kids can play Tarzan and never leave the hotel. There is also a game room that will keep the young ones occupied for hours if need be.

Seattle Downtown YMCA *(see p. 39)* This Y welcomes families and has rooms with or without private baths. You get to use all of the athletic facilities here; for facilities like these, you'd have to stay at the most expensive hotel in Seattle.

Located at a marina on the west shore of Lake Union, these two houseboats are nothing like the place Tom Hanks was living in *Sleepless in Seattle*. Though much smaller, they still offer a chance to sample the Seattle houseboat life. If you're prone to sea sickness, you might want to pass on these, since boat wakes tend to keep these houseboats rocking throughout the day. While both houseboats have galleys and sundecks, one is 28 feet long and sleeps up to four people and the other is 40 feet long and sleeps up to six people. Both have great views of the lake.

✪ **The M. V. Challenger.** 1001 Fairview Ave. N., Seattle, WA 98109. ☎ **206/340-1201.** Fax 206/621-9208. 15 rms (12 with private bath). $75–$200 double. Rates include full breakfast. Children by reservation only. AE, CB, DC, DISC, MC, V. Free parking.

If you love ships and the sea and want a taste of Seattle's water-oriented lifestyle, don't pass up an opportunity to spend the night onboard a restored and fully operational old tugboat (or one of this inn's other boats). If, however, you need lots of space, this place is definitely not for you. Guest rooms are as small as you would expect berths to be on any small boat. However, you're welcome to visit the bridge of the *Challenger* for a great view of Lake Union and the Seattle skyline, delve into the mechanics of the tug's enormous diesel engine, or simply hang out in the conversation pit in the cozy main cabin. The location, at the south end of Lake Union, puts you a bit of a walk (or a short bus ride) from downtown, but there are lots of waterfront restaurants within walking distance. This is a great place for a weekend getaway or romantic vacation.

INEXPENSIVE

B. D. Williams House Bed and Breakfast. 1505 Fourth Ave. N., Seattle WA 98109-2902. ☎ **800/880-0810** or 206/285-0810. 5 rms (all with private or dedicated bathroom). $75–$150 double. Rates include full breakfast. AE, DC, MC, V.

Located high atop Queen Anne Hill, yet within walking distance of Seattle Center, this restored historic home dates from the turn of the century. Colorful flower gardens surround the inn, and a vegetable garden provides produce for the inn's gourmet breakfasts. An enclosed sunporch and an open veranda are pleasant spaces in which to relax any time of year and no matter what the weather. Most rooms here have excellent views of either Puget Sound, Lake Union, or the downtown city skyline. Both the rooms and the neighborhood are extremely quiet, and walkers will appreciate the nearby parks.

4 First Hill & Capitol Hill

VERY EXPENSIVE

✪ **Sorrento Hotel.** 900 Madison St., Seattle, WA 99104-1297. ☎ **800/426-1265** or 206/ 622-6400. Fax 206/343-6155. 34 rms, 42 suites. A/C MINIBAR TV TEL. $200–$220 double; $240–$1,200 suite. AE, CB, DC, DISC, MC, V. Valet parking $16.

An old-world atmosphere reigns at this small hotel set high on First Hill overlooking the rest of downtown Seattle, and though it is a bit out of the center for a deluxe hotel, it is still convenient to downtown (and there's a complimentary town car to take you downtown). From the wrought-iron gates and palm trees of the courtyard entrance to the plush seating of the octagonal lobby, the Sorrento whispers style and elegance. The Sorrento's posh atmosphere is only duplicated in Seattle by the Four Seasons Hotel. However, here at the Sorrento, the hotel's small size assures every guest of personal service.

No two rooms here are alike, but all are luxuriously appointed and set up for business travelers (rooms even have their own fax machines). More than half the rooms

Seattle Accommodations—North & Northeast

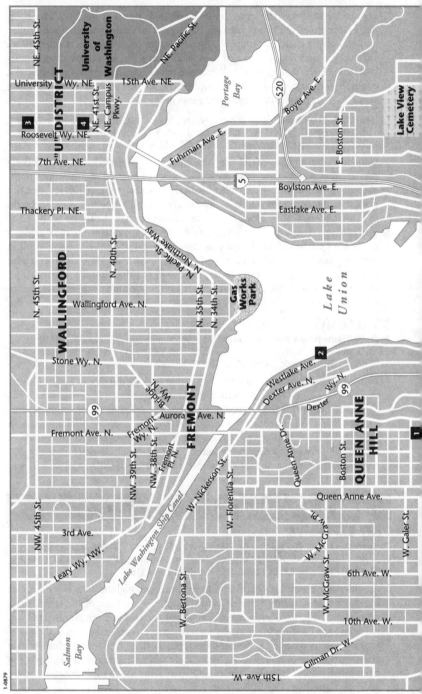

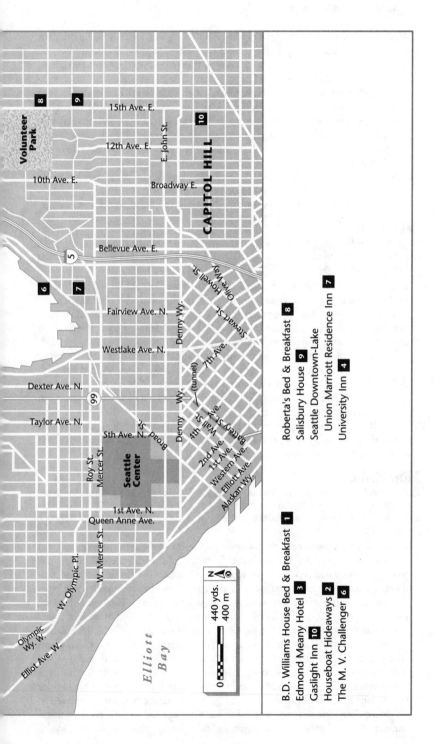

Volunteer Park

15th Ave. E.

12th Ave. E.

E. John St.

10th Ave. E.

Broadway E.

CAPITOL HILL

Bellevue Ave. E.

Howell St.

Olive Way

Fairview Ave. N.

Stewart St.

Denny Wy.

Westlake Ave. N.

7th Ave.

(tunnel)

Dexter Ave. N.

Denny Wy.

4th Ave.

Wall St.

Battery St.

Taylor Ave. N.

2nd Ave.

5th Ave. N.

1st Ave.

Western Ave.

Roy St.

Elliott Ave.

Mercer St.

Seattle Center

Broad St.

Alaskan Wy.

1st Ave. N.

Queen Anne Ave.

W. Mercer St.

W. Olympic Pl.

Olympic Wy. W.

Elliot Ave. W.

Elliott Bay

N

0   440 yds.
0   400 m

B.D. Williams House Bed & Breakfast **1**
Edmond Meany Hotel **3**
Gaslight Inn **10**
Houseboat Hideaways **2**
The M. V. Challenger **6**

Roberta's Bed & Breakfast **8**
Salisbury House **9**
Seattle Downtown–Lake
Union Marriott Residence Inn **7**
University Inn **4**

43

here are suites, and with the least expensive of these going for only $20 more than a deluxe room, consider spending it for a little extra space to spread out. For the complete Seattle experience, ask for a room on the west side of the hotel; you'll have a view of the city and Puget Sound.

Dining/Entertainment: The **Hunt Club,** a dark, clublike restaurant serves superb Northwest cuisine (see chapter 5 for details), and in the adjacent **Fireside Room** bar, you can get lighter and less expensive meals. Several nights a week a pianist provides musical atmosphere in the lounge. Afternoon tea and weekend meals are served in the lobby and Fireside Room. In the summer, there's an Italian "street" cafe in the hotel's courtyard.

Services: Room service, concierge, valet/laundry service, complimentary limousine service to downtown, morning newspaper, massages.

Facilities: Exercise room with the latest Nautilus equipment, salon, flower shop.

EXPENSIVE

Plaza Park Suites. 1011 Pike St., Seattle, WA 98101. ☎ **800/426-0670** or 206/682-8282. Fax 206/682-5315. 26 rms, 168 suites. A/C TV TEL. $125 double; $180–$340 suite. Rates include continental breakfast. AE, DC, DISC, MC, V. Valet parking $13.

Located just a block uphill from the Washington State Convention and Trade Center, this hotel caters primarily to business travelers who need a bit of extra room for getting work done while in town. However, because the hotel is about equidistant between the waterfront and Capitol Hill, it makes a good choice if you are planning on doing a bit of barhopping or nightclubbing on the hill.

While not all the accommodations here are suites, they are definitely the better choice. However, even the suites here are not as big as you would expect, although they do have two TVs, two phones, and two poster king beds. Many rooms here have good views that take in the Space Needle, but many also get a lot of traffic noise from both the freeway and Pike Street.

Services: Room service, valet/laundry service, complimentary downtown shuttle.

Facilities: Small outdoor pool (seasonal), whirlpool spa, fitness room (plus access to nearby athletic club for $7), deli.

MODERATE

✪ **Gaslight Inn.** 1727 15th Ave., Seattle, WA 98122. ☎ **206/325-3654.** 9 rms (5 with private bath), 1 studio and 6 suites (all with private bath). TV. $68–$108 double; $98 studio; $128–$148 suite. Rates include continental breakfast. AE, MC, V. Off-street parking only if staying in studio or suite.

Anyone who is a fan of the arts-and-crafts movement of the early 20th century will enjoy a stay at this 1906 vintage home. Throughout the inn, there are numerous pieces of Stickley furniture, and everywhere you turn, oak trim frames doors and windows. The common rooms are spacious and attractively decorated with a combination western and northwestern flare, and throughout the inn's two house there are lots of art-glass pieces. A library filled with interesting books and magazines makes a comfortable spot for a bit of free time or, if it's cold out, take a seat by the fireplace. In summer, guests can swim in the backyard pool or lounge on the deck. Guest rooms continue the design themes of the common areas with lots of oak furnishings and heavy, peeled-log beds in some rooms. An annex next door has a studio and six suites with kitchens, dining areas, and separate bedrooms and living rooms. One of these suites, done in a contemporary style with an art-glass chandelier, has a fireplace and an outstanding view of the city. Another has a hot tub and its own private garden. Innkeepers Steve Bennet, Trevor Logan, and John Fox together can provide a wealth of information about Seattle and the inn's Capitol Hill environs. Gay visitors to Seattle will find this inn to be a good choice of accommodations.

The Inn at Virginia Mason. 1006 Spring St., Seattle, WA 98104. ☎ **800/283-6453** or 206/583-6453. Fax 206/223-7545. 79 rms, 3 suites. A/C TV TEL. $98–$155 double; $155–$215 suite. AE, CB, DC, DISC, MC, V. Parking $4.

You may think I've sent you to a hospital rather than a hotel when you first arrive at this small European-style hotel on Pill Hill. The hotel takes its name from the Virginia Mason Hospital, which is next door and is connected to the hotel. Regardless of the fact that most of the guests here are either here on hospital business or to visit relatives who are in the hospital, the hotel is a good choice for its economical rates, quiet location, and proximity to downtown. The hotel keeps good company: the Sorrento Hotel is only a block away.

The lobby is small and casually furnished, though there is a grand piano. Just off the lobby is a little brick courtyard, and up on the roof there is a sundeck. Because this is an old building, room sizes vary a lot, but most have large closets, modern bathrooms (some with windows), and wing-back chairs. Deluxe rooms and suites can be quite large, and some have whirlpool baths, fireplaces, dressing rooms, hair dryers, and refrigerators.

The hotel's **Rhododendron Restaurant** serves Northwest and traditional cuisine. There is live piano music several nights a week. Other amenities include valet/laundry service, concierge, room service, and privileges at a nearby fitness center.

Roberta's Bed and Breakfast. 1147 16th Ave. E., Seattle, WA 98112. ☎ **206/329-3326.** Fax 206/324-2149. 5 rms (4 with private bath). $85–$125 double. Rates include full breakfast. MC, V.

Bibliophiles will be certain to develop an instant rapport with this B&B's namesake innkeeper. Roberta is, to say the least, fond of books and has filled shelves in nearly every room with books both old and new. On a rainy Seattle day, I can think of no better way to spend an afternoon than curled up at Roberta's with a good book. This turn-of-the-century home is on a beautiful tree-lined street just around the corner from Volunteer Park. A big front porch stretches across the front of the house, while inside there are hardwood floors and a mix of antique and modern furnishings. My favorite room is the attic hideaway, which has angled walls, painted wood paneling, lots of skylights, and a claw-foot bathtub. The overall effect of this room is that of a ship's cabin or artist's garret. Breakfast starts with tea or coffee left at your door and continues downstairs in the dining room with a hearty meal that includes home-baked treats.

Salisbury House. 750 16th Ave. E., Seattle, WA 98112. ☎ **206/328-8682.** Fax 206/720-1019. 4 rms (all with private bath). $75–$125 double. Rates include full breakfast. AE, MC, V.

This grand old house on tree-lined 16th Avenue East has a wide porch that wraps around two sides. Sit down in one of the porch chairs and enjoy one of Seattle's prettiest streetscapes. Inside there's plenty to admire as well. Two living rooms (one with a wood-burning fireplace) and a second-floor sun porch provide plenty of spots for relaxing and meeting other guests. On sunny summer days, breakfast may even be served in the small formal garden in the backyard. Guest rooms all have queen-size beds with down comforters, and one even has a unique canopy bed hung with pink satin. One of the other rooms has an old claw-foot tub in the bathroom. Breakfasts here are deliciously filling and might include fresh fruit, juice, quiche, fresh-baked muffins or bread, or oatmeal pancakes. Cathryn and Mary Wiese, mother and daughter, are the friendly innkeepers.

5 The University District

Located 15 to 20 minutes from downtown Seattle, the U District will likely appeal to younger travelers. The neighborhood offers less expensive accommodations than downtown, yet is still fairly convenient to Seattle's major attractions. Also nearby are the Burke Museum, Henry Art Gallery, the Woodland Park Zoo, and, of course, the University of Washington. As you would expect in a university neighborhood, there are lots of cheap restaurants in the neighborhood, and this fact, combined with the lower hotel rates here, makes this a good choice for anyone on a budget.

EXPENSIVE

✪ **Edmond Meany Hotel.** 4507 Brooklyn Ave. NE, Seattle, WA 98105. ☎ **800/899-0251** or 206/634-2000. 155 rms. A/C TV TEL. $129–$169 double. AE, DC, MC, V. Free parking.

Fresh from a complete renovation, the Edmond Meany Hotel is now one of Seattle's hippest hotels. Although it is no longer as economical as it once was, it is still considerably cheaper than comparable downtown hotels and the modern art deco styling will surround you in retro style unlike anything else you'll find in the city. If you need to be near the university, this is the top choice in the neighborhood, especially if you want a view of downtown Seattle, distant mountains, and various lakes and waterways. Every room here is a large corner room, which means plenty of space to spread out and plenty of views from the higher floors. Boldly styled furnishings will appeal to anyone with an appreciation for contemporary furniture design. Though the tiled combination baths are small, they do have hair dryers and a small shelf above the pedestal sink.

Dining/Entertainment: The **Pleiades Restaurant,** down in the basement, is as brashly contemporary in styling as the rest of the hotel and serves moderately priced creative meals with a Northwest slant. There's a bar to one side of the restaurant. Just off the lobby is a stylish little cafe where you can get your espresso fix throughout the day.

Services: Room service, valet/laundry service, complimentary newspaper.

Facilities: Unfortunately, there's no swimming pool here but there is a fitness room.

MODERATE

Chambered Nautilus Bed and Breakfast Inn. 5005 22nd Ave. NE, Seattle, WA 98105. ☎ **800/545-8459** or 206/522-2536. Fax 206/528-0898. 6 rms (all with private bath). $79–$109 double. Rates include full breakfast. AE, MC, V.

Located on an apartment-lined street in the University District, this inn sits high above the street atop an ivy-covered embankment and out of view of the street. The shady forest surrounding the inn gives it a very secluded feel; you'd hardly know you're in the middle of the city. If you have trouble climbing stairs, this inn is definitely not for you. There are a lot of stairs between parking and the guest rooms, especially if you are in one of the third-floor view rooms (which just happen to be the best in the house). Owners/innkeepers Joyce Schulte and Steve Poole bought this inn not too long ago and have since imparted to it a bit of their own personalities.

✪ **University Inn.** 4140 Roosevelt Way NE, Seattle, WA 98105. ☎ **800/733-3855** or 206/632-5055. Fax 206/547-4937. 102 rms, 12 junior suites. A/C TV TEL. $102–$112 double; $132 junior suite. Rates include continental breakfast. AE, DC, DISC, MC, V.

Located within easy walking distance of the university, this renovated 1960s vintage hotel offers surprisingly attractive rooms, many of which have views of Lake Union.

Although the standard rooms have only showers in their bathrooms, these rooms compensate for this lack with small balconies. The deluxe rooms are more spacious and those on the west side of the hotel have unusual pushed-out windows that provide glimpses of Lake Union (best views are in winter). For even more room and the best views, opt for one of the junior suites, which have large windows, microwaves, small refrigerators, coffeemakers, and telephones in the bathrooms (ask for room 331; it's got a view of Mount Rainier). Facilities include a small outdoor pool (seasonal), whirlpool spa, and a tiny exercise room. Along with your simple breakfast, you can grab a free copy of the paper. Filling breakfasts, as well as lunch, are available in the inn's **Portage Bay Cafe.**

6 Near Sea-Tac Airport

EXPENSIVE

Doubletree Seattle Airport. 18740 International Blvd., Seattle, WA 98188. ☎ **800/547-8010** or 206/246-8600. Fax 206/431-8687. 838 rms, 12 suites. A/C TV TEL. $144–$195 double ($99–$109 weekends); $189–$650 suite. AE, CB, DC, DISC, MC, V. Free parking.

Big, sprawling, and glitzy, this convention hotel can be a mob scene, but the interesting lakeside setting and Northwest styling keep it popular. Seven wings and a 14-story tower almost guarantee that you'll get lost trying to find your room, so make it easy on yourself and request a tower room with a view. A glass elevator will whisk you up to your floor, providing a great view of the airport all the way. Rooms here are uniformly large, so whether you book a room with two doubles, a queen, or a king-size bed, you'll have plenty of space to move around. Guest rooms all have coffeemakers and irons and ironing boards.

Dining/Entertainment: **Maxi's,** up on the 14th floor, is an elegant, large restaurant that serves Northwest cuisine. The adjacent lounge is on three levels so that you can enjoy the view no matter where you're sitting. Down on the first floor you'll find **SeaPorts,** a seafood restaurant open for lunch and dinner. The **Coffee Garden** is a very casual lobby coffee shop.

Services: Room service, concierge, free airport shuttle, car-rental desk, valet/laundry service.

Facilities: Outdoor pool, exercise room, gift shop, business center, beauty salon, barbershop.

✪ **Seattle Sea-Tac Marriott.** 3201 S. 176th St., Seattle, WA 98188. ☎ **800/228-9290** or 206/241-2000. Fax 206/248-0789. 459 rms, 5 suites. A/C TV TEL. $144 double ($89–$144 weekends); $225–$550 suite. AE, CB, DC, DISC, MC, V. Free parking.

With its steamy atrium garden full of tropical plants, a swimming pool, and two whirlpool tubs, this resort-like hotel may keep you so enthralled you won't want to leave. You can't pick a better place to stay in the airport area. In the atrium, there are even waterfalls and totem poles for that Northwest outdoorsy feeling, and best of all, it's always sunny and warm in here, unlike in the real outdoorsy Northwest. In the lobby, a huge stone fireplace and moose head hanging on the wall conjure up images of a remote mountain lodge. To get the most out of your stay here, try to get one of the rooms with a view of Mount Rainier.

Dining/Entertainment: **Yukon Landing Restaurant** will have you thinking you're in the middle of the gold rush. Moose, deer, and elk heads mounted on wooden walls, stone pillars, rough-hewn beams, and deer-antler chandeliers all make this rustic restaurant very popular. The **Lobby Lounge** is its own little greenhouse overlooking the atrium.

Services: Room service, free airport shuttle, car-rental desk, valet/laundry service.
Facilities: Indoor swimming pool, whirlpool spa, health club, sauna, game room.

MODERATE

WestCoast Sea-Tac Hotel. 18220 International Blvd., Seattle, WA 98188. ☎ **800/426-0670** or 206/246-5535. Fax 206/246-9733. 146 rms. A/C TV TEL. $90–$114 double. AE, CB, DC, DISC, MC, V. Free parking.

Located almost directly across from the airport's main entrance, this modern hotel has been recently renovated and provides comfortable accommodations designed for business travelers. European styling prevails and there's a grand piano in the lobby (feel free to play whenever the urge strikes). The guest rooms have queen- or king-size beds, work desk, and are generally quite large (if you need space, this is the place). In superior king rooms, you get evening turndown service, coffee and a newspaper in the morning, plush terry-cloth robes, hair dryers, and an honor bar. The hotel backs to a small lake, but only a few rooms have lake views.

Dining/Entertainment: Gregory's Bar and Grill, a moderately priced restaurant with unremarkable food, is across the parking lot from the main hotel facility. Five nights a week, there is karaoke music in the attached lounge, which has an aeronautical theme.

Services: Room service, free airport shuttle, valet/laundry service.
Facilities: Seasonal outdoor pool, whirlpool spa, sauna.

INEXPENSIVE TO MODERATE

Among the better and more convenient inexpensive chain motel choices are **Motel 6 (Sea-Tac South),** 18900 47th Ave. S., Seattle, WA 98188 (☎ 206/241-1648), charging $37 to $48; **Motel 6 (Sea-Tac Airport),** 16500 International Blvd., Seattle, WA 98188 (☎ 206/246-4101), charging $41 to $51 for a double; **Super 8 Motel,** 3100 S. 192nd St., Seattle, WA 98188 (☎ 206/433-8188), charging $69 to $82 for a double; and **Travelodge Seattle Airport,** 2900 S. 192nd St., Seattle, WA 98188 (☎ 206/241-9292), charging $39 to $85 double.

7 The Eastside

Home to Bill Gates, Microsoft, countless high-tech spin-off companies, and seemingly endless suburbs, the Eastside lies across Lake Washington from Seattle proper and is comprised of the fast-growing cities of Kirkland, Bellevue, Redmond, Bothell, and a few other smaller communities. As the presence of Bill Gates's media-hyped mansion attests, there are some pretty wealthy neighborhoods here on the Eastside, but wealth doesn't necessarily equal respect, and the Eastside is still much derided by Seattle citizens as uncultured and nothing more than a bedroom community. However, Seattleites' attitudes aside, should you be out this way on high-tech business or visiting friends, you may find an Eastside hotel more convenient than one in downtown Seattle, and surprisingly, two of the most luxurious hotels in the entire Seattle area are here on this side of Lake Washington. If it isn't rush hour, you can usually get from the Eastside to downtown Seattle in about 20 minutes via the famous floating I-90 and Wash. 520 bridges.

VERY EXPENSIVE

✪ **Bellevue Club Hotel.** 11200 SE Sixth St., Bellevue, WA 98004. ☎ **800/579-1110** or 425/454-4424. Fax 425/688-3101. 64 rms, 3 suites. A/C TV TEL. $190–$230 double; $370–$995 suite. AE, DC, MC, V.

From the moment you drive up to this hotel, which epitomizes contemporary North-west styling in its gardens, architecture, and interior design, you know this is some-place special. Strikingly landscaped gardens surround the entrance and an arbor draped with wisteria lead to the front door. There are works of contemporary art throughout the public areas, including plenty of colorful art-glass pieces. Style, how-ever, is only part of the story here. The "club" in this hotel's name refers to a state-of-the-art health club that should make this the top choice of the fit.

Even if you aren't into aerobic workouts, this hotel has much to offer. Simply put, you won't find more elegant rooms anywhere in Seattle. Guest rooms here are out-rageously plush, with the high-ceilinged garden rooms among our favorites. These come with a floor-to-ceiling wall of glass, massive draperies, and a private patio fac-ing onto a beautiful garden. Luxurious European fabrics are everywhere, giving rooms a very romantic feel (although the hotel is most popular with business travelers). In the bathrooms, which are resplendent in granite and glass, you'll find whirlpool tubs (in most rooms) and even dumbbells. Three telephones, fax machines, irons and iron-ing boards, in-room safes, and hair dryers are all standard.

Dining/Entertainment: The same elegant contemporary styling seen in the lobby is to be found in the **Polaris Restaurant,** which is part of the club complex. North-west flavors predominate on the menu here. There's also a lounge.

Services: Concierge, 24-hour room service, valet/laundry service, complimentary morning newspaper and overnight shoeshine.

Facilities: The "Club" in this hotel's name is a massive full-service health club that has everything from an indoor running track to a 50-meter pool to indoor squash courts and outdoor tennis courts. At press time, there were plans to add a spa also.

Hyatt Regency Bellevue at Bellevue Place. 900 Bellevue Way NE, Bellevue, WA 98004. ☎ **800/233-1234** or 425/462-1234. Fax 425/646-7567. 382 rms, 29 suites. A/C TV TEL. $165–$225 double ($99–$129 weekends); $250–$1,000 suite. AE, CB, DC, DISC, MC, V. Valet parking $11; self-parking $7.

Located across the street from the Northwest's largest shopping mall and connected to a smaller and more exclusive shopping center, the Hyatt Regency Bellevue is a sure bet for anyone who likes to shop. This high-rise also offers from its upper floors some good views of Lake Washington, the Seattle skyline, and the Cascade Range, with the best views being those from the south side of the building. Decor in the public areas is an interesting mixture of traditional European styling and Oriental art and antiques. While all the rooms are very comfortable and have coffeemakers, hair dryers, and irons and ironing boards, for a bit extra, you can opt for a couple of different types of upgraded rooms. Opt for a Regency Club room ($25 extra) and you'll get the best views and access to a concierge lounge that serves complimentary breakfast, lunch, and evening hors d'oeuvres. There are also business-plan rooms that come with fax machines, free local phone calls, and a complimentary breakfast.

Dining/Entertainment: Eques, the hotel's main dining room, is located just off the lobby and serves rather traditional and conservative American cuisine. The decor, as the name implies, incorporates various horse images. An adjacent lounge provides a quiet spot for a drink. **Chadfield's Sports Pub** features green-marble counters, hardwood floors (covered with peanut shells), and plenty of televisions for monitoring the big game. Light snacks and sandwiches are served in the pub.

Services: 24-hour room service, valet/laundry service.

Facilities: The adjacent health club ($7 for 1 day; $12 for 3 days) is large and well-equipped (lap pool, steam room, sauna, whirlpool spa, weight room, aerobics room).

✪ **The Woodmark Hotel on Lake Washington.** 1200 Carillon Point, Kirkland, WA 98033-7351. ☎ **800/822-3700** or 425/822-3700. Fax 425/822-3699. 100 rms, 25 suites. A/C MINIBAR TV TEL. $180–$230 double; $250–$1,250 suite. AE, DC, JCB, MC, V. Valet parking $11; self-parking $9.

Despite all the lakes and bays in the Seattle area, it has a surprising dearth of waterfront hotels, and although Kirkland's Woodmark Hotel is 20 minutes from downtown Seattle (on a good day), it is still the metro area's premier waterfront lodging and the most resort-like hotel in the area. Surrounded by a luxury residential community and upscale shopping plaza, the Woodmark looks out over a wide lawn to the very same waters that Bill Gates views from his nearby Xanadu. Doormen and stunning flower arrangements await at the portico (which is flanked by a day spa), while inside the lobby, a wall of glass frames a view of the lake.

While there are plenty of lake-view rooms here, you'll pay as much as a $50 premium for these rooms. Creek-view rooms, which are the least expensive, offer a pleasant view of an attractively landscaped salmon stream. In the Woodmark's guest rooms you'll find such welcome features as floor-to-ceiling windows that open, a tiny television and a hair dryer in the bathroom, a large work desk, two telephones, and a coffeemaker.

Dining/Entertainment: At **Waters,** an upscale lake-view bistro, you can dine on an eclectic melange of flavors. For afternoon tea and cocktails throughout the day, there is the cozy **Library Bar,** which often has live piano music in the evenings. In addition, there are complimentary late-night snacks and drinks available.

Services: Room service, concierge, courtesy local shopping van, complimentary newspaper, shoeshine service, laundry/valet service, complimentary use of laptop computer, cellular phone, pager.

Facilities: Exercise room, day spa, marina, business center.

MODERATE

Best Western Bellevue Inn. 11211 Main St., Bellevue, WA 98004. ☎ **800/421-8193** or 425/455-5240. Fax 206/455-0654. 179 rms. $100–$140 double. AE, DC, DISC, JCB, MC, V. Free parking.

The Bellevue is one of the few hotels in the Seattle area that captures the feel of the Northwest in design and landscaping. The sprawling two-story hotel is roofed with cedar-shake shingles and lushly planted with rhododendrons, ferns, azaleas, and fir trees. Try to book a poolside first-floor room. These rooms, though a bit dark, have sunken, rock-walled patios. Bathrooms include plenty of counter space, and there are built-in hair dryers. There are also coffeemakers and minirefrigerators in all rooms.

The hotel gives out complimentary passes to a local athletic club and offers complimentary local van service, valet/laundry service, and the services of a rental-car desk. You may also make use of an outdoor pool, an exercise room, and a newsstand.

Jonah's is a rather lackluster restaurant that serves standard American fare. The adjoining bar is popular as an after-work hangout for business travelers.

Seattle Dining 5

Over the past few years Seattle has begun to develop a reputation as one of the country's top restaurant cities. This reputation has brought in the likes of Planet Hollywood and a restaurant by California celebrity chef Wolfgang Puck (with a second on the way at press time). The city has also been drawing more and more top-notch chefs eager to make a start.

While Seattle's reputation has risen on the shoulders of its creative Northwest cuisine, the past few years saw the city in the throes of the Mediterranean/rustic Italian dining trend that swept the nation. Although there still seems to be an Italian restaurant on every corner in Seattle, and new ones still opening, a new trend is slowly developing: pan-Asian or Euro-Asian restaurants with boldly contemporary interior decor.

Although a few years back this style of cooking might have been dubbed Pacific Rim (another name for Northwest cuisine), the new moniker is more appropriate. Pan-Asian restaurants such as Seattle's own Wild Ginger and Wolfgang Puck's ObaChine spread the flavors of Asia across their menus and, in the case of ObaChine, mix them all together. In the Westin Hotel, Hawaiian restaurateur Roy Yamaguchi has opened a mainland outpost serving his highly creative Euro-Asian cuisine. A consequence of this trend is that eating Asian food no longer limits you to low-budget and characterless settings. Of course, in the hands of accomplished chefs, the food itself also leaps out of the realm of the mundane. A few more Seattle restaurants have been hopping on the pan-Asian bandwagon this year, and still others are acknowledging the trend by incorporating Asian dishes into their menus. So, are you ready for sushi egg rolls with fiery Burmese dipping sauce on a bed of Sumatran smoked eel curry?

One Seattle dining trend that has not changed is the city's near obsession with seafood. You may be aware that wild salmon in the Northwest are rapidly disappearing from the region's rivers, but this doesn't bar nearly every menu in the city from featuring salmon. Much of it is now hatchery fish, or fish imported from Canada or Alaska. Along with the salmon, there are nearly a dozen varieties of regional oysters available. Dungeness crabs are another Northwest specialty, which though not as large as king crabs, are quite a bit heftier than the blue crabs of the eastern United States. You may also run across such unfamiliar clams as the razor clam or the geoduck (pronounced "gooey duck"). The former is shaped like a straight razor and can be chewy if not prepared properly, and the latter is a bivalve of prodigious proportions (as much as 12 pounds) that usually shows up only in stews and chowders.

With so much water all around, you would be remiss if you didn't eat at a **waterfront restaurant** while in Seattle. You'll find them on virtually every body of water in the Seattle area, offering views of everything from marinas to Mount Rainier, the Olympic Mountains to the Space Needle. We have listed waterfront restaurants in appropriate neighborhood categories below. Downtown, you'll find Anthony's Pier 66 and Elliott's; in the Queen Anne Hill/Lake Union area, you'll find McCormick's Harborside, Kamon on Lake Union, and Palisade; in the north Seattle section, you'll find Ivar's Salmon House, Ponti, and Ray's Boathouse; in west Seattle, you'll find Salty's on Alki; in east Seattle, you'll find Leschi Lakecafe; and on the Eastside, you'll find Yarrow Bay Grill.

If you're looking for someplace to eat after midnight, there are ever more decent options in Seattle (especially downtown) for **late-night dining.** In the listings below, check out Flying Fish, Palace Kitchen, Trattoria Mitchelli, and 13 Coins.

Want to do **brunch?** No problem, there are some great options around the city. Try Cafe Flora, Ivar's Salmon House, McCormick and Schmick's Harborside, Palisade, Ponti Seafood Grill, Salty's on Alki, the Space Needle, or, over on the Eastside, Yarrow Bay Grill.

1 Best Bets

- **Best Spot for a Romantic Dinner:** At **Chez Shea,** Corner Market Building, Suite 34, 94 Pike St., (☎ **206/467-9990**), in a quiet corner of Pike Place Market, candlelit tables, subdued lighting, views of ferries crossing the bay, and superb meals add up to the perfect combination for a romantic dinner. Gaze into the eyes of your companion and share bites of polenta torta and king-salmon with cumin-macadamia butter. It just doesn't get much better than this.
- **Best Place to Close a Deal: Il Terrazzo Carmine,** 411 First Ave. S. (☎ **206/467-7797**), tucked away in a hidden corner of Pioneer Square, is one of Seattle's premier power-lunch spots. Upscale Italian food is the order of the day, and, of course, the bar will fix you a martini or two.
- **Best Spot for a Celebration:** From the number of people, young and old, who show up at **Anthony's Pier 66,** 2201 Alaskan Way (☎ **206/448-6688**), it seems obvious that this is now a favorite of Seattleites in the mood to celebrate. The view, the decor, the food, all say tonight is a special night.
- **Best Decor:** With a saltwater tide pool pond meandering through the middle of the dining room, beautiful koa wood details everywhere, and art-glass chandeliers, **Palisade,** Elliott Bay Marina, 2601 W. Marina Place (☎ **206/285-1000**), has the most memorable decor of any Seattle restaurant. Never mind that it also has a 180° view of Elliott Bay.
- **Best View:** There's no question here, the **Space Needle Restaurant and Emerald Suite,** Seattle Center, 219 Fourth Ave. N. (☎ **206/443-2100**), have the best views in Seattle—360° of them. Sure it's expensive, and it's not the best food Seattle has to offer, but there's no other place in town with such a view.
- **Best Wine List: Canlis,** 2576 Aurora Ave. N. (☎ **206/283-3313**), has been around for almost 50 years and has had plenty of time to develop an extensive and well-thought-out wine list.
- **Best Value:** For little more than you'd pay to eat at your local cheap Chinese joint, you can savor the culinary artistry of Wolfgang Puck, California's most famous

chef, at **ObaChine,** 1518 Sixth Ave. (☎ **206/749-9653**), a pan-Asian bistro extraordinaire.

- **Best for Kids:** Located on the south shore of Lake Union, **Cucina!Cucina!,** Chandler's Cove, Fairview Ave. N. (☎ **206/447-2782**), is Seattle's most popular family restaurant because of all the things they do here to make dining out fun for kids. Adults like it, too.
- **Best French:** With classic flavors, ingredients flown in from France, and a heavy hand with the black truffles, **Virazon,** 1329 First Ave. (☎ **206/233-0123**), near Pike Place Market, is Seattle's most traditional French restaurant.
- **Best Italian:** With so many Italian restaurants in Seattle these days, it's tough deciding which is the best. If you've got the bucks, though, **Il Terrazzo Carmine,** 411 First Ave. S. (☎ **206/467-7797**), in Pioneer Square, is as likely a candidate as any for a big night on the town.
- **Best Northwest Cuisine:** Chef Thierry Rautureau at **Rover's,** 2808 E. Madison St. (☎ **206/325-7442**), combines his love of Northwest ingredients with his classic French training to produce his own distinctive take on Northwest cuisine.
- **Best Seafood:** Chef Tom Douglas seems to be able to do no wrong, and at **Etta's Seafood,** 2020 Western Ave. (☎ **206/443-6000**), he focuses his culinary talents on more than just his famed crab cakes.
- **Best Steaks:** The **Metropolitan Grill,** 818 Second Ave. (☎ **206/624-3287**), in downtown Seattle serves corn-fed, aged beef grilled over mesquite wood. Steaks just don't get any better than this.
- **Best Burger:** Peppered bacon, kasseri cheese, and grilled onions on a thick, juicy burger all inside a chewy Italian roll—this is the combination that makes the **Belltown Pub** burger the best in town (2322 First Ave.; ☎ **206/728-4311**).
- **Best Vegetarian:** Interesting and diverse preparations with vegetables and their friends—grains, legumes, nuts, and pasta—come out of the kitchen at **Café Flora,** 2901 E. Madison St. (☎ **206/325-9100**).
- **Best Pizza:** It looks gooey, crusty, and tempting, and tastes even better at **Pizzeria Pagliacci,** 426 Broadway E. (☎ **206/324-0730**), with several different locations around Seattle.
- **Best Desserts:** At **Dilettante Chocolates,** 416 Broadway E. (☎ **206/329-6463**), almost everything has chocolate in it, which is absolutely fine with us. The cases are packed with all manner of cakes, tortes, and truffles.
- **Best Late-Night Dining:** Chef Christine Keff has, with her **Flying Fish** restaurant in Belltown, 2234 First Ave. (☎ **206/728-8595**), brought Seattle something it has been hungering for: a great place to eat if you're hungry at, say, 11:30 on a Wednesday night.
- **Best Outdoor Dining:** While in Seattle there are lots of waterfront restaurants with great decks overlooking various bodies of water, for something a little different, try the shady garden courtyard at **Serafina,** 2043 Eastlake Ave. E. (☎ **206/323-0807**), a rustic Italian restaurant near Lake Union.
- **Best Espresso: Torrefazione**, 320 Occidental Ave. S. (☎ **206/624-5847;** 622 Olive Way, ☎ 206/624-1429), serves its brew in hand-painted Italian crockery, and has delectable pastries to go with your espresso.

2 Restaurants by Cuisine

AMERICAN
Canlis (Lake Union, Queen Anne Hill, Magnolia, *E*)

Leschi Lakecafe (First Hill, Capitol Hill, East Seattle, *M*)
Merchants Café (Downtown, *I*)

BAKERIES & PASTRY SHOPS

A la Francaise (Downtown, *I*)
The Crumpet Shop (Downtown, *I*)
Dilettante Chocolates (First Hill,
 Capitol Hill, East Seattle, *I*)
The Famous Pacific Dessert
 Company (First Hill, Capitol Hill,
 East Seattle, *I*)
Le Panier (Downtown, *I*)
Macrina (Downtown, *I*)
Three Girls Bakery (Downtown, *I*)

CAFES & COFFEE BARS

Still Life in Fremont Coffeehouse
 (Downtown, *I*)
Torrefazione (Downtown, *I*)
Zio Rico (Downtown, *I*)

CHINESE/ASIAN

Hing Loon (Downtown, *I*)
Kamon on Lake Union (Lake Union,
 Queen Anne Hill, Magnolia, *M*)
ObaChine (Downtown, *M*)
Wild Ginger Asian Restaurant and
 Satay Bar (Downtown, *M*)

CONTINENTAL

Canlis (Lake Union, Queen Anne
 Hill, Magnolia, *E*)
The Georgian (Downtown, *E*)

EASTERN EUROPEAN

Labuznik (Downtown, *M*)

FRENCH

Café Campagne (Downtown, *M*)
Campagne (Downtown, *E*)
The Painted Table (Downtown, *M*)
Virazon (Downtown, *E*)

GEORGIAN

Pirosmani (Lake Union, Queen Anne
 Hill, Magnolia, *M*)

INTERNATIONAL

Belltown Pub (Downtown, *I*)
Marco's Supperclub (Downtown, *M*)
Queen City Grill (Downtown, *M*)
Shea's Lounge (Downtown, *M*)

ITALIAN/EUROPEAN

Assaggio (Downtown, *M*)
Cafe Juanita (Kirkland, *M*)
Café Lago (Fremont, Wallingford,
 the University District, *M*)
Cucina!Cucina! (Lake Union, Queen
 Anne Hill, Magnolia, *I*)
Il Bistro (Downtown, *E*)
Il Terrazzo Carmine (Downtown, *E*)
Isabella (Downtown, *M*)
La Buca (Downtown, *M*)
The Pink Door (Downtown, *M*)
Serafina (Lake Union, Queen Anne
 Hill, Magnolia, *M*)
Trattoria Mitchelli (Downtown, *M*)

JAPANESE

Kamon on Lake Union
 (Lake Union, Queen Anne Hill,
 Magnolia, *M*)
Nikko (Downtown, *E*)

MEDITERRANEAN

Andaluca (Downtown, *M*)
Pirosmani (Lake Union, Queen Anne
 Hill, Magnolia, *M*)

NATURAL FOODS

Gravity Bar (Downtown, *I*)

NORTHWEST

Andaluca (Downtown, *M*)
Chez Shea (Downtown, *E*)
Dahlia Lounge (Downtown, *M*)
Flying Fish (Downtown, *M*)
Fuller's (Downtown, *E*)
The Georgian (Downtown, *E*)
The Herbfarm (Fall City, *VE*)
The Hunt Club (First Hill, Capitol
 Hill, East Seattle, *E*)
Kamon on Lake Union (Lake Union,
 Queen Anne Hill, Magnolia, *M*)
Kaspar's (Lake Union, Queen Anne
 Hill, Magnolia, *E*)
The Painted Table (Downtown, *M*)
Palace Kitchen (Downtown, *M*)
Palisade (Lake Union, Queen Anne
 Hill, Magnolia, *M*)

Key to abbreviations: *E*=Expensive; *I*=Inexpensive; *M*=Moderate; *VE*=Very Expensive

Rover's (First Hill, Capitol Hill,
East Seattle, *E*)
Shea's Lounge (Downtown, *M*)
The Space Needle and Emerald
Suite Restaurant (Lake Union,
Queen Anne Hill,
Magnolia, *E*)
Theôz (Downtown, *M*)
Yarrow Bay Grill (Kirkland, *M*)

PIZZA

Pizzeria Pagliacci (First Hill, Capitol
Hill, East Seattle, *I*)

SEAFOOD

Anthony's Pier 66 and Bell Street
Diner (Downtown, *E*)
The Brooklyn Seafood, Steak, and
Oyster House (Downtown, *E*)
Elliott's (Downtown, *M*)
Emmett Watson's Oyster Bar
(Downtown, *I*)
Etta's Seafood (Downtown, *M*)
Flying Fish (Downtown, *M*)
Ivar's Salmon House (Fremont,
Wallingford, the University
District, *M*)
Kaspar's (Lake Union, Queen Anne
Hill, Magnolia, *E*)

McCormick and Schmick's
(Downtown, *M*)
McCormick and Schmick's
Harborside (Lake Union,
Queen Anne Hill, Magnolia, *M*)
McCormick's Fish House and Bar
(Downtown, *M*)
Ponti Seafood Grill (Fremont,
Wallingford, the University
District, *M*)
Ray's Boathouse and Cafe (Fremont,
Wallingford, the University
District, *M*)
Salty's on Alki (West Seattle, *M*)

STEAK

Metropolitan Grill (Downtown, *E*)
Ray's Boathouse and Cafe (Fremont,
Wallingford, the University
District, *M*)

THAI

Siam on Broadway
(First Hill, Capitol Hill,
East Seattle, *I*)

VEGETARIAN

Café Flora (First Hill, Capitol Hill,
East Seattle, *M*)

3 Downtown (Including the Waterfront, Pioneer Square, Belltown & the International District)

EXPENSIVE

✪ **Anthony's Pier 66 and Bell Street Diner.** 2201 Alaskan Way. ☎ **206/448-6688.**
Reservations recommended (and only accepted) upstairs at Pier 66. Main dishes $17–$27 (Pier 66), $9–$22 (Bell Street Diner). AE, DISC, MC, V. Pier 66 Sun–Thurs 5–9:15pm, Fri–Sat 5–10:15pm; Bell Street Diner Sun–Thurs 11am–10pm, Fri–Sat 11am–11pm. SEAFOOD.

There are a lot of mediocre restaurants on the Seattle waterfront, but if you head up to the north end of the waterfront you'll find not only excellent food but an exceedingly stylish restaurant that features art glass and a boldly contemporary styling throughout. There are actually two restaurants here (three if you count the walk-up window out front), with the up-market crowd heading upstairs for the likes of applewood-grilled salmon, and the more cost-conscious staying downstairs at the Bell Street Diner where meals are much easier on the wallet. For the higher prices, you get the better views as long as you don't get stuck at the counter that overlooks the exhibition kitchen. In summer the decks are the place to be.

The Brooklyn Seafood, Steak, and Oyster House. 1212 Second Ave. ☎ **206/224-7000.**
Reservations recommended. Main courses $13–$33. AE, DC, DISC, MC, V. Mon–Fri 11am–3pm; Mon–Thurs 5–10pm, Fri 5–10:30pm, Sat 4:30–10:30pm, Sun 4:30–10pm. SEAFOOD.

Seattle Dining—Downtown

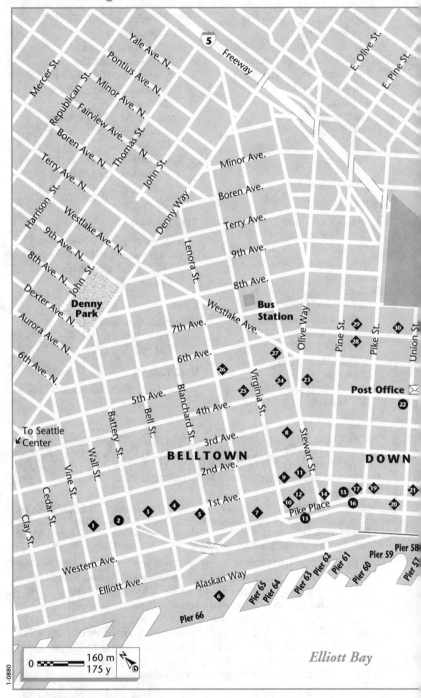

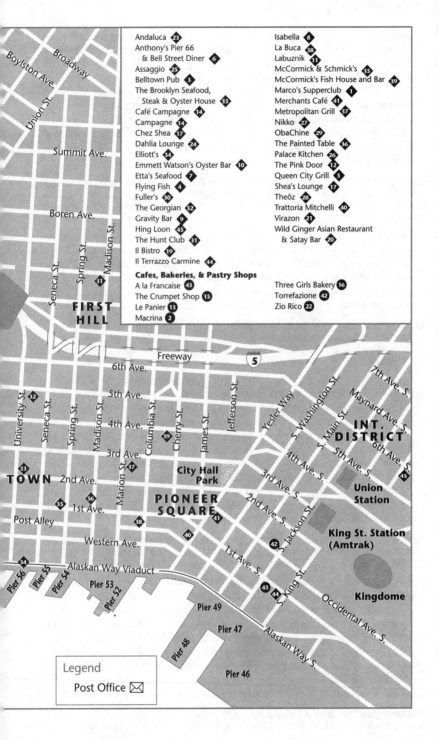

Designed to look as if it's been here for decades, The Brooklyn is housed in one of the city's oldest buildings. The specialty here is definitely oysters, with about 10 different types piled up at the oyster bar on any given night. If oysters on the half shell don't appeal to you, there are plenty of other tempting appetizers ranging from grilled salmon sausages to roasted garlic and goat cheese. Alder-planked meats and fishes are another specialty here. This type of cooking is similar to smoking or grilling and originated with the Native Americans of the Northwest. In addition, there are simply prepared grilled steaks, and such dishes as seafood pasta in parchment, and grilled black tiger prawns with a vanilla bean and lime sauce. There are even a couple of vegetarian dishes on the menu. After 5pm, there is free valet parking.

Campagne. Inn at the Market, 86 Pine St. ☎ **206/728-2800.** Reservations recommended. Main dishes $20–$30; tasting menu $55; 3-course family dinners for 2 or 3 persons $30 per person, for 4 or more $25 per person. AE, CB, DC, MC, V. Daily 5:30–10pm (cafe dining until midnight). FRENCH.

Cheerful and unpretentious, Campagne is one of the most enjoyable French restaurants in Seattle. Large windows let in precious sunshine and provide a view of Elliott Bay over the top of Pike Place Market. The menu here leans toward country French, with such dishes as house-cured duck prosciutto with a chilled fig and melon timbale, arugula and shaved Reggiano cheese; grilled lamb; and roasted baby chicken stuffed with basmati rice and fava beans. Family dinners are available, and change daily.

✪ Chez Shea. Corner Market Building, Suite 34, 94 Pike St., Pike Place Market. ☎ **206/467-9990.** Reservations highly recommended. Main dishes $25–$26 (à la carte dishes available Tues–Thurs and Sun); fixed-price 4-course dinner $39. AE, MC, V. Tues–Sun 5:30–10pm. NORTHWEST.

Quiet, dark, and intimate, Chez Shea is one of the finest restaurants in Seattle. A dozen candlelit tables, with views across Puget Sound to the Olympic Mountains, are the perfect setting for a romantic dinner. The menu changes with the season, and ingredients come primarily from the market below. On a recent spring evening, dinner started with an asparagus-watercress flan and then moved on to a carrot bisque. There are usually five choices of entree, and among these were rabbit braised in wine with balsamic vinegar, sweet peppers, leeks, and rosemary, and halibut sautéed with blood orange coulis with gaeta olives, red onion, coriander, white wine, and garlic. Though dessert is à la carte, you'll find it impossible to let it pass you by. While there are equally fine restaurants in the city, none has quite the quintessential Seattle atmosphere as Chez Shea.

Fuller's. Sheraton Seattle Hotel and Towers, 1400 Sixth Ave. ☎ **206/621-9000.** Reservations recommended. Main dishes $18–$30; tasting menu $55; lunches $10–$15. AE, CB, DC, DISC, JCB, MC, V. Mon–Fri 11:30am–2pm; Mon–Sat 5:30–10pm. NORTHWEST.

Fuller's, named for the founder of the Seattle Art Museum, is dedicated to both the culinary and the visual arts of the Northwest. Each dish is as artfully designed as it is superbly prepared, and surrounding you in this elegant and newly renovated dining room are works of art by the Northwest's best artists. Fuller's menu changes seasonally, but Asian and Mediterranean flavors have predominated of late. A recent menu included an appetizer of smoked ahi tuna with cucumber wasabi vinaigrette and daikon sprouts; two main dishes were saffron and coriander marinated demi rack of lamb and grilled veal chop with morel mushrooms. Lunch, with its lower prices, is especially popular. The wine list reflects the seasonal changes on the menu.

The Georgian. Four Seasons Olympic Hotel, 411 University St. ☎ **206/621-1700.** Reservations recommended. Main dishes $20–$36. AE, CB, DC, MC, V. Mon–Fri 6:30–11am, Sat

6:30am–noon, Sun 7am–1pm; Mon–Thurs 5:30–10pm, Fri–Sat 5:30–10:30pm. CONTINENTAL/ NORTHWEST.

Nowhere in Seattle is there a more elegant restaurant—to dine at The Georgian is to dine in a palace. The soaring ceiling is decorated with intricate moldings, and the huge windows are framed by luxurious curtains. The attentive service will convince you that your table is the only one being served. Menu offerings are a mingling of Northwest and Continental cuisines, but veal or New York tenderloin with mushrooms and aged Black Angus steak are the signature dishes. As you would expect, the wine list is well suited to both the food and the restaurant's ambience.

Il Bistro. 93-A Pike St. and First Ave. (inside Pike Place Market). ☎ **206/682-3049.** Reservations recommended. Pastas $10–$16; main dishes $16–$26.50. AE, CB, DC, MC, V. Mon–Sat 11:30am–3pm; Sun–Thurs 5:30–10pm, Fri–Sat 5:30–11pm; bar nightly until 2am. ITALIAN.

You'll find Il Bistro to the left of the famous Pike Place Market sign. The entrance is from the ramp that leads into the bowels of the market, and once inside you'll feel as if you're dining in a wine cellar. Il Bistro takes Italian cooking very seriously and puts the Northwest's bountiful ingredients to good use. The region is damp most of the year and brings forth excellent crops of wild and cultivated mushrooms. Watch for them on the menu; they're always a treat.

The menu lists such mouthwatering starters as calamari sautéed with fresh basil, garlic vinegar, and white wine. Pasta can be a genuine revelation when served with shiitake mushrooms, hot pepper flakes, vodka, and tomato cream. Long before you arrived, the choice of which main dish to order was decided by the hundreds of loyal fans who insist that the rack of lamb with wine sauce is the best in Seattle. Don't take their word for it—have it yourself. A wine list featuring Italian, Northwest, and California wines and a selection of single-malt scotches and grappas rounds out the experience.

✪ **Il Terrazzo Carmine.** 411 First Ave. S. ☎ **206/467-7797.** Reservations recommended. Pastas $9.50–$14; main dishes $18.50–$26. AE, DC, DISC, MC, V. Mon–Fri 11:30am–2:30pm and 5:30–10pm, Sat 5:30–10pm. ITALIAN.

Considered by many to be the finest Italian restaurant in Seattle, Il Terrazzo Carmine is tucked into the back of an office building in the Pioneer Square area and overlooks a hidden waterfall terrace. This is a big-time power lunch spot and suits are de rigueur for men. What the wealthy come for is a rarefied atmosphere, professional service, and reliable fine Italian fare. Nowhere else in town will you find the likes of sweetbreads ragout and both beef and tuna carpaccio. Among the pastas, you're likely to encounter venison-stuffed ravioli and pappardelle with duck. If you're a steak eater, consider the *bistecca piemontese,* made with dry-aged Black Angus New York steak and served with truffle oil, radiccio, and endive.

✪ **Metropolitan Grill.** 818 Second Ave. ☎ **206/624-3287.** Reservations recommended. Main dishes lunch $7.50–$20, dinner $17–$35. AE, CB, DC, DISC, JCB, MC, V. Mon–Fri 11am–3:30pm and 5–11pm; Sat 4–11pm, Sun 4:30–10pm. STEAK.

Another reliable restaurant for aspiring financial whizzes and their mentors, the Metropolitan is dedicated to carnivores. When you walk in, you'll see various cuts of meat, from filet mignon to triple-cut lamb chops, displayed on ice. Green-velvet booths and floral-design carpets strike the keynote of the sophisticated atmosphere, and mirrored walls and a high ceiling trimmed with elegant plasterwork make the dining room feel larger than it actually is. Perfectly cooked steaks are the primary attraction, and a baked potato and a pile of thick-cut onion rings complete the perfect steak dinner.

Nikko. Westin Hotel Seattle, 1900 Fifth Ave. ☎ **206/322-4641.** Reservations recommended. Dinners $14–$35; sushi $3.25–$20. AE, CB, DC, MC, V. Mon–Fri 11:30am–2pm and 5:30–10pm, Sat–Sun 5:30–10pm. JAPANESE.

With knock-out decor that merges traditional Japanese styling with contemporary design elements, this is Seattle's trendiest Japanese restaurant. Black-slate floors, blond shoji-screen walls, indirect and subtle lighting, and original art on the walls are just some of the details that make Nikko an attractive place for a meal. Expert sushi chefs, a display teppan-grill bar, and an extensive menu that makes the most of the Northwest's abundance of seafood assure you that Nikko is more than just a pretty place to assuage a hunger. There are even family-style dinners that allow you to sample a wide assortment of dishes, if you dine in a group of four or more.

✪ **Virazon.** 1329 First Ave. ☎ **206/233-0123.** Reservations recommended. Main dishes $16–$39; 5-course tasting menu $49. AE, DC, MC, V. Mon 11:30am–2:30pm, Tues–Thurs 11:30am–2:30pm and 5:30–9:30pm, Fri–Sat 11:30am–2:30pm and 6–10pm. FRENCH.

There are several French restaurants in the Pike Place Market vicinity, but none is as authentic as Virazon. This is high-end French, the cuisine of legend, with truffles making frequent appearances (a black and white soup of black truffles and celery root; a salad with truffles, peas, white corn, and poached quail eggs; crab and lobster cakes with peas, basil, truffles, and a champagne sauce). Foie gras caviar, squab, and frogs legs also show up. While the classic dishes on the menu will be tempting to gastronomes, it is the tasting menu that is the restaurant's biggest draw. Let chef Astolfo Rueda create a truly memorable dinner for you. Though the restaurant is located on busy First Avenue, inside you'll find a quiet, refined atmosphere perfect for a romantic dinner or other special occasion.

MODERATE

✪ **Andaluca.** Mayflower Park Hotel, 407 Olive Way. ☎ **206/382-6999.** Reservations recommended. Main dishes $14.50–$23. AE, CB, DC, DISC, MC, V. Mon–Thurs 11:30am–2:30pm and 5–10pm, Fri–Sat 11:30am–2:30pm and 5–11pm, Sun 4–9pm. NORTHWEST/MEDITERRANEAN.

Located in the basement of the Mayflower Park Hotel, this sumptuous restaurant mixes the traditional and the contemporary like no other restaurant in town. To step into the restaurant is to enter a world of vibrant artistry, both in decor and cuisine. Chef Don Curtiss continues to build his reputation with such dishes as traditional Spanish zarazuela shellfish stew and, at press time, paella (on Sunday nights). The menu is divided into small plates and large plates, so no matter the size of your hunger, you'll find something to fill it. While the menu changes frequently, you might find a spicy octopus dish on the small plate menu, but it's the Dungeness crab tower, made with avocado, palm hearts, and gazpacho salsa, that has taken Seattle diners by storm. Don't miss it.

Assaggio. 2010 Fourth Ave. ☎ **206/441-1399.** Reservations recommended. Pastas $9–$15, main dishes $14–$20. AE, DC, DISC, MC, V. Mon–Fri 11:30am–2:30pm and 5–10pm, Sat 5–10pm. ITALIAN.

Located on the ground floor of the Hotel Claremont, Assaggio has become one of Seattle's favorite Italian restaurants. This large, casual restaurant has an old-world feel, with a high ceiling, arches, Roman-style murals on the walls, and a wait staff in white aprons and loud ties (definitely an American touch). However, what really recommends this place is the excellent food. For a starter, you might try the grilled radicchio wrapped in pancetta (Italian ham) and topped with a red onion-balsamic vinaigrette. Pastas come from all over Italy, but it's hard to beat the pappardella boscaiola with prosciutto ham, wild mushrooms, Marsala and Barolo wine, and a touch of cream.

Of course there are traditional pizzas, but there are also such other standbys as osso buco and veal saltimboca.

Café Campagne. 1600 Post Alley. ☎ **206/728-2233.** Reservations not accepted. Main dishes $8–$15. AE, MC, V. Mon–Sat 8am–11pm, Sun brunch 8am–3pm. FRENCH.

This cozy little cafe is an offshoot of the Inn at the Market's popular Campagne, and though it is located in the heart of the Pike Place Market neighborhood, it's a world away from the market madness. The menu changes with the season but might include a hearty country-style pâté or baked marinated goat cheese on the appetizer menu. Entrees include filling sandwiches such as the popular lamb burger with aioli or roast pork tenderloin on foccacia with apricot mustard. Main courses are served à la carte, so if you're particularly hungry, peruse the list of side dishes, which might include baby artichokes stewed in olive oil with lemon and garlic. The cafe also doubles as a wine bar and has a good selection of reasonably priced wines by the glass or by the bottle.

Dahlia Lounge. 1904 Fourth Ave. ☎ **206/682-4142.** Reservations highly recommended. Main dishes $16–$22. AE, DC, DISC, MC, V. Mon–Fri 11:30am–2:30pm; Mon–Thurs 5:30–10pm, Fri–Sat 5:30–11pm, Sun 5–9pm. NORTHWEST.

The neon chef holding a flapping fish may suggest that the Dahlia is little more than a roadside diner, but a glimpse inside at the stylish decor will likely have you thinking otherwise. One look at the menu, one bite of any dish, will convince you that this is one of Seattle's finest restaurants. Mouth-watering and succulent Dungeness crab cakes, a bow to Chef Tom Douglas's Maryland roots, are the house specialty and should not be missed. Lobster-shiitake potstickers are also a perennial favorite. The menu, influenced by the far side of the Pacific Rim, changes regularly. The lunch menu features many of the same offerings at slightly lower prices.

Elliott's. Pier 56, Alaskan Way. ☎ **206/623-4340.** Reservations recommended. Main dishes $14–$30. AE, DISC, MC, V. Sun–Thurs 11am–11pm, Fri–Sat 11am–11:30pm (the oyster bar stays open later). SEAFOOD.

While most of its neighbors are content to coast along on tourist business, Elliott's actually aims to keep locals happy by serving some of the best seafood in Seattle. Although the restaurant is right on the waterfront, the view really isn't that great, so if you're looking for a drop-dead view, try elsewhere. However, if you're looking for superbly prepared fresh seafood, Elliott's is a good bet. The oyster bar, which *Fortune* magazine called one of the five best in the country, does usually have a great selection of fresh oysters. If you prefer your oysters cooked, consider the pan-seared oyster sampler, which includes a trio of boldly flavored dipping sauces.

✪ **Etta's Seafood.** 2020 Western Ave. ☎ **206/443-6000.** Reservations recommended. Main dishes $8.50–$23. AE, DC, DISC, MC, V. Mon–Thurs 11:30am–10pm, Fri 11:30am–11pm, Sat 9am–11pm, Sun 9am–10pm. SEAFOOD.

A makeover of Seattle chef Tom Douglas's original Cafe Sport, Etta's is located in the Pike Place Market area. Of course, it serves Douglas's signature crab cakes (crunchy on the outside, creamy on the inside), which are not to be missed. Consider the seared ahi tuna if it's on the menu. This almost-sushi has a wonderful texture. Don't ignore your side dishes, either; they can be exquisite and are usually enough to share around the table. If you're not a lover of seafood, don't be afraid: Even though it makes up most of the menu, there are other fine options. Stylish contemporary decor sets the mood and assures that this place is as popular with locals as it is with tourists.

⭕ **Flying Fish.** 2234 First Ave. ☎ **206/728-8595.** Reservations recommended. Main dishes $9–$20. AE, MC, V. Daily 5pm–midnight. NORTHWEST/SEAFOOD.

Chef Christine Keff has been on the Seattle restaurant scene for many years now and in Flying Fish has hit on something the city really wants. Not only are there the bold combinations of vibrant flavors demanded by the city's well-traveled palates, but the hip Belltown restaurant serves dinner midnight every night, keeping late-night partiers from going hungry. Every dish here is a work of art, and with small plates, large plates, and platters for sharing, diners are encouraged to sample a wide variety of the kitchen's creations. On a recent night, the smoked rock shrimp spring rolls were positively sculptural, and the hot-and-sour squid salad was a fiery melange of flavors that alone make this restaurant worth coming back to again and again. Desserts are often so decorated that they're almost parties in their own right.

Isabella. 1909 Third Ave. ☎ **206/441-8281.** Reservations recommended. Pastas $9.50–$15, main dishes $17.50–$26.50. AE, DISC, MC, V. Mon–Thurs 11:30am–10pm, Fri 11:30am–11pm, Sat 5–11pm. ITALIAN.

Although Isabella is on a block just out of the mainstream of downtown traffic, it has maintained a loyal following for its romantic setting and bold flavors. The sumptuous decor goes against the local trend toward hard-edged contemporary designs, and the menu flaunts the vibrant flavors of fresh herbs. Although the menu is primarily southern Italian in focus, that doesn't mean you shouldn't expect the likes of grilled lamb chops with a Dijon peppercorn sauce or a mixed seafood grill. However, it is the restaurant's rich and creamy risottos that are Isabella's real claim to fame. The wine list, unfortunately, sticks strictly to Italian wines and doesn't offer much in a low price range. Lunches, mostly pastas and pizzas, are very reasonably priced.

La Buca. 102 Cherry St. ☎ **206/343-9517.** Reservations recommended on weekends. Lunch $7–$10, dinner $10–$16. AE, DC, DISC, MC, V. Mon–Sat 11:30am–2:30pm; Mon–Sun 5pm–10pm. ITALIAN.

Walk down the flight of stairs into this Pioneer Square area and you'll be dining in the Seattle underground. Dark and cavernous with brick arches supporting the ceiling, La Buca is reminiscent of a huge wine cellar. The menu is primarily southern Italian, but goes far beyond spaghetti and meatballs. The dishes show off La Buca's mouth-watering fare: A recent menu featured pan-roasted chicken breast served with a gorgonzola and toasted pistachio sauce; polenta with a topping of lamb ragout; rigatoni with roasted chicken and roasted pepper sauce; and beef rollantina stuffed with provolone cheese, Italian parsley, and garlic and roasted with a red wine, rosemary, and tomato sauce.

Labuznik. 1924 First Ave. ☎ **206/441-8899.** Reservations recommended. Main dishes $13–$29. AE, DC, DISC, MC, V. Tues–Sat 5–10pm. EASTERN EUROPEAN.

At Labuznik, the meat-and-potatoes meals of Eastern Europe have never been forgotten. Instead, they have been perfected. In Czech, *labuznik* means "lover of good food." Dine here and you'll be a happy labuznik when you leave. The tasty but tongue-twisting *vepro knedlo zelo* translates into a filling plate of roast pork with sauerkraut and dumplings. The veal Orloff is deliciously rich with mushrooms, capers, pickles, and cream. A meal here would not be complete without the Sacher torte. A lighter and less expensive menu is also available.

McCormick and Schmick's. 1103 First Ave. ☎ **206/623-5500.** Reservations recommended. Main dishes $7–$27. AE, DC, DISC, MC, V. Mon–Fri 11:30am–11pm, Sat 4:30–11pm, Sun 4:30–10pm. SEAFOOD.

Force your way past the crowds of business suits at the bar and you'll find yourself in a classic fish house—cafe curtains, polished brass, leaded glass, wood paneling, waiters in black bow ties. Daily fresh sheets featuring well-prepared seafood dishes the likes of Louisiana catfish with bay shrimp Creole sauce, traditional crab cakes with tartar sauce, or blue marlin grilled with Hunan barbecue sauce and crispy leeks have made McCormick and Schmick's extremely popular. Late afternoons and late evenings, bar appetizers are only $1.95, and early dinner specials ($12.95) are available weekdays from 3 to 5:30pm and Sunday between 5 and 6pm. If the restaurant is crowded and you can't get a table, consider sitting at the counter and watching the cooks perform feats with fire.

McCormick's Fish House and Bar. 722 Fourth Ave. (at Columbia St.). ☎ **206/682-3900.** Reservations recommended. Main dishes $9–$20. AE, CB, DC, DISC, MC, V. Mon–Fri 11:30am–11pm, Sat 4:30–11pm, Sun 4:30–10pm. SEAFOOD.

A recent menu here listed almost 30 different seafoods from such far-flung locations as Massachusetts, Chile, Hawaii, Idaho, and, of course, Washington—to give you some idea of how committed McCormick's is to bringing you the very best. However, most of the listed seafoods were from the Northwest. The ambience is old-fashioned, with dark-wood booths and a tile floor around the long bar, and service is usually fast. The clientele tends to be very upscale, especially in the bar after nearby financial offices let out. Both traditional and imaginative Northwest-style cuisine, such as Copper River salmon cakes with cranberry-lime aioli or white sturgeon topped with roasted corn chipotle relish, is served.

Marco's Supperclub. 2510 First Ave. ☎ **206/441-7801.** Reservations highly recommended. Main courses lunch $7–$11, dinner $11–$17. AE, MC, V. Mon–Fri 11:30am–2pm; daily 5:30–11pm. INTERNATIONAL.

This Belltown restaurant, furnished with thrift-store crockery and reupholstered yard-sale furnishings, has a casual ambience that belies the high-quality meals emanating from the kitchen. The menu draws on cuisines from around the world, so even jaded gourmets may find something new here. A recent menu included such unusual offerings as fried sage leaves with a medley of dipping sauces, Thai-style mussels, and Korean barbecue with spicy soba noodle salad for appetizers. Among the entrees, you're likely to find such memorable dishes as Jamaican jerk chicken with sautéed greens and sweet potato puree or sesame-crusted ahi tuna with stir-fried veggies and ginger-steamed rice. If you enjoy creative cookery at reasonable prices, check this place out.

✪ **ObaChine**. 1518 Sixth Ave. ☎ **206/749-9653.** Reservations recommended. Main courses $8.25–$16.50. AE, DC, MC, V. Daily 11:30am–midnight. ASIAN.

Celebrity chef Wolfgang Puck moved into Seattle in early 1997 with this pan-Asian restaurant and satay bar. The main dining room, with its more formal, though still very reasonably priced, menu is upstairs, while the satay bar, with its exhibition kitchen, is the lively street-level space. As you would expect of a chef who made his name keeping the jaded citizens of Los Angeles and Santa Monica happy, ObaChine is a very stylish place, the sort of place where you're not sure whether to ogle the decor or peruse the menu. While the menu is short and at first seems cobbled from those of countless other Asian restaurants, closer inspection reveals that ObaChine has mixed up the flavors of Asia in an entirely new way. There are tandoori shrimp egg rolls, seared scallops with plum wine–black bean sauce and yam-wasabi puree, and tea-leaf baked 10-spice salmon. Whatever else you order, don't miss the banana and walnut spring rolls with caramel dipping sauce.

Life in the Espresso Lane

"I'll take a double half-caf tall skinny latte with a shot of hazelnut syrup, hold the foam." It may sound like a foreign language, but it doesn't take long to decipher the complexities of espresso. The following primer should soon have you speaking (and understanding) coffeespeak like a Seattle native.

First, a little background. Coffee originated centuries ago in the highlands of east Africa in the region that is today Ethiopia. Legend has it that a goatherd noticed that his goats acted differently after eating the berries of a particular bush. Trying the berries himself, the goatherd found that they made him more alert, definitely a bonus in the goatherding business, what with lions, tigers, and hyenas stalking the flock.

Coffee consumption has changed radically over the ages. The Italians introduced espresso, the French rounded things off with milk, and Seattle raised it to an American obsession transmuting espresso in much the same way that pizzas were transfigured when they crossed the Atlantic to the new world. Where else but in the United States would you find such bizarre concoctions as Milky Way coffee (espresso, chocolate milk, and caramel syrup)? However, despite the occasional cookie-coffee aberrations, coffee-making today is a fine art that may have reached its zenith in the coffee bars, cafes, coffee carts, and drive-through coffee windows of Seattle.

There are two basic types of coffee beans: robustus and arabica. The former are the cheaper, lower quality beans and are used primarily in standard American supermarket coffees. The latter are the higher quality beans, with richer flavor, and are used for gourmet coffees and espresso. Flavor in either of these beans is determined in large part by the way the raw bean is roasted. Most regular coffees are given a light to medium roasting that produces a rougher, less complex flavor. A dark or espresso roast provides a dark oily looking bean that produces a well-rounded, rich, deep flavor. Roasting coffee beans is an art that produces immense variations in flavors and, which in turn causes educated coffee drinkers to develop loyalties to different coffee roasters.

Espresso isn't quite ubiquitous throughout the United States, so, for those of you who are not yet cruising in the espresso lane, here are some important definitions and examples of how to order coffee Seattle-style:

Espresso—a specially roasted and ground coffee that has hot water forced through it to make a small cup of dense, flavorful coffee. Straight espresso is definitely an

---

The Painted Table. Alexis Hotel, 92 Madison St. ☎ **206/624-3646.** Reservations recommended. Main dishes $16–$25; lunch main dishes $8–$16. AE, CB, DC, DISC, MC, V. Mon–Fri 6:30–10am and 11:30am–2pm, Sat–Sun 7:30am–noon; daily 5:30–10pm. NORTHWEST/FRENCH.

At The Painted Table it isn't just what's on the dish that's a work of art, it's the dish itself. Every table is set with hand-painted plates done by West Coast ceramic artists. Should you take a fancy to your plate, you can take it home with you for between $45 and $70. The restaurant's atmosphere and service are upscale casual and every dish is beautifully arranged. The potato-crusted Alaskan halibut with grilled portobello mushroom is one of our favorites. Chile-rubbed ahi tuna with tarragon corn broth is another winner. For dessert, a banana split made with a sweet Peruvian banana, three different types of chocolate, plus a chocolate mousse, is the chef's take on an old favorite.

acquired taste. Espresso developed in Italy, where today it is often drunk with a twist of lemon. European shots of espresso are smaller than American shots. Different coffeehouses serve different size shots, which means you might get more or less coffee flavor in your drink.

Latte—a shot of espresso topped off with steamed milk at roughly a three-to-one ratio. The correct term for this drink is *caffè latte* (with the accent on the final *es*). This translates as coffee milk, but in the Northwest, folks just say, "I'll have a latte (pronounced *lah*-tay)," which really means, "I'll have a milk." Oh well, so much for learning a second language.

Single—one shot of espresso. You say, "I'll have a single latte."

Double—two shots of espresso. You say, "I'll have a double latte."

Tall—a latte with extra milk. A tall usually comes with one shot of espresso, but you can also get two shots. You say, "I'll have a double tall latte."

Grande—a 16-ounce latte with two shots of espresso. This is pretty high-test, so leave it to the pros until you've worked your way up the latte ladder.

Skinny—skimmed milk. You say, "I'll have a tall, skinny latte." You can also get lattes made with 2 percent milk or with whole milk.

Half-Caf—a drink made with half decaffeinated coffee. You say, "I'll have a double tall, skinny, half-caf latte." They say, "Why bother?"

Foam—formed by steaming milk, this is the topping on a latte. Some people want it and some people don't.

Flavorings—sweet syrups with different flavors for giving your latte a bit more complexity. They're sort of the wine cooler of the espresso lane. You can get everything from caramel to mango.

Cappuccino—espresso with hot milk and usually a sprinkling of cinnamon on top. A cappuccino's color is same as that of a Capuchin monk's habit and thus the name.

Macchiato—an espresso with a dollop of foamed milk on top to insulate the coffee and keep it hotter just a little bit longer.

Mocha—espresso, steamed milk, and chocolate. Slap some whipped cream on top and you've got the ultimate high-octane, high-calorie pick-me-up.

Americano—a single shot of espresso topped off with water to make an approximation of traditional American-style coffee but with more flavor.

Café au lait—regular brewed or drip-filter coffee mixed with hot or steamed milk. This doesn't have the intense flavor of a latte and isn't readily available in Seattle.

Palace Kitchen. 2030 Fifth Ave. ☎ **206/448-2001.** Reservations recommended. Main dishes $14–$19. AE, DISC, MC, V. Daily 5pm–1am. NORTHWEST.

This is chef Tom Douglas's third restaurant (Dahlia Lounge and Etta's Seafood are the other two), and it's also the most casual. The atmosphere is urban chic, with cement pillars, simple wood booths, and a few tables in the window, which overlooks the monorail tracks. The menu is short and features a nightly selection of unusual cheeses and a different preparation from the applewood grill each night of the week (North Carolina ribs on Monday, cured pork loin with ricotta ravioli on Thursday, pheasant with porcini risotto on Sunday). Any night of the week you can start a meal with goat cheese fondue or salt cod cakes on sorrel, but it's the olive poppers that are the biggest hit. Night owls will be glad to know they have the Palace Kitchen to turn to for a decent meal after midnight.

The Pink Door. 1919 Post Alley. ☎ **206/443-3241.** Reservations recommended. Pastas $10–$12.50; main dishes $13–$18. AE, MC, V. Tues–Sat 11:30am–10pm (bar food Tues–Thurs till 11:30pm, Fri–Sat till 1am). ITALIAN.

If we didn't tell you about this one, you'd never find it. There's no sign out front, only the pink door for which the restaurant is named (look for it between Stewart and Virginia streets). On the other side of the door, stairs lead to a cellarlike space, which in summer is almost always empty because people would rather dine on the deck with a view of Elliott Bay. What makes this place so popular is not just the good food, but the fun goings-on. Tuesday through Thursday, there's a tarot card reader in residence, and on weekends there's usually an accordionist. Sometimes there are even magicians. Be sure to start your meal with the fragrant roasted garlic and ricotta-Gorgonzola spread or the *bagna cauda,* a hot anchovy, herb, and olive oil dipping sauce.

Queen City Grill. 2201 First Ave. ☎ **206/443-0975.** Reservations recommended. Main dishes $9–$20. AE, DC, DISC, MC, V. Mon–Thurs 11:30am–11pm, Fri 11:30am–midnight, Sat 5pm–midnight, Sun 5–11pm. INTERNATIONAL.

Battered wooden floors that look as if they were salvaged from an old hardware store and high-backed wooden booths give the Queen City Grill the look of age. If you didn't know better, you'd think this place had been here since the Great Fire of 1889. The spare decor and sophisticated lighting underscore an exciting menu. Some people come here just for the crab cakes (with just the right amount of roasted pepper/garlic aioli) but everything else is just as inspired. Seafood is the specialty, so you might start with tuna carpaccio accompanied by a lime, ginger, and mustard sauce. The chicken–wild rice gumbo is an unusual and tasty soup.

Shea's Lounge. Corner Market Building, Suite 34, 94 Pike St., Pike Place Market. ☎ **206/467-9990.** Reservations for 6 or more people only. Main courses $8.50–$13. AE, MC, V. Tues–Sun 4:30pm to 10 or 11pm. NORTHWEST/INTERNATIONAL.

This is the lounge for the ever-popular Chez Shea, one of the Pike Place Market's hidden treasures, and is one of the most sophisticated little spaces in Seattle. Romantic lighting and a view of the bay make this a popular spot with couples, and whether you just want a cocktail and an appetizer or a full meal, you can get it here. The menu features gourmet pizzas (green apple, blue cheese, and walnuts, for example), sandwiches, combination appetizer plates, a few soups and salads, and five nightly specials such as Moroccan chicken pie. You might start with an asparagus-watercress flan with red pepper–shallot confetti. The desserts, though pricey, are divinely decadent. This is a great spot for a light meal.

Theôz. 1523 Sixth Ave. ☎ **206/749-9660.** Reservations recommended. Main dishes $10.50–$24. AE, MC, V. Mon–Thurs 11am–2pm and 5–10pm, Fri 11am–2pm and 5–11pm, Sat 5–11pm, Sun 5–10pm. NORTHWEST.

With chef Emily Moore, formerly of The Painted Table, at the helm, Theôz has become an instant hit. Its location directly across the street from Wolfgang Puck's much touted ObaChine, hasn't hurt things either (what a block!). With a very spare and sophisticated interior, Theôz lets the food make all the architectural statements. Food is layered and dressed and decorated until each plate is a work of art (sound like The Painted Table?). The menu, which is broken into small and large plates, is overwhelmingly tempting and laced with the unfamiliar. How about some beautiful little lotus chips or banana leaf tamales? Or try something from the clay oven, perhaps pork loin and ribs with red chile–banana sauce, Tehuantepec mashed potatoes, and garlic greens. However, whatever you do, don't eat so much that you can't fit in a desert like the chocolate piano, a tiny baby grand with brownies for legs, cake for a body, and chocolate mousse where the wires should be. Astounding!

Trattoria Mitchelli. 84 Yesler Way. ☎ **206/623-3883.** Reservations for 6 or more people only. Pastas $6.85–$8; main dishes $9–$14.50. AE, DC, MC, V. Tues–Fri 7am–4am, Sat 8am–4am, Sun 8am–11pm, Mon 7am–11pm. ITALIAN.

Located in the hearty of Pioneer Square, Trattoria Mitchelli is a cozy place with a friendly old-world atmosphere. The white-tiled waiting area has large windows that let in the warm summer air and salty breezes. An old circular bar in the counter room is a popular after-work and late-night gathering spot; candles flicker in Chianti bottles, and conversation is lively. There is a selection of chicken and veal dishes, all of which are worth trying. The pizza kitchen and bar features pizza and calzone baked in a wood oven. If you're a night owl, keep Mitchelli's in mind—they serve full meals until 4am.

✪ **Wild Ginger Asian Restaurant and Satay Bar.** 1400 Western Ave. ☎ **206/623-4450.** Reservations not necessary. Satay $2–$8; main dishes $8.50–$18. AE, DC, DISC, MC, V. Mon–Thurs 11:30am–3pm and 5–11pm, Fri 11:30am–3pm and 5pm–midnight, Sat 11:30am–3pm and 4:30pm–midnight, Sun 4:30–11pm. Satay until 1am every night. CHINESE/ASIAN.

With chef Jeem Han Lock winning the 1997 "Best Chef of the Northwest" award from the James Beard Foundation, Wild Ginger has gone from being a longtime local favorite to national stardom. Even celebrity chef Wolfgang Puck copied Wild Ginger's concept at ObaChine, his first Seattle restaurant.

Pull up a comfortable stool around the large satay grill and watch the cooks grill little skewers of anything from fresh produce to fish to pork to prawns to lamb. Each skewer is served with a small cube of sticky rice and a dipping sauce. Order three or four satay sticks and you have a meal. If you prefer to sit at a table and have a more traditional dinner, Wild Ginger can accommodate you. Try the Panang beef curry (flank steak in pungent curry sauce of cardamom, coconut milk, Thai basil, and peanuts). The lunch menu contains many of the dinner entrees, but at lower prices.

INEXPENSIVE

✪ **Belltown Pub.** 2322 First Ave. ☎ **206/728-4311.** Reservations not accepted. Main dishes $7–$17. AE, MC, V. Sun–Thurs 11:30am–11pm, Fri–Sat 11:30am–midnight. INTERNATIONAL.

Located in an old sleeping bag factory in Belltown, this lively pub serves a surprisingly varied menu. However, what people really come here for are the burgers, which are the best in Seattle—thick, juicy, well-flavored, and set on thick, chewy rolls. Accompany your burger with a pint from one of the 20 microbrew taps. There are tables on the sidewalk in summer, and huge wooden booths for when the weather is inclement.

Emmett Watson's Oyster Bar. 1916 Pike Place no. 16. ☎ **206/448-7721.** Reservations not accepted. Soups $2–$7; main dishes $5–$9. No credit cards. Summer Mon–Thurs 11:30am–9pm, Fri–Sat 11:30am–10pm, Sun 11:30am–8pm. Winter Mon–Thurs 11:30am–8pm, Fri–Sat 11:30am–9pm, Sun 11:30am–6pm. SEAFOOD.

Tucked away in a rare quiet corner of Pike Place Market (well, actually, it's across the street in the market overflow area), Emmett Watson's exudes regional character and local color. The battered booths are tiny, but there's also courtyard seating. Named for a famous Seattle newspaper columnist, there are clippings and photos all over the walls of the restaurant. Oysters on the half shell are the raison d'être for this little place, but the fish dishes are often memorable as well. Service is infamously slow, but it's worth the wait for such tasty treats as a bowl of garlicky salmon chowder that's a meal in itself.

✪ Gravity Bar. 113 Virginia St. ☎ **206/448-8826.** Reservations not necessary. Meals $4–$7.25; juices $2–$4.75. MC, V. Downtown Mon–Thurs 11am–9pm, Fri 11am–10pm, Sat 10am–10pm, Sun 10am–8pm; Broadway Sun–Thurs 10am–10pm, Fri–Sat 10am–11pm. NATURAL FOODS.

If you're young and hip and concerned about the food that you put into your body, this is the place to go in downtown Seattle. The postmodern, neoindustrial decor (lots of sheet metal on the walls, bar, and menus) is the antithesis of the wholesome juices and meals they serve here. The juice list includes all manner of unusual combinations, all with catchy names like Martian Martini or 7 Year Spinach. Despite what you might think after reading this description, you'll also encounter espresso, beer, or wine here—which might come with unique additions (Guinness with apple juice, for example). Be there or be square. There's another Gravity Bar on Capitol Hill at 415 E. Broadway (☎ 206/325-7186).

Hing Loon. 628 S. Weller St. ☎ **206/682-2828.** Reservations not necessary. Main dishes $5–$9. Sun–Thurs 10am–midnight, Fri–Sat 10am–2am. CHINESE.

Bright fluorescent lighting, big Formica-top tables, void of atmosphere—this is the sort of place you would pass by without a thought if you were aimlessly searching for a restaurant in the International District. With so many choices in a few square blocks, it is easy to be distracted by fancy decor. Forget the rest and take a seat in Hing Loon. Seafood is the house specialty and none is done better than the oysters with ginger and green onion on a sizzling platter. For a veggie dish, don't miss the eggplant in Szechuan sauce. The restaurant makes all its own noodles, so you can't go wrong ordering chow mein or chow funn (wide noodles)—but be prepared for a large helping. If you're feeling really daring, try the cold jellyfish. Pork dishes tend to be fatty.

Merchants Café. 109 Yesler Way. ☎ **206/624-1515.** Reservations not necessary. Main dishes and sandwiches $5–$15. AE, DISC, MC, V. Mon 11am–4pm, Tues–Thurs 11am–9pm, Fri 11am–2pm, Sat 10am–2pm. AMERICAN.

Merchants Café is Seattle's oldest restaurant and looks every bit of its 100-plus years. A well-scuffed tile floor surrounds the bar, which came around the Horn in the 1800s. An old safe and gold scales are left over from the days when Seattle was the first, or last, taste of civilization for Yukon prospectors. At one time the restaurant's basement was a card room and the upper floors were a brothel. In fact, this may be the original Skid Row saloon (Yesler Way was the original Skid Road down which logs were skidded to a sawmill). Straightforward sandwiches and steaks are the mainstays of the menu.

4 Lake Union, Queen Anne Hill & Magnolia

EXPENSIVE

✪ Canlis. 2576 Aurora Ave. N. ☎ **206/283-3313.** Reservations highly recommended. Main dishes $20–$32. AE, CB, DC, DISC, MC, V. Mon–Sat 5–11pm. AMERICAN/CONTINENTAL.

Canlis has been in business since 1950, and has become a Seattle tradition. However, traditions tend to lose their appeal for younger generations, and to reconnect with the movers and shakers of today's Seattle, this restaurant recently went through a major remodeling. With a mix of contemporary styling and Asian antiques, the restaurant definitely seems poised to take on the 21st century. The mix of Asian and classic American and Continental fare keeps both traditionalists and more adventurous diners content. If so inclined you could start with sashimi or escargots and then go on to a filet mignon from the restaurant's famed copper grill or Dungeness crab cakes with orange butter. This is the perfect place to close a big deal or celebrate a very special occasion. To finish, why not go all the way and have the Grand Marnier soufflé? While jackets are no longer required for men, this is still the sort of place that just makes you want to get dressed up.

Kaspar's. 19 W. Harrison St. ☎ **206/298-0123.** Reservations recommended. Main courses $15–$20; Vintner's dinners $35–$45; chef's table dinners $50 for 5-course and $75 for 7-course; wine bar appetizers $2.50–$7.50. AE, MC, V. Tues–Sat 4:30–10pm. NORTHWEST/SEAFOOD.

Located in the Lower Queen Anne neighborhood, Kaspar's has long been a favorite with Seattleites, and offers many dining options for various hungers and pocketbooks. For the connoisseur and oenophile there are vintner's dinners; for the ultimate in personal service, try a chef's table dinner and dine in the kitchen with chef Kaspar Donier. For light meals, drinks, and desserts, there's the wine bar. The menu here places an emphasis on seafood and draws on worldwide influences, such as an Asian antipasto plate that includes a crab sushi roll, smoked ahi, and a vegetable spring roll. Alaskan halibut might come with crab-corn cannelloni and sun-dried tomato sauce. Kaspar's is also rightly famous for its desserts.

The Space Needle and Emerald Suite Restaurants. Seattle Center, 219 Fourth Ave. N. ☎ **206/443-2100.** Reservations required. Main dishes $25–$48. Sun brunch $18–$24. AE, CB, DC, MC, V. Mon–Sat 8–10:30am, 11am–3:30pm, and 4–10:30pm; Sun 8am–2:45pm and 5–10:30pm. NORTHWEST.

While Seattleites will be quick to tell you that the prices here are outrageous and the food is not nearly as good as that served at dozens of other less high profile restaurants around town, the Space Needle and Emerald Suite Restaurants stay packed day in and day out. People come simply because it's such a unique experience to dine 500 feet above the city in a revolving restaurant. The Space Needle Restaurant offers the same views as the Emerald Suite, but in a more casual setting. Menus at both restaurants are almost identical (prices are a bit higher in the Emerald Suite). The best thing about eating here is you don't have to pay for the elevator ride!

MODERATE

Kamon on Lake Union. 1177 Fairview Ave. N. ☎ **206/622-4665.** Reservations recommended. Main dishes $12–$25; sushi $3–$7. AE, DC, JCB, MC, V. Mon–Thurs 11:30am–2:30pm and 5–9:30pm; Fri–Sat 5–10:30pm; Sun 5–9:30pm. JAPANESE/NORTHWEST/CHINESE/ASIAN.

Of the many big waterfront restaurants at the south end of Lake Union, Kamon is still my favorite. There are, of course, the views across the lake to the sunset sky and the Space Needle, but there are also traditional and contemporary Asian-inspired dishes. Sushi fans can take a seat at the long sushi bar, but, if it's summer, I'd much rather be sitting out on the deck. If you prefer a bit more lively entertainment with your meal, try a teppanyaki dinner and watch the chef cook your meal right at your table. Japanese, Chinese, Thai, and Indonesian dishes all show up on the menu, and for those with a more nouvelle leaning, there are such dishes as pasta with smoked scallops in a ginger cream sauce, as well as raspberry teriyaki chicken.

McCormick and Schmick's Harborside. 1200 Westlake Ave. N. ☎ **206/270-9052.** Reservations recommended. Main dishes $7.50–$20. AE, DC, JCB, MC, V. Mon–Sat 11:30am–11pm; Sun 10am–11pm. SEAFOOD.

This is the best location of any of Seattle's McCormick and Schmick's restaurants and overlooks the marinas on the west side of Lake Union. The menu, which changes daily, includes seemingly endless choices of appetizers, sandwiches, salads and creative entrees. Just be sure to order something with seafood in it, like a seared rare ahi with Asian cucumber salad, a crab cake sandwich, or grilled halibut topped with a

Seattle Dining—North & Northeast

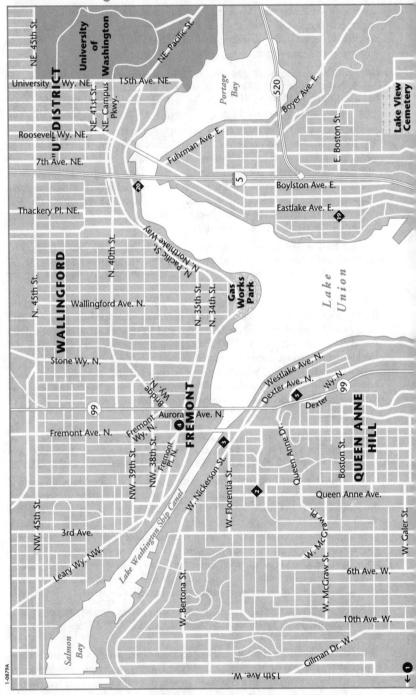

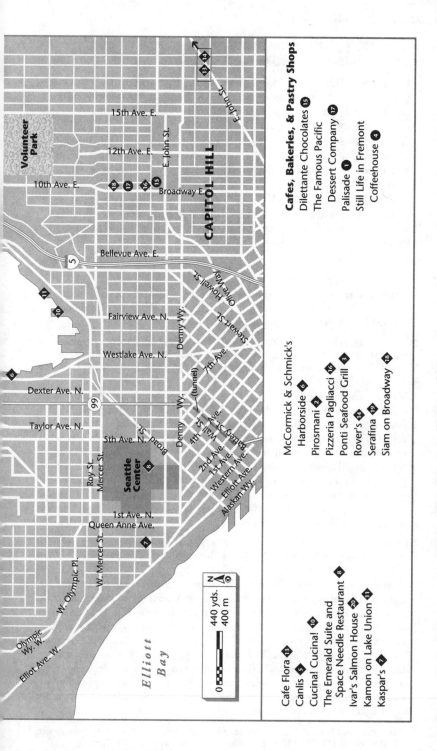

Cafes, Bakeries, & Pastry Shops

Dilettante Chocolates 15
The Famous Pacific
Dessert Company 17
Palisade 1
Still Life in Fremont
Coffeehouse 4

McCormick & Schmick's
Harborside 6
Pirosmani 2
Pizzeria Pagliacci 16
Ponti Seafood Grill 3
Rover's 14
Serafina 19
Siam on Broadway 18

Cafe Flora 13
Canlis 5
Cucina! Cucina! 10
The Emerald Suite and
Space Needle Restaurant 8
Ivar's Salmon House 20
Kamon on Lake Union 11
Kaspar's 7

🅜 Family-Friendly Restaurants

Ivar's Salmon House *(see p. 75)*   This restaurant is built to resemble a Northwest Coast Native American longhouse and is filled with artifacts that kids will find fascinating. If they get restless, they can go out to the floating patio and watch the boats passing by.

Gravity Bar *(see p. 68)*   If you're traveling with teenagers, they'll love this place where Seattle's young and hip and health-conscious crowd comes to dine. The decor is postmodern neoindustrial and the food is wholesome, with juices called Martian Martini and 7 Year Spinach.

Cucina!Cucina! *(see p. 73)*   Every day's a party at this lively Italian restaurant on Lake Union, and kids always get special treatment (pictures to color, puzzles to do, pizza dough to shape and then let the kitchen cook). Birthdays are even better!

---

hazelnut butter and tart cherry chutney. Sure, there are meat dishes on the menu, but why bother, unless you came here for the excellent view. There are early dinner specials ($13.95) between 3 and 6:30pm.

✪ **Palisade.** Elliott Bay Marina, 2601 W. Marina Place. ☎ **206/285-1000.** Reservations recommended. Main dishes $14–$30. AE, DC, DISC, MC, V. Mon–Thurs 11:30am–2pm and 5–9:30pm, Fri 11:30am–2pm and 5–10pm, Sat 11:30am–2pm and 4:30–10pm, Sun 10am–2pm and 4:30–9pm. NORTHWEST.

With a panorama that sweeps from downtown to West Seattle and across the sound to the Olympic Mountains, Palisade has one of the best views of any Seattle waterfront restaurant. It also happens to have great food and the most inventive interior design of any restaurant in town (a saltwater pond, complete with fish, sea anemones, and starfish, is in the middle of the dining room). The building itself is a cross between an old lighthouse and Chinese palace. The extensive menu features dishes prepared on a searing grill, in a wood-fired oven, in a wood-fired rotisserie, and in an applewood broiler. What this all adds up to is many choices of flavorful seafoods and meats. Palisade is not easy to find, but it is more than worth the trouble to find it. Call for directions.

Pirosmani. 2220 Queen Anne Ave. N. ☎ **206/285-3360.** Reservations recommended, especially on weekends. Main dishes $16–$22. AE, DC, MC, V. Tues–Sat 5:30–10pm. GEORGIAN/MEDITERRANEAN.

Named after the Georgian Republic's most famous artist, Pirosmani is a small, informal restaurant in a Victorian home in the upper Queen Anne district. Chef Laura Dewell pulls her uncommon gastronomic references both from Georgia (formerly of the USSR) and the sunny Mediterranean. For starters, you might whet your appetite with such dishes as juicy traditional Georgian pork and beef dumplings seasoned with mint, onion, green pepper, and paprika, or eggplant over a puree of walnuts and herbs with Georgian cheese and a yogurt-garlic sauce. The detail and attention given to each dish, such as lamb with dried sour cherries and herbs accompanied by layered pasta with mozzarella and feta, makes each one distinctive. Save room for one of the light and unusually flavored desserts.

✪ **Serafina.** 2043 Eastlake Ave. E. ☎ **206/323-0807.** Reservations recommended. Pastas $9.50–$15; entrees $13–$19. MC, V. Mon–Thurs 11:30am–2pm and 5:30–10pm, Fri 11:30am–2pm and 5:30–11pm, Sat 5:30–11pm, Sun 5:30–10pm. ITALIAN.

The atmosphere is rustic and serves to underscore the earthy, Italian, country-style dishes served here. This is one of our favorite dining spots, with just a touch of sophistication and a casual ambience. In the summer, try to get a table in the romantic garden courtyard. The antipasti Serafina is always a good choice for a starter and changes daily, though it's hard to resist prosciutto and figs. Among the pastas you might find the likes of penne with leeks, pears, and prawns. For a main dish try a classic Umbrian preparation of roasted Italian sausages with grapes served over soft polenta.

INEXPENSIVE

Cucina!Cucina! Chandler's Cove, Fairview Ave. N. ☎ **206/447-2782.** Reservations accepte at lunch only. Main dishes $6–$15. AE, DISC, MC, V. Sun–Thurs 11:30am–11pm, Fri–Sat 11:30am–midnight. ITALIAN.

Although it is part of a chain headquartered in Bellevue, Cucina!Cucina! is popular not only for its waterfront view but for its lively it's-always-a-party atmosphere. Located at the south end of Lake Union, this restaurant is also a favorite of Seattle families because of all the special attention kids are given here. But just because families are welcome doesn't mean this place isn't fun for adults, too. In summer, the deck is the place to be.

5 First Hill, Capitol Hill & East Seattle

EXPENSIVE

The Hunt Club. Sorrento Hotel, 900 Madison St. ☎ **206/343-6156.** Reservations recommended. Main dishes $24–$33. AE, CB, DC, DISC, MC, V. Mon–Thurs 7–10am, 11am–2:30pm, and 5:30–10pm; Fri 7–10am, 11am–2:30pm, and 5:30–11pm; Sat 7am–2:30pm, 5:30–11pm; Sun 7am–2:30pm, 5:30–10pm. NORTHWEST.

The Hunt Club is just the sort of place its name would indicate—dark, intimate, well suited to business lunches and romantic celebrations. Mahogany paneling lines the walls, and if you need a little privacy, folding louvered doors can create private dining areas. The menu, which changes weekly, balances French, Italian, and Asian influences while stirring in a generous helping of Northwest ingredients. Whether you're having a quick meal in the lounge, a light lunch, or a four-course dinner, you'll find creativity a keystone of the menu. The best way to start a meal is with the Sorrento seafood appetizer plate, which includes a trio of delicately flavored preparations. You might then move onto something as unusual as spice-grilled ostrich fillet with blackberries or something more familiar such as filet mignon with merlot beef essence. Just be sure to save room for one of the outstanding desserts.

✪ **Rover's.** 2808 E. Madison St. ☎ **206/325-7442.** Reservations required. Main dishes $23–$39; 5-course tasting menu $49.50–$59.50; chef's grand menu $89.50. AE, DC, DISC, MC, V. Tues–Sat 5:30–9:30pm. NORTHWEST.

Tucked away in a quaint clapboard house behind a chic little shopping center in the Madison Valley neighborhood is one of Seattle's most acclaimed restaurants. Rover's chef, Thierry Rautureau, received classic French training before falling in love with the Northwest and all the wonderful ingredients it has to offer an imaginative chef. Voilá! Northwest cuisine with a French accent. The menu changes frequently, and the delicacies therein are enough to send the most jaded of gastronomes into fits of indecision. To make life easier, many guests simply opt for one of the five-course dinners and leave the decision making to a professional—the chef. Rest assured you won't be disappointed. If, on the other hand, you must have the seared sea scallops with foie gras and a chestnut puree or roasted guinea-fowl with green lentils, cherry chutney, and huckleberry vinegar sauce, by all means order from the menu.

MODERATE

✪ **Café Flora.** 2901 E. Madison St. ☎ **206/325-9100.** Reservations taken for 8 or more. Main dishes $7.25–$14. MC, V. Tues–Fri 11:30am–10pm, Sat 9am–2pm and 5–10pm, Sun 9am–2pm and 5–9pm. VEGETARIAN.

Big, bright, and airy, this Madison Valley cafe will dispel any ideas about vegetarian food being boring. This is meatless gourmet cooking and draws on influences from around the world—a vegetarian's dream come true. While the menu changes weekly, unusual pizzas are always on the menu. Just to get you in the mood consider these recent offerings: a Provençal appetizer plate that included a tapenade (kalamata olives, orange zest, and capers), herbed goat cheese, roasted eggplant pâté, and crostini; portobello Wellington with a mushroom-pecan pâté and sautéed leeks in a puff pastry; and a pea and Gorgonzola risotto with a ragout of morels, tomatoes, roasted garlic, thyme, and sherry. Of course none of these will likely be available when you visit, but you get the picture.

Leschi Lakecafe. 102 Lakeside Ave. ☎ **206/328-2233.** Reservations recommended. Main dishes $9–$20. AE, DISC, MC, V. Mon–Thurs 11:30am–2pm and 5–9pm, Fri 11:30am–2pm and 5–10pm, Sat 11:30am–3pm and 5–10pm, Sun 9am–2pm and 5–9pm. AMERICAN.

While views across Elliott Bay from the downtown waterfront are all well and good, they don't include a view of Mount Hood. Leschi Lakecafe, however, does, at least when The Mountain is out, it does. This casual restaurant on the shore of Lake Washington was the ferry terminal for Eastside ferries back before they built the floating bridges. While the view's the thing here, the menu offers enough variety to satisfy most people, and the specials can be real winners. While the menu includes such contemporary offerings as Northwest bouillabaisse and peach-soy marinated chicken, it also includes ale-battered fried seafood for those who like to keep things simple. Be sure to try the Leschi's ice cream, even if you only get a petite serving— although when we were last there, the chocolate mousse in a chocolate tulip cup was irresistible.

INEXPENSIVE

Pizzeria Pagliacci. 426 Broadway E. ☎ **206/324-0730.** Reservations not accepted. Pizza $9–$17. AE, MC, V. Sun–Thurs 11am–11pm, Fri–Sat 11am–1am. PIZZA.

Pagliacci's pizza was voted the best in Seattle, and they now have three popular locations. Although you can order a traditional cheese pizza, there are much more interesting pies on the menu, like pesto pizza or the sun-dried tomato primo. It's strictly counter service, but there are plenty of seats at each of the bright restaurants. For those in a hurry or who just want a snack, there is pizza by the slice. Pagliacci is also at 550 Queen Anne Ave. N. (☎ 206/285-1232) and at 4529 University Way NE (☎ 206/632-0421).

Siam on Broadway. 616 Broadway E. ☎ **206/324-0892.** Reservations recommended on weekends. Main dishes lunch $5.50–$9, dinner $6.50–$10.50. AE, MC, V. Mon–Thurs 11:30am–10pm, Fri 11:30am–11pm, Sat 5–11pm, Sun 5–10pm. THAI.

At the north end of Broadway, on Capitol Hill, you'll find one of Seattle's best Thai restaurants, the small and casual Siam on Broadway. The tom yum soups, made with either shrimp or chicken, are the richest and creamiest I've ever had—also some of the spiciest. If you prefer your food less fiery, let your server know. Just remember that they mean it when they say superhot. The phad Thai (spicy fried noodles) is excellent, and the nua phad bai graplau (spicy meat and vegetables) is properly fragrant with chiles and basil leaves. A second much larger restaurant, Siam on Lake Union, is located at 1880 Fairview Ave. E. (☎ 206/323-8101).

6 North Seattle (Including Fremont, Wallingford & the University District)

MODERATE

Café Lago. 2305 24th Ave. E. ☎ **206/329-8005.** Reservations accepted for 6 or more Sun–Thurs only. Main courses $11–$19. DISC, MC, V. Sun and Tues–Thurs 5–9:30pm, Fri–Sat 5–10pm. ITALIAN.

This casual trattoria is located in the Montlake district just south of the University of Washington, and bakes some of the best rustica-style pizzas in Seattle. These gourmet pizzas are as visually appealing as they are delicious and include such ingredients as bresaola, an air-dried beef, and coppa, a peppered pork shoulder. If you're here with a few friends, by all means, start with the big antipasto plate, which comes with roast garlic, eggplant, roasted red peppers, and several different cheeses among other things. The lasagnas and raviolis, made with handmade pasta, may be even more popular than the pizzas.

Ivar's Salmon House. 401 NE Northlake Way. ☎ **206/632-0767.** Reservations recommended. Main dishes $11–$27; fish bar $4.50–$7.50. AE, MC, V. Main restaurant, Mon–Fri 11:30am–2:30pm and 4:30–11pm, Sat noon–11pm, Sun 10am–2pm and 4–10pm. Fish bar, Sun–Thurs 11:30am–10pm, Fri–Sat 11am–11pm. SEAFOOD.

This Ivar's commands an excellent view of the Seattle skyline from the north end of Lake Union, and floating docks out back act like magnets for weekend boaters who abandon their own galley fare in favor of the restaurant's clam chowder and famous alder-smoked salmon. The theme here is Northwest Coast Indian, and the building has even won an award from the Seattle Historical Society for its replica of a tribal longhouse. Inside are many artifacts, including long dugout canoes and historic photographic portraits of Native American chiefs. Both kids and adults love this place.

Ponti Seafood Grill. 3014 Third Ave. N. ☎ **206/284-3000.** Reservations recommended. Main dishes $12.50–$23.50. AE, DC, MC, V. Mon–Thurs 11:30am–2:30pm and 5–10pm, Fri 11:30am–2:30pm and 5–11pm, Sat 5–11pm, Sun 10am–2:30pm and 5–10pm. SEAFOOD.

Situated at the south end of the Fremont Bridge overlooking the Lake Washington Ship Canal, Ponti is one of Seattle's most elegant and sophisticated restaurants. The menu here has an international flavor, though it also offers some solidly northwestern creations. On a recent evening, the appetizers included a decadent dish of smoked salmon served with a corn pancake, vodka crème fraîche, chives, and caviar. The pasta menu always includes some highly creative dishes such as Thai curry penne with broiled scallops, Dungeness crab meat, ginger-tomato chutney, and fresh basil chiffonade, and the daily listing of fresh seafoods might include the likes of grilled Copper River salmon with a subtle ginger beurre blanc and mushroom salsa. If possible, save room for a piece of the Chocolate Lover's torte, with chocolate mousse and ganache in a pool of raspberry sauce. Three-course early dinners ($13.95) are served between 5 and 6pm. Lunches are less expensive than dinner and equally well prepared.

Ray's Boathouse and Cafe. 6049 Seaview Ave. NW. ☎ **206/789-3770.** Reservations not accepted upstairs; recommended on weekends downstairs. Main dishes $14–$32 (in Boathouse), $9–$16 (in Cafe). AE, CB, DC, DISC, MC, V. Daily 11:30am–10pm. SEAFOOD/STEAK.

If you're looking for a waterfront restaurant with reliably good food and a different perspective than available from the Seattle downtown waterfront, head out to Ballard, where you'll find Ray's at the mouth of the Lake Washington Ship Canal. Instead of seeing the city, you'll see the bluff in Discovery Park, a marina, and the Olympic

Mountains across the Sound. Ray's is actually two distinctly different restaurants (as are several Seattle waterfront restaurants). Upstairs are the cafe and lounge, where you'll find a boisterous crowd of suntanned boating types. Waiting times of up to an hour here are not unusual, but no one seems to mind. Downstairs, everything is quiet, cozy, and sophisticated.

7 West Seattle

MODERATE

Salty's on Alki. 1936 Harbor Ave. SW. ☎ **206/937-1600.** Reservations recommended. Main dishes $10–$37. AE, DISC, MC, V. Mon–Fri 11am–2:30pm and 4:30–10pm, Sat noon–3pm and 4–10pm, Sun 4–10pm. SEAFOOD.

Although the prices are almost as out of line as those at the Space Needle and the service can be abysmal, this restaurant has *the* waterfront view in Seattle, and the food is usually pretty good. Because the restaurant is set on the northeast side of the Alki Peninsula, it faces downtown Seattle on the far side of Elliott Bay. Come at sunset for dinner and watch the setting sun sparkle off skyscraper windows as the lights of the city twinkle on. Monday through Friday there are sunset dinner specials starting at 4:30pm. On sunny summer days, lunch on one of the two decks is a sublimely Seattle experience.

8 The Eastside

VERY EXPENSIVE

✪ **The Herbfarm.** 32804 Issaquah–Fall City Rd., Fall City. ☎ **206/784-2222.** Reservations required. Fixed-price 9-course dinners $115; 6-course lunches $60. AE, MC, V. Seatings Thurs–Sat only. Closed mid-Feb to Mar. NORTHWEST.

The Herbfarm, the most highly acclaimed restaurant in the Northwest, is known across the nation for its extraordinarily lavish meals. Throughout the year, the menu changes every week or two, with different themes to match the seasons. Wild gathered vegetables, Northwest seafoods and meats, organic vegetables, wild mushrooms, and of course the generous use of fresh herbs are the ingredients from which the restaurant's chef creates his culinary extravaganzas. Dinners are paired with complimentary wines, often from northwestern wineries.

This restaurant is so incredibly popular that reservations are taken only twice a year (once in the spring and once in the fall). However, 25% of seats are held available for reservations made one week in advance. These seats can be reserved at 1pm each Friday.

Unfortunately, a fire destroyed the restaurant (although not the rest of the farm) in 1996, but at press time, a new Herbfarm restaurant was scheduled to open in June of 1998. A bed-and-breakfast inn, with six suites and a wine room will also (hopefully) open in June.

MODERATE

Cafe Juanita. 9702 NE 120th Place, Kirkland. ☎ **425/823-1505.** Reservations recommended. Main dishes $14–$20. MC, V. Daily 5:30–9:30pm. ITALIAN.

Hard to find and housed in a little 1950s brick building, this Italian restaurant is one of Kirkland's long-time favorites. With a sort of fern bar feel and windows that look out into the trees of a greenway behind the restaurant, Cafe Juanita is a casual sort of place, with the menu printed on a blackboard each day. However, this is not to imply that the food is casual. The wine racks just inside the door should clue you in to the fact that meals here are meant to be savored.

Yarrow Bay Grill. 1270 Carillon Point, Kirkland. ☎ **425/889-9052.** Reservations recommended. Main dishes $15–$27. AE, DC, DISC, MC, V. Mon–Sat 11:30am–2pm and 5:30–10:30pm, Sun 10am–2:30pm and 5–10pm. NORTHWEST.

The combination of Northwest cuisine and a view across Lake Washington to Seattle has made this restaurant, in the upscale Carillon Point retail, office, and condo development, a favorite of Eastside diners. The setting is decidedly nouveau riche and about as close as you get to a Southern California setting in the Northwest. The menu is not so long that you can't make a decision, yet long enough to provide some serious options. A portobello tempura combines two of our favorite flavors into one tasty dish. There are also Thai-style crab cakes with a lemongrass–sweet mustard sauce. Entrees are equally divided between seafoods and meats, with at least one vegetarian dish on the menu daily. Keep in mind that the menu changes daily, and nearly every table has a view. There is also a more casual and less expensive restaurant downstairs from the Grill.

9 Cafes, Bakeries & Pastry Shops

CAFES & COFFEE BARS

Unless you've been on Mars the past few years, you're likely aware that Seattle has become the espresso capital of America. Seattleites are positively rabid about coffee. Coffee isn't just a hot drink or a caffeine fix anymore, it's a way of life. Espresso and its creamy cousin latte (made with one part espresso to three parts milk) are the stuff that this city runs on, and you will never be more than about a block from your next cup. There are espresso carts on the sidewalks, drive-through espresso windows, espresso bars, espresso milk shakes, espresso chocolates, even eggnog lattes at Christmas. The ruling coffee king is Starbucks, a chain of dozens of coffee bars where you can buy your java by the cup or by the pound. They sell some 36 types and blends of coffee, and you can find their shops all over the city. SBC, formerly Stewart Brothers Coffee and also known as Seattle's Best Coffee, doesn't have as many shops as Starbucks, but it does have a very devoted clientele. Rapidly gaining ground in the Seattle coffee wars is the Tully's chain, which seems to be opening an espresso bar on every corner that doesn't already have a Starbucks or an SBC. However, serious espresso junkies swear by Torrefazione and Cafe Apassionato. If you see one of either of these chains, check it out and see what you think.

Coffee bars and cafes are now almost as popular as bars as places to hang out and visit with friends. Among my favorite Seattle cafes are the following:

Still Life in Fremont Coffeehouse, 709 N. 35th St. (☎ 206/547-9850). Fremont is Seattle's most eclectic neighborhood, and Still Life reflects this eclecticism. It's big and always crowded. Good vegetarian meals.

Torrefazione, 320 Occidental Ave. S. (☎ 206/624-5773), and also at 622 Olive Way (☎ 206/624-1429). With its hand-painted Italian crockery, Torrefazione has the feel of a classic Italian cafe. The one in the Pioneer Square area has much more atmosphere. Great pastries.

Zio Rico, 1415 Fourth Ave. (☎ 206/467-8616). This is the most elegant cafe in Seattle, with big, comfortable easy chairs and lots of dark wood paneling. A great place to sit and read the *Wall Street Journal.*

BAKERIES & PASTRY SHOPS

A la Francaise, 415 First Ave. S. (☎ 206/624-0322). This Pioneer Square French bakery has the most authentic feel of any bakery or pastry shop in Seattle, right down to the sidewalk tables surrounded by a low wall with flower-filled planters on top. Great breads and pastries!

The Crumpet Shop, 1503 First Ave. (☎ **206/682-1598**). If coffee isn't your cup of tea, check out this tea shop in Pike Place Market. As the name implies, crumpets are the specialty.

Dilettante Chocolates, 416 Broadway E. (☎ **206/329-6463**). This chocolate shop turned pastry bakery also happens to be Seattle's leading proponent of cocoa as the next drink to take the country by storm. If you don't order something with chocolate here, you're missing the point. Can you say, "To die for"? I knew you could.

The Famous Pacific Dessert Company, 516 Broadway E. (☎ **206/328-1950**). At this Capitol Hill pastry extravaganza, you can indulge in more than 30 cakes and tortes.

Le Panier, 1902 Pike Place (☎ **206/441-3669**). Located in the heart of Pike Place Market, this French bakery is a great place to get a croissant and a latte and watch the market action.

Macrina, 2408 First Ave. (☎ **206/448-4032**). This Belltown bakery is a great place for a quick and cheap breakfast or lunch. In the morning, the smell of baking bread wafts down First Avenue and draws in many a passing stranger.

Three Girls Bakery, 1514 Pike Place, Stall no. 1 (☎ **206/622-1045**). With a wall of glass cases full of baked goods and a window facing onto one of the busiest spots in Pike Place Market, this bakery is a favorite place to grab a few pastries or other goodies to go. They do, however, also have a counter in back where you can sit down.

10 Quick Bites

If you're just looking for something quick and cheap and don't want to resort to McDonald's or Burger King, consider grabbing a wrap. It can be just about anything in a tortilla and has become the food of choice in Seattle these days. Keep your eyes out for a **Taco del Mar** (90 Yesler St., 1336 First Ave., Third Avenue and Marion Street, 725 Pike St., and 607 Broadway E. are just a few convenient locations) or a **Todo Wraps** (of which there are many all around the city). In Belltown, **Mondo Burrito,** 2121 First Ave. (☎ **206/728-9697**), serves some of the best burritos in the city.

Of course there are dozens of places to get a quick meal in Pike Place Market, and a lot of them are pretty good. Our favorites are the **Burrito Window** on First Avenue (just a few steps south of the market information booth), **My Favorite Piroshky,** on Pike Place (around the corner from this same information booth), and the lunch counter at the **Three Girls Bakery** (see above), which is also on Pike Place.

There are also a couple of food courts downtown—one in **Westlake Center** shopping mall, 400 Pine St., and one in the **Columbia Center** (Seattle's tallest building) at Fourth Avenue and Columbia Street.

If you're downtown at lunch and just want a gourmet sandwich and pasta s alad that you can grab out of a case, stop by **Briazz,** 1400 Fifth Ave. (☎ **206/ 343-3099**).

What to See & Do in Seattle

6

In the past few years, as Seattle has become one of the nation's most talked about and popular cities, life on the city's cultural front has been changing dramatically. However, despite new and renovated museums, Seattle's natural surroundings are still the city's primary attraction. You can easily cover all of Seattle's museums and major sights in 2 or 3 days, and with the help of the itineraries below, you should have a good idea of what not to miss. The itineraries outlined below will provide a good overview of the history, natural resources, and cultural diversity that have made Seattle the city it is today.

Once you've seen what's to see indoors, you can begin exploring the city's outdoor life. A car is helpful, though not entirely necessary, for sampling the city's outdoor activities. However, if you want to head farther afield, say to Mount Rainier, the Olympic Mountains, or a Puget Sound or ocean beach, you'll definitely need a car.

SUGGESTED ITINERARIES

If You Have 1 Day

Day 1   Start your day in the historic Pioneer Square District and take the earliest Seattle Underground Tour you can (see my "Good Times in Bad Taste" feature below). You'll have fun and get a good idea of Seattle's early history. From Pioneer Square, walk down to the waterfront and head north. You'll pass numerous overpriced seafood restaurants (most with good views and some good food), as well as quite a few fish-and-chip counters. At Pier 55 you can get a 1-hour harbor tour cruise, and at Pier 59 you'll find the Seattle Aquarium, where you can learn about the sea life of the region. Directly across from the aquarium is the Pike Hill Climb, which leads from the waterfront up the hill to Pike Place Market. In the market, you can buy fresh salmon and Dungeness crabs packed to go, peruse the produce and flower vendors, and explore the dark depths of the market for unusual shops. From Pike Place Market, walk to the monorail station in Westlake Center shopping mall, which is at the corner of Pine Street and Fourth Avenue. The monorail will take you to Seattle Center, where you can ride an elevator to the top of the Space Needle, Seattle's best-known landmark. Finish the day with dinner at one of the city's many restaurants serving seafood or Northwest cuisine.

If You Have 2 Days

Day 1 Start your first day in Pioneer Square, as outlined above. After the Seattle Underground Tour, head over to the nearby International District (Chinatown) and have lunch in a Chinese restaurant. Hing Loon is our favorite. After lunch, head over to the waterfront for a harbor cruise, a stop at the aquarium and Ye Olde Curiosity Shop, and then dine here on the waterfront at Elliott's or Anthony's Pier 66.

Day 2 Start your second day at Pike Place Market, and be sure to arrive early as the fruit, vegetable, flower, and fish vendors are opening. You'll likely be in the company of several of the city's finest chefs, many of whom do their shopping here. From the market it is only two blocks to the new Seattle Art Museum. After touring the museum, take the lunch tour to Tillicum Village. You'll see Northwest Native American dances while dining on alder-smoked salmon. When you return to Seattle, head for Seattle Center and the Space Needle.

If You Have 3 Days

Days 1–2 Follow the two-day strategy outlined above.

Day 3 Do something very Seattle. Rent a sea kayak on Lake Union or go in-line skating at Green Lake. Wander around the funky Fremont neighborhood and maybe go to the Woodland Park Zoo or the Burke Museum depending on your interests.

If You Have 5 Days or More

Days 1–3 Follow the 3-day strategy, as outlined above.

Days 4–5 Take a trip out of the city to Mount Rainier, Snoqualmie Falls, Bainbridge Island, or Mount St. Helens. All these trips can be turned into overnighters or longer (see chapter 10 for details on the first three; see chapter 20 for an excursion to Mount St. Helens).

1 The Top Attractions

The Seattle Waterfront. Alaskan Way from Yesler Way N. to Bay St. and Myrtle Edwards Park.

This is the city's single most popular attraction, and much as in San Francisco's Fishermen's Wharf area, there is much to recommend both for and against the waterfront. Yes it's very touristy, with tacky gift shops, saltwater taffy, T-shirts galore, and lots of overpriced restaurants, but it's also home to the Seattle Aquarium, the Omnidome Film Experience, and Ye Olde Curiosity Shop (king of the tacky gift shops). Several cruise-boat companies dock here, and there are also companies offering sailboat and sea kayak tours. The waterfront is also the best place to hire a horse-drawn carriage for a spin around the downtown.

At the south end of the waterfront, near Pioneer Square, you'll find the Washington State Ferries terminal at Pier 52 (a ferry ride makes for a cheap cruise). At Pier 54, you'll find companies offering sea kayak tours, sportfishing trips, jet-boat tours, and bicycle rentals. At Pier 55, boats leave for 1 1/2-hour harbor cruises, as well as on the Tillicum Village excursions to Blake Island. At Pier 57, you'll find the Bay Pavilion, which has a vintage carousel and a video arcade to keep the kids busy. At Pier 59, you'll find the Seattle Aquarium and the Omnidome Film Experience and a waterfront park. Continuing up the waterfront, you'll find Pier 66, the Bell Street Pier, which has a rooftop park with free binoculars. This is also where you'll find Anthony's, the hippest restaurant on the waterfront, and by the summer of 1998, the Odyssey Maritime Discovery Center, dedicated to the history of shipping and fishing in Puget Sound should be open. At Pier 67, you'll find the Edgewater hotel, which is a great place to take in the sunset over a drink or dinner. Next door, at Pier 69, is the dock for the ferries that ply between Seattle and Victoria. Sunset and jazz

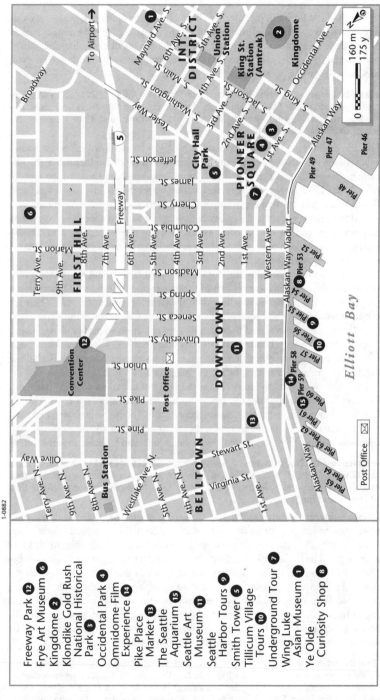

Seattle Attractions

Freeway Park **12**
Frye Art Museum **6**
Kingdome **2**
Klondike Gold Rush National Historical Park **3**
Occidental Park **4**
Omnidome Film Experience **14**
Pike Place Market **13**
The Seattle Aquarium **15**
Seattle Art Museum **11**
Seattle Harbor Tours **9**
Smith Tower **5**
Tillicum Village Tours **10**
Underground Tour **7**
Wing Luke Asian Museum **1**
Ye Olde Curiosity Shop **8**

1-0882

81

cruises also leave from this pier. At Pier 70, you'll find the *Spirit of Puget Sound* cruise ship, as well as a nightclub. Just north of this pier is grassy Myrtle Edwards Park, a nice finale to a very pleasant waterfront. This park has a popular bicycling and skating trail, and is the northern terminus for the Waterfront Streetcar, which can take you back to your starting point.

✪ **Pike Place Market.** Between Pike St. and Pine St. (at First Ave.). ☎ **206/682-7453.** Free admission (tours $5). Mon–Sat 9am–6pm, Sun 11am–5pm. Closed New Year's Day, Easter, Memorial Day weekend, July 4, Labor Day, Thanksgiving, Christmas. Bus: 15 or 18. Waterfront Streetcar: To Pike Place Market stop.

Pike Place Market, originally a farmers' market, was founded in 1907 when housewives complained that middlemen were raising the price of produce too high. The market allowed shoppers to buy directly from producers, and thus save on grocery bills. By the 1960s, however, the market was no longer the popular spot it had been. World War II had deprived it of nearly half its farmers when Japanese Americans were moved to internment camps. The postwar flight to the suburbs almost spelled the end for the market, and the site was being eyed for a major redevelopment project. However, a grassroots movement to save the 9-acre market culminated in its being declared a National Historic District.

Today it is once again bustling, but the 100 or so farmers and fishmongers who set up shop here are only a small part of the attraction. More than 200 local craftspeople and artists can be found selling their creations throughout the year. There are excellent restaurants, and hundreds of shops fill the market area. Street performers, including mimes, a pianist, and hammered-dulcimer players, serenade milling crowds. There is an information booth almost directly below the large Pike Place Market sign where you can pick up a free map and guide to the market. Watch for Rachel the giant piggy bank and the flying fish at the Pike Place Fish stall.

For a glimpse behind the scenes at the market, you can take a Market Classroom Tour on Wednesday mornings in summer or on Saturday mornings other months. On these tours you'll learn about the market's history, get tips on shopping here, and maybe meet a restaurant chef or two as they shop for fresh market ingredients. Call the above number for information on scheduled tours and to make a reservation.

The Space Needle. 203 Sixth Ave. N., Seattle Center. ☎ **206/443-2111.** Admission $8.50 adults, $7 seniors, $4 ages 5–12, ages 4 and under free (no charge if dining in rotating restaurant). Daily 8am–midnight. Valet parking $5. Bus: 1, 15 or 18. Monorail: From Westlake Center at Pine St. and Fourth Ave.

From a distance it resembles a flying saucer on top of a tripod, and when it was built it was meant to suggest future architectural trends. Erected for the 1962 World's Fair, the 600-foot-tall Space Needle is the quintessential symbol of Seattle. At 518 feet above ground level, the views from the observation deck are stunning. There are displays identifying more than 60 sites and activities in the Seattle area, and high-powered telescopes let you zoom in on distant sights. You'll also find a history of the Space Needle, a lounge, and two very expensive restaurants. If you don't mind standing in line and paying quite a bit for an elevator ride, make this your first stop in Seattle so you can orient yourself (there are, however, cheaper alternatives if you just want a view of the city; see "Panoramas" below for details).

✪ **Seattle Art Museum.** 100 University St. ☎ **206/654-3100.** Admission $6 adults, $4 seniors and students, ages 12 and under free. Free first Thurs of each month (free for seniors on first Fri of each month). Admission ticket also valid at Seattle Asian Art Museum if used within 1 week. Tues–Sun 10am–5pm (Thurs until 9pm). Also open on Martin Luther King Day, Presidents' Day, Memorial Day, and Labor Day. Closed Thanksgiving, Christmas, and New Year's Day. Bus: 15, 18 or any bus using the bus tunnel.

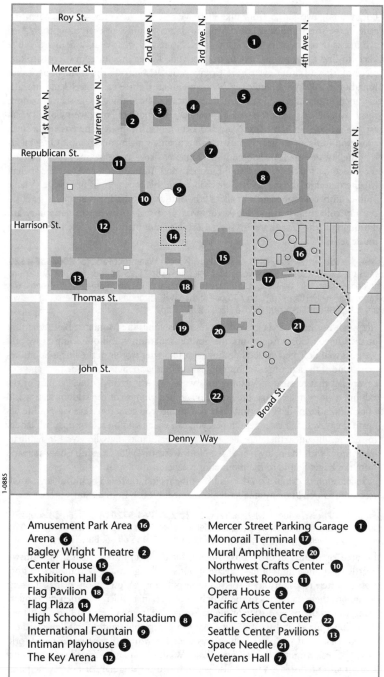

Seattle Center

Amusement Park Area **16**
Arena **6**
Bagley Wright Theatre **2**
Center House **15**
Exhibition Hall **4**
Flag Pavilion **18**
Flag Plaza **14**
High School Memorial Stadium **8**
International Fountain **9**
Intiman Playhouse **3**
The Key Arena **12**

Mercer Street Parking Garage **1**
Monorail Terminal **17**
Mural Amphitheatre **20**
Northwest Crafts Center **10**
Northwest Rooms **11**
Opera House **5**
Pacific Arts Center **19**
Pacific Science Center **22**
Seattle Center Pavilions **13**
Space Needle **21**
Veterans Hall **7**

83

Located only two blocks from Pike Place Market and presenting a stark cement facade to the street, the Seattle Art Museum is a repository for everything from African masks to old masters to Andy Warhol. No matter what your taste in art, you're likely to find a few rooms here to interest you. To see the museum's most striking piece of art you don't even have to buy a ticket. Outside the front door stands Jonathon Borofsky's *Hammering Man,* an animated three-story steel sculpture that hammers unceasingly and at first glance appears to be nothing more than a shadow. Inside you'll find one of the nation's premier collections of Northwest Coast Indian art and artifacts and an equally large collection of African art. There is also a small collection of Asian art at this museum, but Seattle's main collection of Oriental art is at the Seattle Asian Art Museum in Volunteer Park (see below for details). Up on the museum's top floor, you'll find European and American art, covering the ancient Mediterranean to the medieval, Renaissance, and Baroque periods in Europe. A large 18th-century collection and a smaller 19th-century exhibition lead up to a large 20th-century collection that includes a room devoted to Northwest contemporary art. Throughout the year there are special exhibits mounted here, as well as film and music series.

✪ **The Seattle Aquarium.** 1483 Alaskan Way, Pier 59, Waterfront Park. ☎ **206/386-4320.** Admission $7.75 adults, $7 seniors, $5.15 ages 6–18, $1.95 ages 3–5 (joint Aquarium-Omnidome tickets also available). Labor Day to Memorial Day, daily 10am–5pm; Memorial Day to Labor Day, daily 10am–7pm. Bus: 15 or 18; then walk through Pike Place Market to the waterfront. Waterfront Streetcar: To Pike Place Market stop.

Although not nearly as large and impressive as either the Monterey Bay Aquarium or the Oregon Coast Aquarium, the Seattle Aquarium is still quite impressive and presents well-designed exhibits dealing with the water worlds of the Puget Sound region. One of the aquarium's most popular exhibits is an interactive tide pool and discovery lab that re-creates Washington's wave-swept intertidal zone. As part of the exhibit, a video microscope provides a magnified glimpse of the seldom-seen world of plankton. From the underwater viewing dome, you get a fish's-eye view of life beneath the waves, and each September, you can watch salmon return up a fish ladder to spawn. Of course there are also plenty of small tanks that allow you to familiarize yourself with the many fish of the Northwest. In 1998, an exhibit on waterways from the Puget Sound to the mountains is scheduled to open.

In addition to exhibits on the sea life of the region, there is a beautiful large coral-reef tank, as well as many smaller tanks that exhibit fish from distant waters.

Museum of Flight. 9404 E. Marginal Way S. ☎ **206/764-5720.** Admission $8 adults, $7 seniors, $4 ages 6–15, free for ages 5 and under. Free first Thurs 5–9pm. Daily 10am–5pm (until 9pm Thurs). Closed Thanksgiving and Christmas. Take exit 158 off I-5. Bus: 174.

Located right next door to busy Boeing Field, 15 minutes south of downtown Seattle, this museum will have aviation buffs walking on air. Within the six-story glass-and-steel repository are displayed some of history's most famous planes. To start things off, there's a replica of the Wright brothers' first glider, and then the exhibits bring you to the present state of flight. Suspended in the Great Hall are 20 planes, including a DC-3 and the first air force F-5 supersonic fighter. You'll also see the famous Blackbird spy plane, which was once the world's fastest jet. A rare World War II Corsair fighter rescued from Lake Washington and restored to its original glory is also on display. Visitors also get to board the original Air Force One presidential plane. An exhibit on the U.S. space program features an Apollo command module. And while any air-and-space museum lets you look at mothballed planes, not many have their own air-traffic control tower and let you watch aircraft taking

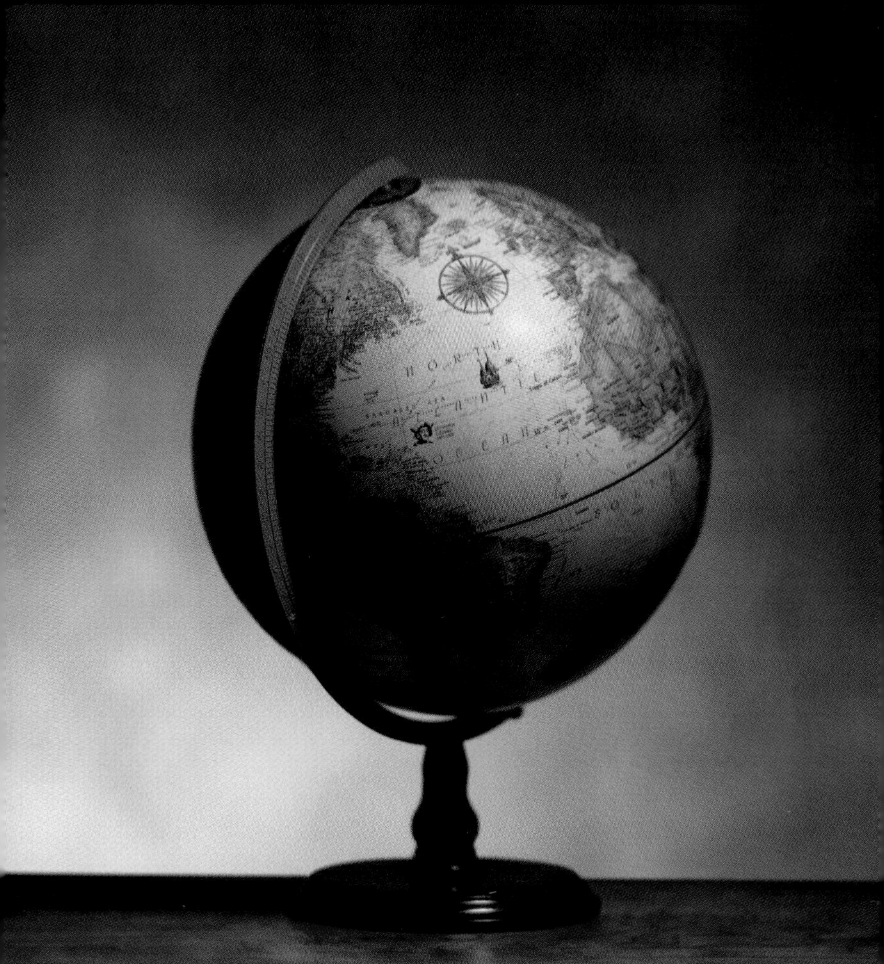

In case you want to be welcomed there.

We're here to see that you're always welcomed at establishments everywhere. That's why millions of people carry the American Express® Card – for peace of mind, confidence, and security, around the world or just around the corner.

do more

AMERICAN EXPRESS

Cards

In case you're
running low.

We're here to help with more than 118,000 Express Cash

locations around the world. In order to enroll, just call

American Express before you start your vacation.

do more

AMERICAN
EXPRESS

Express
Cash

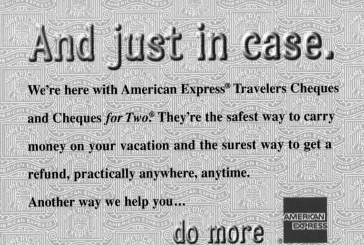

And just in case.

We're here with American Express® Travelers Cheques
and Cheques *for Two.*® They're the safest way to carry
money on your vacation and the surest way to get a
refund, practically anywhere, anytime.

Another way we help you...

do more

AMERICAN
EXPRESS

**Travelers
Cheques**

off and landing at an active airfield. See my "North of the City" excursion in chapter 10 for information on a tour of the Boeing plant.

✪ **Woodland Park Zoo.** 5500 Phinney Ave. N. ☎ **206/684-4800.** Admission $8 adults; $7.25 seniors, college students and disabled; $5.50 children ages 6–17; $3.25 ages 3–5; ages 2 and under free. Mar 15–Oct 30 daily 9:30am–6pm; Oct 31–Mar 14 daily 9:30am–4pm. Parking $3.50. Bus: 5.

Located in north Seattle, this sprawling zoo has outstanding exhibits focusing on such bioclimatic zones as Alaska, tropical Asia, the African savanna, and the tropical rain forest. The brown bear enclosure is an amazing reproduction of an Alaskan stream and hillside, and in the savanna, zebras gambol and antelopes and giraffes graze contentedly. An elephant forest provides plenty of space for the zoo's pachyderms. The tropical nocturnal house has fascinating exhibits that allow visitors to see nocturnal creatures when they are at their most active. The gorilla and orangutan habitats also are memorable. For the little ones, there is a farm animals area and a petting zoo.

Omnidome Film Experience. Pier 59, Waterfront Park. ☎ **206/622-1868.** Admission $6.95 adults, $5.95 seniors and ages 6–18, $4.95 ages 3–5, under age 3 free (a second film costs only $3 more; Omnidome-Aquarium combination tickets available). Sun–Thurs 10am–9pm, Fri–Sat 10am–11pm. Closed Thanksgiving and Christmas. Bus: 15 or 18; then walk through Pike Place Market to the waterfront. Waterfront Streetcar: To Pike Place Market stop.

The Omnidome, for those who have never experienced it, is a movie theater with a 180° screen that fills your peripheral vision and puts you right in the middle of the action. People with hangovers or those who get motion sickness should stay away! This huge wraparound theater is located adjacent to the Seattle Aquarium, and for many years now has featured a film about the eruption of Mount St. Helens. In late 1997 a feature on whales was scheduled to open and various other special features are shown throughout the year.

2 Other Museums

ART MUSEUMS

Frye Art Museum. 704 Terry Ave. (at Cherry St.). ☎ **206/622-9250.** Free admission. Tues–Sat 10am–5pm (Thurs until 9pm), Sun noon–5pm. Closed Thanksgiving, Christmas, and New Year's Day. Bus: 3, 4, or 12.

Located on First Hill, this recently renovated and expanded museum is primarily an exhibit space for the extensive personal art collection of Charles and Emma Frye, Seattle pioneers who began collecting art in the 1890s. The collection focuses on late 19th-century and early 20th century representational art by European and American painters. There are works by Thomas Hart Benton, Edward Hopper, Albert Bierstadt, and Pablo Picasso, as well as a large collection of engravings by Winslow Homer. In the museum's new wings, you'll find special exhibits that change monthly. The special exhibitions are often in striking contrast to the styles seen in the permanent collection.

✪ **Henry Art Gallery.** University of Washington, 15th Ave. NE and NE 41st St. ☎ **206/543-2280.** Admission $5 adults, $3.50 students and seniors, ages 12 and under free. Free Thursday from 5 to 8pm. Tues–Sun 11am–5pm (Thurs until 8pm). Closed Thanksgiving, Christmas, and New Year's Day. Bus: 7, 43, 70, 71, 72, or 73.

This museum on the University of Washington campus was greatly expanded in 1997 and now has nearly three times the exhibit space that it once had. This new space has loads of potential and is well lit by pyramidal and cubic skylights that can be seen near the main museum entrance. Expect the museum to stage many more interesting exhibits in the years to come. The focus here is on contemporary art with retrospectives of individual artists, as well as exhibits focusing on specific themes or media. Photography and video are both well represented, and for the most part, the exhibits are the most challenging to be seen in the Seattle area. There's also a cafe here and a small sculpture courtyard.

✪ **Seattle Asian Art Museum.** 1400 E. Prospect St., Volunteer Park (14th Ave. E. and E. Prospect St.). ☎ **206/654-3100.** Admission $6 adults, $4 students and seniors, ages 12 and under free. Free to all on first Thurs of each month (free for seniors on first Fri of each month). Admission ticket also valid at Seattle Art Museum if used within 1 week. Tues–Sun 10am–5pm (Thurs until 9pm). Closed Thanksgiving, Christmas, and New Year's Day. Bus: 10.

Housed in the renovated art deco building that once served as the city's main art museum, the Asian art collection has an emphasis on Chinese and Japanese art but also includes pieces from Korea, Southeast Asia, South Asia, and the Himalayas. Collections of Chinese terra-cotta funerary art, snuff bottles, and Japanese *netsukes* (belt decorations) are among the museum's most notable. One room is devoted almost exclusively to Japanese screens and painting while another holds Japanese folk art, including several old kimonos. The central hall is devoted to the stone religious sculptures of South Asia (primarily India). Special exhibits change every six months and there are frequent lectures and concerts.

HISTORICAL & CULTURAL MUSEUMS

Burke Museum. 17th Ave. NE and NE 45th St. ☎ **206/543-5590.** Donation, $3 adults, $2 students and seniors, $1.50 ages 6–18. Daily 10am–5pm. Closed July 4, Thanksgiving, Christmas, and New Year's Day. Bus: 70, 71, 72, or 73.

Located in the northwest corner of the University of Washington campus, the Burke Museum features exhibits on the natural and cultural heritage of the Pacific Rim. It is noteworthy primarily for its Northwest Coast Indian art collection and an active schedule of special exhibits. Down in the basement, there is a large collection of minerals and fossils. In front of the museum stand replicas of totem poles carved in the 1870s and 1880s. There is also an ethnobotanical garden displaying plants used by northwestern tribes. At press time the museum was about to reopen after an extensive renovation aimed at providing better space and all-new exhibits.

Klondike Gold Rush National Historical Park. 117 S. Main St. ☎ **206/553-7220.** Free admission. Daily 9am–5pm. Closed Thanksgiving, Christmas, and New Year's Day. Bus: 15, 18, 21, 22, or 23. Waterfront Streetcar: To Occidental Park stop.

It isn't in the Klondike (which isn't even in the United States) and it isn't really a park (it's a single room in an old store), but it is a fascinating little museum. "At 3 o'clock this morning the steamship Portland, from St. Michaels for Seattle, passed up [Puget] Sound with more than a ton of gold on board and 68 passengers." When the *Seattle Post-Intelligencer* published that sentence on July 17, 1897, it started a stampede. Would-be miners heading for the Klondike goldfields in the 1890s made Seattle their outfitting center and helped turn it into a prosperous city. When they struck it rich up north, they headed back to Seattle, the first U.S. outpost of civilization, and unloaded their gold, making Seattle doubly rich. It seems only fitting that this museum should be here. Film buffs can catch a free screening of Charlie

Insider Tip

Campus parking is very expensive on weekdays and Saturday mornings, so try to visit the Burke Museum on a Saturday afternoon or a Sunday.

Chaplin's film *The Gold Rush* the first Sunday of each month. Another unit of the park is in Skagway, Alaska.

Museum of History and Industry. 2700 24th Ave. E. ☎ **206/324-1126.** Admission $5.50 adults, $3 seniors and ages 6–12, $1 for ages 2–5, under age 2 free. Tues by donation. Daily 10am–5pm. Closed Thanksgiving, Christmas, and New Year's Day. Bus: 25, 43, or 48.

If the Seattle Underground Tour's vivid description of life before the fire has you curious about what the city's more respectable citizens were doing back in the 1880s, you can find out here, where re-created storefronts provide glimpses into their lives. Located at the north end of Washington Park Arboretum, this museum explores various aspects of Seattle's history, with frequently changing exhibits on more obscure aspects of the city's past. While many of the exhibits will be of greatest interest to Seattle residents, anyone wishing to gain a better understanding of the history of Seattle and the Northwest will find the displays here of interest. There is a Boeing mail plane from the 1920s, plus an exhibit on the 1889 fire that leveled the city. This museum also hosts touring exhibitions that address Northwest history.

NW Seaport/Maritime Heritage Center. 1002 Valley St. ☎ **206/447-9800.** Free admission. Mon–Sat 10am–4pm, Sun noon–4pm (until 5pm daily in summer).

Although this marine heritage center at the south end of Lake Union is currently little more than a shipyard for the restoration of three historic ships, it has grand plans for the future. If you're a fan of tall ships and the age of sail, you can pay a visit to the 1897 schooner *Wawona,* which is currently under restoration. Most months of the year, there are Friday lunchtime folk music concerts on the deck of this boat. Nearby, in Chandler's Cove, you'll find the Puget Sound Maritime Museum Exhibit, 901 Fairview N. (☎ **206/624-3028**), with more exhibits on Northwest maritime heritage. Together these two centers are working to turn the adjacent Navy Reserve Training Center into a maritime museum.

Wing Luke Asian Museum. 407 Seventh Ave. S. ☎ **206/623-5124.** Admission $2.50 adults, $1.50 students and seniors, 75¢ ages 5–12, under 5 free. Free on Thurs. Tues–Fri 11am–4:30pm, Sat–Sun noon–4pm. Closed New Year's Day, Easter, July 4, Veteran's Day, Thanksgiving, Christmas eve, and Christmas day. Bus: Any bus using the bus tunnel.

Located in the heart of Seattle's International District (Chinatown) and named for the first Asian American to hold public office in the Northwest, this museum explores the role various Asian cultures have played in the settlement and development of the Northwest. Despite much persecution over the years, Asians, primarily Chinese and Japanese, have played an integral role in developing the Northwest, and today the connection of this region with the far side of the Pacific is opening up both economic and cultural doors. Many of the museum's special exhibits are meant to help explain Asian customs to non-Asians.

SCIENCE MUSEUMS

Pacific Science Center. 200 Second Ave. N., Seattle Center. ☎ **206/443-2001.** Admission $7.50 adults, $5.50 ages 6–13 and seniors, $3.50 ages 2–5, under 2 free. IMAX $5.50 adults, $4.50 ages 6–13 and seniors, $3.50 ages 2–5. Laser show $6 for evening performances ($3 on Tues). Various discounted combination tickets available. June–Sept, daily 10am–6pm; Oct–May, Mon–Fri 10am–5pm, Sat–Sun and holidays 10am–6pm. Closed Thanksgiving and Christmas. Bus: 1, 2, 3, 4, 6, 13, 15, 16, 18, 19, 24, or 33. Monorail: To Seattle Center.

Although its exhibits are aimed primarily at children, the Pacific Science Center is fun for all ages. The main goal of this sprawling complex at Seattle Center is to teach kids about science and to instill a desire to study it. To that end, there are dozens of fun hands-on exhibits addressing the biological sciences, physics, and chemistry. Kids

Good Times in Bad Taste

If you love bad jokes and have a fascination with the bizarre (or maybe this de-
scribes your children), you won't want to miss Bill Speidel's Underground Tour
and a visit to Ye Olde Curiosity Shop. Together these two should reassure you that
espresso, traffic jams, and stadium controversies aside, Seattle really does have a sense
of humor.

If you have an appreciation of off-color humor and are curious about the seamier
side of Seattle history, **Bill Speidel's Underground Tour,** 610 First Ave. (☎ 206/
682-4646), will likely entertain and enlighten you. The tours lead down below street
level in the Pioneer Square area where still can be found vestiges of Seattle businesses built before the great fire of 1889. Learn the low-down dirt on early Seattle,
a town where plumbing was problematic and a person could drown in a pothole.
(Tours held daily; $6.50 adults, $5.50 seniors, $5 students ages 13–17, $2.75 children ages 6–12).

Ye Olde Curiosity Shop, 1001 Alaskan Way, Pier 54 (☎ 206/682-5844), is a
cross between a souvenir store and Ripley's Believe It or Not! It's weird! It's tacky!
It's always packed! See Siamese-twin calves, a natural mummy, the Lord's Prayer
on a grain of rice, a narwhal tusk, shrunken heads, a 67-pound snail, fleas in dresses,
walrus and whale oosiks (the bone of the male reproductive organ)—in fact, all the
stuff that fascinated you as a kid. The collection of oddities was started in 1899 by
Joe Standley, who had developed a more-than-passing interest in strange curios.

---

learn how their bodies work, blow giant bubbles, and experiment with robots. There
is a planetarium for learning about the skies (plus laser shows for the fun of it). Even
more interesting are the many special exhibits, so be sure to check the schedule when
you're in town. There are also special events, including a bubble festival. An IMAX
theater has daily showings of short films on its $3^1/_2$-story-high screen.

3 Neighborhoods

The **International District,** centered between Fifth Avenue S. and Eighth Avenue S.
(between S. Main Street and S. Lane Street), is Seattle's large and prosperous Asian
neighborhood. Called the International District rather than Chinatown because so
many Asian nationalities have made this area home, this neighborhood has been the
center of the city's Asian communities for more than 100 years. You can learn about
the district's history at the Wing Luke Museum (see above), where you can also pick
up a walking-tour map of the area. There are of course many restaurants, import
stores, and food markets. In fact, the huge Uwajimaya (see "Markets" in chapter 8
for details) is all of these rolled up in one. Both the **Nippon Kan Theatre,** 628 S.
Washington St. (☎ 206/467-6807), and the **Northwest Asian-American Theater,**
409 Seventh Ave. S. (☎ 206/340-1049), feature performances with an Asian flavor.
At the corner of Maynard Avenue S. and S. King Street, you'll find Hing Hay Park,
the site of an ornate and colorful pavilion given to the city by Taipei, Taiwan.

The **Fremont District,** which begins at the north end of the Fremont Bridge near
the intersection of Fremont Avenue N. and N. 36th Street, is Seattle's funkiest,
funnest, and most unusual neighborhood. "Welcome to the Center of the Universe"
reads the sign on the Fremont Bridge, and from this point onward, you know you
are in a very different part of Seattle, maybe even a different dimension. This funky
neighborhood also goes by the name Republic of Fremont, and has as its motto

"De Libertas Quirkas," which roughly translated means "free to be peculiar." At this crossroads business district, you'll find unusual outdoor art, the Fremont Sunday Market, several vintage clothing and furniture stores, a brew pub, and many more unexpected and unusual shops, galleries, and cafes. On summer Saturday nights, there are outdoor movies, and in June, there is the wacky Solstice Parade, a countercultural promenade with giant puppets, wizards, fairies, face paint, and hippies of all ages. Among the public artworks in the neighborhood are *Waiting for the Interurban* (at the north end of the Fremont Bridge), the *Fremont Troll* (under the Aurora Bridge on N. 36th Street), and *The Rocket at the Center of the Universe* (at the corner of Evanston Avenue N. and N. 35th Street). For a walking tour of Fremont, see chapter 7.

4 Totem Poles

Totem poles are the quintessential symbol of the Northwest, and although this Native American art form actually comes from farther north (in British Columbia), there are quite a few totem poles around Seattle. In Occidental Park, just off Pioneer Square at Occidental Avenue South and South Washington Street you'll find four totem poles that were carved by local artist Duane Pasco. The tallest is the 35-foot-high *The Sun and Raven,* which tells the story of how Raven brought light into the world. Next to this pole is *Man Riding a Whale.* This type of totem pole was traditionally carved to help villagers during their whale hunts. The other two figures that face each other are symbols of the Bear Clan and the Welcoming Figure.

A block away, in the triangular park of Pioneer Place, you can see Seattle's most famous totem pole. The pole you see here now is actually a copy of the original, which arrived in Seattle in 1890 after a band of drunken men stole it from a Tlingit village up the coast. In 1938 the pole was set afire by an arsonist. The Seattle city fathers sent a $5,000 check to the Tlingit village requesting a replacement. Supposedly, the response from the village was, "Thanks for paying for the first totem pole. If you want another, it will cost another $5,000." The city paid up, and so today Pioneer Square has a totem pole and Seattle has a clear conscience.

Up near Pike Place Market, at Victor Steinbrueck Park, which is at the intersection of Pike Place, Virginia Street, and Western Avenue, are two 50-foot-tall totem poles. To see the largest concentration of authentic totem poles, visit the University of Washington's Burke Museum (see above for details).

5 Panoramas

If you've ever seen a photo of the Space Needle framed by the high-rises of downtown Seattle, then you've probably seen a photo taken from **Kerry Viewpoint** on Queen Anne Hill. If you want to take your own drop-dead photo of the Seattle skyline from this elevated perspective, head north from Seattle Center on Queen Anne Avenue N. and turn left on W. Highland Drive. When you reach the park, you'll immediately recognize the view—it's on the cover of virtually every Seattle tourist booklet available.

For a more far-reaching panorama that takes in everything from the Cascades to the Olympics, head up to **Volunteer Park** on Capitol Hill. Here you'll find an old water tower surrounded by attractive gardens. A winding staircase leads to the top of the water tower, from which you get 360° views. To find the water tower, park near the Seattle Asian Art Museum if you can and walk back out to the parking lot to where the road splits. The view from directly in front of the museum isn't bad either.

If you don't want to deal with the crowds at the Space Needle, but still want an elevated downtown view, head to the big, black **Columbia Seafirst Center** at the corner of Fourth Avenue and Columbia Street. At 943 feet, this is the tallest building in Seattle (twice as tall as the Space Needle) and the building with the greatest number of stories west of the Mississippi. Up on the 73rd floor, you'll find an observation deck. Admission is $5 for adults and $3 for seniors and children.

6 Parks & Public Gardens

In addition to the parks and gardens listed here, you'll find the Carl S. English, Jr. Ornamental Gardens adjacent to the Hiram M. Chittenden Locks in the Ballard neighborhood of north Seattle (see "Where to See Salmon," below, for details).

PARKS

For much of Seattle's population, it is the city's many parks that make this such a livable city. In the downtown area, **Myrtle Edwards Park,** at the north end of the waterfront, provides a great spot for enjoying sunsets over Puget Sound and the Olympic Mountains. **Freeway Park,** at Sixth Avenue and Seneca Street, is one of Seattle's most unusual parks. Built right on top of busy Interstate 5, this green space is more a series of urban plazas, with lots of terraces, waterfalls, and cement planters creating walls of greenery. You'd never know there's a roaring freeway beneath your feet.

For serious communing with nature, however, nothing will do but **Discovery Park.** Occupying a high bluff and sandy point jutting into Puget Sound, this is Seattle's largest and wildest park. You can easily spend a day wandering the trails and beaches here.

Up on Capitol Hill, you'll find one of Seattle's largest and most popular parks. **Volunteer Park,** E. Prospect Street and 14th Avenue E., is surrounded by the elegant mansions of Capitol Hill and is a popular spot for suntanning and playing Frisbee. The park is also home to the Seattle Asian Art Museum, an amphitheater, a water tower with a superb view of the city, and a conservatory filled with tropical and desert plants.

On the east side of Seattle, along the shore of Lake Washington, you'll find not only swimming beaches but also large **Seward Park,** which has been home in recent years to a pair of bald eagles. While this park's waterfront areas are its biggest attraction, it also has a dense forest with trails winding through it.

In north Seattle, you'll find several parks worth visiting. These include the unique **Gasworks Park** at the north end of Lake Union on N. Northlake Way and Meridian Avenue N. This park has, in the middle of its green lawns, the rusting hulk of an old industrial plant. This park's Kite Hill is the city's favorite kite-flying spot. North of here, on Green Lake Way N. near the Woodland Park Zoo, you'll find **Green Lake Park,** which is a center for exercise buffs who jog, bicycle, and skate around the park on a paved path. It's also possible to swim in the lake, and there are plenty of grassy areas. Due east of Green Lake several miles, on the shore of Lake Washington at Sand Point, is the large **Magnusson Park.** This park is a former military base and for that reason doesn't have the feel of other Seattle parks. However, the meadows, beaches, and adjacent Sound Garden (a series of aural sculptures for which Seattle's famous grunge rock band was named) make this an interesting spot to visit. The park is off Sand Point Way NE.

North of the Ballard district, you'll find two very pleasant waterfront parks: **Golden Gardens** and **Carkeek.** The former, on Seaview Avenue NW, is best known as the site of one of Seattle's best beaches, but it is also a very pleasant spot for a sunset stroll. Carkeek Park, on NW Carkeek Park Road, is farther north and is a wild bit of forest surrounded by suburbia. Within the park, trails meander among the trees and lead down to a beach (which is unfortunately backed by railroad tracks).

Over in West Seattle, off Fauntleroy Ave. SW just north of the ferry dock for ferries to Vashon Island and the Kitsap Peninsula, you'll find **Lincoln Park,** which offers wooded trails, a beach, and even a public swimming pool, and all with excellent views across Puget Sound.

PUBLIC GARDENS

Washington Park Arboretum. 2300 Arboretum Dr. E. ☎ **206/543-8800.** Free admission. Daily dawn to dusk; visitor center Mon–Fri 10am–4pm, Sat–Sun 10am–4pm. Enter on Lake Washington Blvd. off E. Madison St. or take Wash. 520 off I-5 north of downtown, take the Montlake exit, and go straight through the first intersection. Bus: 11, 43, or 84.

Acres of trees and shrubs stretch from the far side of Capitol Hill all the way to the Montlake Cut, a canal connecting Lake Washington to Lake Union. Within the 200-acre arboretum, there are 5,000 varieties of plants and quiet trails that are pleasant throughout the year but most beautiful in spring, when azaleas, cherry trees,

On the Trail of Dale Chihuly

For many years now Northwest glass artist Dale Chihuly, one of the founders of the Pilchuck School for glass art north of Seattle, has been garnering nationwide media attention for his fanciful and color-saturated contemporary glass art. From tabletop vessels to massive window installations, his creations in glass have a depth and richness of color treasured by collectors across the country. His sensuous forms include vases within bowls that are reminiscent of Technicolor birds' eggs in giant nests. His ikebana series, based on the traditional Japanese flower-arranging technique, are riotous conglomerations of color that twist and turn like so many cut flowers waving in the wind.

So where do you go to see the works of this master of molten glass? There's no one place in Seattle to see a collection of his work, but there are numerous public displays around the city. Up on the third floor of the **Washington State Convention and Trade Center,** Pike Street and Eighth Avenue, there is a case with some beautifully lighted vases. In the lobby of the **Sheraton Seattle Hotel,** 1400 Sixth Ave., there are works by Chihuly and other Northwest glass artists from the Pilchuck School. If you want to dine surrounded by art glass, including work by Chihuly, make a reservation at the Sheraton's ever-popular Fuller's. The **City Centre shopping arcade,** 1420 Fifth Ave., has displays by numerous glass artists, including Chihuly. Don't miss the large wall installation that is beside this upscale shopping arcades lounge (out the back door of FAO Schwartz). Also at City Centre, you'll find the **Foster/White Gallery,** which represents Chihuly in Seattle and always has a few of his pieces on display (and yes, they are for sale). The main Foster/White Gallery, 311¹/₂ Occidental Ave. S., is in Pioneer Square, and another satellite gallery is located in Kirkland at 126 Central Way.

If you're willing to drive to Chihuly's home town of **Tacoma,** 32 miles south of Seattle, you can see the largest museum exhibit of Chihuly's work at the **Tacoma Art Museum,** 1123 Pacific Ave. (☎ **253/272-4258**), open Tuesday to Wednesday and Friday to Saturday from 10am to 5pm, Thursday 10am to 7pm (until 8pm on the third Thursday of each month), Sunday from noon to 5pm. Just up the street from here, at Tacoma's restored Union Station (now the federal courthouse), some of the artist's larger pieces have been installed.

rhododendrons, and dogwoods are all in flower. Sadly, much of the arboretum has been neglected over the decades and plants and paths are no longer as well maintained as they ought to be. The north end of the arboretum, a marshland that is home to ducks and herons, is popular with kayakers, canoeists (see "Sea Kayaking, Canoeing, Rowing & Sailing" in "Outdoor Activities," below, for places to rent a canoe or kayak), and bird watchers. A boardwalk with views across Lake Washington meanders along the water in this area.

Japanese Gardens. Washington Park Arboretum, Lake Washington Blvd. E. (north of E. Madison St.). ☎ **206/684-4725.** Admission $2 adults; $1 seniors, the disabled, and ages 6–18. Mar–Apr, daily 10am–6pm; May, daily 10am–7pm; June–Aug, daily 10am–8pm; Sept–Oct, daily 10am–6pm; Nov, daily 10am–4pm. Closed Dec–Feb. Bus: 11.

Situated on 3 1/2 acres of land, the Japanese Gardens are a perfect little world unto themselves. Babbling brooks, a lake rimmed with Japanese irises and filled with colorful koi (Japanese carp), and a cherry orchard (for spring color) are peaceful any time of year. Unfortunately, noise from a nearby road can be distracting at times. A special Tea Garden encloses a Tea House, where, between April and October, on the third Saturday of each month at 1:30pm, you can attend a traditional tea ceremony.

Volunteer Park Conservatory. E. Prospect Street and 14th Avenue E. ☎ **206/322-4112.** Free admission. May 1–Sept 15, daily 10am–7pm; Sept 16–Apr 30, 10am–4pm. Bus: 10.

This stately old Victorian conservatory, built in 1912, houses a large collection of tropical and desert plants, including palm trees, orchids, and cacti.

7 Where to See Salmon

While numbers of salmon in the Puget Sound region have dwindled dangerously low in recent years, it is still possible in various places to witness the annual return of salmon.

In the autumn, on the waterfront, you can see returning salmon at the **Seattle Aquarium.** At **Hiram M. Chittenden Locks,** 3015 NW 54th St. (☎ **206/783-7059**), between July and August, you can view salmon both as they leap up the locks' fish ladder and through underwater observation windows. These locks, which are used primarily by small boats, connect Lake Union and Lake Washington with the waters of Puget Sound, and depending on the tides and lake levels, there is a difference of 6 to 26 feet on either side of the locks. The Carl S. English, Jr. Botanical Garden, which contains more than 500 species of plants, is adjacent to the locks. The locks and park are open daily from 7am to 9pm and the visitors center is open June through September daily from 10am to 7pm and October through May Thursday through Monday from 11am to 5pm (closed Thanksgiving, Christmas, and New Year's Day). Take bus 17 or 46. East of Seattle, in downtown **Issaquah,** there is a salmon hatchery at 125 Sunset Way (☎ 425/391-9094), where salmon can be seen year round. However, it is in October that adult salmon can be seen returning to the hatchery. Each year in October, the city of Issaquah holds a Salmon Days Festival to celebrate the return of the natives.

8 Especially for Kids

Listed below you'll find several attractions that are aimed almost exclusively at kids, however, for a few other attractions that will appeal to both kids and adults, see the "Top Attractions," above, for the following Seattle attractions: **Pacific Science Center, The Seattle Aquarium, Omnidome Film Experience,** and **Woodland Park Zoo.** Also, check out Ye Olde Curiosity Shop. And what could be more fun than exploring the creepy world of the Seattle Underground (see my "Good Times in Bad Taste" feature above).

You can also take the kids to a sports event. Seattle supports professional football, basketball, and baseball teams (see "Spectator Sports" below). You might also be able to catch a performance at the Seattle Children's Theatre or the Northwest Puppet Center. See "Children's Theater" in chapter 9 for details.

The Children's Museum. Center House, Seattle Center. ☎ **206/298-2521.** Admission $4.50. Daily 10am–5pm. Closed Thanksgiving, Christmas, and New Year's Day. Bus: Bus: 15 or 18. Monorail: from Westlake Center at the corner of Pine St. and Fourth Ave.

Seattle's Children's Museum is located in the basement of the Center House at Seattle Center. The museum includes plenty of hands-on cultural exhibits, a child-size neighborhood, an imagination station, a mountain wilderness area, a global village, and other exhibits to keep the little ones busy learning and playing for hours.

Enchanted Village and Wild Waves. 36201 Enchanted Pkwy. S., Federal Way. ☎ **206/661-8000.** Enchanted Village, $11 adults, $9 children ages 3–9, free for children 2 and under, $7 seniors; Enchanted Village and Wild Waves together, $19.95 adults, $17.95 children ages 3–9, free for children 2 and under, $10 seniors. Mid-May to early Sept; call for hours. By car from Seattle, take I-5 south to Exit 142-B, Puyallup.

The littlest kids can watch the clowns and ride on miniature trains, merry-go-rounds, and the like at Enchanted Village. The older kids, teenagers, and adults will want to spend the hot days of summer riding the wild waves, tubing down artificial streams, and swooshing down water slides.

Seattle Center. 305 Harrison St. ☎ **206/684-7200** or 206/728-1585. Free admission; pay per ride or game (various multiride tickets available). June–Labor Day, daily noon–11pm; Labor Day to June, weekends noon–11pm (schedule sometimes varies in winter months). Bus: 15 or 18. Monorail: from Westlake Center at the corner of Pine St. and Fourth Ave.

If you want to keep the kids entertained all day long, go to Seattle Center. This 74-acre amusement park and cultural center was built for the Seattle World's Fair in 1962 and stands on the north edge of downtown at the end of the monorail line. The most visible building at the center is the Space Needle (see above), which provides an outstanding panorama of the city from its observation deck. However, of much more interest to children are the Fun Forest rides (a roller coaster, log flume, merry-go-round, and Ferris wheel), arcade games, and minigolf. Seattle Center is also the site of the Children's Museum and Seattle Children's Theatre. This is Seattle's main festival site, and in the summer months hardly a weekend goes by without some festival or another filling its grounds.

9 Organized Tours

For information on the Seattle Underground tour, see my "Good Times in Bad Taste" feature above. For information on touring the Boeing plant, see my "North of the City" excursion in chapter 10.

WALKING TOURS

If you'd like to explore downtown Seattle with a knowledgeable guide, join one of the informative walking tours offered by **See Seattle Walking Tours** (☎ 425/226-7641). The tours visit Pike Place Market, the waterfront, the Pioneer Square district, and the International District. Tour prices range from $15 to $30.

If you'd like an insider's glimpse of life in Seattle's International District, book a tour with **Chinatown Discovery Tours** (☎ 206/236-0657). On these walking tours, which last from 1¹/₂ to 3 hours, you'll learn the history of this colorful and historic neighborhood. **A Touch of Chinatown** ($9.95) is a brief introduction to the neighborhood. The **Chinatown by Day** tour ($24.95) includes a six-course lunch. **Nibble Your Way Through Chinatown** ($14.95) provides a sampling of flavors from around the International District. The **Chinatown by Night** tour ($34.95) includes an eight-course banquet.

BUS TOURS

If you'd like an overview of Seattle's main tourist attractions, or if you're pressed for time during your visit, you can pack in a lot of sights on a tour with **Gray Line of Seattle** (☎ **800/426-7532** or 206/626-5208). Half-day tours are $24 for adults, $12 for children; full-day tours are $33 for adults, $16.50 for children. Tours outside the city are also available.

From May through October, Gray Line also offers a **Trolley Tour** on one of those buses made up to look like an old trolley. The tour is actually a day pass to use the trolley, which follows a set route around downtown Seattle. The trolley goes along the waterfront and also stops at Seattle Center, Pike Place Market, the Seattle Art Museum, and Pioneer Square. A two-day pass is $13 for adults and $6.50 for children. Because buses in downtown are free, the Waterfront Streetcar is less than $1 most of the day, and the monorail will get you to Seattle Center for $1, the trolley is not a very good deal.

BOAT TOURS

In addition to the boat tours and cruises mentioned below, you can do your own low-budget cruise simply by hopping on one of the ferries operated by Washington State Ferries. Try the Bainbridge Island or Bremerton ferries out of Seattle for a 2-hour round-trip. For a longer and more scenic trip, drive north to Anacortes and ride the ferries through the San Juan Islands, perhaps spending a few hours in the town of Friday Harbor before returning. It's also possible to take the first ferry of the day from Anacortes, ride all the way to Sidney, British Columbia, and then catch the next ferry back to Anacortes.

Located at Blake Island State Marine Park across Puget Sound from Seattle and only accessible by tour boat or private boat, Tillicum Village was built in conjunction with the 1962 Seattle world's fair. The "village" is actually just a large restaurant and performance hall fashioned after a traditional Northwest Coast Indian longhouse, but with totem poles standing vigil out front, the forest encircling the longhouse, and the waters of Puget Sound stretching out into the distance, Tillicum Village is a beautiful spot. **Tillicum Village Tours,** Pier 56 (☎ **206/443-1244**), operates tours that include the scenic boat ride to and from the island, a dinner of alder-smoked salmon, and a performance of traditional masked dances. After the dinner and dances, you can strike out on forest trails to explore the island (you can even return on a later boat if you want to spend a couple of extra hours hiking). There are even beaches on which to relax. Tours cost $50.25 for adults, $46.50 for seniors, $32.50 for children ages 13 to 19, $20 for children ages 6 to 12, and $10 for children ages 4 to 5. Tours are offered daily from May to October; other months schedule varies. If you were going to opt for only one tour while in Seattle, this should be it—it's unique and truly northwestern.

Seattle is a city surrounded by water, and if you'd like to see it from various aquatic perspectives, you can take one of the cruises offered by **Argosy Cruises,** Pier 55 (☎ **206/623-4252**), which offers the widest array of cruises in the Seattle area. There's a Seattle harbor cruise (departs from Pier 55; $13.40 adults, $6.45 children ages 5 to 12); a cruise through the Hiram Chittenden Locks to Lake Union (departs from Pier 57; $21.70 adults, $11.10 children ages 5 to 12), and two cruises around

Lake Washington (one departs from Chandler's Cove at the south end of Lake Union and the other departs from downtown Kirkland on the east side of the lake; $17.10 adults, $8.75 children ages 5 to 12). The latter two cruises will take you past the fabled Xanadu built by Bill Gates on the shore of Lake Washington.

From June through August **Clipper Navigation,** Pier 69 (☎ **800/888-2535,** 206/ 448-5000, or 250/382-8100 in Victoria), operates 2-hour sunset cruises that circumnavigate Bainbridge Island. Fares are $16 for adults and $8 for children. In July and August, some of the cruises also include live jazz music ($20 for adults, $10 for children).

You can explore the mazelike waterways of the Puget Sound on an all-day cruise aboard the *San Juan Explorer,* which is also operated by Clipper Navigation. This cruise heads up the east side of Whidbey Island and through Deception Pass before reaching the San Juan Islands. You then get four hours in the town of Friday Harbor before starting the return trip to Seattle. The round-trip fare is $59 for adults, $54 for seniors, and $29.50 for children. Discounted advance purchase fares are also available, and overnight stays can be arranged.

Various *Victoria Clipper* ferries, operated by Clipper Navigation, ply the waters between Seattle and Victoria, British Columbia, with several departures daily in summer. A high-speed catamaran passenger ferry takes 3 to 5 hours to reach Victoria, and a turbo-jet passenger ferry takes only 2 hours (this is the fastest passenger boat in the western hemisphere). If you leave on the earliest ferry, you can spend the better part of the day exploring Victoria and be back in Seattle for a late dinner. Round-trip fares range from $88 to $109 for adults, $78 to $99 for seniors, and $44 to $54.50 for children ages 1 to 11. Discounted advance-purchase tickets are also available. Some scheduled trips also stop in the San Juan Islands. Various tour packages are also available, including an add-on tour to Butchart Gardens.

Clipper Navigation also operates a car ferry, the *Princess Marguerite III,* between Seattle and Victoria during the summer months. This ship takes 4¹/₂ hours to make the journey and the round-trip fare is $98 for a car and driver and $58 for adult passengers, $50 for seniors, and $29 for children ages 1 to 11.

If you'd like a bit of dining and dancing with your cruise around Puget Sound, book a cruise on the **Spirit of Puget Sound,** Pier 70 (☎ **206/443-1442**). This big sleek yacht does lunch, dinner, and moonlight party cruises. Adult fares range between $31.50 and $33 for lunch and between $55.50 and $59.25 for dinner.

Want a boat tour that's really all about raw power? Try a ride on the turbo-charged *Rocket,* a 70-foot tour boat operated by **Pier 54 Adventures,** Pier 54 (☎ **206/ 623-6364**). Powered by twin V-12 engines, this boat absolutely flies over the waters of Puget Sound. Fares for the 30-minute outings are $10 for adults, $9 for seniors, and $7 for children.

Looking for a quieter way to see Seattle from the water? Pier 54 Adventures also offers sailboat rides in their replica of the *Spray,* the sailboat Joshua Slocum used in his 1895 solo voyage around the world (the first such trip ever). Cruises are $15 to $25 for adults, $13.50 to $22.50 for seniors, and $10 to $15 for children. The higher fare is for the sunset cruise. **Let's Go Sailing,** Pier 56 (☎ **206/624-3931**), offers 1¹/₂- and 2¹/₂-hour sailboat cruises. The longer excursions are at sunset. Cruises are $20 to $35 for adults, $18 to $32 for seniors, and $15 to $28 for children under age 12. Over on Lake Union, **Sailing in Seattle,** 1900 Westlake Ave. N. (☎ **206/ 298-0094**), offers 2¹/₂-hour cruises for $35.

SCENIC FLIGHTS

Seattle is one of the few cities in the United States where floatplanes are a regular sight in the skies and on the lakes of the area. If you'd like to see what it's like to take off and land from the water, you've got a couple of options. **Seattle Seaplanes,** 1325 Fairview Ave. E. (☎ **800/637-5553** or 206/329-9638), which takes off from the southeast corner of Lake Union, offers 20-minute scenic flights over the city for $42.50. **Sound Flight,** 243 W. Perimeter Rd., Renton (☎ **800/825-0722**), which leaves from the south end of Lake Washington, offers a variety of scenic flights of varying lengths, with rates starting at $59. You could also book a flight on **Kenmore Air** (☎ **800/543-9595** or 206/486-1257) for an excursion to the San Juan Islands or Victoria. This company flies from Lake Union at 950 Westlake Ave. N. and from the north end of Lake Washington.

If you'd rather pretend you're back in the days of *The English Patient,* you can go up in a 1927 biplane with **Galvin Flying Service** (☎ **206/763-9706**), which flies out of Boeing Field. A 20-minute flight along the Seattle waterfront costs $79 for one person and $89 for two.

A RAILWAY EXCURSION

If you happen to be a fan of riding the rails, consider the **Spirit of Washington Dinner Train,** 625 S. Fourth St., Renton (☎ **800/876-RAIL** or 206/227-RAIL). Running from Renton, at the south end of Lake Washington, to the Columbia Winery near Woodinville, at the north end of the Lake, this train rolls past views of the lake and Mount Rainier. Along the way, you're fed a tasty and filling lunch or dinner. At the turn-around point, you get to tour a winery and taste some wines. Dinner tours range from $57 to $69; lunch tours range from $47 to $59. The higher prices are for seatings in the dome car, which definitely has finer views.

A COUPLE OF UNUSUAL TOURS

If you're interested in tapping into Seattle's microbrew scene, consider taking a **Brew Hops Tour** (☎ **206/283-8460**). This company offers both lunch and dinner tours to several Seattle breweries and brewpubs. Tours are $35 per person.

If your tastes run to the macabre, you might be interested in the Private Eye on Seattle tour offered by **Windsor and Hatten Legal Investigators** (☎ **206/622-0590**). These somewhat bizarre van tours are led by a retired private investigator who shares his stories of interesting and unusual cases he handled over the 40 years he was a private dick in the Emerald City. Tours are $20 per person.

10 Outdoor Activities

BEACHES

Alki (rhymes with *sky*) **Beach,** across Elliott Bay from downtown Seattle, is Seattle's most popular beach and is the nearest approximation you'll find in the Northwest to a Southern California beach scene. The paved path that runs along this 2¹/₂-mile-long beach is popular with skaters, walkers, and cyclists, and the road that parallels the beach is lined with shops and restaurants. But the views across Puget Sound to the Olympic Mountains confirm that this is indeed the Northwest.

For a more northwestern beach experience (which usually includes a bit of hiking or walking), head to one of the area's many waterfront parks. Lincoln Park, south of Alki Beach in West Seattle has bluffs and forests backing the beach. Northwest of downtown Seattle, you'll find **Discovery Park,** where miles of beaches are the primary destination of most park visitors. North of Ballard, on Seaview Avenue NW, **Golden Gardens Park** has lawns and shade trees. There are also several parks along the shores of Lake Washington that have small stretches of beach, many of which are actually popular with swimmers. **Mount Baker Beach** and **Seward Park,** both southeast of downtown Seattle along Lake Washington Boulevard, are two good places to hang out by the water and do a little swimming.

BICYCLING

During the summer, **Terrene Tours** (☎ 206/325-5569) rents bicycles from Pier 54 on the waterfront. Rental rates are $10 for two hours and $16 for up to four hours. This company also offers guided bicycle tours around both the immediate Seattle vicinity and farther afield in Washington.

Gregg's Green Lake Cycle, 7007 Woodlawn Ave. NE (☎ 206/523-1822); and the **Bicycle Center,** 4529 Sand Point Way NE (☎ 206/523-8300)—both rent bikes by the hour, day, or week. Rates range from $3 to $5 per hour and $15 to $30 per day. These shops are both convenient to the **Burke-Gilman Trail** and the **Sammamish River Trail.** The former is a 12¹/₂-mile trail created from an old railway bed. It starts at **Gasworks Park** and continues to **Kenmore Logboom Park** at the north end of Lake Washington by way of the University of Washington. Serious riders can then connect to the Sammamish River Trail, which leads to Marymoor Park at the north end of Lake Sammamish. Linking the two trails together adds up to a 50-mile round-trip ride. Marymoor Park is the site of Seattle's velodrome, a bicycle racetrack. There are lots of great picnicking spots along both trails. Bicycles can also be rented on the Seattle waterfront at Pier The West Seattle bike path along **Alki Beach** is another good place to ride.

From spring through early fall, Lake Washington Boulevard between **Seward Park** and **Mount Baker Beach** is closed to motor vehicles on the second Saturday and third Sunday of each month for Bicycle Saturdays and Sundays.

BOARDSAILING

Local Seattle waters are ideal for boardsailing, and depending on conditions can be excellent for beginners or the experienced. **Urban Surf,** 2100 N Northlake Way (☎ 206/545-WIND), will rent you a board and give you lessons if you need them. Rates are $35 per day for a board. Lessons are $100 for two 3-hour sessions. Magnuson Park, on Lake Washington north of the University District, and Gasworks Park on Lake Union, Alki Beach in West Seattle, and Golden Gardens Park north of Ballard are some of the area's popular boardsailing spots.

FISHING

While salmon and steelhead runs have dwindled dangerously low all over the Northwest, it is still possible to do a lot of fishing in the waters off Seattle. **Sport Fishing of Seattle,** Pier 54 (☎ 206/623-6364), offers year-round fishing for both salmon and bottom fish. For a half day of fishing, they charge $65 for adults and $50 for children. If you'd rather do some saltwater fly-fishing, contact **A Spot Tail Salmon Guide** (☎ 206/283-6680), a guide service operated by Keith Richards, who charges $350 for one or two people to do a full day of angling.

GOLF

While Seattle isn't a name that springs immediately to mind when one thinks of golf, the sport is as much a passion here as it is all across the country these days. There are more than a dozen public golf courses in the Seattle area. Seattle also has three conveniently located municipal golf courses—**Jackson Park Golf Course,** 1000 NE 135th St. (☎ 206/363-4747); **Jefferson Park Golf Course,** 4101 Beacon Ave. S. (☎ 206/762-4513); and **West Seattle Golf Course,** 4470 35th Ave. SW (☎ 206/ 935-5187)—all three of which charge very reasonable greens fees of $18.50.

Harbour Pointe, 11817 Harbour Pointe Blvd., Mukilteo (☎ **206/355-6060** or 800/233-3128), the number-two ranked public golf course in Washington state, is just a few miles north of Seattle near the city of Everett. This course abounds in water hazards (each of the first 10 holes have water), and on the 11th hole you're treated to a fine view of Puget Sound. Greens fees range from $30 to $45. One hour north of Seattle, in the town of Stanwood, you'll find the **Kayak Point Golf Course,** 15711 Marine Dr. (☎ **800/562-3094**), which *Golf Digest* rated the best public course in the Northwest. Greens fees range from $23 to $27.

HIKING

Within Seattle itself, there are several large natural parks that are laced with enough trails to allow for a few good long walks. Among these are Seward Park on Lake Washington Boulevard southeast of downtown and Lincoln Park south of Alki Beach in West Seattle. However, the city's largest natural park and Seattleites favorite quick dose of nature is **Discovery Park,** northwest of downtown at the western tip of the Magnolia neighborhood. This park covers more than 500 acres and has many miles of trails and beaches to hike. There are gorgeous views, forest paths, and meadows for lazing in after a long walk.

For more challenging hiking in the real outdoors, head east of Seattle on I-90. Rising abruptly from the floor of the Snoqualmie Valley outside the town of North Bend is **Mount Si,** with a tiring trail to its summit, but a payoff of awesome views. Farther east on I-90, as at Snoqualmie Pass and before you reach it, there are several trailheads. Some trails lead to mountain summits, others to glacier-carved lakes, and still others past waterfalls deep in the forest. Due to their proximity to Seattle, these trails can be very crowded, and you will need a parking permit to leave your car at national forest trailheads (though not at the Mount Si trailhead, which is on state land). For more information, contact the **North Bend Ranger District** (☎ **206/ 888-1421**).

HORSEBACK RIDING

Down at the south end of Lake Washington on the outskirts of the city of Renton, you can rent horses at **Aqua Barn Ranch,** 15227 SE Renton–Maple Valley Hwy. (☎ **206/255-4618**). East of Seattle, near Issaquah, **Tiger Mountain Outfitters,** 24508 SE 133rd St. (tel. **206/392-5090**), leads guided rides into Tiger Mountain State Forest. Reservations are required.

HOT-AIR BALLOONING

Seattle really isn't known as a hot-air ballooning center, but if you'd like to try floating over the Northwest landscape not far outside the city, contact **Over the Rainbow** (☎ **206/364-0995**), which flies over the vineyards of the Woodinville area. Fares range from $110 for a weekday breakfast flight with champagne and continental breakfast to $140 for a weekend flight with a picnic dinner at the end of the flight.

IN-LINE SKATING

Seattle has developed a reputation as one of the nation's hot in-line skating destinations. Throughout the city there are dozens of miles of paved paths that are perfect for skating. You can rent in-line skates at **Greg's Green Lake Cycle,** 7007 Woodlawn Ave. NE (☎ **206/523-1822**) for about $12 per day or $4 per hour. The trail around Green Lake in north Seattle and the Burke-Gilman trail (see the description under "Bicycling," above) are both good places for skating and are convenient to Gregg's. Other place to try include Myrtle Edwards Park and the waterfront, and the paved path along Lake Washington Boulevard north of Seward Park.

JOGGING

The waterfront, from Pioneer Square north to Myrtle Edwards Park, where a paved path parallels the water, is a favorite downtown jogging route. The residential streets of Capitol Hill when combined with roads and sidewalks through Volunteer Park are another good choice. If you happen to be staying in the University District, you can access the 12^1/$_2$-mile-long Burke-Gilman Trail or run the ever-popular trail around Green Lake.

PARASAILING

This sport, in which people are strapped into a parachute and towed behind a boat, may be more closely associated with the beaches of Mexico and other warm-weather vacation destinations, but it's also possible to parasail in Seattle. On the waterfront, rides are available at Pier 57 from **Pier 57 Parasailing** (☎ **206/622-5757**), which charges $49 for a 10-minute flight for one person and $89 for a 10-minute tandem flight (300-pound limit). Flights are offered daily in the summer from 11am to sunset. You can also try parasailing over in Kirkland on the east side of Lake Washington. **Lake Washington Parasail** (☎ **206/822-SAIL**) operates out of Kirkland Marina Park at the end of Kirkland Avenue and charges $42 for a ride.

PARKS

See "Parks & Gardens," earlier in this chapter.

SEA KAYAKING, CANOEING, ROWING & SAILING

On the waterfront, at Pier 54, **Outland Adventures** (☎ **206/623-6364**), offers guided 1^1/$_2$-hour sea kayak tours. Tours are $35 per person and are in very stable double kayaks.

If you'd rather head out on your own, try **Northwest Outdoor Center,** 2100 Westlake Ave. N. (☎ **206/281-9694**), which is located on Lake Union and will rent you a sea kayak for between $8 and $12 per hour. You can also opt for guided tours lasting from a few hours to several days, and there are plenty of classes available for those who are interested.

Moss Bay Rowing and Kayak Center, 1001 Fairview Ave. N. (☎ **206/682-2031**) rents sea kayaks at the south end of Lake Union near Chandler's Cove. Rates range from $8 per hour for a single to $12 per hour for a double.

The **University of Washington Waterfront Activities Center,** on the university campus behind Husky Stadium (☎ **206/543-9433**), is open to the public and rents canoes and rowboats for $5 per hour. With the marshes of the Washington Park Arboretum directly across a narrow channel from the boat launch, this is an ideal place for the inexperienced to rent a boat.

The Center for Wooden Boats, 1010 Valley St. (☎ **206/382-BOAT**), a museum that rents classic boats, is at Waterway 4 at the south end of Lake Union. Dedicated to the preservation of historic wooden boats, the center is unique in that many exhibits can be rented and taken out on Lake Union. There are rowboats and large and small sailboats. Rates range from $15 to $38 per hour. Individual sailing instruction is also available. From June 1 to Labor Day, the center is open daily from 11am to 7pm; the rest of the year, Wednesday through Monday from noon to 6pm.

SKIING

One of the reasons Seattleites put up with long, wet winters is because they can go skiing within an hour of the city, and with many slopes set up for night skiing, it's possible to leave work and be on the slopes before dinner, ski for several hours, and be home in time to get a good night's rest. The ski season in the Seattle area generally runs from mid-November to the end of April.

Equipment can be rented at the ski areas listed below, and at **REI,** 222 Yale Ave. N. (☎ **206/223-1944**).

Cross-Country Skiing   In the Snoqualmie Pass area, less than 50 miles east of Seattle on I-90, **Ski Acres/Hyak Nordic Center** (☎ **206/434-6646**), offers rentals, instruction, and many miles of groomed trails. Ski Acres even has lighted trails for night skiing. The trail fee runs $6 to $8.

There are also several sno-parks along I-90 at Snoqualmie Pass. Some of these have groomed trails while others have trails that are marked but not groomed. When renting skis, be sure to get a **Sno-Park permit.** These are required if you want to park at a cross-country ski area. Sno-park permits are available at ski shops.

Downhill Skiing   Jointly known as **The Pass,** Alpental, Ski Acres, Snoqualmie, and Hyak ski areas (☎ **206/236-PASS** or 206/236-1600 for snow conditions) are all located at Snoqualmie Pass less than 50 miles east of Seattle off of I-90. Together, these four ski areas offer more than 65 ski runs, rentals, and lessons. Adult lift ticket prices range from $15 to $18 for midweek night skiing to $28 for a weekend all-day pass. Call for hours of operation.

TENNIS

Seattle Parks and Recreation operates dozens of outdoor tennis courts all over the city. The most convenient are at **Volunteer Park,** 15th Ave. East and East Prospect St., and at **Lower Woodland Park,** West Green Lake Way North. If it happens to be raining and you had your heart set on playing tennis, there are indoor public courts at the **Seattle Tennis Center,** 2000 Martin Luther King Jr. Way S. (☎ **206/ 684-4764**). Rates here are $14 for singles and $18 for doubles for 1¼ hours. This center also has outdoor courts for $4 for 1½ hours.

11 Spectator Sports

With professional football, baseball, basketball, women's basketball, and ice hockey teams, as well as the various University of Washington Huskies teams, Seattle is obviously a city of sports fans. However, even sports fans have their limits, and the stadium battles of the past few years have tried the patience of both sports fans and Seattleites who couldn't care less who's in the American League playoffs or heading to the Super Bowl. First there was the partial collapse and restoration of the Kingdome roof, paid for by taxpayers. Then the Mariners demanded a new stadium. Seattle voters said no they wouldn't pay for a new stadium, but the state legislature figured out a way to get the stadium built (and keep the Mariners in town) without raising Seattle property taxes. Then the owner of the Seahawks football team started talking about moving his team somewhere else because he didn't want to play in the Kingdome either. When Microsoft cofounder Paul Allen stepped in and offered to buy the Seahawks if the city would build a new stadium, the entire state got to vote on whether to build a separate football stadium. By a slim margin the citizens of Washington state voted to tax themselves so that they could keep the Seahawks in Seattle. As things now stand, the Kingdome will soon be torn down to make way for the new football stadium. The Seattle SuperSonics basketball team, by the way, got a new arena (actually a renovated existing arena) with no controversy at all.

So, as it currently stands, there will in a few years be two new stadiums, one for baseball and one for football, standing side by side where the Kingdome now stands.

And the Kingdome, alas, will be torn down. But, as they say, it ain't over till the fat lady sings, and it is likely that the latest stadium vote will be challenged in court.

TicketMaster (☎ 206/628-0888) sells tickets to almost all sporting events in the Seattle area. If they're sold out, try **Pacific Northwest Ticket Service** (☎ 206/232-0150).

BASEBALL

Of all of Seattle's major league sports teams, none is more popular than the American League's **Seattle Mariners** (☎ 206/628-9400). The team would probably be almost as popular even without Ken Griffey Jr., but with this powerhouse hitter slamming in the home runs with astounding regularity, the team has developed a devoted following. For the time being (until their new stadium is completed) the Mariners play in the Kingdome. Ticket prices range from $5 to $22 and are usually fairly readily available. Expect these prices to go up when the new stadium is finally completed. Tickets are available at the Kingdome box office or through TicketMaster (☎ 206/622-HITS). Parking is next to impossible in the Kingdome neighborhood, so plan to leave your car behind.

Up in Everett, north of Seattle, the **Everett Aquasox** (☎ 206/258-3673), a farm team of the Seattle Mariners, play Class-A ball and have also developed a dedicated following in the past few years. Tickets are $5 to $7 and are available at the Aquasox Stadium Store, 3802 Broadway, Everett and through TicketMaster (☎ 206/628-0888).

BASKETBALL

The NBA's **Seattle SuperSonics** (☎ 206/281-5800) have been putting in good showings in the past few years, but haven't quite gotten their act together. They play in the completely remodeled and updated Key Arena in Seattle Center. Tickets are $8 to $60 and are available at the arena box office and through TicketMaster (☎ 206/628-0888). Tickets can generally be had even on short notice.

With an instant following among women's basketball fans weaned on the University of Washington Huskies women's basketball team, the **Seattle Reign** (☎ 206/285-5225) of the newly formed American Basketball League, was an instant hit in Seattle. The women of the Reign play ball at the Mercer Arena at Seattle Center. Tickets are $8 to $35 and are available through TicketMaster.

If not for the popularity of the University of Washington Huskies women's basketball team, Seattle may not have gotten a pro women's basketball team. For information on the women's and men's Huskies basketball games, contact **University of Washington Sports** (☎ 206/543-2200).

FOOTBALL

With five bad seasons in a row, the NFL's **Seattle Seahawks** (☎ 206/827-9777) are the least loved of Seattle's pro ball teams. Nevertheless, the people of the state obviously didn't want to see the Seahawks leave town or they wouldn't have voted for a new stadium. Until the new stadium is built, they'll likely be playing in the Kingdome. Tickets cost $19 to $38. Parking in the Kingdome area is nearly impossible during games, so take the bus if you can.

Not surprisingly, the **University of Washington Huskies** (☎ 206/543-2200), who play in Husky Stadium on the university campus, have a more loyal following. Big games (Nebraska or Washington State) sell out as soon as tickets go on sale in the summer. Other games can sell out in advance, but there are usually obstructed-view tickets available on the day of the game. Ticket prices range from $28 to $30.

HOCKEY

The Western Hockey League's **Seattle Thunderbirds** (☎ 206/448-PUCK) play major junior ice hockey at the Key Arena in Seattle Center. While Seattle isn't really a hockey town, the Thunderbirds have quite a following. Tickets are available by calling the above number or TicketMaster (☎ **206/628-0888**).

HORSE RACING

The new **Emerald Downs** (☎ **888/931-8400** or 206/288-7711) race track has brought horse racing and pari-mutuel betting back to the Seattle area after an absence of several years beginning with the closure of Longacres Race Track. This state-of-the-art track is located in the city of Auburn off Wash. 167, which is reached from I-405 at the south end of Lake Washington. To reach the track, take the 15th Avenue NW exit. Admission prices range from $3 to $5.50. The season runs from March to September.

MARATHON

The **Seattle Marathon** takes place in November. There's a runners' hot line in Seattle that you can call for more information on this and other races in the area (☎ **206/524-RUNS**).

12 Day Spas

If you prefer being pampered to paddling a kayak, facials to fishing, or massages to mountain climbing, then you'll be glad to know that Seattle has plenty of day spas scattered around the metro area. These facilities offer such treatments as massages, facials, seaweed wraps, mud baths, and the like. Seattle day spas include **Aveda**, Alexis Hotel, 1015 First Ave. (☎ **206/628-9605**); **Le Salon Paul Morey,** Rainier Square Concourse, 1301 Fifth Ave. (☎ **206/624-4455**); **Marketplace Salon and Day Spa,** 2001 First Ave. (☎ **206/441-5511**); **Robert Leonard,** 2033 Sixth Ave. (☎ **206/441-9900**); and **Ummelina,** 1523 Sixth Ave. (☎ **206/624-1370**); and, over in Kirkland at Carillon Point, **Spa Csaba,** 1250 Carillon Point (☎ **206/803-9000**). At these spas, a wide variety of treatments are available. Expect to pay at least $150 for a half day of pampering and $300 or more for a full day.

7

Strolling Around Seattle

Downtown Seattle is easy to explore on foot (if you don't mind hills). Foremost, of course, you should see the Pike Place Market and the waterfront, which together form the busiest neighborhood in Seattle. You really don't need a guided tour of this area: Just follow the hordes of people.

WALKING TOUR 1
Pioneer Square Area

Start: Pioneer Place at the corner of Yesler Way and First Avenue.
Finish: Washington Street Public Boat Landing.
Time: Approximately 2 hours, not including shopping, dining, and museum and other stops.
Best Times: Weekdays, when the neighborhood and the Seattle Underground Tour are not so crowded.
Worst Times: Weekends, when the area is very crowded.

In the late 19th century, the Pioneer Square area was the heart of downtown Seattle, so when a fire raged through these blocks in 1889, the city was devastated. However, residents and merchants quickly began rebuilding and set about to remedy many of the problems with infrastructure that had faced Seattle in the years before the fire. Today this small section of the city is all that remains of old Seattle. Since one architect, Elmer Fisher, was responsible for the design of many of the buildings constructed after the fire, the neighborhood has a distinctly uniform architectural style.

While wandering these streets, don't bother looking for a place called Pioneer Square, you won't find it. The name actually applies to the whole neighborhood, not a park surrounded by four streets as you would surmise. Do keep your eye out for old manhole covers, many of which were cast with maps of Seattle or Northwest Coast Indian designs.

Start your tour of this historic neighborhood at the corner of Yesler Way and First Avenue on:

1. **Pioneer Place,** the triangular park at the heart of Pioneer Square. The totem pole here is a replacement of one that burned in 1938. The original pole had been stolen from a Tlingit village up the coast in 1890. Legend has it that after the pole burned, the city fathers sent a check for $5,000 requesting a new totem pole.

The Tlingit response was, "Thanks for paying for the first one. Send another $5,000 for a replacement." The cast-iron pergola in the park was erected in 1905 as a shelter for a large underground lavatory. Facing the square are several historic buildings, including the gabled Lowman Building and three buildings noteworthy for their terra-cotta facades. One of these is:

2. The Pioneer Building, one of the architectural standouts of this neighborhood. It houses an antiques mall and:

3. Doc Maynard's, 610 First Ave. (☎ 206/682-4649), a nightclub featuring live rock bands. By day this is also the starting point of the Underground Tour, which takes a look at the Pioneer Square area from beneath the sidewalks. The tour is a great introduction to the history of the area (if you don't mind off-color jokes) and actually spends quite a bit of time aboveground (duplicating much of the walking tour outlined here). Forming the south side of Pioneer Place is:

4. Yesler Way, the original Skid Row. In Seattle's early years, logs were skidded down this road to a lumber mill on the waterfront, and the road came to be known as Skid Road. These days it's trying hard to live down its reputation, but there are still quite a few people down on their luck here.

☕ **TAKE A BREAK**   Across Yesler Way from the pergola is Merchants Cafe, 109 Yesler Way (☎ 206/624-1515), the oldest restaurant in Seattle. If it happens to be time for lunch or dinner, this is a good place to stop. Meals are moderately priced and well prepared.

From Pioneer Place, walk up James Street past a triangular parking deck (a monstrosity that prompted the movement to preserve the rest of this neighborhood). At the corner of Second Avenue, turn left to reach:

5. Ruby Montana's Pinto Pony, 603 Second Ave. (☎ 206/621-PONY), a cluttered shop selling (and displaying) all manner of retro-kitsch both new and vintage. If pink flamingos and Elvis clocks are your style, Ruby's is your store. Right next door is:

6. Laguna, 609 Second Ave. (☎ 206/682-6162), which specializes in midcentury pottery, primarily from California. Fiesta, Bauer, and Weller are all well represented. Across the street and half a block toward Yesler Way, you'll come to:

7. The Linda Cannon Gallery, 520 Second Ave. (☎ 206/233-0404), which among other things sells early works by popular comic artist Lynda Barry. Right next door is:

8. Smith Tower, which when completed in 1914 was the tallest building west of the Mississippi. The ornate lobby and elevator doors are reason enough for a visit to this building, but there is also a great view of the city from an observatory near the top of the building. However, the observatory is only open to visitors on the Seattle Underground tour.

From Smith Tower, continue down Second Avenue on the opposite side of the street (keeping right when Second Avenue S. Extension forks to the left). At the corner of S. Main Street, you'll find the shady little:

9. Waterfall Park, with a roaring waterfall that looks as if it had been transported here straight from the Cascade Range. The park is built on the site of the original United Parcel Service (UPS) offices and makes a wonderful place for a rest or a picnic lunch. Turn right onto Main Street and in 1 block you'll come to cobblestoned:

10. Occidental Park, with four totem poles carved by Northwest artist Duane Pasco. This shady park serves as a gathering spot for homeless people, so you may not want to linger. However, on the west side of the park is the:

Walking Tour 1—Pioneer Square Area

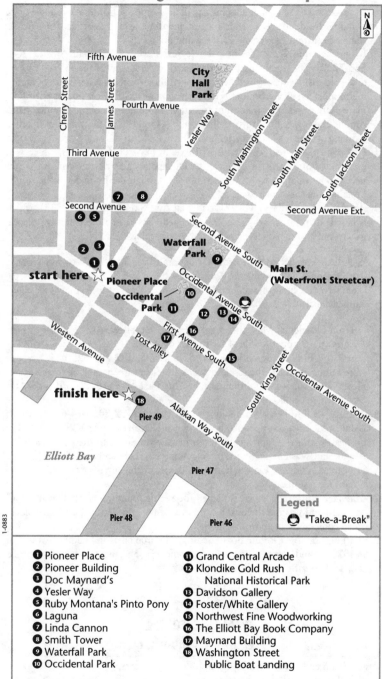

N

Fifth Avenue

City Hall Park

Cherry Street

James Street

Fourth Avenue

Yesler Way

South Washington Street

South Main Street

South Jackson Street

Third Avenue

Second Avenue Ext.

Second Avenue

7 **8**

6 **5**

Second Avenue South

Waterfall Park

2 **3**

9

1 **4**

start here ☆ **Pioneer Place**

Occidental Avenue South

Main St. (Waterfront Streetcar)

Occidental Park

10

11

12 **13**

14

First Avenue South

16

Post Alley

17

15

Western Avenue

South King Street

Occidental Avenue South

finish here ☆ **18**

Pier 49

Alaskan Way South

Elliott Bay

Pier 47

Pier 48

Pier 46

Legend
☕ "Take-a-Break"

1-0883

1 Pioneer Place
2 Pioneer Building
3 Doc Maynard's
4 Yesler Way
5 Ruby Montana's Pinto Pony
6 Laguna
7 Linda Cannon
8 Smith Tower
9 Waterfall Park
10 Occidental Park

11 Grand Central Arcade
12 Klondike Gold Rush
        National Historical Park
13 Davidson Gallery
14 Foster/White Gallery
15 Northwest Fine Woodworking
16 The Elliott Bay Book Company
17 Maynard Building
18 Washington Street
        Public Boat Landing

11. **Grand Central Arcade,** a shopping and dining center created from a restored brick building. Inside, there are craft and antique stores as well as art galleries. Across Main Street from Occidental Park is a unit of:

12. **Klondike Gold Rush National Historical Park,** 117 S. Main St. (☎ **206/ 553-7220**). The small museum is dedicated to the history of the 1897–98 Klondike gold rush, which helped Seattle grow from an obscure town into a booming metropolis. The waterfront streetcar, which connects Pioneer Square with Pike Place Market and other waterfront attractions, stops in front of the historical park. Around the corner from this small museum is Occidental Mall, where you'll find a couple of Seattle's best galleries, including:

13. **Davidson Galleries,** 313 Occidental Ave. S. (☎ **206/624-7684**), which sells everything from 16th-century prints to contemporary art by Northwest artists. You never know what to expect when you walk through the front door here. Right upstairs from this gallery is:

14. **Foster/White Gallery,** 311½ Occidental Ave. S. (☎ **206/622-2833**), which is best known for its art glass. This is famed glass artist Dale Chihuly's Seattle gallery and always has several of his works on display.

🌀 **TAKE A BREAK** Across Occidental Park from these two galleries is **Torrefazione,** 320 Occidental Ave. S. (☎ **206/624-5773**), which many people claim serves the best coffee in Seattle. Be sure to get your coffee in one of the hand-painted cups.

From Occidental Mall, turn right onto Jackson Street. At the corner of First Avenue on the opposite side of the street, you'll see:

15. **Northwest Fine Woodworking,** 101 S. Jackson St. (☎ **206/625-0542**), a large store selling exquisite, hand-crafted wooden furniture, as well as some smaller pieces. Well worth a visit. From here, head up First Avenue to the corner of Main Street, where you'll find:

16. **The Elliott Bay Book Company,** 101 S. Main St. (☎ **206/624-6600**), which is one of the city's most popular bookstores and has an extensive selection of books on Seattle and the Northwest. From here, walk north to the corner of First Avenue and Washington Street, passing numerous shops and bars, all of which are in historic buildings. On the northwest corner of this intersection you'll see the beautifully restored:

17. **Maynard Building,** which is named for Seattle founding father David "Doc" Maynard and was the site of the city's first bank. Turn left here and in 1 block, you'll come to the waterfront and the:

18. **Washington Street Public Boat Landing.** This iron open-air building was erected in 1920 and today serves as a public dock where people can tie up their boats while they are in Seattle.

WALKING TOUR 2
Fremont Neighborhood

Start: South end of Fremont Bridge near Ponti restaurant.
Finish: Trolleyman Pub at the corner of Phinney Avenue and 34th Street.
Time: Approximately 2 hours, not including time spent dining.
Best Times: Sunday, during the Fremont Sunday Market.
Worst Times: Early morning or evening, when shops are closed.

Walking Tour 2—Fremont Neighborhood

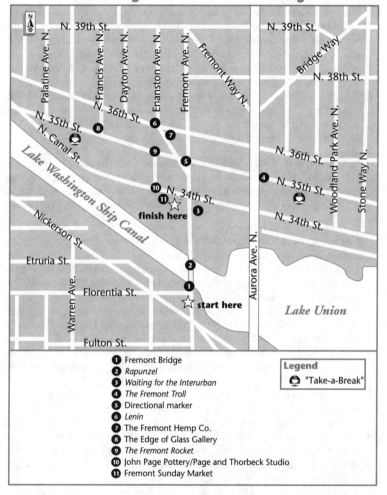

1. Fremont Bridge
2. *Rapunzel*
3. *Waiting for the Interurban*
4. *The Fremont Troll*
5. Directional marker
6. *Lenin*
7. The Fremont Hemp Co.
8. The Edge of Glass Gallery
9. *The Fremont Rocket*
10. John Page Pottery/Page and Thorbeck Studio
11. Fremont Sunday Market

Legend

🛑 "Take-a-Break"

Seattle's Fremont neighborhood marches to a different beat than the rest of the city. Styling itself the Republic of Fremont and the center of the universe, this small, tight-knit neighborhood is the funnest and funkiest neighborhood in the city. Fremont residents have focused on art as a way to draw the community together, and in so doing they have created a corner of the city where silliness reigns.

Start your tour by finding a parking spot around the corner from Ponti restaurant at the south end of the:

1. **Fremont Bridge.** This bridge is the busiest drawbridge in the United States and spans the Lake Washington Ship Canal. "Welcome to the center of the Universe" reads the sign in the middle of the bridge. As you approach the north side of the bridge, glance up and in the window of the bridge-tender's tower, you'll see:

2. *Rapunzel,* a neon sculpture of Rapunzel, complete with neon tresses cascading down the wall of the tower. As you finally make landfall in the Republic of Fremont, you will see at the end of the bridge on the opposite side of the street from Rapunzel, Seattle's most beloved public sculpture.

3. *Waiting for the Interurban* features several people waiting for the trolley that no longer runs from Fremont to downtown Seattle. These folks, frozen in time as they are, are frequently dressed up by local residents, with costumes changing with the season. Continue east along N. 34th Street from this statue, and then turn left and uphill underneath the Aurora Bridge, which towers high above. At the top of the hill, you will see, lurking in the shadows beneath the bridge:

4. *The Fremont Troll.* This massive monster is in the process of crushing a Volkswagen Beetle. No need to run in fear, though, a wizard seems to have put a spell on the troll and turned it into cement. Turn left at the troll and walk a block down N. 35th Street to the best little cafe in the neighborhood.

☕ **TAKE A BREAK Still Life in Fremont Coffeehouse,** 709 N. 35th St. (☎ 206/547-9850), is a classic hippie hangout, with a swinging screen door, wood floors, and lots of alternative newspapers on hand at all times. Although oatmeal is a specialty, they also serve soups, salads, sandwiches, pastries, and good espresso.

From Still Life in Fremont, it's only a few steps down the hill to the corner of N. Fremont Avenue and Fremont Place. This is the center of the center of the universe, and it is here that you will find Fremont's:

5. Directional marker. This old-fashioned signpost has arrows point to such important locations as the center of the universe (straight down), the *Fremont Troll, Rapunzel,* Atlantis, and the North Pole. If you're still in doubt as to where you are, you can consult the handy nearby mapboard, which has a neighborhood map. From the signpost, continue west (away from the intersection) on Fremont Place, and in 1 block (at the corner of N. 36th Street), you will see a larger than life statue of:

6. *Lenin.* This 20-foot-tall statue in no way reflects the attitudes of the many very capitalistic merchants in the neighborhood. Directly behind comrade Lenin, you will find:

7. The Fremont Hemp Co., local purveyor of all natural hemp clothing, the officially sanctioned and politically correct attire for strolling the streets of Fremont. Continuing west along N. 36th Street for another couple of blocks you will come to:

8. The Edge of Glass Gallery, 513 N. 36th St. (☎ **206/547-6551**), where you can often see art-glass artists at work. Even if there's no one blowing glass, there are plenty of beautiful pieces of art glass to see. From here, backtrack to Evanston Avenue and turn right. In 1 block, you will see:

9. The Fremont Rocket. Although there is speculation that this rocket was used by the aliens who founded Fremont, the truth is far stranger. You can read the entire history of the rocket on another mapboard below the rocket (if you haven't already figured it out, the locals don't want you getting lost in their neighborhood, so they've put up maps all over to help you find your way from one famous Fremont locale to the next). Downhill from the rocket on Evanston Avenue, you will come to:

10. John Page Pottery/Page and Thorbeck Studio, 604 N. 34th St., which makes pottery for the stars (no, not the stars at which the rocket is aimed but stars like Oprah Winfrey and Darryl Hannah). Classic ranch motifs are a favorite with customers here. Surrounding this studio/shop are the parking lots that on Sundays are the site of the:

11. Fremont Sunday Market, which is a combination flea market and produce market. This is also where old films are shown (under the stars; yes, the ones the rocket is aimed at) on summer Saturday nights.

☕ **WINDING DOWN From the Sunday market area, it is 3 blocks west (away from the bridge) to the **Trolleyman Pub,** 3400 Phinney Ave. N., which is one of Seattle's best brewpubs and home of the Redhook Ale Brewery.

Seattle Shopping 8

As the largest U.S. city in the region, Seattle has always been where the Northwest shopped. Nordstrom, Eddie Bauer, and REI (all of which were founded in Seattle) have become familiar to shoppers all across the country, and these stores remain some of the busiest in the city. However, in the past few years, as Seattle has developed a national reputation as a great place to put down roots, the retail face of the city has begun to change considerably.

National retailers have been taking over the storefronts of downtown Seattle, opening up flashy new stores and cashing in on the city's newfound popularity. The names and merchandise at these stores are familiar from stores in other cities as well as from mail-order catalogs. Banana Republic, Nike, Levi Strauss, Ann Taylor, FAO Schwartz, Barney's New York, and others have stores in Seattle now, so if you forgot to pick up that dress in Chicago or those running shoes in New York, have no fear, you can find them here.

Seattle does, however, have one last bastion of local merchandising—**Pike Place Market.** Whether shopping is your passion or merely an activity in which you occasionally indulge, you should not miss this historic market, which is actually one of Seattle's top tourist attractions. Once the city's main produce market—and quite a few produce stalls remain—this sprawling collection of buildings is today filled with hundreds of unusual shops.

After tasting the bounties of the Northwest, it's hard to go back to Safeway, Sanka, and Chicken of the Sea. Sure you can get coffee, wine, and seafood where you live, but do a little food shopping in Seattle and you'll be tapping the source. Washington State wines, coffee from the original Starbucks, and fish that flies—these are a few of the culinary treats that await you here.

1 The Shopping Scene

Although Seattle is a city of neighborhoods, and even out in the 'hoods you'll find great little shops, ground zero of the Seattle shopping scene is the corner of **Pine Street and Fifth Avenue.** Within 1 block of this intersection are two major department stores—Nordstrom and The Bon Marché—and an upscale urban shopping mall. Fanning out east and south from this intersection are blocks of upscale stores that have begun to take on a very familiar look. Small local shops are rapidly being replaced by national and international boutiques and megastores. Here in this neighborhood you'll now

Hours

Shops in Seattle are generally open Monday through Saturday from 9 or 10am to 5 or 6pm, with shorter hours on Sunday. The major department stores usually stay open later on Friday evenings, and many shopping malls stay open until 9pm Monday through Saturday.

---

find Ann Taylor, Barney's New York, NIKETOWN, the Original Levi's Store, the Warner Bros. Studio Store, Banana Republic, and FAO Schwartz. However, you'll also still find a few local stores in the neighborhood.

The city's main tourist shopping district is the **Pike Place Market** neighborhood. Here you'll find dozens of T-shirt and souvenir shops, as well as import shops and stores appealing to teenagers and twenty-somethings. Pike Place Market itself is a fascinating warren of cubbyholes that pass for shops. While produce usually isn't something you stock up on while on vacation, there are several market shops that sell ethnic cooking supplies that are not as perishable as a dozen oysters or a geoduck clam. While you may never find anything here you really need, it's still fun to look (at least that's what millions of Seattle visitors each year seem to think). Just west of Pike Place Market is the Seattle **waterfront,** where you'll find many more gift and souvenir shops.

In the **Pioneer Square area,** Seattle's historic district, you'll find the city's greatest concentration of art galleries, some of which specialize in Native American art. This neighborhood also has several antiques stores.

As the center of both the gay community and the city's youth culture, **Capitol Hill** has the most eclectic selection of shops in the city. Beads, imports, CDs, vintage clothing, politically correct merchandise, and gay-oriented goods fill the shops along Broadway. Capitol Hill's main shopping plaza is the Broadway Market, which has lots of small shops.

Even funkier than Capitol Hill, the **Fremont** neighborhood just north of Lake Union is filled with retro stores selling vintage clothing, midcentury furniture and collectibles, and curious crafts. A couple of miles east of Fremont is the **Wallingford** neighborhood, which is anchored by an old schoolhouse that has been converted into a shopping arcade with interesting crafts, fashions, and gifts. The **University District,** also in north Seattle, has everything necessary to support a student population and goes upscale with the University Village shopping center.

2 Shopping A to Z

ANTIQUES & COLLECTIBLES

For an absolutely astounding selection of antiques, head north of Seattle to the town of **Snohomish** (near Everett),where you'll find more than 150 antiques shops.

Clarke and Clarke Tribal Arts. 524 First Ave. S. ☎ **206/447-7017.**

This small shop near the Kingdome specializes in tribal antiques and art from around the world. Antique silk Chinese robes, Japanese samurai swords, African wood carvings, masks from Oaxaca, Mexico, and Middle Eastern copper pots are just some of the items you'll find here.

The Crane Gallery. 100 W. Roy St. ☎ **206/622-7185.**

Chinese, Japanese, and Korean antiquities are the focus of this shop in the Queen Anne neighborhood, which prides itself on selling only the best pieces. Imperial Chinese porcelains, bronze statues of Buddhist deities, rosewood furniture, Japanese ceramics, netsukes, snuff bottles, and Chinese archaeological artifacts are just some of the quality antiques you'll find here. Some Southeast Asian and Indian objects are also available.

Honeychurch Antiques. 1008 James St. ☎ **206/622-1225.**

For high-quality Asian antiques, including Japanese wood-block prints, textiles, furniture, and ivory and wood carvings, few Seattle antiques stores can approach Honeychurch Antiques. Regular special exhibits give this shop the feel of a tiny museum. An annex, called **Glenn Richards/The Honeychurch Warehouse,** is located at 964 Denny Way and specializes in new and old architectural elements from Asia.

Jean Williams Antiques. 115 S. Jackson St. ☎ **206/622-1110.**

If your taste in antiques runs to 17th-, 18th-, and 19th-century French and English furniture, this Pioneer Square antique dealer may have something to add to your collection.

Laguna. 609 Second Ave. ☎ **206/682-6162.**

Twentieth-century art pottery is the specialty of this shop near Pioneer Square. Pieces by such midcentury pottery factories as Catalina Island, Roseville, Bauer, Weller, and Franciscan are stacked on the shelves here. This is a great place to look for dinnerware and vintage tiles.

Manifesto Vintage Posters. 2030 First Ave. ☎ **206/269-0898.**

This Belltown gallery specializes in vintage posters from around the world and usually has more than 2,000 posters in stock. Subjects include travel, movies, and advertising. The posters aren't cheap, but even if you can't afford to buy, the shop is fun to visit.

ANTIQUE MALLS & FLEA MARKETS

The Downtown Antique Market. 2218 Western Ave. ☎ **206/448-6307.**

Housed in a turn-of-the-century warehouse 3 blocks north of Pike Place Market, this antiques mall has more than 80 dealers and a wide variety of antiques and collectibles.

Fremont Sunday Market. 600 N. 34th St. ☎ **206/282-5706.**

Crafts, imports, antiques, collectibles, fresh produce, and live music all combine to make this Seattle's second favorite public market (after Pike Place Market). The market is open from the end of April through Christmas.

Pioneer Square Antique Mall. 602 First Ave. ☎ **206/624-1164.**

This underground antique mall is in the heart of Pioneer Square right beside the ticket booth for the Seattle Underground tour and contains 80 stalls selling all manner of antiques and collectibles. Look for glass, old jewelry, and small collectibles here.

ART GALLERIES

The Pioneer Square area has for many years been Seattle's main art gallery district, and although there are still quite a few galleries in the neighborhood, over the past few years many galleries have moved to other locations around the metropolitan area. Still, there are enough galleries left around Pioneer Square that anyone interested in art should be sure to wander around south of Yesler Way.

GENERAL ART GALLERIES

Carolyn Staley. 313 First Ave. S. ☎ **206/621-1888.**

A wide range of old prints, including a large collection of Japanese wood-block prints, are on view at this Pioneer Square gallery. Whatever your personal interest, you'll likely find something intriguing in the gallery's large collection.

Davidson Galleries. 313 Occidental Ave. S. ☎ **206/624-7684.**

Located in the heart of the Pioneer Square neighborhood, this gallery is divided into three different areas of focus—contemporary paintings and sculptures, often by Northwest artists; contemporary prints by American and European artists; and antique prints, some of which date back to the 1500s.

Greg Kucera Gallery. 608 Second Ave. ☎ **206/624-0770.**

A low-key setting in the Pioneer Square area serves as one of Seattle's most reliably cutting-edge galleries in Seattle. Both emerging artists and those with international reputations find their way into this gallery, often in the same show.

Linda Cannon Gallery. 520 Second Ave. ☎ **206/233-0404.**

This gallery near Pioneer Square sells, among many new works, older pieces by now-famous cartoonist Lynda Barry. Because these latter pieces are resales of works from the early part of Barry's career, you never know what you might find.

Lisa Harris Gallery. 1922 Pike Place. ☎ **206/443-3315.**

Landscapes and figurative works, by both expressionist and realist Northwest and West Coast artists, are a specialty of this gallery, which is located on the second floor of a building in Pike Place Market.

ART GLASS

Edge of Glass Gallery. 513 N. 36th St. ☎ **206/547-6551.**

Located in the Fremont district, this gallery doubles as a studio where there are glass-blowing demonstrations Thursday through Sunday afternoons.

Foster/White Gallery. 311½ Occidental Ave. S. ☎ **206/622-2833.**

If you are enamored of art glass, as we are, be sure to stop by one or all of the three Foster/White galleries. These galleries represent Dale Chihuly in Seattle and always have a few works by this master glass artist for sale. Some of Chihuly's pieces even sell for less than $10,000! Other glass artists who have trained at the Pilchuck School of Glass are also represented.

Another Foster/White Gallery is located in the City Centre shopping mall, 1420 Fifth Ave. (☎ **206/340-8025**), and a third is in Kirkland at 126 Central Way (☎ **206/822-2305**).

The Glass Eye. 1902 Post Alley, Pike Place Market. ☎ **206/441-3221.**

The Glass Eye is one of Seattle's oldest art-glass galleries and specializes in glass made from Mount St. Helens ash. These hand-blown pieces all contain ash from the volcano's 1980 eruption. Works by artists from around the country are available and many pieces are small enough to carry home.

Glasshouse. 311 Occidental Ave. S. ☎ **206/682-9939.**

Located in the Pioneer Square area, this gallery also houses a studio where you can observe art glass being created. Many of the area's top glass artists are represented.

Vetri. 1408 First Ave. ☎ **206/667-9608.**

With a wide variety of art glass by dozens of artists, some of whom have studied at the Pilchuck School, this gallery is riotously colorful and will give you a good idea of the broad spectrum of work being created by contemporary glass artists. They also represent William Morris, whose works have the look of ancient artifacts.

NATIVE AMERICAN ART

Flury and Company. 322 First Ave. S. ☎ **206/587-0260.**

This Pioneer Square gallery specializes in prints by photographer Edward S. Curtis, who is known for his portraits of Native Americans. The gallery also has an excellent selection of antique Native American art.

✪ **The Legacy.** 1003 First Ave. ☎ **800/729-1562** or 206/624-6350.

The Legacy is Seattle's oldest and finest gallery of contemporary and historic Northwest Coast Indian and Alaskan Eskimo art and artifacts. You'll find a large selection of masks, boxes, bowls, baskets, ivory artifacts, jewelry, prints, and books for the serious collector.

Northwest Tribal Art. 1417 First Ave. ☎ **206/467-9330.**

Located next to Pike Place Market, this is one of Seattle's most important galleries selling Northwest Coast Indian and American Eskimo art. Traditional and contemporary wood carvings, masks, fossilized ivory carvings, soapstone carvings, scrimshaw, jewelry, drums, and even totem poles are available.

Stonington Gallery. 2030 First Ave. ☎ **206/443-6580.**

This is one of Seattle's top galleries specializing in contemporary Native American art and crafts. Here you'll find a good selection of Northwest Coast Indian masks, totem poles, mixed-media pieces, prints, and carvings. There is also a good selection of books about Northwest Native American art.

BOOKS

Bowie and Company Booksellers. 314 First Ave. S. ☎ **206/624-4100.**

Located in the Pioneer Square area, this bookstore specializes in old, rare, out-of-print, and hard-to-find books. There are many signed editions in stock. A recent catalog listed such books as a 1945 edition of *The Oregon Trail* (illustrated and signed by Thomas Hart Benton; $150), a 1921 *The Boy's Life of Edison* (signed by Thomas Edison; $1,450), and a first edition of Tom Robbins's *Another Roadside Attraction* ($150). Books on cooking are a specialty here.

Elliott Bay Book Company. 101 S. Main St. ☎ **206/624-6600.**

With battered wooden floors and a maze of rooms full of books, this is the bookstore of choice for Seattle book lovers. There's an excellent selection of books on Seattle and the Northwest, so if you want to learn more about the region or are planning further excursions, stop by. The store is located just south of Pioneer Square.

Shorey's Book Store. 1109 N. 36th St. ☎ **206/633-2990.**

Shorey's has been in business since 1890, and will be happy to find you books from the year they opened (or from any other year, for that matter). Rare, antiquarian, and out-of-print books are their specialty. With more than a million items in stock, Shorey's is sure to have that obscure tome you've been seeking for years. If they don't have it, they'll search the world to find it for you. The store's motto is "The oldest, the biggest, the best!" You'll find the store north of Lake Union to the east of Fremont, off Stone Way.

67 Books. 322 Second Ave. ☎ **206/447-9229.**

The name says it all. This Pioneer Square–area bookstore carries only 67 books at any given time (and they aren't best-sellers). The owner-chosen books cover a wide and eclectic range of interests and each is displayed on a pedestal. It would be hard to visit this store and not find a book you'd like to have.

CHOCOLATE

Bernard C. City Centre, 1420 Fifth Ave. ☎ 206/340-0396.

Seattle isn't known for its chocolate, and Bernard C. isn't a local chocolatier (Bernard is headquartered in Calgary, Canada, but originally came from Belgium), but the traditional Belgian-style filled chocolates here are the best we've had outside Belgium (way better than Godiva). There's another, larger store in Kirkland at 128 Central Way (☎ 425/822-8889).

COFFEE

All over the city, almost every corner, you'll find espresso bars, cafes, and coffeehouses, and while you can get coffee back home, you might want to pick up some of whichever local coffee turns out to be your favorite. If you are a latte junkie, you might want to make a pilgrimage to the shop that started it all.

✪ Starbucks. 1912 Pike Place, Pike Place Market. ☎ 206/448-8762.

Seattle has developed a reputation as a city of coffeeholics, and Starbucks is one reason why. This company has coffeehouses all over town, but this is the original. With some 36 types of coffee available by the cup or by the pound, you can do a bit of taste-testing before making a decision.

CRAFTS

The Northwest is a leading center for craftspeople, and one of the places to see what they are creating is Pike Place Market. Although there are quite a few permanent shops within the market that sell local crafts, you can meet the artisans themselves on weekends when they set up tables on the main floor.

Crackerjack Contemporary Crafts. Wallingford Center, 1815 N. 45th Ave. ☎ 206/547-4983.

With colorful and imaginative crafts by more than 250 artists from around the country, this shop in the eclectic Wallingford Center shopping arcade (an old schoolhouse) is a great place to check for something interesting and unique to bring home from a trip to Seattle.

✪ Fireworks Fine Crafts Gallery. 210 First Ave. S. ☎ 206/682-8707.

Playful, outrageous, bizarre, beautiful—these are just some of the terms that can be used to describe the eclectic collection of Northwest crafts on sale at this Pioneer Square gallery. Cosmic clocks, wildly creative jewelry, and artistic picture frames are some of the fine and unusual items you'll find here. Other stores are at Westlake Center, 400 Pine St. (☎ 206/682-6462) and Bellevue Square, Bellevue Way, Bellevue (☎ 206/688-0933). At press time, a fourth gallery was planned for the University Village shopping plaza in the University District.

John Page Pottery/Page and Thorbeck Studio. 604 N. 34th St. ☎ 206/632-6178.

Billing themselves as the potters to the stores, the owners of this Fremont pottery studio and retail shop specialize in dinnerware with classic Western ranch motifs. Clients have included Oprah Winfrey, Robin Williams, and Darryl Hannah. You can pick up a single piece of pottery or commission an entire set of dishes.

✪ Northwest Fine Woodworking. 101 S. Jackson St. ☎ 206/625-0542.

This store is a showcase for some of the most amazing woodworking you'll ever see. Be sure to stroll through here while in the Pioneer Square area. The warm hues of the exotic woods are soothing and the designs are beautiful. Furniture, boxes, sculptures, vases, bowls, and much more are created by more than 35 Northwest artisans. A second shop is at 122 Central Way, Kirkland, WA (☎ 206/889-1513).

DEPARTMENT STORES

The Bon Marché. Third Ave. and Pine St. ☎ **206/506-6000.**

Seattle's other department store is every bit as well stocked as next-door-neighbor Nordstrom and with such competition in the neighborhood tries every bit as hard to keep its customers happy. You'll find nearly anything you could possibly want at this store.

✪ **Nordstrom.** 1501 Fifth Ave. ☎ **206/628-2111.**

Known for personal service, Nordstrom stores have gained a reputation for being among the premier department stores in the United States. The company originated here in Seattle (opening its first store in 1901), and its customers are devotedly loyal. Whether it's your first visit or your 50th, the knowledgeable staff will help you in any way they can. Prices are comparable to those at other department stores, but you also get the best service available. There are very popular sales in January (for men), June (for women and children), July (for men and women), and November (for women and children). In August 1998, Nordstorm is scheduled to open at 500 Pine Street in what used to be the Frederick and Nelson department store. There are other Nordstroms at area shopping malls.

DISCOUNT SHOPPING

✪ **The Rack.** 1601 Second Ave. ☎ **206/448-8522.**

This is the Nordstorm overflow shop where you'll find discontinued lines as well as overstock, and all at greatly reduced prices. Women's fashions make up the bulk of the merchandise here.

SuperMall. 1101 SuperMall Way. ☎ **206/833-9500** or 800/SAY-VALU.

The outlet mall to end all outlet malls, SuperMall has upper-end fashion outlets including Nordstrom Rack, Off 5th–Saks Fifth Avenue Outlet, Eddie Bauer Outlet, and Ann Taylor Loft. In 1997 they were offering a free bus shuttle from downtown Seattle, so if you need a ride, call and see if they're still offering this deal.

FASHION

In addition to the stores listed below, you'll find quite a few familiar names in downtown Seattle.

ACCESSORIES

Byrnie Utz Hats. 310 Union St. ☎ **206/623-0233.**

Boasting the largest selection of hats in the Northwest, this cramped hat-wearer's heaven looks as if it hasn't changed in 50 years. There are Borsalino Panama hats, Kangol caps, and, of course, plenty of Stetsons.

CHILDREN'S CLOTHING

Boston St. Wallingford Center, 1815 N. 45th Ave. ☎ **206/634-0580.**

With sizes 0 through 14, this store, in the renovated old schoolhouse that is now the Wallingford Center shopping arcade, stocks fun play clothes as well as more dressy fashions for kids. There's lots of 100% cotton clothing, and prices are moderate to expensive.

MEN'S & WOMEN'S CLOTHING

Eddie Bauer. Fifth Ave. and Union St. ☎ **206/622-2766.**

Eddie Bauer got his start here in Seattle back in 1922, and today his chain is one of the country's foremost purveyors of upscale outdoor fashions. A visit to this store is a must for anyone who dresses the Eddie Bauer look. Other Eddie Bauer stores can be found at Bellevue Square mall, University Village mall, Northgate mall, and Southcenter mall.

NIKETOWN. 1500 Sixth Ave. ☎ **206/447-6543.**

Around the country, there are currently eight NIKETOWNs selling all things Nike and only things Nike. If you don't live near one of these high-tech megastores and you do wear swooshes, then this store should definitely be on your shopping itinerary, even if you aren't in the market for a new pair of basketball shoes.

Paragon. 2200 First Ave. ☎ **206/448-9048.**

One of Seattle's favorite trendy boutiques, Paragon specializes in men and women's clothing for the 21 to 50 age group—fashions that can be worn to the office and then for a night out. A visit to Paragon is a social experience, since there's a coffee cart parked outside and the employees are chatty and get to know their customers well, even if it is only for half an hour!

Seattle Pendleton. 1313 Fourth Ave. ☎ **206/682-4430.**

For northwesterners, and many other people across the nation, Pendleton is and always will be the name in classic wool fashions. This store features tartan plaids and Indian-pattern separates, accessories, and blankets. Other Pendleton stores are at Southcenter Mall, Bellevue Square, and Tacoma Mall.

MEN'S CLOTHING

The Forum. 95 Pine St. ☎ **206/624-4566.**

Located in the Pike Place Market neighborhood, The Forum features sophisticated fashions from the likes of Perry Ellis, Girbaud, and Robert Comstock. A second store is in Bellevue Square mall.

WOMEN'S CLOTHING

Alhambra. 101 Pine St. ☎ **206/621-9571.**

Alhambra stocks an eclectic collection of women's clothing, jewelry, and home furnishings. When we visited there was a fun and quirky selection of dressy straw hats.

Ardour. 1115 First Ave. ☎ **206/292-0660.**

The fashions here are romantic without being fussy and are something of a cross between the Seattle and the Paris looks. There are lots of soft, natural-looking fabrics and handmade sweaters. There are also shoes, jewelry, and other accessories. You can put together a very nice ensemble here, though it won't be cheap.

Baby and Co. 1936 First Ave. ☎ **206/448-4077.**

Claiming stores in Seattle and on Mars, this up-to-the-minute store stocks fashions that can be trendy, outrageous, or out-of-this-world. Whether you're into earth tones or bright colors, you'll likely find something you can't live without.

Boutique Europa. 1420 Fifth Ave. (in City Center). ☎ **206/587-6292.**

In this store, you'll find classically tailored and casual clothing with a European flair, such as knit dresses from Italy and boiled wool jackets.

Local Brilliance. 1535 First Ave. ☎ **206/343-5864.**

This shop carries a wide selection of casual and fun fashions by designers from around the Northwest and the rest of the country. Its fashions appeal to a wide range of age groups, and there are also artist-designed hats and jewelry.

Passport. 123 Pine St. ☎ **206/628-9799.**

Soft and easygoing is the current style at this large store near Pike Place Market. Velvet, cotton, rayon, and other natural fibers are the fabrics of choice here.

✪ **Ragazzi's Flying Shuttle.** 607 First Ave. ☎ **206/343-9762.**

Fashion becomes art and art becomes fashion at this chic boutique-cum-gallery on Pioneer Square. Hand-woven fabrics and hand-painted silks are the specialties here, but of course such sophisticated fashions require equally unique body decorations in the form of exquisite jewelry creations. Designers and artists from the Northwest and the rest of the nation find an outlet for their creativity at the Flying Shuttle.

GIFTS/SOUVENIRS

Pike Place Market is the Grand Central Station of Seattle souvenirs, with stiff competition from Seattle Center and Pioneer Square.

Made in Washington. Pike Place Market (Post Alley at Pine St.). ☎ **206/467-0788.**

Whether it's salmon, wine, or Northwest crafts, you'll find a selection of Washington State products in this shop. It's an excellent place to pick up gifts for all those who didn't get to come to Seattle with you. Other Made in Washington locations include Westlake Center (☎ 206/623-9753); Bellevue Square, Bellevue (☎ 206/454-6907); Gilman Village, Issaquah (☎ 206/392-4819); and Northgate Shopping Center (☎ 206/361-8252).

Ruby Montana's Pinto Pony. 603 Second Ave. ☎ **206/621-PONY.**

Definitely not your run-of-the-mill souvenir shop, Ruby Montana's bills itself as the "Outfitters for the Cosmic Cowpoke." Retro-kitsch is the name of the game at this Pioneer Square shop, with wind-up robots, pig lights to hang from your Christmas tree, wacky salt-and-pepper shakers, Betty Boop stuff, lava lamps, pink flamingos, and, yes, even some cowboy motif items.

Ye Olde Curiosity Shop. 1001 Alaskan Way, Pier 54. ☎ **206/682-5844.**

If you can elbow your way into this waterfront institution, you'll find every inch of space, horizontal and vertical, covered with souvenirs and crafts, both tacky and tasteful. Surrounding all this merchandise are the weird artifacts that have made this one of the most visited shops in Seattle.

HOUSEWARES, HOME FURNISHINGS & GARDEN ACCESSORIES

The Complete Gardener. 205 Pine St. ☎ **206/623-7818.**

Residents of Seattle and the rest of the Northwest are absolutely crazy about gardening (it's the weather), so it was a natural thing for a garden store to appear in the middle of the city's main tourist shopping district. Take home a few fancy tools, some fragrant soaps, or all the makings for your very own bonsai tree (a pot, a small conifer or other tree, special bonsai tools, bonsai wire, potting soil, and decorative bonsai rocks).

Kasala. 1505 Western Ave. ☎ **206/623-7795.**

Boldly styled contemporary furnishings are this store's main business, and you probably don't want to ship a couch home. However, they also have lots of easily packed accent pieces—vases, candlesticks, picture frames—that are just as wildly modern as the furniture.

Sur La Table. 84 Pine St. ☎ **206/448-2244.**

Gourmet cooks will not want to miss an opportunity to visit Sur La Table, where every imaginable kitchen utensil is available. There are a dozen different kinds of whisks, an equal number of muffin tins, all manner of cake decorating tools, tableware, napkins, cookbooks—simply everything a cook would need. The shop is in the heart of Pike Place Market.

JEWELRY

Dashasa. Fourth and Pike Bldg., 1424 Fourth Ave. ☎ **206/623-0519.**

If you're looking for someone to design a custom contemporary piece of jewelry, stop by this tiny shop tucked away in the Fourth and Pike Building. Each piece of jewelry they create is a tiny work of art, and they offer computer imaging as well.

European Creations. Fourth and Pike Bldg., 1424 Fourth Ave. ☎ **206/628-0338.**

Located across the hall from the jeweler mentioned above, this jewelry design studio was founded by two master jeweler brothers from St. Petersburg. They specialize in custom jewelry using a wax-casting process and incorporating images from the past into contemporary designs.

Fox's Gem Shop. 1341 Fifth Ave. ☎ **206/623-2528.**

This is Seattle's premier jeweler, and among other elegant lines, they feature the Tiffany Collection. Displays here, including an 11,000-year-old mastodon skeleton, make shopping here a bit like visiting a museum.

MALLS/SHOPPING CENTERS

Bellevue Square. Bellevue Way and NE 8th Ave., Bellevue. ☎ **206/454-2431.**

Over in Bellevue, on the east side of Lake Washington, you'll find one of the area's largest shopping malls, with more than 200 stores. There's even an art museum, the Bellevue Art Museum, here in the mall.

Broadway Market. 401 Broadway E. ☎ **206/322-1610.**

Located in the stylish Capitol Hill neighborhood, the Broadway Market is a trendy little shopping center with a decidedly urban neighborhood feel. The mall houses numerous small shops and restaurants with reasonable prices.

City Centre. Sixth Ave. and Union St. ☎ **206/223-8999.**

This upscale downtown shopping center is the Seattle address of such familiar high-end retailers as Barneys New York, Benetton, FAO Schwartz, and Ann Taylor. There is also a Foster/White Gallery selling works by Dale Chihuly and other Northwest glass artists, and works of art by these and other glass artists are on display throughout City Centre. Bernard C. Chocolates is also here, and there is a very comfortable lounge where you can rest your feet out of the Seattle weather.

Rainier Square. 1326 Fifth Ave.

Built on the bottom floors of several skyscrapers, Rainier Square is a loose association of about 30 shops ranging from Eddie Bauer to Port Chatham Packing Company (smoked salmon).

Westlake Center. 400 Pine St. ☎ **206/467-1600.**

This is Seattle's premier downtown, upscale, urban shopping mall and is in the heart of Seattle's main shopping district. Under this roof are more than 80 specialty shops, including Godiva Chocolatier, Cache, Victoria's Secret, The Limited, and Made in Washington. There's also an extensive food court here. This mall is also the southern terminus for the monorail to Seattle Center.

MARKETS

✪ **Pike Place Market.** Pike St. and First Ave. ☎ **206/682-7453.**

Pike Place Market is one of Seattle's most famous landmarks and tourist attractions. It shelters not only produce vendors, fishmongers, and butchers, but also artists, craftspeople, and performers. There are hundreds of shops and dozens of restaurants (including some of Seattle's best) tucked away in hidden nooks and crannies on the numerous levels of the market. With so much to see and do, a trip to Pike Place Market can easily turn into an all-day affair.

Uwajimaya. 519 Sixth Ave. S. ☎ **206/624-6248.**

Typically, your local neighborhood supermarket has a section of Chinese cooking ingredients; it's probably about 10 feet long, with half that space taken up by various brands of soy sauce. Now imagine your local supermarket with nothing but Asian foods, housewares, produce, and toys. That's Uwajimaya, Seattle's Asian supermarket in the heart of the International District.

RECREATIONAL GEAR

The North Face. 1023 First Ave. ☎ **206/622-4111.**

The North Face is one of the country's best-known names in the field of outdoor gear, and here in their downtown shop, you can choose from among their diverse selection.

Patagonia Seattle. 2100 First Ave. ☎ **206/622-9700.**

Patagonia has built up a very loyal clientele based on the durability of its outdoor gear and clothing. Sure the prices are high, but these clothes are built to last.

REI. 222 Yale Ave. N. ☎ **206/223-1944.**

Recreational Equipment, Incorporated (REI), was founded here in Seattle back in 1938 and today is the nation's largest co-op selling outdoor gear. In 1996, REI opened an awesome flagship store just off I-5 not far from Lake Union. The store, a cross between a high-tech warehouse and a mountain lodge, is massive and houses not only anything you could ever need for pursuing your favorite outdoor sport, but also has a 65-foot climbing pinnacle, a rain room for testing raingear, a mountain-bike trail for test-driving bikes, a footwear test trail, even a play area for kids. With all this under one roof, who needs to go outside?

SALMON

If you think the fish at Pike Place Market looks great, but you could never get it home on the plane, think again. Any of the seafood vendors in Pike Place Market will pack your fresh salmon or Dungeness crab in an airline-approved container that will keep it fresh for up to 48 hours. Alternatively, you can buy vacuum-packed smoked salmon that will keep for years without refrigeration.

✪ **Pike Place Fish.** 86 Pike Place, Pike Place Market. ☎ **800/542-7732** or 206/682-7181.

Located just behind Rachel, the life-sized bronze pig, this fishmonger is famous for flying fish. Pick out a big silvery salmon, ask them to fillet it, and watch the show. They'll also deliver your packaged order to your hotel, ready to carry onto your plane.

Port Chatham Smoked Seafood. Rainier Sq., 1310 Fourth Ave. ☎ **800/872-5666** or 206/ 623-4645.

Northwest Coast Indians relied heavily on salmon for sustenance, and to preserve the fish they used alder-wood smoke. This tradition is still carried on today to produce one of the Northwest's most delicious food products. This store sells smoked sock-eye, king salmon, rainbow trout, and oysters—all of which will keep without refrigeration until the package is opened.

Other stores are in Bellevue Square mall and Southcenter mall.

Totem Smokehouse. 1906 Pike Place, Pike Place Market. ☎ **800/972-5666** or 206/443-1710.

Located at street level in Pike Place Market, this is another good source of vacuum-packed smoked salmon, and while prices aren't cheap, it sure is tasty fish.

TOYS

Archie McPhee. 3510 Stone Way N. ☎ **206/545-8344.**

You may already be familiar with this temple of the absurd through its mail-order catalog. Now imagine wandering through aisles full of goofy gags. Give yourself plenty of time and take a friend.

FAO Schwartz. City Centre, 1420 Fifth Ave. ☎ **206/442-9500.**

Yes, the toy store of the rich and famous is in Seattle, too. Want to know what Madonna's kid will be getting for Christmas this year? Stop by and see.

✪ **Magic Mouse.** 603 First Ave. ☎ **206/682-8097.**

Adults and children alike have a hard time pulling themselves away from this, the funnest toy store in Seattle. It is conveniently located in Pioneer Square and has a good selection of European toys.

Wood Shop Toys. 320 First Ave. S. ☎ **206/624-1763.**

Just 2 blocks away from Magic Mouse is another Seattle favorite that sells wooden toys, puppets, and lots of nostalgia toys that will appeal to adults as much as they appeal to kids. This place is worth a look even if you're not in the market for toys.

WINE

The Northwest is rapidly becoming known as a producer of fine wine. Its relatively dry summer with warm days and cool nights provides a perfect climate for growing grapes. After you have sampled Washington or Oregon vintages, you might want to take a few bottles home.

Pike and Western Wine Merchants. 1934 Pike Place, Pike Place Market. ☎ **206/441-1307.**

Visit this shop for an excellent selection of Washington and Oregon wines, as well as those from California, Italy, and France. The extremely knowledgeable staff will be happy to send you home with the very best wine available in Seattle.

Seattle After Dark

Though Seattleites spend much of their free time enjoying the city's natural surroundings, they have not overlooked more cultured evening pursuits. In fact, the winter weather that keeps people indoors and a long-time desire to be the cultural mecca of the Northwest have fueled a surprisingly active and diverse nightlife here. In recent years, Seattle has become something of an arts Mecca. The Seattle Opera is ranked as one of the top operas in the country, and its stagings of Wagner's Ring series have achieved near-legendary status. The Seattle Symphony receives accolades, and the Seattle Repertory Theatre has won Tony awards for its productions. There are more equity theaters in Seattle than in any U.S. city other than New York, and a thriving fringe theater keeps the city's lovers of avant-garde theater contentedly discoursing in cafes about the latest hysterical or thought-provoking performances. Music lovers will also find a plethora of classical, jazz, and rock offerings.

The biggest news on the Seattle performing arts scene is the construction of the new Benaroya Hall performing arts center downtown adjacent to the Seattle Art Museum. This state-of-the-art performance hall will serve as home for the Seattle Symphony and Seattle Opera and will move classical music performances back downtown from the Seattle Center Opera House. Benaroya Hall is scheduled to open in 1998.

Much of the evening entertainment is clustered in the Seattle Center and Pioneer Square areas. The former hosts theater, opera, and classical music performances; the latter is a nightclub district. The Belltown area north of Pike Place Market also has quite a few bars and nightclubs and a number of alternative performance spaces.

While winters are a time for enjoying the performing arts, summers are a time of outdoor festivals, and while these take place during daylight hours as much as they do after dark, you'll find information on these festivals and performance series in this chapter.

For half-price, day-of-show tickets to a wide variety of performances all over the city, stop by **Ticket/Ticket** (☎ **206/324-2744**), which has two sales booths: one in Pike Place Market and one on Capitol Hill. The Pike Place Market location, First Avenue and Pike Street, is open Tuesday through Sunday from noon to 6pm. The other booth is on the second floor of the Broadway Market, 401 Broadway E., and is open Tuesday through Saturday from 10am to 7pm and Sunday from noon to 6pm. Ticket/Ticket levies a service charge of 50¢ to $3, depending on the ticket price. If you want to pay full price with your credit card, call **Ticketmaster Northwest** (☎ **206/292-ARTS** or 206/628-0888).

To find out what's going on when you are in town, pick up a free copy of *Seattle Weekly,* which is Seattle's arts-and-entertainment newspaper. You'll find it in bookstores, convenience stores, grocery stores, newsstands, and other places around the city. On Friday, the *Seattle Times* includes a section called "Tempo," which is a guide to the week's arts and entertainment offerings.

1 The Performing Arts

Although a new downtown symphony hall was under construction at press time, the main venues for the performing arts in Seattle are still primarily clustered in Seattle Center, the special events complex that was built for the 1962 Seattle world's fair. Here, in the shadow of the Space Needle, you'll find the Opera House, Bagley Wright Theater, Intiman Playhouse, Seattle Children's Theatre, Seattle Center Coliseum, and Memorial Stadium.

OPERA & CLASSICAL MUSIC

The **Seattle Opera** (☎ **206/389-7676**), which currently performs at the Seattle Center Opera House but will move to the new Benaroya Hall when it opens in 1998, is considered one of the finest opera companies in the country and is *the* Wagnerian opera company. The stagings of Wagner's four-opera *The Ring of the Nibelungen* are breathtaking spectacles that draw crowds from around the country. In addition to classical operas, the season usually includes a more contemporary musical. Ticket prices range from $30 to $97.

Each year, under the baton of Gerard Schwarz, the **Seattle Symphony** (☎ **206/ 215-4747**), which also performs at the Seattle Center Opera House and will later move to Benaroya Hall, offers an amazingly diverse musical season that runs from September to May. There are evenings of classical, light classical, and pops, plus morning concerts, children's concerts, guest artists, and much more. Ticket prices range from $8 to $65.

The **Northwest Chamber Orchestra** (☎ **206/343-0445**), a perennial favorite with Seattle classical music fans, is a showcase for Northwest performers. The annual Baroque Festival in the autumn is the highlight of the season, which runs from September to April. Performances are held primarily in Kane Hall on the University of Washington campus, although there is also a series of concerts at the Seattle Art Museum. Ticket prices range from $18 to $25.

Other classical music companies to keep an eye and ear out for while in town include the **Bellevue Philharmonic Orchestra** (☎ **425/455-4171**), the **Early Music Guild** (☎ **206/325-7066**), and **Philharmonia Northwest** (☎ **206/392-7694**).

THEATER
MAINSTREAM THEATERS

The **Seattle Repertory Theater** (☎ **206/443-2222**), which performs at the Bagley Wright Theater, Seattle Center, 155 Mercer St., has been around for more than 30 years. As Seattle's top professional theater, it stages the most consistently entertaining productions in the city. In 1997, the Rep cranked up its rep another pair of notches with the addition of the new Leo K. Theatre and the hiring of Sharon Ott right after she won a Tony for transforming the Berkeley Rep into the best regional theater in the country. Expect many good things to come out of these changes. The Rep's season runs from October to May with six plays performed in the main theater and three more in the more intimate Leo K. Theatre. Productions range from classics to world premieres to Broadway musicals. Ticket prices range from $10 to $40.

With a season that runs from May to October, the **Intiman Theatre Company** (☎ **206/269-1900**), which performs at the Intiman Playhouse, Seattle Center, 201 Mercer St., picks up where the Seattle Rep leaves off, filling in the gap left by those months when the Seattle Rep's lights are dark. The fact that the two theaters are side by side at Seattle Center makes it easy to remember which way to go on performance nights. Ticket prices range from $18.50 to $31; $10 for standing room only.

Performing in the historic Eagles Building theater adjacent to and reached via the Washington State Convention and Trade Center, **A Contemporary Theater (ACT)**, 700 Union St. (☎ **206/292-7676**), offers slightly more adventurous productions than the other major theater companies in Seattle. However, it is not nearly as avant-garde as some of the smaller companies. The season runs from the end of April to mid-November. Ticket prices range from $16.25 to $30.50.

Located on the shore of Green Lake in north Seattle, **The Bathhouse Theatre,** 7312 W. Green Lake Way N. (☎ **206/524-9108**), is known for its revivals of classic musicals and stagings of old radio revues. Ticket prices range from $12.60 to $25.

CHILDREN'S THEATER

If it's a rainy day and you'd like to keep the kids entertained for a couple of hours, there are a couple of excellent options in downtown Seattle. The **Seattle Children's Theatre,** Charlotte Martin Theatre at Seattle Center, Second Avenue N. and Thomas Street (☎ **206/441-3322**), stages both entertaining classics and thought-provoking dramas. Shows appeal to children of different ages, so call to see what's being staged (tickets $11.50 to $17.50). Drawing on international themes and traditional tales from around the world, the innovative **Northwest Puppet Center,** 9123 15th Ave. NE. (☎ **206/523-2579**), stages performances that will appeal to adults as well as children. Puppet companies from around the world perform throughout the year. There is also a puppet museum here (tickets $7.50 adults, $5.50 children).

FRINGE THEATER

With such a burgeoning mainstream performing-arts community, it is not at all surprising that Seattle has developed the sort of fringe theater life once only associated with such cities as New York, London, and Edinburgh. The city's more avant-garde performance companies have been grabbing their share of the limelight with daring, outrageous, and thought-provoking productions.

A perusal of a few local entertainment publications recently turned up the following fringe theater performances (all taking place in the same 2-week period): *The Shadow of Drek* (which included a *Star Trek* send-up), *Lucky Stiff* (a musical about a Monte Carlo competition for $6 million), *Wuthering! Heights! The! Musical!* (a spoof of small-town musicals), *The whY Files* (a parody of the hit TV show), *Lady Chatterly's Lover,* and *The Return of the Sirens of Swing* (a cabaret piece about three singing sisters).

Seattle's newfound interest in fringe theater finds its greatest expression each spring, when the **Seattle Fringe Theater Festival** (☎ **206/320-9588**), a showcase for small, self-producing theater companies, takes over various Capitol Hill venues. There are usually performances by more than 70 theater groups from around the country.

Even if you don't happen to be in town for Seattle's annual fringe binge, check out the following venues for way-off Broadway productions, performance art, poetry jams, and spoken word performances:

- **Annex Theater,** 1916 Fourth Ave. (☎ **206/728-0933**)—thought-provoking dramas and comedies, cabaret theater.

- **Book-It Theater,** 1219 Westlake Ave., Suite 301. (☎ 206/216-0833)—works by local playwrights.
- **Empty Space Theatre,** 3509 Fremont Ave. N. (☎ 206/547-7500)—mostly comedy, popular with a young crowd.
- **The Group Theater,** Seattle Center House, 305 Harrison St. (☎ 206/441-1299)—multicultural theater.
- **New City Theater,** 1634 11th Ave. (☎ 206/323-6800)—performance art, works by local playwrights.
- **Northwest Asian-American Theater,** Theatre Off Jackson, 409 Seventh Ave. S. (☎ 206/340-1049)—works by Asian-American writers, actors, and musicians.
- **Theater Schmeater,** 1500 Summit St. (☎ 206/324-5801)—best known for its stage adaptations of *The Twilight Zone* episodes.
- **Velvet Elvis Arts Lounge Theatre,** 107 Occidental Ave. S. ☎ 206/624-8477)—performance art, poetry nights, alternative video productions, jazz.

DANCE

Although Seattle has a well-regarded ballet company and a theater dedicated to contemporary dance and performance art, Seattle is not nearly as devoted to dance as it is the theater and classical music. However, this said, there is hardly a week that goes by without some sort of dance performance being staged somewhere in the city. Touring companies of all types, the University of Washington Dance Department faculty and student performances, UW World Dance series (see below for details), and the Northwest New Works Festival (see below for details) each spring all bring plenty of creative movement to the stages of Seattle. When you're in town, check *Seattle Weekly* or the *Seattle Times* for a calendar of upcoming performances.

The **Pacific Northwest Ballet,** Seattle Center Opera House, 321 Mercer St. (☎ 206/441-2424 for information, or 206/292-ARTS for tickets), is Seattle's premier dance company. During the season, which runs from September to June, the company presents a wide range of classics, new works, and (the company's specialty) pieces choreographed by George Balanchine (tickets $14 to $69). If you happen to be in Seattle in December, try to get a ticket to this company's performance of *Nutcracker.* In addition to outstanding dancing, you'll enjoy sets and costumes by children's book author Maurice Sendak.

Much more adventurous choreography is the domain of **On the Boards,** 153 14th Ave. (☎ 206/325-7901), which, although it stages a wide variety of performance art, is best known as Seattle's premier modern-dance venue (tickets $8 to $22). In addition to dance performances by Northwest artists, there are a variety of productions each year by internationally known artists. The Northwest New Works Festival, a barrage of contemporary dance and performance art held every spring, is the season's highlight.

MAJOR PERFORMANCE HALLS

With ticket prices for shows and concerts as high as they are these days, it pays to be choosy about what you see, but sometimes where you see it is just as important. Seattle has two restored historic theaters that are as much a part of a performance as what goes on up on the stage.

The **5th Avenue Theatre,** 1308 Fifth Ave. (☎ 206/625-1418), which first opened its doors in 1926 as a vaudeville house, is a loose re-creation of the imperial throne room in Beijing's Forbidden City. In 1980, the theater underwent a complete renovation that restored this Seattle jewel to its original splendor, and today the astounding interior is as good a reason as any to see a show here. Don't miss an opportunity to attend a performance here. Broadway shows are the theater's mainstay (tickets $20 to $65).

The **Paramount Theatre,** Pine Street and Ninth Avenue (☎ **206/682-1414**), one of Seattle's few historic theaters, has been restored to its original beauty and today shines with all the brilliance it did when it first opened. New lighting and sound systems have brought the theater up to contemporary standards. The theater stages everything from rock concerts to Broadway musical (tickets $20 to $65).

PERFORMING ARTS SERIES

When Seattle's own resident performing arts companies aren't taking to the dozens of stages around the city, various touring companies from around the world are. If you're a fan of Broadway shows, check the calendars at the Paramount Theatre and the 5th Avenue Theatre, both of which regularly serve as Seattle stops for touring shows.

The **International Music Festival of Seattle,** P.O. Box 2166, Seattle, WA 98111-2166 (☎ **206/233-0993**), usually held in late June and early July, is a classical music series focusing primarily on chamber music. Performances are held at Meany Hall, the Seattle Art Museum, and the Meydenbauer Center in Bellevue (tickets $23 to $25).

The **UW World Series** (☎ **206/543-4880**), held at Meany Hall on the University of Washington campus, is actually several different series including a chamber music series, a classical piano series, a world dance series, and a world music and theater series. Together these four series keep the Meany Hall stage busy between October and April. Special events are also scheduled. Tickets are $21 to $40.

Seattle loves the theater and each spring, the city binges on the fringes with the **Seattle Fringe Theater Festival** (see "Fringe Theater," above).

Summer is a time of outdoor festivals and performance series in Seattle, and should you be in town during the sunny months, you'll have a wide variety of al fresco performances from which to choose. The city's biggest summer music festivals are the Northwest Folklife Festival over Memorial Day weekend and Bumbershoot over Labor Day weekend. See the Seattle Calendar of Events in chapter 2 for details.

AT&T Summer Nights at the Pier (☎ **206/281-8111** for information, or 206/628-0888 for tickets) presents a summer's worth of big-name acts at Pier 62/63 on the waterfront. Blues, jazz, rock, and folk acts generally pull in a 30-something to 40-something crowd (tickets range from $10 to $35). **Greenstage** (☎ **206/935-5606**) stages Shakespeare in the parks at green spaces around the metro area. There are usually two plays done in repertory over the space of the summer. Call for schedule and locations. Out at **Woodland Park Zoo** (☎ **206/684-4800**), there are a couple of different music series each summer, including one for children. The Zoo Tunes series usually brings in big names in jazz, easy listening, and blues. In Fremont, there are Saturday night movie screenings projected against the wall of an old building. People set up seats in a parking lot for these fun and funky evenings. Over in Woodinville, which is on the east side of Lake Washington, Chateau Ste. Michele, Washington's largest winery, stages the area's most enjoyable outdoor summer concert series. The **Summer Festival On The Green** (☎ **206/488-3300**) is held at the winery's amphitheater, which is surrounded by beautiful estatelike grounds. Of course, plenty of wine is available.

2 The Club & Music Scene

If you have the urge to do a bit of clubbing and barhopping while in Seattle, there's no better place to start than in Pioneer Square. Good times are guaranteed whether you want to hear a live band, hang out in a good old-fashioned bar, or dance. The Belltown neighborhood, north of Pike Place Market is another good place to stumble from one club to the next, although here you'll get a bit more exercise and cover a few more blocks.

FOLK, COUNTRY & ROCK

While the distinctive Seattle sound has lost its hold on the American consciousness, Seattle is still a lively city if you're into rock 'n' roll. Currently, as elsewhere in the country, lounge music and 1970s nostalgia are all the rage. Martinis are being sipped as much as microbrews are being quaffed, and Frank Sinatra wannabes are showing up in clubs all over town.

The Pioneer Square area is Seattle's main live music neighborhood (almost everything but classical), and the clubs have banded together to make things easy on music fans. The "Joint Cover" plan lets you pay one admission to get into 10 or so clubs. The charge is $5 on weeknights and $8 on weekends (occasionally $12 for national-act nights). Participating clubs currently include The Fenix, Fenix Underground, Doc Maynard's, The Central Saloon, Colourbox, The Bohemian Cafe, and a few other night spots. Most of these clubs are short on style and hit-or-miss when it comes to music (which makes the joint cover a great way to find out where the good music is on any given night).

A few noteworthy Pioneer Square clubs include **The Central Saloon,** 207 First Ave. S. (☎ **206/622-0209**), which was established in 1892 and is the oldest saloon in Seattle; **Doc Maynard's,** 610 First Ave. (☎ **206/682-4649**), which by day is the starting point of the family oriented Underground Tour; and **Fenix/Fenix Underground,** 315 and 323 Second Ave. (☎ **206/467-1111**), two clubs that together book what usually is the best music in Pioneer Square.

✪ The Backstage. 2208 NW Market St. ☎ **206/781-2805.** Cover $6–$20.

This is Seattle's top venue for contemporary music of all kinds and packs in the crowds most nights. The audience ranges from drinking age up to graying rock 'n' rollers. The music ranges from Afro pop to zydeco, with lots of new and old national acts hitting the stage.

Ballard Firehouse. 5429 Russell St. ☎ **206/784-3516.** Cover $3–$20.

An eclectic assortment of musical styles finds its way onto the bandstand of this converted firehouse in the old Scandinavian neighborhood of northwest Seattle. Now it's just the music that's hot, and that's the way they want to keep it. You'll see everything from up-and-comers to revival bands back on tour to cash in on 1970s nostalgia. People having dinner here get the best tables.

Crocodile. 2200 Second Ave. ☎ **206/728-0316.** Cover $2–$9.

With its rambunctious and wild decor, this Belltown establishment is a combination nightclub, bar, and restaurant. There's live rock Tuesday through Sunday nights. The music calendar here is always eclectic with everything from rock to folk to jazz. In the summer of 1997, the Crocodile staged Lounge-a-Palooza I, with lounge acts crooning for the lounge lizards.

Showbox. 1426 First Ave. ☎ **206/628-3151.**

Located across the street from Pike Place Market, this club used to be a comedy venue but has been booking a lot of name rock acts lately. You never know who might be playing here; maybe Rickie Lee Jones, maybe George Clinton, maybe Better than Ezra. Definitely *the* downtown rock venue for performers with a national following.

Sit and Spin. 2219 Fourth Ave. ☎ **206/441-9484.** Cover free to $6.

It's a club, it's a juice bar, it's a cafe, it's a Laundromat! This Belltown cafe/club is all of these and more. A popular hangout for the city's young scene-makers, Sit and Spin books an eclectic range for music. Decor is 1950s funky and the food is good.

Grave Matters

While the 1994 suicide of Kurt Cobain of the Seattle band Nirvana didn't spell the end of grunge music, it did cause a lot of problems for his widow, Courtney Love. After Cobain was cremated, Love did not immediately inter his ashes. Lacking a grave to which to make their pilgrimages, fans created a de facto memorial in the tiny Veretta Park, which adjoined Cobain and Love's property, the site of his suicide. After 2 years in which beer cans, syringes, and graffiti accumulated and branches, flowers, and dirt disappeared, Love was quoted in the *Seattle Post-Intelligencer* as saying, "I'm knocking down the greenhouse where Kurt died because it's become bigger than the Space Needle!" Fans may never have an appropriate memorial for Cobain; rumors have circulated over the years that Love scattered his ashes around some of Cobain's favorite hang-outs.

Grunge music aside, Seattle hasn't produced a lot of famous rock stars over the years. However, one native son (who supposedly hated his hometown), continues to attract fans decades after his death. Jimi Hendrix, guitarist extraordinaire and wizard of feedback, is buried in **Greenwood Memorial Park,** 350 Monroe Ave. NE, in Renton, a southern suburb of Seattle. Just look for the grave with a guitar carved on it.

Martial arts master and movie star Bruce Lee and his son Brandon Lee (who died while making a film about his father), may never have had the following that Jimi Hendrix did, but their fans are no less dedicated to their memories. The graves of father and son can both be found in **Lake View Cemetery,** just north of Volunteer Park on Capitol Hill. Seattle founding fathers Arthur Denny, Henry Yesler, and "Doc" Maynard are also buried at Lake View.

JAZZ & BLUES

Art Bar. 1516 Second Ave. ☎ **206/622-4344.** Cover free to $3.

With funky thrift-store decor and very eclectic taste in art, this bar is a Bohemian hangout par excellence. Some nights there is live jazz and other nights a DJ spins tunes (not necessarily jazz), but mostly, the Art Bar is just someplace for the city's more artistic types to get together.

✪ **Dimitriou's Jazz Alley.** 2033 Sixth Ave. ☎ **206/441-9729.** Cover $10–$18.50.

This is Seattle's premier jazz club. Cool and sophisticated, Dimitriou's books only the best performers, including name acts, and is reminiscent of New York jazz clubs.

New Orleans Creole Restaurant. 114 First Ave. S. ☎ **206/622-2563.** No cover weeknights (unless there's a national act playing); weekends $8 (joint cover).

If you like your food and your jazz hot, check out the New Orleans. Tuesday is Cajun night, but the rest of the week you can hear Dixieland, R&B, jazz, and blues.

Patti Summers Cabaret. Pike Place Market, First Ave. and Pike St. ☎ **206/621-8555.** No cover.

Located in a dark and dated cellar space in the Pike Place Market, this club has been the home of jazz pianist Patti Summers for many years. Summers performs several nights each week.

Prego. Madison Hotel, 512 Madison St. ☎ **206/583-0300.** No cover.

This is jazz with a view. Prego, an Italian restaurant at the top of the Madison Hotel, features live jazz several nights a week. Although this is meant as music to dine by, it's still fun to have a drink in the lounge and listen to a little light music while gazing out over the city.

2218. 2218 First Ave. ☎ **206/441-2218.** No cover.

This Belltown restaurant and club features live jazz most nights of the week. Tuesday nights expect crooning à la old Blue Eyes and Harry Connick Jr. On Friday and Saturday nights there are currently piano soloists early in the evening and dancing to recorded music later.

COMEDY, CABARET & DINNER THEATER

Cabaret de Paris. Rainier Sq., Fourth Ave. and Union St. ☎ **206/623-4111.** $37–$39 for dinner and show.

Throughout the year this club stages a wide variety of entertaining programs of music, dance, and humor. Updated torch songs and numbers from classic musicals assure that the shows here will appeal to both young and old alike. The Christmas shows are especially funny. Over the years the cabaret's satirical musical reviews poking fun at Seattle have always been big hits.

Comedy Underground. 222 S. Main St. ☎ **206/628-0303.** Admission $4–$10.

Located in the Pioneer Square area, where the Seattle Underground tour has proved that too much time beneath the city streets can lead even normal people to tell bad jokes, this is Seattle's most convenient comedy club.

Entros. 823 Yale St. N. ☎ **206/624-0057.** Game pass $10 to $15.

This place is part dinner theater, part weird-and-wacky game center. Housed in an old industrial building near Lake Union, Entros entertains with all kinds of strange games before, during, and after meals. In fact, you don't even have to eat here to enjoy the games. The games defy categorization, but they're all loads of fun; you just have to check it out yourself.

Mystery Cafe Dinner Theatre. The Bon Marché, Third Ave. and Stewart St. ☎ **206/ 324-8895.** $38 for dinner and show.

The patented formula of allowing the audience to become part of the staged murder mystery has been around for a while now and remains a fun way to spend an evening if you're a fan of murder mysteries or games. Here, the suspects also serve the three-course meal. Shows are Friday and Saturday night at 8pm. The Mystery Cafe had plans to move at press time, but you should still be able to track them down by calling the above number.

DANCE CLUBS

Downunder. 2407 First Ave. ☎ **206/728-4053.** Cover free on Thurs, $5 Fri, and Sat.

Located in the Belltown neighborhood north of Pike Place Market, the Downunder doesn't necessarily play underground music, but it is down a flight of stairs from street level. Wild decor, light shows, and high-energy music attract a Generation X crowd. Techno to grunge. Open Thursday, Friday and Saturday 9pm to 4am.

Iguana Cantina. 2815 Alaskan Way. ☎ **206/728-7071.** Cover $5–$9.

This cavernous place on the waterfront is popular with Seattle's singles set. There's live Top 40 dance music most nights, and the restaurant has great views of Elliott Bay. Open Wednesday to Sunday.

Kid Mohair. 1207 Pine St. ☎ **206/625-4444.** Cover $4.

Billing itself as a cigar bar and nightclub, this classy little dance club is currently one of Seattle's hot dance spots. Things don't start happening here until around midnight.

Vogue. 2018 First Ave. ☎ **206/443-0673.** Cover $5–$10.

Although this Belltown club where the band Nirvana gave its first public performance of "Smells Like Teen Spirit" is much changed from the early days of grunge and no longer does live shows, it is still a fun place if you don't mind a young, pierced crowd. These days, it hosts 1980s New Wave nights as well as World Beat nights.

3 The Bar Scene

BARS

FX McRory's. 419 Occidental Ave. S. ☎ **206/623-4800.**

The clientele is upscale, and you're likely to see members of the Seahawks or the SuperSonics at the bar. The original Leroy Neiman paintings on the walls lend class to this sports bar. You'll also find Seattle's largest selection of bourbon (more than 140 varieties) and microbrew beers and ales. There's also an oyster bar and good food.

McCormick and Schmick's. 1103 First Ave. ☎ **206/623-5500.**

The mahogany paneling, sparkling cut glass, and waiters in bow ties lend this restaurant bar a touch of class, but otherwise this place could have been the inspiration for *Cheers.* Very popular as an after-work watering hole of Seattle money-makers, McCormick and Schmick's is best known for its excellent and inexpensive happy-hour snacks.

Oliver's. Mayflower Park Hotel, 405 Olive Way. ☎ **206/623-8700.**

Oliver's is martini central for Seattle, and year after year bartender Mike Rule keeps winning the award for best martini in town in the Martini Classic Challenge (which also happens to be sponsored by the Mayflower Park Hotel). Only you can decide whether Oliver's shakes up the perfect martini.

The Pink Door. 1919 Post Alley. ☎ **206/443-3241.**

Better known as Pike Place Market's unmarked restaurant, the Pink Door has a very lively after-work bar scene, and while many of the people sipping Campari-laced martinis are waiting for a table on the deck, others are here to have their palms read—yes, the Pink Door has its own resident palm reader.

Two Bells Tavern. 2313 Fourth Ave. ☎ **206/441-3050.**

Although little more than an old tavern and local hangout for Belltown residents, the Two Bells has a commitment to art. While the barstools and tables have seen better days, the walls are usually hung with interesting artwork.

The Virginia Inn. 1937 First Ave. ☎ **206/728-1937.**

Of all the bars in Belltown, that oh-so-stylish neighborhood north of Pike Place Market, the Virginia Inn has long been a favorite of everyone from artists to grunge rockers to the after-work crowd. With lots of burnished wood and a few tables out on the sidewalk, it's a comfortable place to sip a martini or microbrew.

BREWPUBS

Big Time Brewery and Alehouse. 4133 University Way NE. ☎ **206/545-4509.**

Located in the University District and decorated to look like a turn-of-the-century tavern complete with a 100-year-old back bar and a wooden refrigerator, the Big Time serves as many as 12 of its own brews at any given time, and some of these can be pretty unusual.

Lounging Around in Seattle

Whether it was named for the maker of the vermouth that flavored the gin or by a guy running for the ferry to Martinez on San Francisco Bay, the martini has been around for well over a century. Over the years it has been a symbol of sophistication and a symbol of power. In its current revival, in part driven by the 20-something generation, it is either a relatively cheap display of wealth in a downsized economy (and goes hand in hand with cigars) or it is a retro indulgence akin to wearing bell bottoms and disco dancing.

Today anything goes in the world of martinis, and often it seems the fruitier the better. However, whether you consider a drink made with tequila, cranberry juice, or blue Curaçao to still be a martini, there is no denying that martini madness is sweeping the country, and Seattle is no exception.

If you're a traditionalist and are looking for the very best classic martini in town, **Oliver's,** 405 Olive Way (☎ **206/623-8700),** in the Mayflower Park Hotel, is the place for you. Bartender Mike Rule has perfected his martini and, by winning the hotel's annual Martini Challenge (held in October) for 4 years in a row, from 1993 to 1996, solidly established Oliver's reputation for serving the best martini in town (the happy hour hors d'oeuvres aren't bad either). It doesn't hurt that this classy little bar is a gorgeous space with floor to ceiling windows.

Obviously, cultivating a taste for martinis can prove very deleterious to your wallet. With most premium martinis costing somewhere between $6 and $7, a night on the town can really set you back. One solution is to start your evening at the **Martini-Manhattan Memorial Bar,** 619 Pine St. (☎ **206/621-VONS),** which is sort of a downsized version of TGIFriday's (you know, lots of junk all over the walls and ceiling). Happy hour here boasts the best $2 martinis in town, and from

Elysian Brewing Company. 1221 E. Pike St. ☎ **206/860-1920.**

Although the brewery at this Capitol Hill brewpub is one of the smallest in the city, the pub itself is quite large and has a industrial feel that says local brewpub all over it. The stout and strong ales are especially good.

Hales Ales Brewery and Pub. 4301 Leary Way NW. ☎ **206/782-0737.**

Located about a mile west of the Fremont Bridge heading toward Ballard, this is the area's *other* brewpub, and while Red Hook Ales' Trolleyman gets most of the attention, Hales brews fine ales as well. This brewery, which has a second brewpub over in downtown Kirkland on the Eastside, doesn't bottle any of its brews, so if you want to try a Hales, you'll just have to stop by one of its pubs.

Hart Brewery Pub. 1201 First Ave. S. ☎ **206/682-3377.**

Located south of the Kingdome in a big old warehouse, this pub is part of the brewery that makes Thomas Kemper lagers and Pyramid ales. Brewery tours and beer tastings are offered, but this is most popular as a place for dinner and drinks, especially before and after sporting events at the Kingdome. There's good pub food, too.

The Pike Pub and Brewery. 1415 First Ave. ☎ **206/622-6044.**

Located in an open, central space inside Pike Place Market, this brewpub makes excellent stout and pale ale and on Thursdays taps a cask and offers $1.50 pints. There's live instrumental music a couple of nights a week, and, with its comfortable the wall of Bombay Sapphire gin bottles all set up for rapid-fire dispensing of libations, it's obvious that this place keeps the martinis flowing.

If the lounge scene is as important to you as the martini you drink and retro is your thing, then you belong at **The Back Door Ultra Lounge,** 503 Third Ave. (☎ 206/622-7665), which is located at the back of the Appointment Restaurant in the Pioneer Square area. This is the quintessential funky retro lounge, with exotica parties, cheap martinis, and walls covered with bad art from the 1950s and 1960s. Too cool.

After making the scene at the Back Door, check out **Marcus's,** 88 Yesler Way (☎ 206/624-3323), which claims to be Seattle's only underground martini and cigar bar. In this case, underground means just that—martini drinking in the Seattle underground. You'll find this bar in Pioneer Square under the Taco del Mar.

If you can get started early enough in the evening on a Saturday night, you can cut the rug to a live big band over at **Seattle Center House** at the base of the Space Needle. The bands play from 8 to 11pm and admission is $5. There are even ballroom dancing lessons ($2) from 7 to 8pm. Young and old make this scene, and those cats and kittens sure can dance.

OK, so maybe accordions aren't exactly essential to the martini scene, but they're just so much fun that you'd be a fool not to drop by the bar at **The Pink Door,** 1919 Post Alley (☎ 206/443-3241), a very popular Italian restaurant in Pike Place Market. There's no sign out front, which kind of gives this place the feel of a speakeasy. Through the door, down the stairs, through the dining room, and there you are. Accordion madness strikes every Friday and Saturday night. They also happen to do some interesting martinis here.

Cheers! And remember olives are fattening.

---

couches, the Pike makes a great place to get off your feet after a day of exploring the market.

Trolleyman Pub/Red Hook Ale Brewery. 3400 Phinney Ave. N. ☎ **206/548-8000.**

This is the taproom of the Redhook Ale Brewery, one of the Northwest's most celebrated microbreweries, and is located in a restored trolley barn on the Lake Washington Ship Canal. You can sample the ales brewed here, have a bite to eat, and even tour the brewery if you're interested. Red Hook has a second brewery and pub at 14300 NE 145th St. (☎ 206/483-3232) in Woodinville on the east side of Lake Washington.

IRISH PUBS

✪ **Kells.** 1916 Post Alley, Pike Place Market. ☎ **206/728-1916.** Cover Fri–Sat only, $3.

This friendly Irish pub has the look and feel of a casual Dublin pub and stays absolutely packed most nights of the week. They pull a good Guinness stout and feature live traditional Irish music Wednesday through Saturday. This is also a restaurant serving traditional Irish meals.

Murphy's. 1928 N. 45th St. ☎ **206/634-2110.**

Located north of Lake Union in the Wallingford neighborhood, this pub is a reasonable facsimile of an Irish pub. Wednesday is a popular open-mike night, and there are live bands on Friday and Saturday nights.

4 The Gay & Lesbian Nightlife Scene

Capitol Hill is Seattle's main gay neighborhood, and it is here that you'll find the greatest concentration of gay and lesbian bars and dance clubs. The *Seattle Gay News* (☎ 206/324-4297) is the community's newspaper and is available at gay bars and nightclubs.

BARS

C. C. Attle's. 1501 E. Madison St. ☎ **206/726-0565.**

Located across the street from Thumpers, this bar has a 1940s look and is known for its cocktails.

Crescent. 1413 E. Olive Way. ☎ **206/720-8188.**

If you're a karaoke kind of guy, the Crescent on Sunday night is the place for you. Saturday nights are dance and cruise nights.

Mr. Paddywhacks. 722 E. Pike St. ☎ **206/322-4024.**

With male dancers performing nightly, this club is a very popular cruising bar. If you're looking to meet someone while you're in town, this is the place.

Safari Sports Bar and Grille. 1518 11th Ave. ☎ **206/328-4250.**

Just as the name implies, this is a sports bar, and great place to catch a Mariners, Sonics, or Seahawks game.

The Seattle Eagle. 314 E. Pike St. ☎ **206/621-7591.**

If you like to hang with the leather-and-Levi's set, drop by this bar in the Capitol Hill area.

Thumpers. 1500 E. Madison St. ☎ **206/328-3800.**

Perched high on Capitol Hill with an excellent view of downtown Seattle, Thumpers is a classy bar done up in oak. The seats by the fireplace are perfect on a cold and rainy night.

Wildrose. 1021 E. Pike St. ☎ **206/324-9210.**

This friendly restaurant/bar is a long-time favorite with the Capitol Hill lesbian community and claims to be the oldest women's bar on the West Coast. Nonsmokers take note—there are smoke-free sections here.

DANCE CLUBS

The Easy. 916 E. Pike St. ☎ **206/323-8343.**

This Capitol Hill bar is popular with the lesbian singles crowd and doubles as a dance club.

Neighbours. 1509 Broadway. ☎ **206/324-5358.** Cover Sun–Thurs, $1; Fri–Sat, $5.

This has been the favorite dance club of Capitol Hill's gay community for years, and recently, word has gotten out to straights. Still, the clientele is primarily gay. Friday and Saturday buffets are extremely popular. As at other clubs, different nights of the week feature different styles of music.

Re-Bar. 1114 Howell St. ☎ **206/233-9873.** Cover $3–$10

Each night there's a different theme, with the DJs spinning everything from world beat to funk and soul. Although this club isn't strictly gay, Thursday is currently Queer Disco night. Saturday nights also attract a primarily gay crowd.

Timberline. 2015 Boren Ave. ☎ **206/622-6220.**

If the boot-scootin' boogie is your favorite dance, the Timberline is the place to be. You'll find more men line dancing here than in any other club in town.

5 More Entertainment

MOVIES

Movies come close behind coffee and reading as a Seattle obsession. The city supports a surprising number of theaters showing foreign, independent, and nonmainstream films, as well as first-run movies. These include the **Varsity,** 4329 University Way NE (☎ 206/632-3131); **Grand Illusion,** NE 50th Ave. and University Way NE (☎ 206/523-3935); **Neptune,** NE 45th Ave. and Brooklyn St. NE (☎ 206/633-5545); **Harvard Exit,** 807 E. Roy St. (☎ 206/323-8986); and the **Egyptian,** 801 E. Pine St. (☎ 206/323-4978).

The Seattle International Film Festival takes place each May and early June, with around 150 films shown at various theaters. Check local papers for details.

GAME CENTERS

Techies would you like to have us all believe that game centers (basically video arcades raised to the highest level) are the entertainment world's wave of the future. These parlors of virtual reality appeal primarily to the Pac-Man generation and offer a noisy escape into the high-tech world of virtual reality.

Gameworks. 1511 Seventh Ave. ☎ **206/521-0952.**

Feeling more like a nightclub than a video arcade on steroids, this much-hyped entertainment center is hoping to be the wave of the future for the video-game generation. The Indy race car game, with racers sitting in cars that bounce and bank in conjunction with the view on the screen ahead, is a favorite here. However, Vertical Reality is the game that has people standing in line. In this one, you're strapped into a chair that rises and falls depending on how many bad guys you shoot or hits you take.

Wizards of the Coast Game Center. 4518 University Way NE. ☎ **206/675-1608.**

Not nearly as glitzy as Gameworks, this place doubles as both a video-game arcade and a center for devotees of the hit fantasy game Magic. There's also an Internet war games area. The huge minotaur that glares at you as you descend into the dungeon-like basement is way cooler than anything at Gameworks.

POOL & BILLIARDS

Belltown Billiards. 90 Blanchard St. ☎ **206/448-6779.**

With live jazz on Sunday, plenty of tables, and a convenient Belltown location partially below street level, this place has the feel of a classic billiard parlor.

Jillian's Billiard Club. 731 Westlake Ave. N. ☎ **206/223-0300.**

This up-market chain billiard hall overlooking Lake Union attracts a lot of suits in the after-work hours. There are two floors and enough pool tables so that you almost never have to wait. Other table games, including table tennis, are also available.

6 Only in Seattle

While Seattle has plenty to offer in the way of performing arts, some of the city's best after-dark offerings have nothing to do with the music. There's no better way to start the evening (that is if the day has been sunny or only partly cloudy) than to catch the **sunset from the waterfront.** The Bell Street Pier and Myrtle Edwards Park are two of the best and least commercial vantages for taking in nature's evening light show. Keep in mind that sunset can come as late as 10pm in the middle of summer.

Want the best view of the city lights? Hold off on your elevator ride to the top of the **Space Needle** until after dark. Alternatively, you can hop a ferry and sail off into the night. Now, what could be more romantic?

Well, I suppose a **carriage ride** could be as romantic. Carriages are to be found parked and waiting for customers, couples and families alike, on the waterfront.

For a cheap date, nothing beats the **first Thursday art walk.** On the first Thursday of each month, galleries in Pioneer Square and Belltown stay open until 8 or 9pm. There are usually appetizers and drinks available and sometimes live music. On those same first Thursdays, the Seattle Art Museum, the Seattle Asian Art Museum, the Henry Art Gallery, and the Museum of Flight all stay open late and waive their usual admission charge. With the exception of the Museum of Flight, all of these art museums, as well as the Frye Art Museum, are open late every Thursday, though you'll have to pay on those other nights (except at the Frye, which never charges an admission).

Elliott Bay Book Co., 101 S. Main St. (☎ **206/624-6600**), is not only a great place to hang out after dark (or during the day for that matter), but it also schedules frequent readings by touring authors. Stop by or call to check the schedule. There are also frequent art lectures at the Seattle Art Museum and Seattle Asian Art Museum.

Want to learn to dance? Up on Capitol Hill, there are **brass dance steps** inlaid into the sidewalk along Broadway. Spend an evening strolling the strip and you and your partner could teach yourselves several classic dance steps in between noshing a piroshky and savoring a chocolate torte.

Excursions from Seattle 10

After you've explored Seattle for a few days, consider heading out of town on a day trip. Within an hour to an hour and a half of the city you can find yourself in the mountains, inside the world's largest building, cruising up a fjordlike arm of Puget Sound, or strolling through a town you may recognize from a hit TV series. The four excursions listed below are all fairly easy day trips that will give you glimpses of the Northwest outside the Emerald City. Another possible excursion is to visit Mount St. Helens National Volcanic Monument. I list this excursion as a day trip from Portland simply because it takes about an hour less to reach the monument from Portland than it does from Seattle.

1 Mount Rainier

Weather forecasting for Seattleites is a simple matter: Either "the Mountain" is out and the weather is good, or it isn't (out or good). "The Mountain" is of course Mount Rainier, the 14,410-foot-tall dormant volcano that looms over Seattle on clear days. Mount Rainier may look as if it were on the edge of town, but it's actually 90 miles southeast of the city.

The mountain and some 235,400 acres surrounding it are part of Mount Rainier National Park, which was established in 1899 as the fifth U.S. national park. From downtown Seattle, the easiest route to the mountain is via I-5 south to exit 127. Then take Wash. 7 south, which in some 30 miles becomes Wash. 706. The route is well marked.

WHAT TO SEE & DO

You'd be well advised to leave as early as possible, especially if you are heading to the mountain on a summer weekend. Traffic along the route and crowds at the park can be daunting. Before leaving, you might contact the park for information. Write or call **Mount Rainier National Park,** Tahoma Woods, Star Route, Ashford, WA 98304 (☎ 360/569-2211). Keep in mind that during the winter only the Henry M. Jackson Memorial Visitor Center at Paradise is open, and then only on weekends. Park entrances other than the Nisqually entrance are closed by snow throughout the winter.

Mount Rainier National Park admission is $10 per motor vehicle or $5 per person for pedestrians and bicyclists. Just past the main southwest entrance (Nisqually), you'll come to Longmire, site of the National Park Inn, Longmire Museum (exhibits on the park's natural and human history), a hiker information center that issues backcountry permits, and a ski-touring center where you can rent cross-country skis in winter. The road then climbs to Paradise (elevation 5,400 feet), the aptly named mountainside aerie that affords a breathtaking close-up view of the mountain. Paradise is the park's most popular destination, so expect crowds. During July and August the meadows here are ablaze with wildflowers. The circular Henry M. Jackson Memorial Visitor Center provides 360° panoramic views, and a short walk away is a spot from which you can look down on Nisqually Glacier. Many miles of other trails lead out from Paradise, looping through meadows and up onto snowfields above timberline. It's not unusual to find plenty of snow at Paradise as late as July. In 1972 the area set a world's record for snowfall in one year: 93.5 feet!

In summer you can continue beyond Paradise to the Ohanapecosh Visitor Center, where you can walk through a forest of old-growth trees, some more than 1,000 years old. Continuing around the mountain, you'll reach the turnoff for Sunrise. At 6,400 feet, Sunrise is the highest spot accessible by car. A beautiful old log lodge serves as the visitor center. From here you can see not only Mount Rainier, seemingly at arm's length, but also Mounts Baker and Adams. Some of the park's most scenic trails begin at Sunrise.

If you want to see a bit of dense forest or hike without crowds, head for the park's Carbon River entrance in the northwest corner. This is the least visited region of the park because it only offers views to those willing to hike several miles uphill. At 3 miles, there's a glacier plowing through the middle of the rain forest, and at about 5 miles you reach meadows and in-your-face views of the northwest flank of Mount Rainier. Carbon River is formed by the lowest-elevation glacier in the contiguous 48 states.

WHERE TO STAY

Besides the two accommodations listed below, there are several campgrounds in Mount Rainier National Park. While the campgrounds don't take reservations (arrive early for the best chance of getting a site), the inns do, and you should call months in advance for summer weekends.

National Park Inn. P.O. Box 108, Ashford, WA 98304. ☎ **360/569-2275.** 25 rms (18 with private bath). $61 double without bath; $84–$113 double with bath. AE, CB, DC, DISC, MC, V. Free parking.

Located in Longmire, in the southwest corner of the park, this rustic lodge opened in 1920 and was fully renovated in 1990. Because this lodge attracts fewer visitors than Paradise's, it is often easier to find a room here, although you don't get the same breathtaking views. The inn's front veranda does have a view of the mountain, though, and it is here that guests often gather at sunset on clear days. This lodge stays

Impressions

There is a great deal in the remark of the discontented traveller: "When you have seen a pine forest, a bluff, a river, and a lake, you have seen all the scenery of western America. Sometimes the pine is three hundred feet high, and sometimes the rock is, and sometimes the lake is a hundred miles long. But it's all the same don't you know. I'm getting sick of it."

—Rudyard Kipling

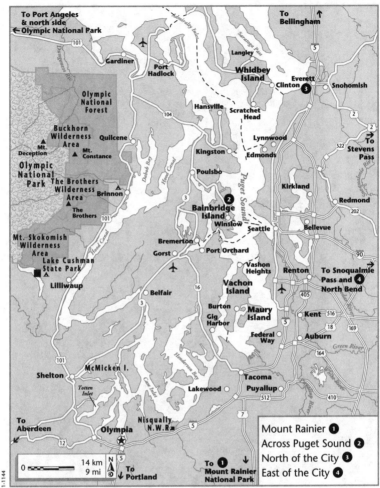

open in the winter, which makes it popular with cross-country skiers. Guest rooms vary in size and have rustic furnishings.

The inn's restaurant has a limited menu that nevertheless manages to offer something for everyone. There's also a lounge with a river-rock fireplace that's perfect for winter-night relaxing. A gift shop and cross-country ski rental shop are adjacent to the inn.

Paradise Inn. P.O. Box 108, Ashford, WA 98304. ☎ **360/569-2275.** 126 rms (95 with private bath), 2 suites. $65 double with shared bath; $92–$118 double with bath; $124 suite. AE, CB, DC, DISC, MC, V. Free parking. Closed early Oct–mid-May.

Built in 1917 high on the flanks of Mount Rainier in an area aptly known as Paradise, this rustic lodge offers breathtaking views of the mountain and nearby Nisqually Glacier. Cedar-shake siding, huge exposed beams, cathedral ceilings, and a gigantic stone fireplace all add up to a quintessential mountain retreat. However, this inn has seen a lot of use over the years and could stand a good renovation. Guest rooms vary in size. The best reason to stay here is that there are miles of trails and meadows

Mount Rainier National Park

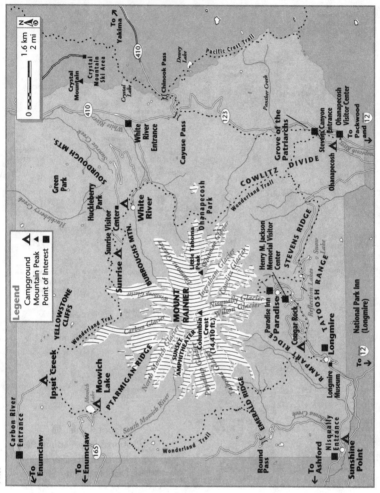

spreading out from the lodge, making this the perfect spot for some relatively easy alpine exploring.

The inn's large dining room serves three meals a day. The Sunday brunch is legendary. A snack bar and lounge are dining options. There is also a gift shop on the premises.

2 Across Puget Sound: Bainbridge Island, Naval History & Antiques

Outlined here is a possible day trip that starts on one ferry and ends on another. The excursion takes in the quiet and picturesque bedroom community of Bainbridge Island, which is popular for its miles of waterfront, its sound-and-mountain views, and its rural feel. Continuing on, you can visit a Native American museum, a Scandinavian town, a museum dedicated to undersea exploration, a mothballed destroyer, and a town full of antiques malls. There's more here than you can easily do in one day, so you should pick and choose what interests you the most.

Start the trip by taking the **Bainbridge Island ferry** from the ferry terminal at Pier 52 on the Seattle waterfront. The fares are $5.90 ($7.10 from mid-May to mid-October) for a car and driver one way, $3.50 for adult car passengers or walk-ons, and $1.75 for seniors and children ages 5 to 11. For a current sailing schedule, contact **Washington State Ferries** (☎ **800/84-FERRY** within Washington State, or 206/464-6400). On board, you can see the Seattle skyline, and on a clear day, Mount Rainier to the southeast and the Olympic Mountains to the west.

If you'd like to get closer to the water and do a little paddling in a sea kayak, turn left as you get off the ferry and head to Waterfront Park, where you'll find **Bainbridge Island Boat Rentals** (☎ **206/842-9229**), which rents single sea kayaks ($10 per hour) and double kayaks and swan boats ($15 per hour). They also rent canoes and rowboats.

Just up the hill from the Bainbridge Island ferry terminal is the island's main shopping district where you'll find some interesting shops and restaurants. If you'd like to sample the local wine, drop in at the **Bainbridge Island Vineyards and Winery,** 682 Wash. 305 (☎ **206/842-WINE**), which is located ¹/₄ mile up the hill from the ferry landing. The winery is open Wednesday through Sunday from noon to 5pm. Down at the south end of the island, you'll find **Fort Ward State Park** (☎ **206/842-4041**) on the quiet shore of Rich Passage. The park offers picnicking and good bird watching. The **Bainbridge Island Historical Museum,** 7650 NE High School Rd. (☎ **206/842-2773**), which is housed in a restored one-room schoolhouse built in 1908, is located at Strawberry Hill Park 1 mile west of Wash. 305. Museum hours change with the seasons; call for current hours. Donation requested. Garden enthusiasts will want to call ahead and make a reservation to visit the **Bloedel Reserve,** 7571 NE Dolphin Dr. (☎ **206/842-7631**), which is 6 miles north of the ferry terminal off Wash. 305 (turn right on Agate Point Road). Expansive and elegant grounds are the ideal place for a quiet stroll amid plants from around the world. Nearby, at the northern tip of the island, you'll find **Fay Bainbridge State Park** (☎ **206/842-3931**), which offers camping and great views across the sound to the Seattle skyline.

After crossing the Agate Passage Bridge to the mainland of the Kitsap Peninsula, take your first right, and as you approach the town of **Suquamish,** you will see signs for the grave of Chief Sealth, for whom Seattle was named. To visit the site of the **Old Man House,** which was a large Native American longhouse, return to Wash. 305, continue west, turn left at the Suquamish Hardware building, and watch for the sign. The Old Man House itself is long gone, but you'll find an informative sign and a small park with picnic tables. Continuing a little farther on Wash. 305, you'll see signs for the **Suquamish Museum,** 15838 Sandy Hook Road (☎ **360/598-3311,** ext. 422), on the Port Madison Indian Reservation. The museum houses a compelling history of Puget Sound's native people. May through September, the museum is open daily from 10am to 5pm; October through April, it's open Friday through Sunday from 11am to 4pm. Admission is $2.50 for adults and $1 for children.

Continuing north on Wash. 305, you next come to the small town of **Poulsbo,** which overlooks fjordlike Liberty Bay. Settled in the late 1880s by Scandinavians, Poulsbo was primarily a fishing, logging, and farming town until it decided to play up its Scandinavian heritage. Shops in the Scandinavian-inspired downtown sell all manner of Viking and Scandinavian souvenirs. Between downtown and the waterfront, you'll find Liberty Bay Park, and at the south end of Front Street, you'll find the **Marine Science Center,** 18743 Front St. NE (☎ **360/779-5549**), which houses interpretive displays on Puget Sound. The center is open Tuesday through Saturday from 10am to 4pm, Sunday and Monday from noon to 4pm. Admission is $2 for adults, $1 for seniors and children ages 2 through 12, $5 for families (free admission on the third Tuesday of each month). If you have a sweet tooth, don't miss **Sluys Poulsbo Bakery,** 18924 Front St. NE (☎ 360/697-BAKE), which bakes mounds of goodies, as well as stick-to-your-ribs breads. In May the annual Viking Fest celebrates traditional Scandinavian culture, as do the Midsommarfest and Yule Log Festival. For more information, contact the **Greater Poulsbo Chamber of Commerce,** 19131 Eight Ave. NE (P.O. Box 1063), Poulsbo, WA 98370 (☎ 360/779-4848).

If you have time and enjoy visiting historic towns, continue north from Poulsbo on Wash. 3 to **Port Gamble**. This community was established in 1853 as a company town for the Pope and Talbot lumber mill, which was for many years the oldest operating lumber mill on the West Coast. Along the town's shady streets are many Victorian homes that were restored by Pope and Talbot. Stop by the Port Gamble Country Store, which now houses the **Port Gamble Historical Museum** (☎ 360/297-8074). Admission is $2 for adults and $1 for seniors and students; open daily 10:30am to 5pm from May 1 to Columbus Day, Monday through Friday from 10:30am to 4pm the rest of the year. The same location is home to the **Of Sea and Shore Museum** (☎ 360/297-2426), where admission is free and hours are daily 10am to 5pm. The former museum is a collection of local memorabilia, while the latter exhibits seashells from around the world.

From Port Gamble, head south on Wash. 3 toward Bremerton to begin an exploration of the area's naval history. Between Poulsbo and Silverdale, you will be passing just east of the **Bangor Navy Base,** which is home port for a fleet of Trident nuclear submarines. The base is on Hood Canal, a long narrow arm of Puget Sound. Near the town of Keyport, you can visit the **Naval Undersea Museum,** Garnett Way (☎ 360/396-4148), which is located 3 miles east of Wash. 3 on Wash. 308. The museum examines all aspects of undersea exploration, with interactive exhibits, models, displays that include a deep-sea exploration and research craft, a Japanese kamikaze torpedo, and a deep-sea rescue vehicle. The museum is open daily from 10am to 4pm (closed on Tuesdays between October and May), and admission is free.

Continuing south, you come to **Bremerton,** which is home to the Puget Sound Naval Shipyard, where mothballed U.S. Navy ships have included the aircraft carriers USS *Nimitz* and USS *Midway* and the battleships USS *Missouri* and USS *New Jersey*. Between May 15 and September 30, **Kitsap Harbor Tours,** 290 Washington Ave. no. 7 (☎ 360/377-8924), offers boat tours of the mothballed fleet and shipyard hourly between 11am and 4pm. Tours are $8.50 for adults, $7.50 for seniors, and $5.50 for children ages 5 to 12. One mothballed destroyer, the USS *Turner Joy,* is now operated by the **Bremerton Historic Ships Association** (☎ 360/792-2457) and is open to the public as a memorial to those who have served in the U.S. Navy and who have helped build the navy's ships. The *Turner Joy* is docked about 150 yards east of the Washington State Ferries terminal. In summer the ship is open daily from 10am to 5pm; from October 1 to May 14, the ship is only open Thursday through Monday from 10am to 4pm. Admission is $5 for adults, $4 for senior citizens and the military, and $3 for children ages 5 to 12. Combination Turner Joy Harbor Tour tickets are also available. Nearby is the **Bremerton Naval Museum,** 130 Washington Ave. (☎ 360/479-7447), which showcases naval history and the historic contributions of the Puget Sound Naval Shipyard. The museum is open Monday through Saturday from 10am to 5pm and Sunday from 1 to 5pm; from

Labor Day through Memorial Day, the museum is only open Tuesday through Sunday and closes at 4pm daily. Admission is free.

To return to Seattle, take the car ferry from Bremerton to Seattle. Fares back to Seattle are charged for vehicles and drivers only, not for passengers.

3 North of the City: Jumbo Jets, Wine & Antiques

This driving excursion takes in the world's largest building, a town full of antique stores, wineries, and a picturesque lakeshore community.

Roughly 30 miles north of Seattle on I-5 on the shore of Puget Sound is the city of **Everett.** Though for the most part it has become a bedroom community for Seattle commuters, it is also home to the region's single largest employer: Boeing. It is here in Everett that the aircraft manufacturer has its main assembly plant. This is the single largest building, by volume, in the world and easily could hold 911 basketball courts, 74 football fields, 2,142 average-size homes, or all of Disneyland (with room left over for covered parking). Free guided 1-hour tours of the facility are held Monday through Friday throughout the year. The schedule varies with the time of year, so be sure to call ahead for details and directions to the plant. Children under 50 inches tall are not allowed, and the tours are first-come, first-served. For more information, contact the **Boeing Tour Center,** Wash. 526, Everett (☎ **800/464-1476** or 206/544-1264).

A few miles east of Everett off U.S. 2, you can jump from the jet age to horse-and-buggy-days in the historic town of **Snohomish.** Established in 1859 on the banks of the Snohomish River, this historic town was, until 1897 the county seat. However, when the county seat was moved to Everett, Snohomish lost its regional importance and development slowed considerably. Today, an abundance of turn-of-the-century buildings are the legacy of the town's early economic growth. By the 1960s these old homes began attracting people interested in restoring them to their original condition, and soon antique shops began proliferating in historic downtown Snohomish. Today the town has more than 400 antique dealers and is without a doubt the antique capital of the Northwest. Surrounding the town's commercial core are neighborhoods full of restored Victorian homes. Each year in September, you can get a peek inside some of the town's most elegant homes on the annual Historical Society Home Tour. You can pick up a copy of a guide to the town's antique stores and its historic homes by stopping by or contacting the **Snohomish Chamber of Commerce,** P.O. Box 135, Snohomish, WA 98291 (☎ **360/568-2526**).

While in town, you may want to visit the **Blackman Museum,** 118 Avenue B (☎ **360/568-5235**), which is housed in an 1879 Queen Anne Victorian that has been restored and filled with period furnishings. The museum is open daily from noon to 4pm in summer (Wednesday through Sunday from noon to 4pm other months), and admission is $1 for adults and 50¢ for seniors and children. For another glimpse into the town's past, head over to Pioneer Village, a collection of restored cabins and other old buildings on Second Street. Each of the buildings is furnished with period antiques. Pioneer Village is open the same hours as the Blackman Museum, and admission is $1.50 for adults and $1 for seniors and children.

Heading south from Snohomish to **Woodinville** on Wash. 9 and then Wash. 522 brings you into Puget Sound's small wine region. The first winery you're likely to encounter here is the tiny **Silver Lake Sparkling Cellars,** 17721 132nd Ave. NE, Woodinville (☎ **425/486-1900**), located in an industrial area near the junction of Wash. 522 and Wash. 202. Although this place lacks character, they craft some excellent red wines. From here, head south on Wash. 202 (Woodinville-Redmond Road), where you'll come to **Facelli Winery,** 16120 Woodinville-Redmond NE no. 1 (☎ 206/488-1020), which is open for tastings only on the weekends. Largest and most famous of the wineries in the area is **Chateau Ste. Michelle,** 14111 NE 145th St., Woodinville (☎ 425/488-3300), located in a grand mansion on a historic estate that was established in 1912. The winery, which is the largest in Washington, is known for the consistent quality of its wines. An amphitheater on the grounds stages music performances throughout the summer. To reach the winery, head south from Woodinville on Wash. 202 and watch for signs. Right across the road from Chateau Ste. Michelle, you'll find **Columbia Winery,** 14030 NE 145th St. (☎ 425/488-2776), which unfortunately doesn't seem to have the same touch with wines that its neighbor does. If beer is more to your tastes, you can stop in at the large **Red Hook Brewery,** 14030 NE 145th St. (☎ 425/483-3232), home to the Forecaster's Pub and right next door to Columbia Winery.

Finish your day with a walk around downtown **Kirkland,** which is along the Moss Bay waterfront. You can stroll along the waterfront and stop in at interesting shops and any of more than a dozen art galleries. There are also several decent restaurants in the area. We like **Bistro Provençal,** 212 Central Way (☎ 425/827-3300), a very reasonably priced French restaurant in downtown Kirkland. For two other restaurant recommendations, see "The Eastside" section of chapter 5. To get back to Seattle, take I-405 south to I-90.

4 East of the City: The Snoqualmie Valley

While Seattle has become a sprawling city of congested highways and high housing prices, there is a reason why so many people put up with the city's drawbacks. Less than an hour east lie mountains so vast and rugged that you can hike for a week without ever crossing a road. Between the city and this wilderness lies the **Snoqualmie Valley,** the Seattle region's last bit of bucolic countryside. Here you'll find small towns, pastures full of spotted cows, "U-pick" farms, and even a few unexpected attractions, including an impressive (and familiar) waterfall and, in summer, a medieval fair. While driving the back roads of the Snoqualmie Valley, keep an eye out for historic markers that include old photos and details about its past.

Snoqualmie Falls, the valley's biggest attraction, plummet 270 feet into a pool of deep blue water. The falls are surrounded by a park owned by Puget Power, which operates a hydroelectric plant inside the rock wall behind the falls. The plant, built in 1898, was the world's first underground electric-generating facility. Within the park you'll find two overlooks near the lip of the falls and a half-mile-long trail leading down to the base of the falls. The river below the falls is popular both for fishing and for white-water kayaking. These falls will be familiar to anyone who remembers the opening sequence of the hit David Lynch TV show *Twin Peaks,* which was filmed in this area. (Anyone interested in seeing other *Twin Peaks* filming sites should stop by the **Salish Lodge** [at the top of the falls] before heading into the town of North Bend to the **Mar-T Cafe** [☎ 425/888-1221], where you can still get "damn good pie.") To reach the falls, take I-90 east from Seattle for 35 to 45 minutes and get off at exit 27.

Snoqualmie Falls are located just outside the town of **Snoqualmie,** which is where you'll find the restored 1890 railroad depot used by the **Puget Sound and Snoqualmie Railroad** (☎ 425/746-4025). On weekends between April and October, 40-minute railway excursions, using steam or diesel trains, run between here and the town of **North Bend.** The fares are $6 for adults, $5 for seniors, and $4 for children ages 3 to 12. Be sure to call ahead for a current schedule.

In North Bend, you can learn more about the history of this valley at the **Snoqualmie Valley Historical Museum,** Gardiner-Weeks Park, Park Street (☎ **425/888-3200**), which is only 3 blocks from the railroad depot. Also in North Bend is a large factory outlet mall, if you're in the mood to do some discount shopping. Outside of North Bend rises **Mount Si,** one of the most frequently hiked mountains in the state. This mountain, carved by glaciers long ago, presents a dramatic face to the valley, and if you are the least bit athletic, it is hard to resist the temptation to hike to the top (take lots of water—it's an 8-mile round-trip hike). To reach the trailhead, drive east of downtown North Bend on North Bend Way, turn left on Mount Si Road, turn right after crossing the Snoqualmie River, and continue another 2.5 miles.

Down the Snoqualmie Valley from the falls, you'll come to the town of **Fall City,** which is home to one of the Northwest's best loved farms: **The Herbfarm,** 32804 Issaquah–Fall City Rd. (☎ **206/784-2222**), which has been closed due to a fire and is scheduled to reopen in June of 1998. Started in 1974 with a wheelbarrow full of potted herbs, The Herbfarm has since blossomed into a farm, country store, school, theme gardens, mail-order business, and the region's most famous (and most expensive) restaurant (see "The Eastside" section of chapter 5 for details).

Between Fall City and the town of **Carnation,** you'll pass several "U-pick" farms, where you can pick your own berries during the summer or pumpkins in the fall.

On weekends between late July and early September, the Snoqualmie Valley is also the site of the **Camlann Medieval Faire** (☎ **425/788-1353**), which is located north of Carnation off Wash. 203. This reproduction of a medieval village is home to knights and squires, minstrels, and assorted other costumed merrymakers. There are crafts stalls, food booths, and, the highlight each day, jousting matches. Medieval clothing is available for rent if you don't happen to have any of your own. There are also evening banquets. Faire admission is $8 for adults, $5 for seniors and children ages 6 to 12, free for children 5 and under. Admission to both the faire and the banquet is $35.

WHERE TO STAY

Salish Lodge and Spa. 6501 Railroad Ave. SE (P.O. Box 1109), Snoqualmie, WA 98065. ☎ **800/826-6124,** 800/2SALISH, or 425/888-2556. 91 rms, 4 suites. A/C TV TEL. $129–$269 double; $450–$599 suite. AE, CB, DC, DISC, MC, V. Free parking.

Set at the top of 270-foot Snoqualmie Falls and only 35 minutes east of Seattle on I-90, Salish Lodge is a popular weekend getaway spot for folks from Seattle. With its country lodge atmosphere, the Salish aims for casual comfort and hits the mark. Guest rooms are furnished with wicker and Shaker furnishings and have down comforters on the beds. With fireplaces and whirlpool baths in every room, this lodge is made for romantic weekend getaways. To make this an even more attractive getaway, a full-service spa was added in 1996, making this the only resort hotel in the Northwest with a spa. Anyone who was a fan of *Twin Peaks* should immediately recognize the hotel.

Dining/Entertainment: The lodge's country breakfast is a legendary feast that will likely keep you full right through to dinner when you can dine on creative Northwest cuisine in the **Salish Dining Room.** The dining room also has one of the most extensive wine lists in the state. In the **Attic Lounge,** you can catch a glimpse of the falls through the window.

Services: Room service, concierge, valet/laundry service, complimentary morning coffee and afternoon tea and cookies, baby-sitting.

Facilities: Full-service spa offering a wide range of body treatments and massages, exercise room, whirlpools, general store.

11 Introducing Portland

Situated at the confluence of the Willamette and Columbia rivers, Portland, with a population of 1.7 million people in the metropolitan area, is a city of discreet charms. While Seattle flaunts its attractions and has positioned itself as a major tourist destination, Portland's merits are not nearly so in-your-face as those of its neighbor to the north. Sure the city has museums and nightclubs, a zoo and a strollable waterfront, but to truly understand why so many people want to live here, you must go beyond the obvious, explore its public gardens and funky neighborhoods, hunt out its outdoor art, and visit its crafts galleries and market.

There is a laid-back air about the city that soon seeps into the bones of most visitors. Unlike so many other cities, Portland seems to be set firmly in the slow lane. Sure, people here can't be parted from their cell phones and beepers, but this is the City of Roses, and people still stop and smell those flowers.

Because Portland is so clean, it has been compared to a theme park, but Portland has far too much soul to be just a picture-perfect city of dreams. Sure, spotless streets, a greensward stretching the entire length of the downtown waterfront, and free trolleys give the city an all-American hometown feel straight out of a Jimmy Stewart movie, but Portland also has a quirky side.

This is the city that launched a thousand microbrews, the city that claims both the world's smallest city park and the largest forested urban park in the country. While street kids, attracted by the city's benign climate and lively music scene, congregate in Pioneer Courthouse Square, those with money in their pockets fill the sidewalk tables of the Nob Hill and Hawthorne neighborhoods. Attend a symphony concert and you're likely to see people in shorts and rafting sandals as well as tuxedos and evening dresses. To encourage bicycle commuting, there are now downtown public showers for cyclists.

For a large percentage of the city's population, outdoor sports are still the raison d'être for living here. This is understandable when you consider the geographic setting of the city. After an hour's drive east, you can be on the slopes of Mount Hood skiing, hiking, or mountain biking or at Hood River on the Columbia River catching big air on a sailboard. Just 1 1/2 hours west, and you're walking the beach, hiking coastal trails, or even surfing the chilly waters of the Pacific.

1   Frommer's Favorite Portland Experiences

- **Hanging Out at Powell's.** They don't call Powell's the City of Books for nothing. This bookstore, selling both new and used books, is huge (you have to get a map at the front door). No matter how much time I spend here, it's never enough. A large cafe makes it all that much easier to while away hours reading something you found on the shelves but aren't sure you want to buy.

- **Free Rides on the Vintage Trolleys.** Tri-Met buses and Max light-rail trolleys are all free within a large downtown area known as the fareless square. That alone should be enough to get you on some form of public transit while you're in town, but if you're really lucky, you might catch one of the vintage trolley cars. There aren't any San Francisco–style hills, but these old trolley cars are still fun to ride.

- **People-Watching at Pioneer Courthouse Square.** This is the heart and soul of downtown Portland, and no matter what time of year or what the weather, people gather here. Grab a latte at the Starbucks and sit by the waterfall fountain. In summer, there are concerts here, both at lunch and in the evenings, and any time of year you might catch a rally, performance, or installation of some kind. Don't miss the weather machine show at noon.

- **Beer Sampling at Brewpubs.** They may not have invented beer here in Portland, but they certainly have turned it into an art form. Whether you're looking for a cozy corner pub or an upscale tap room, you'll find a brewpub where you can feel comfortable sampling what local brewmeisters are concocting. Try a raspberry hefeweizen for a true Northwest beer experience.

- **An Afternoon at the Portland Saturday Market.** This large arts-and-crafts market is an outdoor showcase for hundreds of the Northwest's creative artisans. You'll find fascinating one-of-a-kind clothes, jewelry, kitchen wares, musical instruments, and much, much more. The food stalls serve up some great fast food, too.

- **Strolling the Grounds at the Japanese Garden.** This is the best Japanese Garden in the United States, perhaps the best anywhere outside of Japan. My favorite time to visit is in June when the Japanese irises are in bloom. There's no better stress-reducer in the city.

- **Concerts at the Schnitz.** The Arlene Schnitzer Concert Hall is a restored 1920s movie palace and is the city's most impressive place to attend a performance. Even if the show doesn't meet your expectations, you can enjoy the classic architectural details. This theater is home to the Oregon Symphony.

- **Summertime Concerts at the Washington Park Zoo.** Summertime in Portland means partying with the pachyderms. Two evenings a week throughout the summer, you can catch live music at the zoo's amphitheater. Musical styles include blues, bluegrass, folk, ethnic, and jazz. For the price of zoo admission, you can catch the concert and tour the zoo (if you arrive early enough). Picnics are encouraged, but no alcohol is allowed into the zoo (however, beer and wine are on sale during concerts).

- **Summer Festivals at Waterfront Park.** Each summer, Tom McCall Waterfront Park, which stretches along the Willamette River in downtown Portland, becomes the staging ground for everything from Rose Festival events to the Oregon Brewers Festival. Some festivals are free and some have small cover charges, but all are lots of fun.

- **First Thursday Art Walk.** On the first Thursday of every month, Portland goes on an art binge. People get dressed up and go gallery hopping from art opening to art opening. There are usually hors d'oeuvres and wine available, and sometimes there's even live music. The galleries stay open until 9pm, and there are usually free shuttles to get you from one gallery district to another.

Portland Orientation

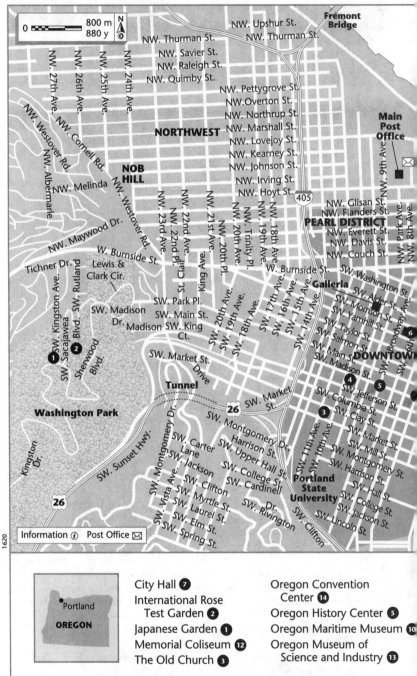

0 | 800 m / 880 y

NW. Upshur St.
Fremont Bridge
NW. Thurman St.
NW. Thurman St.
NW. Savier St.
NW. Raleigh St.
NW. Quimby St.
NW. Pettygrove St.
NW. Overton St.
NW. Northrup St.
NORTHWEST NW. Marshall St.
NW. Lovejoy St.
NW. Kearney St.
NW. Johnson St.
NW. Irving St.
NW. Hoyt St. 405
Main Post Office

NW. 27th Ave.
NW. 26th Ave.
NW. 25th Ave.
NW. 24th Ave.
NW. Westover Rd.
NW. Cornell Rd.
NW. Albermarle
NW. Melinda

NOB HILL

NW. 23rd Ave.
NW. 22nd Ave.
NW. 22nd pl.
NW. 21st Ave.
NW. 20th Pl.
NW. Trinity Pl.
NW. 20th Ave.

NW. Maywood Dr.
NW. Westover Rd.
Tichner Dr.
W. Burnside St.
Lewis & Clark Cir.

NW. Glisan St.
NW. Flanders St.
PEARL DISTRICT
NW. Everett St.
NW. Davis St.
NW. Couch St.

NW. Park Ave.
NW. 8th Ave.
NW. 9th Ave.

NW. 18th Ave.
NW. 19th Ave.
W. Burnside St.

Galleria
SW. Washington St.
SW. Alder St.
SW. Morrison St.
SW. Yamhill St.
SW. Taylor St.
SW. Salmon St.
SW. Main St.
SW. Madison St.
DOWNTOWN

Broadway Ave.
SW. 6th Ave.

SW. Park Pl.
SW. Main St.
SW. Madison Dr.
Madison SW. King Ct.

SW. 20th Ave.
SW. 19th Ave.
SW. 18th Ave.
SW. 17th Ave.
SW. 16th Ave.
SW. 15th Ave.
SW. 14th Ave.

SW. Kingston Ave.
SW. Sacajawea
Sherwood Blvd.
SW. Rutland

1 2

SW. Market St. Drive
Tunnel
26
SW. Market St.

SW. Jefferson St
SW. Columbia St.
SW. Clay St.
SW. Market St.
SW. Mill St.
SW. Montgomery St.
SW. Harrison St
SW. Hall St
SW. College St.
SW. Jackson St.
SW. Lincoln St.

4 5
3

Washington Park

Kingston Dr.

SW. Sunset Hwy.
SW. Montgomery Dr.
SW. Carter Lane
SW. Jackson
SW. Clifton
SW. Vista Ave.
SW. Myrtle St.
SW. Laurel St.
SW. Elm St.
SW. Spring St.

SW. Montgomery Dr.
Harrison St.
SW. Upper Hall St.
SW. College St.
SW. Cardinell
Dr.
SW. Rivington
SW. Clifton

Portland State University

SW. 11th Ave.
SW. 10th Ave.

26

1620

Information ⓘ   Post Office ✉

OREGON
• Portland

City Hall ❼
International Rose Test Garden ❷
Japanese Garden ❶
Memorial Coliseum ⑫
The Old Church ❸

Oregon Convention Center ⑭
Oregon History Center ❺
Oregon Maritime Museum ❿
Oregon Museum of Science and Industry ⑬

146

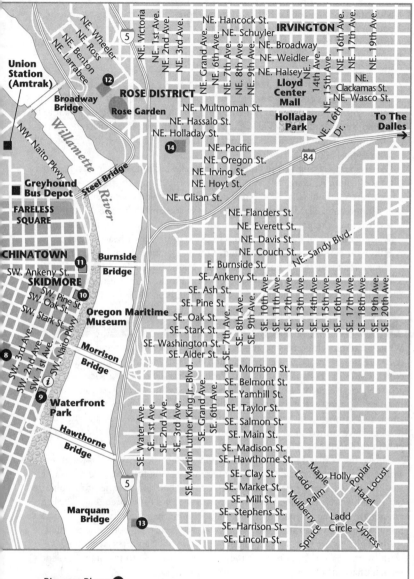

Pioneer Place **8**
Pioneer Courthouse Square **6**
Portland Art Museum **4**
Portland Saturday Market **11**
World Trade Center **9**

- **Mountain-Biking the Leif Ericson Road.** Forest Park is the largest forested city park in the country, and running its length is the unpaved Leif Ericson Road. The road is closed to cars and extends for 12 miles. Along the way, there are occasional views of the Columbia River and the city's industrial neighborhoods. This is a pretty easy ride, without any strenuous climbs.
- **Kayaking Around Ross Island.** Seattle may be the sea kayaking capital of the Northwest, but Portland's not a bad spot for pursuing this sport either. You can paddle on the Columbia or Willamette River, but my favorite easy paddle is around Ross Island in the Willamette River. You can even paddle past the submarine at the Oregon Museum of Science and Industry and pull out at Tom McCall Waterfront Park.
- **Driving and Hiking in the Gorge.** No matter what time of year it is, the drive up the Columbia Gorge is spectacular. If you've got time to spare, take the scenic highway; if not, take I-84. No matter which road you take, be sure to pull off at Multnomah Falls. There are dozens of easily accessible hiking trails throughout the length of the gorge. For an alternative point of view, drive through on the Washington side of the river and stop to climb to the top of Beacon Rock.
- **Hiking and Skiing on Mount Hood.** Less than an hour from Portland, Mount Hood offers year-round skiing and hiking. Timberline Lodge, high on this dormant volcano's slopes, was built by the Works Project Administration during the Great Depression and is a showcase of craftsmanship.

2 The City Today

While Seattle has zoomed into the national consciousness, Portland has, until recently, managed to dodge the limelight and the problems that come with skyrocketing popularity. For many years now Portland has looked upon itself as a small, accessible city, vaguely European in character. *Clean* and *friendly* are the two terms that crop up most often in descriptions of the city. However, as word has spread about overcrowding in Seattle, people looking for the good life and affordable housing have turned to Portland. Today the city is experiencing the same rapid growth that Seattle has gone through for the past decade.

Today, the Portland metropolitan area is facing a battle over how best to develop while still maintaining its distinctive character. As a "big little city," and less interested in growth at any cost as Seattle seems to be, Portland has tried to emphasize quality of life over economic progress, and for now seems to be succeeding. The light-rail system offers an alternative to automobile commuting. The city's Percent for Art program ensures a beautiful downtown, with every new public building required to spend slightly more than 1% of building costs on public art. Special cleaning crews work overtime to pick up trash in the downtown, helping to maintain Portland's reputation as one of the cleanest city's in the country.

To anyone who lives in Portland, however, the city's greatest attributes are its ease of accessibility to the mountains and the coast and the close proximity of idyllic rural settings. Within 30 minutes' drive from downtown, you can be out in the country, and within an hour and a half, you can be walking on the beach, skiing on Mount Hood, fishing in the Sandy River, hiking the Barlow Trail, or sampling a Pinot Noir at a winery. The city's distinct boundary between urban and rural is no accident. Portland's Urban Growth Boundary (UGB) was a demarcation line drawn in the 1970s to prevent the city from experiencing the sort of suburban sprawl characteristic of Californian cities. The UGB has worked well for the past 20 years, but while this city is often cited as a model of urban planning, the truth is that growth guidelines established more than 20 years ago are only now being tested. With ever-increasing pressures from developers, Portland is at a crossroads. Whether it will sprawl beyond its current boundaries or remain a compact city is the big question of the next few years.

For several years now Portland has been extending its light-rail system into its western suburbs of Beaverton and Hillsboro, which are the heart of the region's high-tech industries and home to such companies as Intel, Epson, Fujitsu, and NEC. It is also here that athletic-wear giant Nike is headquartered. Over the life of this book, this MAX light-rail line should finally open, and with it a new chapter in the metropolitan region's growth. Urban planners have redesignated areas around light-rail stations as areas for high-density development in hopes of providing a viable option to commuting by car.

With growth has also come the renovation and gentrification of long neglected neighborhoods throughout Portland. The greatest change in recent years has been in the Pearl District, a neighborhood of old warehouses converted into upscale lofts. This has been the center of the city's art gallery scene for several years now, but with more and more new town houses being built in the area, it is questionable whether gallery owners will be able to pay the escalating rents in upcoming years.

Northwest Portland's Nob Hill area, once filled with funky boutiques, has gone progressively more upscale over the past few years, with the Gap, Pottery Barn, and Urban Outfitters all taking up residence here. Today fans of funky shops and eateries must venture farther from downtown to areas such as the Hawthorne District, Irvington, Sellwood, Southeast Belmont Street, and Multnomah Village. However, the very fact that these neighborhoods are alive and well is a sign that Portland is taking its growth in stride.

Old Town, a neighborhood that should be the busiest in the city, has never managed to slough off its negative image. Home to both the city's finest restored historic buildings and several missions and soup kitchens for the homeless, the area attracts street people and drug dealers, which together keep most other people from venturing into this area except on weekends when the Portland Saturday Market is in full swing. The market is, however, a major point of pride to Portlanders who like to show off the creativity of the region's many craftspeople.

Another positive aspect of Portland's current growth is the restaurant renaissance the city has been experiencing. New restaurants continue to open with astounding regularity all over the city. Where once good restaurants were confined to a few neighborhoods, today you are as likely to find a great French restaurant in an obscure residential neighborhood as you are to find a fine Northwest-style restaurant downtown.

Portland today is growing quickly, though so far with a deliberation that has not compromised the city's values and unique characteristics. Whether this controlled and intelligent growth can continue remains to be seen. However, for now Portland remains a city both cosmopolitan and accessible.

3 A Look at the Past

Portland was once a very inexpensive piece of property. In 1844 it sold for $50, double the original price of Manhattan Island. Before that, however, it had been purchased for just 25¢, although the original purchaser had to borrow the quarter. Remember that there was nothing here at the time. This was a wilderness, and anyone who thought it would ever be anything more was either foolish or extremely farsighted.

Asa Lovejoy and William Overton, the two men who staked the original claim to Portland, were the

Dateline

- **1805** Lewis and Clark expedition passes down the Columbia River on its journey to the Pacific Ocean.
- **1834** Methodist missionaries settle at the confluence of the Columbia and Willamette rivers.

continues

- **1843** Asa Lovejoy and William Overton file a claim for 640 acres on the site of present-day Portland. Filing fee: 25¢.
- **1844** Francis Pettygrove enters into partnership with Lovejoy, buying Overton's share for $50.
- **1845** The name Portland wins over Boston in a coin toss between Pettygrove and Lovejoy.
- **1851** Portland is incorporated.
- **1872** Fire levels most of city.
- **1873** A second fire devastates Portland.
- **1888** First Portland rose show.
- **1905** Centenary celebration of the Lewis and Clark expedition.
- **1907** Annual rose show becomes Portland Rose Festival.
- **1927** Downtown wharves are demolished and a seawall is built.
- **1974** Expressway removed from the west bank of Willamette River to create Waterfront Park.
- **1980** Design for Pioneer Courthouse Square, which has become the city's heart and focal point of downtown activities, is chosen.
- **1990** The Oregon Convention Center, with its twin towers, is completed.
- **1995** The Rose Garden, the city's new basketball stadium, sees its first season.
- **1996** February flood waters come within inches of spilling out of the Willamette River and into downtown Portland.
- **1997** After much controversy, areas are chosen for future expansion of city's urban growth boundary.

latter: farsighted. From this spot on the Willamette River they could see snow-capped Mount Hood 50 miles away; they liked the view and figured other people might also. These two were as disparate as a pair of founding fathers could be. Overton was a penniless drifter. No one is sure where he came from, or where he went when he left less than a year later. Lovejoy had attended Harvard College and graduated from Amherst. He was one of the earliest settlers to venture by wagon train to the Oregon country.

These two men were traveling by canoe from Fort Vancouver, the Hudson's Bay Company fur-trading center on the Columbia River, to the town of Oregon City on the Willamette River. Midway through their journey they stopped to rest at a clearing on the west bank of the Willamette. Overton suggested they stake a claim to the spot. It was commonly believed that Oregon would soon become a U.S. territory and that the federal government would pass out free 640-acre land claims. Overton wanted to be sure that he got his due. Unfortunately, he didn't have the 25¢ required to file a claim. In exchange for half the claim, Lovejoy loaned him the money. Not a bad return on a 25¢ investment!

Wanderlust struck Overton before he could do anything with his claim, and he bartered his half to one Francis Pettygrove for $50 worth of supplies and headed off for parts unknown. Overton must have thought he had turned a pretty deal—from a borrowed quarter to $50 in under a year is a respectable return. Pettygrove, a steadfast Yankee like Lovejoy, was a merchant with ideas on how to make a fortune. Alas, all poor Overton got in the end was a single street named after him.

Pettygrove lost no time in setting up a store on the waterfront, and now with a single building on the site, it was time to name the town. Pettygrove was from Maine and wanted to name the new town for his beloved Portland; Lovejoy was from Boston and wanted that name for the new settlement. A coin was flipped, Pettygrove called it correctly, and a new Portland was born.

Portland was a relative latecomer to the region. Oregon City, Fort Vancouver, Milwaukie, and St. Helens were all doing business in the area when Portland was still just a glimmer in the eyes of Lovejoy and Overton. But in 1846 things changed quickly. Another New Englander, Capt. John Couch, sailed up the Willamette, dropped anchor in Portland, and decided to make this the headquarters for his shipping company.

Impressions

Oregon is seldom heard of. Its people believe in the Bible, and hold that all radicals should be lynched. It has no poets and no statesmen.

—H.L. Mencken, *Americana*, 1925

It's like a town version of New York. You can walk around. People are hanging out in coffee shops.

—Faye Dunaway during a film shoot in Portland

Another enterprising gentleman, a southerner named Daniel Lownsdale, opened a tannery outside town and helped build a road through the West Hills to the wheat farms of the Tualatin Valley. With a road from the farm country and a small port to ship the wheat to market, Portland became the most important town in the region.

With the 1848 discovery of gold in California, and the subsequent demand for such Oregon products as grain and timber, Portland became a booming little town of 800.

By the late 1880s Portland was connected to the rest of the country by several railroad lines, and by 1900 the population had grown to 90,000. In 1905 the city hosted the Lewis and Clark Exposition, that year's World's Fair, which celebrated the centennial of the explorers' journey to the Northwest. The fairgrounds, landscaped by John Olmsted, son and successor to New York City's Central Park designer Frederick Law Olmsted, were a great hit. The city of Portland also proved popular with visitors; by 1910 its population had exploded to 250,000.

By this time, however, there were even more roses than there were people. Since 1888 Portland had been holding an annual rose show, but in 1907 it had blossomed into a full-fledged Rose Festival. Today the annual festival, held each June, is still Portland's favorite celebration. More than 400 varieties bloom in the International Rose Test Gardens in Washington Park, lending Portland the sobriquet "City of Roses."

The 1900s have been a roller-coaster ride of boom and bust for Portland. The phenomenal growth of the city's first 50 years has slowed. While timber and agriculture are still the mainstays of the Oregon economy, the Portland area has developed a high-tech industrial base that has allowed its economy to diversify and continue to prosper.

But, Portlanders tend to have a different idea of prosperity than residents of most other cities. Nature and the city's relationship to it have been an integral part of life here. As far back as 100 years ago the Willamette River was a favored recreation site, with canoe clubs racing on its clean waters. But 20th century industries brought pollution that killed the river. Downtown Portland lost its preeminence as a shipping port, and the wharves were torn down and replaced by a freeway. This was akin to cutting out Portland's very heart and soul. But the freeway didn't last long.

With the heightened environmental awareness of the 1960s and 1970s, Portland's basic character and love of nature began to resurface. A massive cleanup of the Willamette was undertaken; it was eventually so successful that today salmon once again migrate up the Willamette River. The freeway was torn up and replaced with Tom McCall Waterfront Park, a large expanse of lawns, trees, fountains, and promenades. But this is only one in a grand network of parks, a so-called "Emerald Necklace" that was first envisioned by the Olmsteads back in the early 1900s. Today, the city is ringed with parks, including Forest Park, the largest wooded city park in the United States, and Washington Park, which is home to the International Rose Test Gardens, Japanese Garden, Metro Washington Park Zoo, and Hoyt Arboretum. It is this deep-rooted love of nature and the outdoors that seems to have molded this city for more than a century now and will hopefully continue to guide the city in its future growth.

Planning a Trip to Portland

Planning before you leave can make all the difference between enjoying your trip and wishing you had stayed home. For many people, in fact, planning a trip is half the fun of going. You can write to the addresses below for interesting packets of information that are created to get you excited about your upcoming trip.

One of your first considerations should be when you want to visit. Summer is the peak season in the Northwest. That's when the sun shines and outdoor festivals and events take place. During the summer, hotel and car reservations are almost essential; the rest of the year, they are highly advisable. You usually get better rates by reserving at least 1 or 2 weeks in advance.

1 Visitor Information

For information on Portland and the rest of Oregon, contact the **Portland/Oregon Visitors Association,** Three World Trade Center, 26 SW Salmon St., Portland, OR 97204-3299 (☎ **800/ 345-3214** or 503/222-2223; Web site: (www.pova.com). There is also an information booth by the baggage-claim area at Portland Airport.

2 When to Go

While summer is the sunniest season in Portland, and the obvious time to visit, it is also the most crowded time of year here. Although this city is not yet so popular a destination that you can't usually get a room in town at the last minute, you'll definitely have more choices if you plan ahead. If, on the other hand, you visit in one of the rainier months between October and April, you'll find lower hotel room rates and almost as much to see and do.

CLIMATE

This is the section you've all been looking for. You've all heard about the horrible weather in the Northwest. It rains all year, right? Wrong! The Portland area has some of the most beautiful summer weather in the country—warm, sunny days with clear blue skies and cool nights perfect for sleeping. During the months of July, August, and September, it almost never rains. And the rest of the year? Well, yes, it rains in those months and it rains regularly. However, the rain is generally a fine mist and not the torrential downpour most people associate with the word *rain*. In fact, it often rains less yearly in Portland than it does in New York, Boston, Washington, D.C., or Atlanta.

There, now I've let the secret out. Let the stampede begin! Winters here aren't too bad, either. They're warmer than in the Northeast, but there is snow in nearby mountains. In fact, there's so much snow on Mount Hood, only 90 minutes from downtown Portland, that you can ski right through the summer. A raincoat, an umbrella, and a sweater or jacket are all a way of life in this part of the country.

Of course you're skeptical, so here are the statistics.

Portland's Average Temperature & Days of Rain

	Jan	Feb	Mar	Apr	May	June	July	Aug	Sept	Oct	Nov	Dec
Temp. (°F)	40	43	46	50	57	63	68	67	63	54	46	41
Temp. (°C)	4	6	8	10	14	17	20	19	17	12	8	5
Rain (Days)	18	16	17	14	12	10	4	5	8	13	18	19

A CITY OF FESTIVALS

There is nothing Portland enjoys more than a big get-together. Because of the winter weather conditions, these festivals, free concerts, and fairs tend to take place in summer. Not a week goes by then without some sort of event. For a calendar of special events in and around Portland, contact the **Portland Oregon Visitors Association,** Three World Trade Center, 26 SW Salmon St., Portland, OR 97204-3299 (☎ **800/ 345-3214** or 503/222-2223; Web site: (www.pova.com). To find out what's going on during your visit, pick up a free copy of *Willamette Week* or *Portland Guide* (available at the Visitors Association or hotels), or buy the Friday or Sunday *Oregonian.* Some of the larger and more popular special and free events are listed there.

What Things Cost in Portland	U.S. $
Taxi from the airport to the city center	22.00–25.00
Bus or tram ride between downtown points	Free
Local telephone call	.25
Double at The Heathman Hotel (very expensive)	180.00–205.00
Double at Mallory Inn (moderate)	70.00–110.00
Double at Super 8 Portland/Airport (inexpensive)	61.00–73.00
Lunch for one at B. Moloch (moderate)	10.00
Lunch for one at Mayas Taqueria (inexpensive)	6.00
Dinner for one, without wine, at The Heathman (expensive)	32.00
Dinner for one, without wine, at Ristorante Pazzo (moderate)	21.00
Dinner for one, without wine, at Caswell (inexpensive)	8.00
Pint of beer	3.25
Coca-Cola	1.00
Cup of espresso	1.50
Roll of ASA 100 Kodacolor film, 36 exposures	6.00
Admission to the Portland Art Museum	6.00
Movie ticket	6.00–6.50
Oregon Symphony ticket at Arlene Schnitzer Concert Hall	10.00–50.00

Portland Parks and Recreation also sponsors concerts in several parks throughout the city every summer. Write to them in late spring (and include a self-addressed, stamped envelope) at 1120 SW Fifth Ave., Portland, OR 97204, for a free schedule of concerts.

PORTLAND CALENDAR OF EVENTS

February

- **Portland International Film Festival,** various theaters around the city. Tickets usually go on sale around February 1. During the festival, tickets go on sale daily at noon, and weekend shows usually sell out. Mid-February until early March (☎ 503/221-1156).

May

- **Cinco de Mayo Festival,** downtown Portland at Waterfront Park. Hispanic celebration with food and entertainment honoring Portland's sister city, Guadalajara, Mexico. Early May. (☎ **503/823-4572** or 503/222-9807).
- **Mother's Day Rhododendron Show,** Crystal Springs Rhododendron Gardens. Mother's Day (☎ **503/771-8386**).

June

- **Rhythm and Zoo,** Metro Washington Park Zoo. Rhythm and blues concerts are held on Thursday nights from June to August (☎ **503/226-1561**).
- **Your Zoo and All That Jazz,** Metro Washington Park Zoo. Jazz concerts are held on Wednesday nights from June to August (☎ **503/226-1561**).
- ✪ **Portland Rose Festival.** From its beginnings back in 1888, when the first rose show was held, the Rose Festival has blossomed into Portland's biggest celebration. The festivities now span 3$^{1}/_{2}$ weeks and include a rose show, parade, rose queen contest, music festival, car races, footrace, boat races, and even an air show later on in July. For more details, contact the Portland Rose Festival Association, 220 NW Second Ave., Portland, OR 97209 (☎ **503/227-2681** or Ticketmaster at 503/224-4400), for information on schedules and tickets to specific events. Most of the events take place in the first 2 weeks of June, and hotel rooms can be hard to come by. Plan ahead.
- **Peanut Butter and Jam Sessions,** Pioneer Courthouse Square. This is a series of free lunchtime concerts playing everything from classical music to bluegrass to jazz to Japanese taiko drumming. They're held every Tuesday and Thursday, mid-June to mid-August (☎ **503/223-1613**).

July

- **Fourth of July Fireworks,** Fort Vancouver, WA. Since Vancouver's fireworks display is the biggest west of the Mississippi, Portland wisely decided not to try to compete. Vancouver is just across the river, though, so you can see the fireworks from many spots in Portland. For a close-up view, head up to Jantzen Beach. For an elevated perspective, climb up the West Hills (☎ **360/693-5481**).
- **Waterfront Blues Festival,** Waterfront Park. In the second largest blues festival in the country, national and regional acts perform on the bank on the Willamette River in downtown Portland. This is a benefit festival for the Oregon Food Bank, and the suggested admission price is $3 plus two cans of food. Early July (☎ **503/282-0555**).
- **Multnomah County Fair,** Portland Exposition Center. This is a classic county fair, with agricultural displays (cows, chickens, rabbits, goats, vegetables, fruits, flowers, jams, pies, and so on), carnival rides, and live country and rock music. Last week in July (☎ **503/248-5144**).

- **Oregon Brewers Festival,** Waterfront Park. American's largest festival of independent brewers features lots of local microbrew (as well as brews from around the world) and music. Last weekend in July (☎ **503/778-5917** or any brewery in Portland).

August

- **Mount Hood Festival of Jazz,** Mount Hood Community College, Gresham (less than 30 minutes from Portland). For the serious jazz fan, this is the festival of the summer, featuring the greatest names in jazz. Tickets are $29.50 to $45 per day or $60 for a 3-day general admission pass. General admission tickets go on sale in mid-April, and reserved seating tickets go on sale in July. Tickets are available through Ticketmaster. The festival benefits Mount Hood Community College. First weekend in August (☎ **503/666-3810**).
- **The Bite,** Waterfront Park. Portland's finest restaurants serve up sample portions of their specialties at this food and music festival. A true gustatory extravaganza, which also includes wine tasting. Mid-August (☎ **503/248-0600**).

September

- **Rheinlander Oktoberfest,** Oaks Amusement Park. A large and crowded Oktoberfest with lots of polka in the beer hall. Mid-September (☎ **503/232-3000**).
- **North by Northwest (NXNW),** in clubs around the Portland area. The hottest regional bands converge on Portland for this conference and showcase. Mid-September (☎ **503/243-2122** ext. 380, or 512/467-7979.

October

- **Zooboo,** Metro Washington Park Zoo. Family entertainment featuring haunted train rides and games. Mid- to late October (☎ **503/226-1561**).

November

- **Yamhill County Wine Country Thanksgiving,** Yamhill County. About 30 miles outside of Portland, more than two dozen wineries open their doors for tastings of new releases, food, and entertainment. End of November (☎ **503/434-5814**).
- **Christmas at Pittock Mansion,** Pittock Mansion. Each year, this grand château built in French Renaissance style is decorated according to an annual theme. Late November to the end of December (☎ **503/823-3624**).
- **Festival of Lights at The Grotto,** The Grotto. Lighting displays and one of the largest choral festivals in the Northwest. End of November to end of December (☎ **503/254-7371**).

December

- **Holiday Parade of Ships,** Willamette and Columbia rivers. Boats decked out in holiday lights parade and circle on the rivers after nightfall. Month of December.
- **Winter Solstice Festival,** Oregon Museum of Science and Industry. In a 4,000-year-old tradition, the lengthening of the days is celebrated with entertainment, arts and crafts, and special events. December 20 or 21 (☎ **503/797-4000**).

3 Tips for Travelers with Special Needs

FOR TRAVELERS WITH DISABILITIES

Many hotels listed in this book feature special rooms for the disabled, but when making a hotel reservation, be sure to ask.

All MAX light-rail (trolley) system stations have wheelchair lifts, and there are two wheelchair spaces available on each train. Be sure to wait on the platform lift. Many of the Tri-Met buses also are equipped with wheelchair lifts and wheelchair spaces. Look for the wheelchair symbol on buses, schedules, and bus stops. There is also a special door-to-door service provided for people who are not able to use the regular Tri-Met service, but, if visiting Portland, they must have an eligibility card from another public transportation system. Phone ☎ **503/238-4952** for information. **Broadway Cab** (☎ **503/227-1234**) and **Radio Cab** (☎ **503/227-1212**) both have vehicles for transporting persons with disabilities.

For more information, see "Tips for Travelers with Special Needs" in chapter 2.

FOR GAY & LESBIAN TRAVELERS

Gay and lesbian travelers visiting Portland should be sure to pick up a free copy of *Just Out* (☎ **503/236-1252**), a monthly newspaper for the gay community. You can usually find copies at **Powell's Books,** 1005 W. Burnside St. The newspaper covers local news of interest to gays. They also publish a resource guide for lesbians and gays called the *Just Out Pocket Book.* Call the above number to find out where you can get a copy. The guide is a free directory of Portland businesses that welcome gay customers.

4 Getting There

BY PLANE

The Major Airlines   About a dozen carriers service Portland Airport to and from some 100 cities worldwide. The major airlines include **Air Canada** (☎ 800/776-3000, **Alaska Airlines** (☎ 800/426-0333 or 503/224-2547), **America West** (☎ 800/235-9292), **American Airlines** (☎ 800/433-7300), **Continental** (☎ 800/523-3273), **Delta** (☎ 800/221-1212), **Hawaiian** (☎ 800/367-5320), **Horizon Air** (☎ 800/547-9308), **Northwest** (☎ 800/225-2525), **Reno** (☎ 800/736-6247), **Southwest** (☎ 800/435-9792), **TWA** (☎ 800/221-2000), **United Airlines** (☎ 800/241-6522), and **Western Pacific** (☎ 800/930-3030).

Finding the Best Airfare   See "Getting There" in chapter 2 for information on finding the best airfare to Portland.

Portland International Airport (PDX)   Portland International Airport (☎ **503/335-1234**) is located 10 miles northeast of downtown Portland, adjacent to the Columbia River. The airport is relatively small but for several years now has been in the midst of expansions. Currently, the parking garage and airport arrivals and departures entries are being completely redesigned. Expect traffic congestion and construction until sometime in the year 2000. The trip into town is entirely on interstate highways and takes about 20 minutes.

There's an information booth by the baggage-claim area where you can pick up maps and brochures and find out about transportation into the city. Many hotels near the airport provide courtesy shuttle service to and from the airport. Be sure to check at your hotel when you make a reservation.

Here at the airport (where it's currently necessary to take a shuttle to the car-rental area because of airport construction), you'll find the following companies: **Avis** (☎ **800/831-2847** or 503/249-4950); **Budget** (☎ **800/527-0700** or 503/249-6500); **Dollar** (☎ **800/800-4000** or 503/249-4792); **Hertz** (☎ **800/654-3131** or 503/249-8216); and **National** (☎ **800/227-7368** or 503/249-4900). Outside the airport is **Thrifty,** at 10800 NE Holman St. (☎ **800/367-2277** or 503/254-6563).

If you have rented a car at the airport and want to reach central Portland, follow signs for downtown. These signs will take you first to I-205 and then I-84 west, which brings you to the Willamette River. Take the Morrison Bridge exit to cross the river. For more information on renting a car, see "Getting Around" in chapter 13.

If you haven't rented a car at the airport, the best way to get into town is to take the **Raz Transportation Downtown Shuttle** (☎ **503/246-4676** or 503/246-3301) Because of construction at the airport, a bus labeled "Ground Transportation" located outside the baggage claim area will take you out to where the Raz Shuttle is parked. It'll take you directly to your hotel for $9. It operates every 30 minutes from about 6am to midnight daily.

Tri-Met public bus no. 12 leaves the airport approximately every 15 minutes from 5:30am to 11:50pm for the trip to downtown Portland. The trip takes about 40 minutes and costs $1.05. The bus between downtown and the airport operates between 5am and 12:30am and leaves from SW Sixth Avenue and Main Street.

A **taxi** into town costs around $23.

BY CAR

Portland is linked to the rest of the United States by a number of interstate highways and smaller roads. I-5 runs north to Seattle and south as far as San Diego. I-84 runs east as far as Salt Lake City. I-405 arcs around the west and south of downtown Portland. I-205 bypasses the city to the east. U.S. 26 runs west to the coast.

Here are some driving distances from selected cities (in miles):

Los Angeles	1,015
San Francisco	640
Seattle	175
Spokane	350
Vancouver, B.C.	285

BY TRAIN

Amtrak (☎ **800/872-7245**) passenger trains connect Portland with Seattle, San Francisco, Salt Lake City, Chicago, and the rest of the country and stop at historic **Union Station,** 800 NW Sixth Ave. (☎ **503/273-4866**), about 10 blocks from the heart of downtown Portland.

BY BUS

Greyhound Bus Lines connects Portland with the rest of the country. The bus station is at 550 NW Sixth Ave. (☎ **800/231-2222** or 503/243-2357).

13 Getting to Know Portland

Portland's compactness makes it an easy city to explore. Although the airport is in the northeastern part of the city, most important sights and hotels are in the southwestern part. The Willamette River forms a natural dividing line between the eastern and western portions of the city, while the Columbia River forms a boundary with the state of Washington to the north. The West Hills, Portland's prime residential district, are a beautiful backdrop for this attractive city. Covered in evergreens, the hills rise to a height of 1,000 feet at the edge of downtown. Within these hills are Metro Washington Park Zoo, the International Rose Test Garden, the Japanese Gardens, and several other attractions. When you're ready to leave Portland and explore the scenic Oregon countryside, it's easy to drive away on an interstate and be far from the city in 30 minutes.

1 Orientation

VISITOR INFORMATION

The **Portland Oregon Visitors Association Information Center** is at Two World Trade Center, 25 SW Salmon St. (☎ **800/345-3214** or 503/222-2223; Web site: www.pova.com). There is also an information booth by the baggage-claim area at Portland Airport. If you happen to see two people walking down a Portland street wearing matching kelly green hats and jackets, they are probably members of the **Portland Guide** service run by the Association for Portland Progress (☎ **503/224-8684**). They'll be happy to answer any question you have about the city.

CITY LAYOUT

Portland is located in northwestern Oregon at the confluence of the Columbia and Willamette rivers. To the west are the West Hills, which rise to more than 1,000 feet. Some 90 miles west of the West Hills are the spectacular Oregon coast and the Pacific Ocean. To the east are rolling hills that extend to the Cascade Range, about 50 miles away. The most prominent peak in this section of the Cascades is Mount Hood (11,235 feet), a dormant volcanic peak that looms over the city on clear days. From many parts of Portland it's also possible to see Mount St. Helens, another volcano, which erupted spectacularly in 1980.

With about 1.6 million people in the entire metropolitan area, Portland is a relatively small city. This is especially evident when one begins to explore the compact downtown area. Nearly everything is accessible on foot, and the city authorities do everything they can to encourage pedestrians.

Main Arteries & Streets   I-84 (**Banfield Freeway or Expressway**) enters Portland from the east. East of the city is **I-205,** which bypasses downtown Portland and runs past the airport. **I-5 (East Bank Freeway)** runs through on a north-south axis, passing along the east bank of the Willamette River directly across from downtown. **I-405 (Stadium Freeway and Foothills Freeway)** circles around the west and south sides of downtown. **U.S. 26 (Sunset Highway)** leaves downtown heading west toward Beaverton and the coast. **Oregon Hwy. 217 (Beaverton-Tigard Highway)** runs south from U.S. 26 in Beaverton.

The most important artery within Portland is **Burnside Street.** This is the dividing line between north and south Portland. Dividing the city from east to west is the **Willamette River,** which is crossed by eight bridges in the downtown area. From north to south these bridges are named Fremont, Broadway, Steel, Burnside, Morrison, Hawthorne, Marquam, and Ross Island. There are additional bridges beyond the downtown area.

For convenience sake, I'll define downtown Portland as the 300-block area within **Fareless Square.** This is the area in which you can ride for free on the city's public buses and the MAX light-rail system. Fareless Square is bounded by I-405 on the west and south, by Hoyt Street on the north, and by the Willamette River on the east.

Finding an Address   Finding an address in Portland can be easy if you keep a number of things in mind. Almost all addresses in Portland, and even extending for miles beyond the city, include a map quadrant—NE (Northeast), SW (Southwest), and so forth. The dividing line between east and west is the Willamette River; between north and south it's Burnside Street. Any downtown address will be labeled either SW (Southwest) or NW (northwest). An exception to this rule is the area known as North Portland. Streets here have a plain "North" designation. This is the area across the Willamette River from downtown going toward Jantzen Beach.

Avenues run north-south and streets run east-west. Street names are the same on both sides of the Willamette River. Consequently, there is a Southwest Yamhill Street and a Southeast Yamhill Street. In northwest Portland, street names are alphabetical going north from Burnside to Wilson. Naito Parkway (formerly Front Avenue) is the road nearest the Willamette River on the west side, and Water Avenue is the nearest on the east side. Beyond these are numbered avenues. On the west side you'll also find Broadway and Park Avenue between Sixth Avenue and Ninth Avenue. With each block, the addresses increase by 100, beginning at the Willamette River for avenues and at Burnside Street for streets. Odd numbers are generally on the west and north sides of the street, and even numbers on the east and south sides.

Here's an example. You want to go to 1327 SW Ninth Ave. Because it's in the 1300 block, you'll find it 13 blocks south of Burnside and, because it's an odd number, on the west side of the street.

Street Maps   Stop by the **Portland Oregon Visitors Association Information Center,** Two World Trade Center, 25 SW Salmon St. (☎ **800/345-3214** or

---

Impressions

We want you to visit our State of Excitement often. Come again and again. But for heaven's sake, don't move here to live. Or if you do have to move in to live, don't tell any of your neighbors where you are going.

—Gov. Tom McCall, 1971

503/222-2223; Web site: www.pova.com), for a free map of the city; they also have a more detailed one for sale. **Powell's "City of Books,"** 1005 W. Burnside St. (☎ **800/878-7323** or 503/228-4651), has an excellent free map of downtown that includes a walking-tour route and information on many of the sights you'll pass along the way. Members of the **American Automobile Association** can obtain a free map of the city at the AAA offices at 600 SW Market St. (☎ **503/222-6734**) and 8555 SW Apple Way in Beaverton (☎ **503/243-6444**).

NEIGHBORHOODS IN BRIEF

Downtown   This term usually refers to the business and shopping district south of Burnside and north of Jackson Street between the Willamette River and 13th Avenue. You'll find the major department stores, dozens of restaurants, most of the city's performing arts venues, and almost all of the best hotels in this area.

Pearl District   This neighborhood of galleries, artist's lofts, cafes, breweries, and shops is bounded by the Park blocks, Lovejoy Street, I-405, and Burnside Street. Crowds of people come here on First Thursday when the galleries and other businesses are open late.

Chinatown   Portland has had a Chinatown almost since the earliest days. It is entered through the colorful Chinatown Gate at West Burnside Street and Fourth Avenue.

Skidmore District   Also known as Old Town, this is Portland's original commercial core, and centers around Southwest Ankeny Street and Southwest First Avenue. Many of the restored buildings have become retail stores, but despite the presence of the Saturday Market, the neighborhood has never become a popular shopping district, mostly because of its welfare hotels, missions, street people, and drug dealing. Continued attempts to clean up this area are bringing some improvement. There are several nightclubs here.

Northwest/Nob Hill   Located along Northwest 23rd and Northwest 21st avenues, this is Portland's trendiest neighborhood. This is where you'll find many of the city's most talked about restaurants, as well as lots of cafes, boutiques, and more and more national chain stores such as the Gap and Pottery Barn. Surrounding the two main business streets of the neighborhood are blocks of restored Victorian homes on shady tree-lined streets. This is where you'll find the city's liveliest street scene.

Irvington   Though neither as attractive nor as large as the Northwest/Nob Hill neighborhood, Irvington, centered around Broadway in northeast Portland, is almost as trendy. For several blocks along Broadway you'll find unusual boutiques, stores selling imports, and lots of excellent but inexpensive restaurants.

Hollywood District   One of the latest neighborhoods to attract attention in Portland is the Hollywood District of northeast Portland. This area, which centers around the busy commercial activities of Sandy Boulevard near 42nd Avenue, came into being in the early years of this century. The name is taken from the Hollywood Theater, an art deco landmark. Throughout this neighborhood are craftsman-style houses and vernacular architecture of the period.

Sellwood   Situated in the southeast, this is Portland's antique store district and contains many restored Victorian houses. There are also excellent restaurants.

Hawthorne District   This enclave of southeast Portland is full of eclectic boutiques, moderately priced restaurants, and hip college students from nearby Reed College.

2 Getting Around

BY PUBLIC TRANSPORTATION

Free Rides   Portland is committed to keeping its downtown uncongested, and to this end it has invested heavily in its public transportation system. The single greatest innovation and best reason to ride the Tri-Met public buses and the MAX light-rail system is that they're free within an area known as **Fareless Square.** That's right, free! There are 300 blocks of downtown included in Fareless Square, and as long as you stay within the boundaries, you don't pay a cent. Fareless Square covers the area between I-405 on the south and west, Hoyt Street on the north, and the Willamette River on the east.

By Bus   Tri-Met buses operate daily over an extensive network. You can pick up the *Tri-Met Guide,* which lists all the bus routes with times, or individual route maps and time schedules at the **Tri-Met Customer Assistance Office,** behind and beneath the waterfall fountain at Pioneer Courthouse Square (☎ **503/238-7433**). The office is open Monday through Friday from 9am to 5pm.

Outside Fareless Square, fares on both Tri-Met buses and MAX are $1.05 or $1.35, depending on how far you travel.

Seniors 65 years and older pay 50¢ with valid proof of age.

You can also make free transfers between the bus and the MAX light-rail system. A **day ticket** costing $3.25 is good for travel to all zones and is valid on both buses and MAX. Day tickets can be purchased from any bus driver. Nearly all Tri-Met buses pass through the Transit Mall on SW Fifth Avenue and SW Sixth Avenue.

By Light Rail   The **Metropolitan Area Express (MAX)** is Portland's aboveground light-rail system that now connects downtown Portland with the eastern suburb of Gresham. MAX is basically a modern trolley; reproductions of vintage trolley cars operate during certain times on weekends. You can ride MAX for free if you stay within Fareless Square, which includes all the downtown area. However, be sure to buy your ticket before you board MAX if you're traveling out of Fareless Square. Fares are the same as on buses. There are ticket-vending machines at all MAX stops that tell you how much to pay for your destination; these machines also give change. The MAX driver cannot sell tickets. There are ticket inspectors who randomly check tickets. If you don't have one, you can be fined up to $300.

❓ Did You Know?

- The flasher in the famous "Expose Yourself to Art" poster is none other than Bud Clark, the former mayor of Portland.
- Portland is the only city in the United States with an extinct volcano—Mount Tabor—within the city limits.
- Matt Groening, creator of *The Simpsons,* got his start in Portland.
- More Asian elephants have been born in Portland (at the Metro Washington Park Zoo) than in any other city in the United States or Canada.
- Twenty downtown drinking water fountains, each with four individual fountains, were a gift to the city from teetotalling turn-of-the-century timber baron Simon Benson. He wanted his mill workers to have something other than alcohol to drink during the day.

The MAX light-rail system crosses the Transit Mall on SW Morrison Street and SW Yamhill Street. Transfers to the bus are free.

BY CAR

Car Rentals Portland is a compact city, and public transit will get you to most attractions within its limits. However, if you are planning to explore outside the city—and Portland's greatest attractions, such as Mount Hood and the Columbia River Gorge, lie not in the city itself but in the countryside within an hour of the city—you'll definitely need a car.

For the best deal on a rental car, I highly recommend making a reservation at least a week before you arrive in Portland. It also pays to call several times over a period of a few weeks just to ask prices; the last time I rented a car, the same company quoted me different prices every time I called to ask about rates. Remember the old Wall Street adage: Buy low! If you didn't have time to plan ahead, ask about special weekend rates or discounts you might be eligible for. And don't forget to mention that you are a frequent flyer: You might be able to get miles for your car rental. Also, be sure to find out whether your credit card pays the collision-damage waiver, which can add a bundle to the cost of a rental. Currently, daily rates for a compact are around $28 to $40, and weekly rates are around $140 to $190.

The major car-rental companies are represented in Portland, and there are also many independent and smaller car-rental agencies listed in the Portland *Yellow Pages.* At Portland International Airport (where it's necessary to take a shuttle to the car-rental area because of airport construction), you'll find the following companies:

Avis (☎ **800/831-2847** or 503/249-4950), which also has an office downtown at 330 SW Washington St. (☎ 503/227-0220); **Budget** (☎ **800/527-0700** or 503/249-6500), which also has offices downtown at 2033 SW Fourth Ave., on the east side at 2323 NE Columbia Blvd., and in Beaverton at 10835 SW Canyon Rd; **Dollar** (☎ **800/800-4000** or 503/249-4792), which also has an office downtown at NW Broadway and NW Davis St. (☎ 503/228-3540); **Hertz** (☎ **800/654-3131** or 503/249-8216), which also has an office downtown at 1009 SW Sixth Ave. (☎ **503/249-5727**); **National** (☎ **800/227-7368** or 503/249-4900). Outside the airport is **Thrifty,** at 10800 NE Holman St. (☎ **800/367-2277** or 503/254-6563), which also has an office downtown at 632 SW Pine St. (☎ 503/227-6587).

Parking Parking downtown can be a problem, especially if you show up after workers have gotten to their offices on weekdays. There are a couple of very important things to remember when parking downtown:

When parking on the street, be sure to notice the meter's time limit. These vary from as little as 15 minutes (they are always right in front of the restaurant or museum where you plan to spend 2 hours) to long term (read long walk). Most common are 30- and 60-minute meters. You don't have to feed the meters after 6pm or on Sunday.

The best parking deal in town is at the **Smart Park** garages, where the cost is 75¢ per hour or $3 all day on the weekends. Look for the red, white, and black signs featuring Les Park, the friendly parking attendant. You'll find Smart Park garages at First Avenue and Jefferson Street, Fourth Avenue and Yamhill Street, Tenth Avenue and Yamhill Street, Third Avenue and Alder Street, O'Bryant Square, and Naito Parkway and Davis Street. If you make a purchase, the merchant will usually validate your parking ticket, so don't forget to take it along with you.

Rates in other public lots range from about $1 up to about $2.75 per hour.

Special Driving Rules You may turn right on a red light after a full stop, and if you are in the far left lane of a one-way street, you may turn left into the adjacent left lane of a one-way street at a red light after a full stop. Everyone in a moving vehicle is required to wear a seat belt.

BY TAXI

Because most everything in Portland is fairly close, getting around by taxi can be economical. Although there are almost always taxis waiting in line at major hotels, you won't find them cruising the streets—you'll have to phone for one. **Broadway Cab** (☎ **503/227-1234**) and **Radio Cab** (☎ **503/227-1212**) both offer 24-hour radio-dispatched service and accept American Express, Discover, MasterCard, and Visa credit cards. Fares are $2.50 for the first mile and $1.50 for each additional mile.

BY BICYCLE

Bicycles are a very popular way of getting around Portland. For leisurely cycling, try the promenade in Waterfront Park, on the east side of the river between the Hawthorne and Burnside bridges. The Terwilliger Path runs for 10 miles from Portland State University to Tryon Creek State Park in the West Hills. You can pick up a copy of a bike map of the city of Portland at most bike shops. Bicycles can be rented downtown at **Bike Central,** 835 SW Second Ave. and Taylor Street (☎ **503/227-4439**), where rental fees are about $20 to $30 per day, or, in season, **The Bike Gallery,** 821 SW 11th Ave. (☎ **503/222-3821**), where a bike rents for $40 per day.

ON FOOT

City blocks in Portland are about half the size of most city blocks elsewhere, and the entire downtown area covers only about 13 blocks by 26 blocks. These two facts make Portland a very easy place to explore on foot. The city has been very active in encouraging people to get out of their cars and onto the sidewalks downtown. The sidewalks are wide, and there are many small parks with benches for resting, fountains for cooling off, and works of art for soothing the soul.

If you happen to spot a couple of people wearing kelly-green baseball caps and jackets and navy-blue pants, they're probably a pair of **Portland Guides.** These informative souls are there to answer any questions you might have about Portland—"Where am I?" for instance. Their job is simply to walk the streets and answer questions.

FAST FACTS: Portland

Airport   See "Getting There" in chapter 12.

American Express   The **American Express Travel Service Office** (☎ **503/226-2961**) is located at 1100 SW Sixth Ave., which is the corner of Sixth and Main. The office is open Monday through Friday from 9am to 5pm. You can cash American Express traveler's checks and exchange the major foreign currencies here.

Area Code   The area code for the Portland and Salem metropolitan area is **503.** For the rest of Oregon it's **541.**

Baby-Sitters   Call **Wee-Ba-Bee Child Care** (☎ **503/786-3837**) if your hotel doesn't offer baby-sitting services.

Business Hours   Banks are generally open weekdays from 9am to 5pm, with later hours on Friday; some have Saturday morning hours. Offices are generally open weekdays from 9am to 5 or 6pm. Stores typically open Monday through Friday between 9 and 10am and close between 5 and 6pm. Department stores tend to stay open later (until between 7 and 9pm), as do stores in malls. Bars stay open until 1 or 2am; dance clubs often stay open much later.

Car Rentals　See "Getting Around," earlier in this chapter.

Climate　See "When to Go" in chapter 12.

Dentist　If you need a dentist while you are in Portland, contact the **Multnomah Dental Society** for a referral (☎ **503/223-4738** or 503/223-4731).

Doctor　If you need a physician while in Portland, contact the **Medical Society Doctor Referral Service** for a referral (☎ **503/222-0156**).

Driving Rules　See "Getting Around," earlier in this chapter.

Drugstores　See "Pharmacies" below.

Embassies/Consulates　See the appendix "For Foreign Visitors."

Emergencies　For police, fire, or medical emergencies, phone **911.**

Eyeglass Repair　Check out **Binyon's Eyeworld Downtown,** 803 SW Morrison St. (☎ **503/226-6688**).

Hospitals　Three area hospitals are **Legacy Good Samaritan,** 1015 NW 22nd Ave. (☎ **503/229-7711**); **Providence St. Vincent Hospital,** 9205 SW Barnes Rd. (☎ **503/216-1234**), off U.S. 26 (Sunset Highway) before Oregon Hwy. 217; and the **Oregon Health Sciences University Hospital,** 3181 SW Sam Jackson Park Rd. (☎ **503/494-8311**), just southwest of the city center.

Hot Lines　The women's **crisis hot line** number is (☎ **503/235-5333** or toll free in Oregon 888/235-5333). The **Portland Center for the Performing Arts Information Hot line** is (☎ **503/796-9293**).

Information　See "Visitor Information," earlier in this chapter.

Libraries　The **Multnomah County Library,** 801 SW 10th Ave. (☎ **503/ 248-5123**), which reopened in early 1997 after an extensive renovation, is Portland's main library.

Liquor Laws　The legal minimum drinking age in Oregon is **21.**

Lost Property　If you lose something on a bus or the MAX, call ☎ **503/238-4855** Monday through Friday from 9am to 5pm. If you lose something at the airport, call ☎ **503/335-1277.**

Luggage Storage/Lockers　You'll find coin-operated luggage-storage lockers at the **Greyhound Bus Station,** 550 NW Sixth Ave. (☎ **503/243-2357**).

Maps　See "City Layout," earlier in this chapter.

Newspapers/Magazines　Portland's morning daily newspaper is *The Oregonian.* For arts and entertainment information and listings, consult the Arts and Entertainment section of the Friday *Oregonian* or pick up a free copy of *Willamette Week* at Powell's Books and other bookstores, convenience stores, or cafes. Another free weekly tabloid is *Our Town.* The *Portland Guide* is a free weekly tourism guide to Portland and is available at Portland/Oregon Visitors Association and some hotels.

　　6th and Washington News Shop, 617 SW Washington St. (☎ **503/221-1128**), carries a large selection of out-of-town newspapers and magazines. There's also another location of this shop at 832 SW Fourth Ave.

Pharmacies　Convenient to most downtown hotels, **Central Drug,** 538 SW Fourth Ave. (☎ **503/226-2222**), is open Monday to Friday from 9am to 6pm, on Saturday from 10am to 4pm.

Photographic Needs　**Flashback Foto,** 900 SW Fourth Ave. (☎ **503/224-6776**), and 730 SW Alder (☎ **503/224-6775**), offers 1-hour film processing. It's open

Monday through Friday from 7am to 7pm, on Saturday from 9am to 6pm, and on Sunday from noon to 5pm. **Camera World,** SW Sixth Avenue and SW Washington Street (☎ **503/299-4010**), is the largest camera and video store in the city; open Monday through Thursday from 9am to 6pm, Friday from 9am to 8pm, Saturday from 10am to 6pm, and Sunday from 11am to 5pm.

Police   To reach the police, call **911.**

Post Offices   The **main post office,** 715 NW Hoyt St., is open Monday through Friday from 7am to 6:30pm, Saturday from 8:30am to 5pm. There are also convenient post offices at 204 SW Fifth Ave., open Monday through Friday from 8:30am to 5pm, and 1505 SW Sixth Ave., open Monday through Friday from 7am to 6pm, Saturday from 10am to 3pm. The phone number for each of these post offices is ☎ **800/275-8777.**

Radio   **KOPB-FM** (91.5) is the local National Public Radio station.

Rest Rooms   There are public rest rooms underneath Starbucks coffee shop in Pioneer Courthouse Square and in downtown shopping malls.

Safety   Because of its small size and emphasis on keeping the downtown alive and growing, Portland is still a relatively safe city; in fact, strolling the downtown streets at night is a popular pastime. Take extra precautions, however, if you venture into the entertainment district along West Burnside Street or Chinatown at night. Parts of northeast Portland are controlled by street gangs, so before visiting any place in this area, be sure to get very detailed directions so you don't get lost. If you plan to go hiking in Forest Park, don't leave anything valuable in your car. This holds true in the Old Town district as well.

Taxes   Portland is a shopper's paradise—there's no sales tax. However, there is a 9% tax on hotel rooms within the city of Portland. Outside the city, the room tax varies.

Taxis   See "Getting Around," earlier in this chapter.

Television   Channels in Portland are 2 (ABC), 6 (CBS), 8 (NBC), 10 (PBS), 12, 24 (religious), and 49 (Fox). All major cable networks are also available.

Time Zone   Portland is on Pacific time, 3 hours behind the East Coast. In the summer, daylight saving time is observed and clocks are set forward 1 hour.

Transit Info   For bus information, call the **Tri-Met Customer Assistance Office** (☎ **503/238-7433**). They're open Monday through Friday from 9am to 5pm. You can pick up a *Tri-Met Guide* from their office located beneath the waterfall fountain at Pioneer Courthouse Square. For intercity train fares and schedules, call **Amtrak** (☎ **800/872-7245**) or **Union Station** (☎ **503/273-4866**). For intercity bus schedules and fares, call **Greyhound** (☎ **503/243-2357**).

Useful Telephone Numbers   For all kinds of local information, from weather to movie schedules, call the *Oregonian* Inside Line (☎ **503/225-5555**).

Weather   If it's summer, it's sunny; otherwise, there's a chance of rain. This is almost always a sufficient weather forecast in Portland, but for specifics, call **weather information** (☎ **503/243-7575**).

14 Portland Accommodations

The past decade has seen a downtown hotel renaissance in Portland. Several historic hotels have been renovated and other historic buildings have been retrofitted to serve as hotels. These hotels include The Benson, the Governor Hotel, The Heathman Hotel, and the Hotel Vintage Plaza. Today these hotels offer some of Portland's most comfortable and memorable accommodations. This trend is continuing unabated, with the opening in 1996 of the 5th Avenue Suites Hotel in what was once a department store. At press time, another old hotel, the Multnomah, was about to reopen as an Embassy Suites Hotel, and several other new hotels were in planning stages for downtown Portland as well as outlying suburbs.

The city's largest concentrations of hotels are in downtown and near the airport. If you don't mind the high prices, downtown hotels are the most convenient for visitors. However, if your budget won't allow for a first-class business hotel, try near the airport or elsewhere on the outskirts of the city where you are more likely to find inexpensive to moderately priced motels. You'll find the greatest concentration of bed-and-breakfast inns in the Irvington neighborhood of northeast Portland. This area is close to downtown and is generally quite convenient even if you are here on business.

In the following listings, price categories are based on the rate for a double room (most hotels charge the same for a single or double room) in high season and are as follows: **very expensive,** more than $175 per night; **expensive,** $126 to $175 per night; **moderate,** $75 to $125 per night; and **inexpensive,** under $75 per night. Keep in mind that these rates do not include Portland's 9% room tax. Also, keep in mind that these are what hotels call "rack rates," or walk-in rates. Various discounts often reduce these rates, so be sure to ask if they are available. In fact, you can often get a discounted corporate rate simply by flashing a business card (your own, that is). At inexpensive chain motels, there are almost always discounted rates for AAA members and senior citizens. You'll also find that room rates are almost always considerably lower from October through April (the rainy season), and large downtown hotels often offer weekend discounts of up to 50% throughout the year. Some of the large, upscale hotel chains also offer advance-purchase rates similar to those offered by airlines. A few hotels include breakfast in their rates; others offer complimentary breakfast only on certain deluxe floors. Parking rates are per day.

For information on bed-and-breakfast inns in the Portland area, call the **Portland Oregon Visitors Association** (☎ 800/345-3214 or 503/222-2223; Web site: www.pova.com) for a brochure put out by **Metro Innkeepers.** For information on B&Bs in both Portland and Oregon, contact the **Oregon Bed and Breakfast Guild,** P.O. Box 3187, Ashland, OR 97520 (☎ **800/944-6196;** Web site: www.insite.com/obbg/), or write to **Border to Border Bed and Breakfast Directory,** P.O. Box 1283, Grants Pass, OR 97526.

For B&B reservations, call **Northwest Bed and Breakfast Reservation Service,** 610 SW Broadway, Portland, OR 97205 (☎ **503/243-7616,** or 503/370-9033 in Salem; fax 503/316-9118). This service represents more than 75 B&Bs in the Portland and Seattle areas and a total of about 400 homes throughout Oregon, Washington, British Columbia, and Northern California. All homes have been inspected and some offer airport pick-ups. Rates range from $50 to $100 or more for doubles.

Although Portland is not nearly as popular a destination as Seattle, if you are planning to visit during the busy summer months, make reservations as far in advance as possible and be sure to ask if any special rates are available. Most all hotels in the Portland area now offer nonsmoking rooms, and, in fact, most bed-and-breakfast inns are exclusively nonsmoking establishments. Most hotels also offer wheelchair-accessible rooms.

1   Best Bets

- **Best Historic Hotel:** With its sepia-tone murals of Lewis and Clark on the lobby walls and comfortable overstuffed leather chairs by the fireplace, the **Governor Hotel,** SW 10th Ave. and Alder St. (☎ **800/554-3456** or 503/224-3400), built in 1909, captures both the spirit of the Northwest and the luxury of a classic hotel in both its public areas and its guest rooms.
- **Best for Business Travelers:** With fax machines in every room, plenty of room for spreading out your work, a convenient business center, a great restaurant, a health spa, and evening wine tastings, the **5th Avenue Suites Hotel,** 506 SW Washington St. (☎ **800/711-2971** or 503/222-0001), has everything necessary to make a business trip both successful and enjoyable.
- **Best for a Romantic Getaway:** If you're looking for the most romantic room in town, book a starlight room at the **Hotel Vintage Plaza,** 422 SW Broadway, (☎ **800/243-0555** or 503/228-1212). Located on one of the hotel's upper floors, these rooms are basically solariums with curving walls of glass that let you lie in bed and gaze up at the stars. Just be sure to come in the summer when there aren't as many clouds in the sky.
- **Best Lobby for Pretending That You're Rich:** With its walnut paneling, Italian marble, and crystal chandeliers, **The Benson,** 309 SW Broadway (☎ **800/426-0670** or 503/228-2000), is the pinnacle of 19th-century elegance. Order a snifter of brandy, sink into one of the leather chairs by the fireplace, and you too can conjure up your past life as a railroad baron.
- **Best for Families:** With both a shopping mall and a park across the street, the **Doubletree Hotel Portland Lloyd Center,** 1000 NE Multnomah St. (☎ **800/222-TREE** or 503/281-6111), is a great choice if you're traveling with kids. The Rose Garden sports arena is also nearby, as are quite a few good, casual restaurants.
- **Best Moderately Priced Hotel:** Although it is totally unassuming from the outside, **The Riverside,** 50 SW Morrison Ave. (☎ **800/899-0247** or 503/221-0711), is one of Portland's most stylish hotels due to a recent renovation that gave the entire hotel a very contemporary decor. Add to this the fact that Waterfront Park

and the Willamette River are just across the street, and you've got a great deal if you can manage to reserve far enough in advance to get a low rate.

- **Best Budget Hotel:** It's hard to find an inexpensive downtown hotel in any city, and Portland is no exception. However, if you don't mind a bit of faded glory, the **Mallory Hotel,** 729 SW 15th Ave. (☎ **800/228-8657** or 503/223-6311), is the best choice in town. The rooms are far from luxurious, but they suffice, and at less than half the price of hotels only four blocks away, it's a great deal.

- **Best B&B:** With views, a swimming pool, attractive gardens, a secluded feel, and the shops, restaurants, and cafes of Northwest 23rd Avenue only blocks away, the **Heron Haus,** 2545 NW Westover Rd. (☎ **503/274-1846**), is Portland's most luxurious and conveniently located B&B.

- **Best Service:** Though quite unpretentious, the historic **Heathman Hotel,** 1001 SW Broadway (☎ **800/551-0011** or 503/241-4100), is one of Portland's finest hotels and is long on personal service, which extends from complimentary overnight shoe shines to arranging a personal fitness trainer.

- **Best Location:** Though it's only a few blocks from downtown businesses, the **RiverPlace Hotel,** 1510 SW Harbor Way (☎ **800/227-1333** or 503/228-3233), a boutique hotel wedged between the Willamette River and Tom McCall Riverfront Park, feels a world away from the city. In summer, the park hosts countless festivals and if you book the right room, you can have a box seat for a concert in the park.

- **Best Health Club:** If you stay at the **Governor Hotel,** SW 10th Ave. and Alder St. (☎ **800/554-3456** or 503/224-3400), you need only head down to the basement for a total workout at the Princeton Athletic Club. You'll find a lap pool, running track, exercise room, whirlpool spas, saunas, and steam rooms. Sure, it costs an extra $9 a day, but you can bill it to your company.

- **Best Hotel Pool:** Although it's small, the pool at the **Doubletree Hotel Portland Lloyd Center,** 1000 NE Multnomah St. (☎ **800/222-TREE** or 503/281-6111), is set in a sunken garden patio area surrounded by landscaping that is part Japanese garden and part Northwest garden. On a sunny summer day, this cozy little retreat is a great escape from the surrounding city.

- **Best Views:** So, you've seen that photo of the Portland skyline with Mount Hood in the distance and you want that view while you're in town. Sorry, you'll have to sleep in Washington Park for that one. But, the next best bet would be an eastside room on an upper floor of the **Portland Marriott Hotel,** 1401 SW Naito Pkwy. (☎ **800/228-9290** or 503/226-7600).

- **Best West Side Hotel:** If you're here on west side high-tech business or just prefer a little greenery around you, there is no better choice than the **Greenwood Inn,** 10700 SW Allen Blvd. (☎ **800/289-1300** or 503/643-7444). This resortlike hotel has a great restaurant, fun lounge, and very attractive rooms, and all only 15 minutes from downtown Portland.

2 Downtown

VERY EXPENSIVE

The Benson. 309 SW Broadway, Portland, OR 97205. ☎ **800/426-0670** or 503/228-2000. Fax 503/226-4603. 287 rms, 46 junior suites, 9 suites. A/C TV TEL. $205–$215 double ($130–$140 weekends); $245 junior suite ($170 weekends); $350–$700 suite. AE, CB, DC, DISC, ER, JCB, MC, V. Valet parking $12.

The doorman in a top hat is the first tip-off that this is Portland's most traditional and exclusive hotel. The fact that presidents stay here whenever they're in town is another good clue that should you choose to stay here, you'll be enjoying the poshest accommodations in Portland. Built in 1912, The Benson exudes old-world sophistication and elegance. In the French baroque lobby, walnut paneling frames a marble fireplace, Austrian crystal chandeliers hang from the ornate plaster work ceiling, and a marble staircase provides the perfect setting for grand entrances.

The guest rooms, housed in two towers (only one of which is part of the original hotel), vary considerably in size, but all are luxuriously furnished. The deluxe kings are particularly roomy, but it is the corner junior suites that are the hotel's best deal. Not only are these rooms quite large, but the abundance of windows makes them much cheerier than other rooms (and all for only $30 more than a deluxe king). Baths, unfortunately, include little shelf space for spreading out your toiletries.

Dining/Entertainment: In the vaults below the lobby is the **London Grill** (see next chapter), one of Portland's best dining establishments. Open for breakfast, lunch, and dinner, it features fresh seafood specialties and is best known for its tableside preparations. **Piatto** is a much more casual place serving contemporary Italian dishes. The **Lobby Court** has a bar and also serves a buffet lunch Monday through Friday. There's live jazz here in the evenings.

Services: 24-hour room service, concierge, valet parking, valet/laundry service.

Facilities: Exercise room, gift shop.

Governor Hotel. SW 10th Ave. and Alder St., Portland, OR 97205. ☎ **800/554-3456** or 503/224-3400. Fax 503/241-2122. 100 rms, 28 suites. A/C MINIBAR TV TEL. $185–$195 double ($125–$145 weekends); $200 junior suite; $210–$500 suite. AE, CB, DC, JCB, MC, V. Valet parking $13.

This historic hotel is an homage to the Lewis and Clark Expedition, and throughout the hotel, you'll spot references to the famous explorers. However, it is the wall mural in the lobby that most captures the attention. The lobby, though small, has a classically Western feel, with a fireplace and overstuffed leather chairs. Between the lobby and the restaurant, you'll find the Dome Room, with a stunning stained-glass dome skylight. Classic styling aside, it is the presence of one of the city's best athletic clubs in its basement that makes The Governor most appealing to the athletically inclined.

Guest rooms vary considerably in size but all are beautifully decorated. The least expensive rooms are rather small but are nevertheless very comfortable. Still, we'd opt for one of the deluxe guest rooms rather than the standard room. Unfortunately, bathrooms are, in general, quite cramped by today's standards and lack counter space, although their tile work does give them a classic feel. Suites on the other hand are spacious, and some even have huge patios overlooking the city.

Dining/Entertainment: Jake's Grill, a large, old-fashioned restaurant with burnished wood columns and slowly turning overhead fans, is just off the lobby. The menu features grilled steak and seafood.

Services: 24-hour room service; concierge; personal computers and fax machines available; complimentary morning newspaper and coffee; overnight shoeshine; valet/laundry service.

Facilities: Business center, hearing-impaired accommodations. **The Princeton Athletic Club,** down in the lower level of the hotel, includes a lap pool, indoor running track, whirlpool spa, steam rooms, sauna, and exercise room.

✪ **The Heathman Hotel.** 1001 SW Broadway at Salmon St., Portland, OR 97205. ☎ **800/551-0011** or 503/241-4100. Fax 503/790-7110. 151 rms, 47 suites. A/C MINIBAR TV TEL. $180–$205 double (from $140 weekends); $220–$225 junior suite; $275–$675 suite. AE, CB, DC, DISC, MC, V. Parking $12.

Portland Accommodations

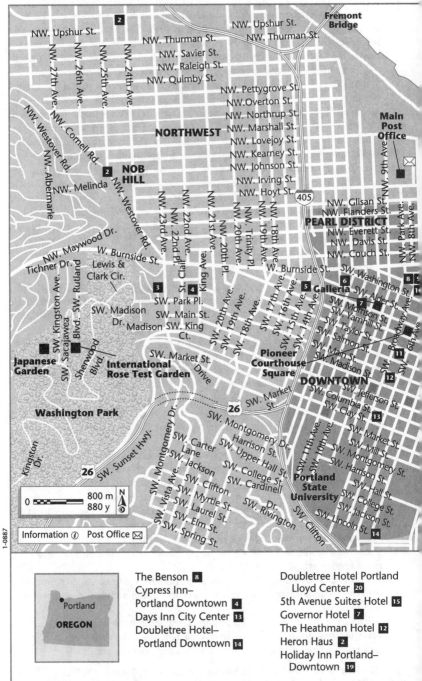

The Benson **8**
Cypress Inn–
Portland Downtown **4**
Days Inn City Center **13**
Doubletree Hotel–
Portland Downtown **14**

Doubletree Hotel Portland
Lloyd Center **20**
5th Avenue Suites Hotel **15**
Governor Hotel **7**
The Heathman Hotel **12**
Heron Haus **2**
Holiday Inn Portland–
Downtown **19**

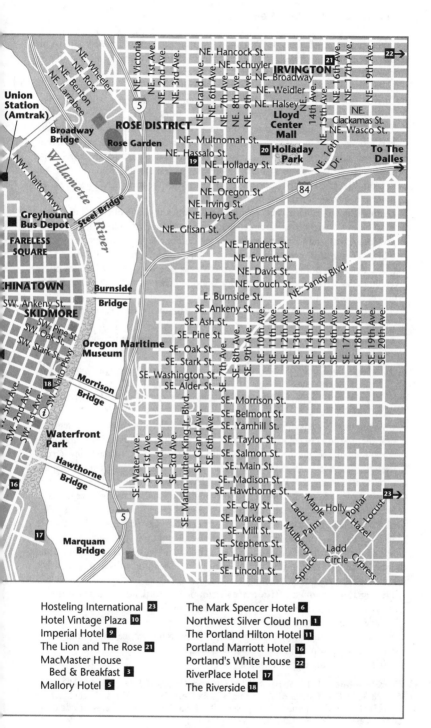

Hosteling International **23**
Hotel Vintage Plaza **10**
Imperial Hotel **9**
The Lion and The Rose **21**
MacMaster House
  Bed & Breakfast **3**
Mallory Hotel **5**

The Mark Spencer Hotel **6**
Northwest Silver Cloud Inn **1**
The Portland Hilton Hotel **11**
Portland Marriott Hotel **16**
Portland's White House **22**
RiverPlace Hotel **17**
The Riverside **18**

The Heathman, which abuts the Portland Center for the Performing Arts and has on display an outstanding collection of art that ranges from 18th-century oil paintings to Andy Warhol prints, is the address of choice for visiting patrons of the arts. Understated luxury and superb service make this one of the finest hotels in the city. While the marble and teak lobby itself is tiny, it opens onto the Tea Court, where the original eucalyptus paneling creates a warm, old-world atmosphere.

The basic rooms here tend to be quite small, but are nonetheless attractively furnished and set up for business travelers. There are no real views to speak of, but rooms on the west side of the hotel do have views of a mural done just for the hotel. One of the best perks is access to a library of 400 movies (no charge). Room service will even send up a free bowl of popcorn to go along with the movie. At press time, all the rooms were scheduled to be refurbished.

Dining/Entertainment: The Heathman Restaurant is one of Portland's finest. The menu emphasizes creatively prepared fresh local produce, seafood, and game. **B. Moloch/Heathman Bakery and Pub,** the hotel's casual, contemporary pub, is two blocks away. Both restaurants have cozy bars. (See chapter 15, "Portland Dining," for details on both restaurants.) In the **Mezzanine Bar,** there is live jazz music several nights a week for most of the year. Afternoon tea is served daily in the **Lobby Lounge,** and there are also evening wine tastings.

Services: 24-hour room service, concierge, valet/laundry service, complimentary newspaper.

Facilities: Privileges at nearby athletic club, on-site fitness suite with a few machines (personal trainers also available).

✪ **Hotel Vintage Plaza.** 422 SW Broadway, Portland, OR 97205. ☎ **800/243-0555** or 503/228-1212. Fax 503/228-3598. 107 rms, 21 suites. A/C MINIBAR TV TEL. $175–$185 double ($140–$165 weekends); $205–$225 suite. All rates include continental breakfast. AE, CB, DC, DISC, MC, V. Valet parking $13.

If you enjoy a good glass of wine and are interested in learning more about regional wines, there is no better Portland hotel to stay than at the Vintage Plaza. Italianate decor and a wine theme are in evidence throughout the hotel. In the lobby, a cozy place with fireplace and the feel of a private living room, there are complimentary evening wine tastings that feature Oregon and Washington wines.

All accommodations are different, and though the standard rooms have much to recommend them, the starlight rooms and two-level suites are the real scene-stealers here. The starlight rooms in particular are truly extraordinary (and cost only $10 more than a regular room). Though small, they have greenhouse-style wall-into-ceiling windows that provide very romantic views at night and let in floods of light during the day. The two-level suites, some with Japanese soaking tubs and one with a spiral staircase, are equally stunning.

Dining/Entertainment: Ristorante Pazzo, one of Portland's best Italian restaurants, is a dark and intimate trattoria serving northern Italian cuisine (see chapter 15, "Portland Dining," for details).

Services: Complimentary evening wine, 24-hour room service, shoeshine service, complimentary morning newspaper, valet/laundry service.

Facilities: Executive gym, business center.

✪ **RiverPlace Hotel.** 1510 SW Harbor Way, Portland, OR 97201-5105. ☎ **800/227-1333** or 503/228-3233. Fax 503/295-6161. 84 rms, 47 suites. A/C TV TEL. $215–$255 double (from $175 weekends outside summer); $250 junior suite; $285–$700 suite. All rates include continental breakfast. AE, CB, DC, JCB, MC, V. Valet parking $14.

With the Willamette River at its back doorstep and the sloping lawns of Waterfront Park to one side, the RiverPlace is Portland's only downtown waterfront hotel. This fact alone would be enough to recommend this hotel, but its quiet boutique-hotel atmosphere would make the RiverPlace an excellent choice even if it were not right on the water. During the summer, the hotel is particularly popular when there are music festivals in the adjacent park.

The river-view standard king rooms here are the hotel's best deal, but the junior suites are only slightly more expensive and provide a bit more space. In general, furnishings here are neither as elegant nor as luxurious as at the Heathman or the Benson, but what you're paying for is, of course, the waterfront locale. More than half the rooms here are suites, and some come with wood-burning fireplaces and whirlpool baths. Planning a long stay in Portland? The hotel can arrange for you to use one of its adjacent condominiums.

Dining/Entertainment: The **Esplanade Restaurant** overlooks the river and serves Northwest and continental fare (see chapter 15 for details). For al fresco summer dining, there's the casual **Patio.** Just off the lobby is a comfortable bar with live piano music and a crackling fire in cool weather.

Services: 24-hour room service, concierge, complimentary shoeshine, valet/laundry service, complimentary morning paper.

Facilities: Whirlpool, sauna, privileges at athletic club.

EXPENSIVE

Doubletree Portland Downtown. 310 SW Lincoln St., Portland, OR 97201. ☎ **800/ 222-TREE** or 503/221-0450. Fax 503/226-6260. 235 rms. 3 suites. A/C TV TEL. $119–$180 double ($89–$99 weekends), $250–$350 suite. AE, CB, DC, DISC, ER, JCB, MC, V. Free parking.

Situated on a shady tree-lined street on the southern edge of downtown Portland, this low-rise hotel offers the convenience of a downtown location and the casual appeal of a resort or suburban business hotel. The design and landscaping reflect the Northwest, and in the courtyard surrounding the swimming pool are lush plantings of evergreens and other shrubs.

The best rooms are those on the third floor overlooking the pool courtyard. Although slightly more expensive, these rooms are quiet and have pleasant views. They also get plenty of that precious Northwest sunlight (when the sun shines), although all the rooms have large windows.

Dining/Entertainment: The **Cityside Restaurant** offers a wide variety of well-prepared meals, with the focus on fresh local seafood. **Club Max** is the hotel's disco, with DJs most evenings and live music occasionally.

Services: Room service, complimentary airport shuttle, valet/laundry service.

Facilities: Outdoor pool in pleasant garden setting, exercise room, gift shop.

✪ **5th Avenue Suites Hotel.** 506 SW Washington St., Portland, OR 97204. ☎ **800/ 711-2971** or 503/222-0001. Fax 503/222-0004. 82 rms. 139 suites. A/C MINIBAR TV TEL. $165 double ($125 weekends), $180–$240 suite ($140 weekends). AE, DC, DISC, JCB, MC, V. Valet parking $14.

Located a block from Pioneer Courthouse Square and within a few blocks of the best shopping in downtown Portland, this unpretentious yet sophisticated hotel is an up-to-the-minute renovation of what was originally a department store (in the lobby, there's a display about the old department store). Ceilings are high, and the art-filled lobby has a marble hearth (though for a gas fireplace) around which guests can gather to enjoy complimentary evening tastings of regional wines. Business travelers, couples, and families with children will all find their needs well met here.

Guest rooms are furnished in a turn-of-the-century country style but also have fax machines for convenience at the turn of this century. Plush upholstered chairs and beds with padded headboards and luxurious comforters assure that business travelers (and others) will be comfortable in their home away from office. Bathrooms have lots of counter space. In the suites, sliding French doors with curtains divide the living room from the bedrooms, but don't provide much privacy.

Dining/Entertainment: The Red Star Tavern and Roast House is a popular American bistro-style restaurant specializing in foods of the Northwest.

Services: 24-hour room service, concierge, complimentary morning coffee and newspaper, complimentary evening wine tasting.

Facilities: Fitness center with numerous exercise machines, day spa offering massages and other body treatments, business center.

The Portland Hilton Hotel. 921 SW Sixth Ave., Portland, OR 97204-1296. ☎ **800/HILTONS** or 503/226-1611. Fax 503/220-2565. 455 rms, 16 suites. A/C TV TEL. $135–$225 double ($109–$119 weekends); $200–$850 suite. AE, CB, DC, DISC, JCB, MC, V. Self parking $14, valet parking $17.

An extensive renovation a few years ago has left the exterior of this high-rise look-ing quite contemporary and the interior looking classically elegant. While business travelers, conventions, and tour groups comprise the bulk of the business here (and keep the lobby bustling with activity), the Hilton is very conveniently located for vacationers as well. Within just a couple of blocks are the Portland Center for the Performing Arts and several museums. An indoor swimming pool and extensive health club also make this a good choice for active travelers.

Rooms here tend to be fairly small, so opt for a double-double or king room if you want a bit more space. Bathrooms, which lack counter space, are also a bit small. However, for the overworked business traveler, there are comfortable chairs and two phones in the rooms. Be sure to request a floor as high as possible to take advantage of the views. The corner rooms with king-size beds are our favorites.

Dining/Entertainment: From its 23rd-floor aerie, **Alexander's** offers a striking panorama of Portland, the Willamette River, and snow-covered Mount Hood (see chapter 15 for details). Back down at lobby level is the informal **Bistro 921** restaurant and bar, with regional and international cuisine.

Services: Room service, concierge, laundry/valet service, overnight shoeshine service.

Facilities: The Portland Hilton Athletic Club features an indoor skylit swimming pool, saunas, steam rooms, an extensive array of exercise machines, fitness trainers, and aerobics classes. Business center.

Portland Marriott Hotel. 1401 SW Naito Pkwy., Portland, OR 97201. ☎ **800/228-9290** or 503/226-7600. Fax 503/221-1789. 503 rms, 6 suites. A/C TV TEL. $145–$205 double ($119–$160 weekends); $300–$450 suite. AE, CB, DC, DISC, ER, JCB, MC, V. Valet parking $13.

Located just across Waterfront Park and Naito Parkway (Front Avenue) from the Willamette River, the Portland Marriott is the flashiest of the city's hotels. A mas-sive portico with Japanese-style landscaping leads guests into a high-ceilinged lobby filled with bright lights.

Most of the guest rooms have small balconies, and if you ask for a room overlook-ing the river, you can throw back the glass door to the balcony, and consider that the view used to be of a noisy freeway (it was torn out to build the park). On a clear day Mount Hood looms in the distance. Unfortunately, the furnishing and carpets are in need of replacement, but if you can overlook a bit of wear and tear, you can enjoy the views and the almost waterfront location.

Dining/Entertainment: Fazzio's Cafe is a family restaurant serving breakfast, lunch, and dinner. **Champions** is a very popular sports bar with all the requisite memorabilia on the walls; on weekends there's dancing to recorded music. The lobby bar attracts a much more sedate crowd.

Services: Room service, concierge floor, valet/laundry service, shoeshine stand, baby-sitting service, massages.

Facilities: Exercise room, indoor pool, whirlpool, saunas, game room, hair salon, gift shop, newsstand, business center.

MODERATE

Days Inn City Center. 1414 SW Sixth Ave., Portland, OR 97201. ☎ **800/899-0248** or 503/221-1611. Fax 503/226-0447. 173 rms. A/C TV TEL. $79–$110 double. AE, CB, DC, MC, V. Free parking.

Although this 1960s vintage hotel lacks much in the way of character or charm, it's the most economical choice if you are looking to stay in downtown Portland. The hotel has been recently renovated and has new carpets and furniture throughout. In the guest rooms, you'll find a couple of unusual touches—a small shelf of hardbound books (mostly *Reader's Digest* condensed books) as well as framed old photos of Portland.

With its brass rails and wood trim, the **Portland Bar and Grill** is popular with the business set for lunch and happy-hour hors d'oeuvres. Hotel amenities include valet/laundry service, room service, and a complimentary newspaper. The hotel also has a seasonal outdoor swimming pool.

Imperial Hotel. 400 SW Broadway, Portland, OR 97205. ☎ **800/452-2323** or 503/228-7221. Fax 503/223-4551. 136 rms. A/C TV TEL. $85–$100 double. AE, CB, DC, DISC, MC, V. Free parking.

Although it doesn't quite live up to its regal name, this older hotel across the street from the Benson is a fine choice if you're on a budget. While the staff may be young and not as polished as at more expensive hotels, they usually are good about seeing to guests' needs. A recent renovation has left the rooms quite up to date, which makes this an excellent choice for budget travelers, and the location can't be beat. In fact, it would be hard to find such reasonably priced downtown accommodations in any comparable city. The corner king rooms, with large windows, should be your first choice, and barring this, at least ask for an exterior room. These might get a little street noise, but they're bigger than the interior rooms and get more sunlight (when the sun shines at all). Rooms have in-room safes, minirefrigerators, and hairdryers. Local phone calls are free. The hotel's restaurant is rather nondescript and unmemorable, but in the lounge, old movie posters hang on the walls and add a bit of retro character. The hotel provides a morning newspaper, valet/laundry service, and room service for its guests.

The Mark Spencer Hotel. 409 SW 11th Ave., Portland, OR 97205. ☎ **800/548-3934** or 503/224-3293. Fax 503/223-7848. 101 rms. A/C TV TEL. $72 double; $99–$109 one-bedroom suite. Lower weekly and monthly rates are also available. Nightly rates include continental breakfast. AE, CB, DC, MC, V. Free parking.

If you're planning an extended stay in Portland and need to be within walking distance of downtown, this is the place for you. Although the hotel is not in the best neighborhood in the city (there are lots of nightclubs and bars in the vicinity), it's just around the corner from Jake's Famous Crawfish, one of Portland's oldest and most popular restaurants, as well as Powell's City of Books. The building itself is quite attractive, with flower baskets hanging from old-fashioned street lamps out front. The Mark Spencer is a favorite of touring Broadway shows when they're in town.

All rooms and suites have kitchenettes, which is the main draw here for people planning on spending a week or more in town. Walk-in closets are also a definite plus for those planning a long stay in town. The hotel offers free housekeeping, coin-operated laundry and valet service, private mailboxes, personal phone lines, and privileges at a nearby athletic club.

✪ **The Riverside.** 50 SW Morrison Ave., Portland, OR 97204-3390. ☎ **800/899-0247** or 503/221-0711. Fax 503/274-0312. 140 rms. A/C TV TEL. $99–$170 double. AE, CB, DC, DISC, MC, V. Free parking.

Overlooking Waterfront Park and located on the MAX light-rail line, this 1960s vintage hotel looks very nondescript from the outside, but inside has been renovated to a 1990s contemporary appearance that makes it one of the most stylish hotels in town. As the name implies, you are only steps from the Willamette River (although not actually on the water), but you are also close to businesses, fine restaurants, and shopping. Guest rooms are as boldly contemporary in design as the lobby and restaurant, which are sort of downscale *Architectural Digest.* If this is your style, make The Riverside your Portland choice.

With its contemporary styling and cozy fireside lounge, the **Riverside Club** offers guests a very stylish place to relax over a drink or enjoy a meal. Large windows look out over the Waterfront Park and the river, and the menu is surprisingly creative. Amenities at the Riverside include room service, valet/laundry service, complimentary newspaper, passes to two fitness clubs.

INEXPENSIVE

✪ **Mallory Hotel.** 729 SW 15th Ave., Portland, OR 97205-1994. ☎ **800/228-8657** or 503/223-6311. Fax 503/223-0522. 136 rms, 26 suites. A/C TV TEL. $70–$110 double; $110 suite. AE, CB, DC, MC, V. Free parking.

The Mallory has long been a favorite of Portland visitors who want the convenience of a downtown lodging but aren't on a bottomless expense account. This is an older hotel in which the lobby, which is done in deep forest green with ornate gilt plaster work trim and crystal chandeliers, has a certain classic (and faded) grandeur. Time seems to have stood still here (there's a doorman in a pith helmet and a lounge straight out of the 1950s). Sometime in 1998, the new west-side Max line will begin service right past the hotel, which will make the Mallory more convenient than ever.

The rooms are not as luxurious as the lobby might suggest and are smaller than comparable rooms at the Imperial or Days Inn, but are comfortable and clean. With rates this low, you might even want to go for one of the king-size suites. These rooms are about as big as they come, with walk-in closets, minirefrigerators, and sofa beds. Amenities include free local calls, 1pm checkout, and valet/laundry service.

The dining room at the Mallory continues the grand design of the lobby. Heavy drapes hang from the windows, and faux-marble pillars lend just the right air of imperial grandeur.

3 Nob Hill & Northwest Portland

EXPENSIVE

✪ **Heron Haus.** 2545 NW Westover Rd., Portland, OR 97210. ☎ **503/274-1846.** Fax 503/243-1075. 6 rms (all with private bath). TV TEL. $125–$250 double. Rates include continental breakfast. MC, V. Free parking.

A short walk from the bustling Nob Hill shopping and dining district of northwest Portland, the Heron Haus B&B offers outstanding accommodations, spectacular views, and tranquil surroundings. There's even a small swimming pool with sundeck. Surprisingly, the house still features some of the original plumbing. In most places this would be a liability but not here, since the plumbing was done by the same man who plumbed Portland's famous Pittock Mansion. Many of that building's unusual bath features are to be found at the Heron Haus as well. One shower has seven

---

🏨 Family-Friendly Hotels

Embassy Suites Hotel *(see p. 183)*   An indoor pool and large atrium make this a safe bet for kids any time of year, and the huge Washington Square Mall is just down the street. Parents will appreciate having their own bedroom.

Doubletree Lloyd Center *(see p. 179)*   Let the kids loose in the huge Lloyd Center Shopping Mall across the street and they'll stay entertained for hours (there's even an ice-skating rink in the mall). There's also a large shady park across from the hotel.

Portland Marriott Hotel *(see p. 174)*   The game room and indoor pool are popular with kids, and just across the street is Tom McCall Waterfront Park, which runs along the Willamette River.

---

shower heads; another has two. In another room there's a modern whirlpool spa that affords excellent views of the city. Several rooms now have fireplaces.

MODERATE

MacMaster House Bed and Breakfast Inn. 1041 SW Vista Ave., Portland, OR 97205. ☎ 800/774-9523 or 503/223-7362. 7 rms (2 with private bath). $75–$90 double with shared bath; $115–$120 double with private bath. Rates include full breakfast. AE, DC, MC, V.

Located adjacent to both Washington Park and the trendy shops and restaurants of the Nob Hill neighborhood, this imposing mansion sits high above the street and is surrounded by huge old rhododendrons that are gorgeous in the spring. The inn is furnished with the sort of authentic eclecticism that characterized the Victorian era; everywhere you turn there is something interesting to catch the eye. Many of the guest rooms have interesting murals on the walls, and there's even a painting on the side of an old tub in the third floor shared bathroom. Three rooms have fireplaces, and one of these has a claw-foot tub. Some of the rooms are on the third floor, and the inn itself is up a flight of stairs from the street, so you need to be in good shape to stay here. Although the inn is not as immaculate as many B&Bs, it makes up for this with loads of character. The inn's resident Dalmatian will undoubtedly greet you at the door when you arrive.

✪ **Northwest Silver Cloud Inn.** 2426 NW Vaughn St., Portland, OR 97210-2540. ☎ 800/205-6939 or 503/242-2400. Fax 503/242-1770. 81 rms. A/C TV TEL. $80–$128 double. All rates include continental breakfast. AE, DC, DISC, MC, V.

This newer hotel is located just north of Portland's trendy Nob Hill neighborhood, and though it faces the beginning of the city's industrial area, it is still a very attractive and comfortable place. Reasonable rates are the main draw here, but the hotel is also within a 5-minute drive of half a dozen of the city's best restaurants. The standard rooms have small refrigerators, while the minisuites come with refrigerators, wet bars, microwave ovens, and a separate seating area. The most expensive rooms are the king rooms with whirlpool tubs. Local phone calls are free, and facilities include a fitness room and a whirlpool spa. Try to get a room away from Vaughn Street. To find the hotel, take I-405 to Ore. 30 west and get off at the Vaughn Street exit.

INEXPENSIVE

Cypress Inn—Portland Downtown. 809 SW King St., Portland, OR 97205. ☎ 503/226-6288. Fax 503/274-0038. 82 rms. A/C TV TEL. $59–$89 double. All rates include continental breakfast. AE, DC, DISC, MC, V. Free parking.

At press time, this motel, which has seen better days but which for the most part is acceptable, had plans to become a Park Lane Inn and Suites and undergo an extensive renovation. When this happens, expect a jump in rates. Because the motel sits a little bit up into the hills west of downtown, it has some nice views over the city, but you'll have to ask for a room with two double beds to get a view. You'd expect to spend quite a bit more for such views, which makes these rooms a good value. Another plus here is that you are within walking distance of both the Nob Hill shopping and restaurant district and Washington Park, which is home to the Japanese Gardens and the International Rose Test Garden. Be sure to avail yourself of the free local phone calls, and complimentary continental breakfast. There's also a courtesy airport shuttle.

4 Jantzen Beach & North Portland

Located on Hayden Island in the middle of the Columbia River, Jantzen Beach, named for the famous swimwear company that got its start here, is a beach in name only. Today this area is a huge shopping mall complex aimed primarily at Washingtonians, who come to Oregon to avoid Washington's sales tax. Jantzen Beach is also home to a pair of large convention hotels that are among the city's only waterfront hotels. Both hotels are, however, in the flight path for the airport, and although the rooms themselves are adequately insulated against noise, the swimming pools and sundecks can be pretty noisy.

EXPENSIVE

Doubletree Hotel Portland Columbia River. 1401 N. Hayden Island Dr., Portland, OR 97217. ☎ **800/222-TREE** or 503/283-2111. Fax 503/283-4718. 351 rms, 10 suites. A/C TV TEL. $129–$180 double ($85–$99 weekend); $225–$350 suite. AE, CB, DC, DISC, ER, JCB, MC, V. Free parking.

Attractive landscaping and an interesting low-rise design that's slightly reminiscent of a Northwest Coast Indian longhouse has kept this hotel popular for many years. Although rush-hour traffic problems can make this a bad choice if you're here to explore Portland, it's a good location if you plan to visit Mount St. Helens or the Columbia Gorge. You're also within walking distance of the mall. The style of this hotel gives it a very resort-like feel. Guest rooms are large, though rather nondescript, but many of them have views of the Columbia River. Be sure to ask for one of these.

Dining/Entertainment: The Coffee Garden, in the lobby, offers coffee shop meals from early morning to evening. Great views of the Columbia River are to be had at **Brickstones Restaurant,** which features an international menu emphasizing fresh local seafoods and produce. For late-night entertainment, there's the **Brickstones Bar,** where there a DJ spins tunes a couple of nights a week. For a quieter atmosphere, try the aptly named **Quiet Bar,** a small glass-walled octagonal building just off the lobby and overlooking the river and the I-5 Bridge. There's also an espresso cart in the lobby.

Services: Room service, complimentary airport shuttle, valet/laundry service.

Facilities: Heated outdoor swimming pool, whirlpool spa, putting green, gift shop, barbershop, beauty salon.

Doubletree Hotel Portland Jantzen Beach. 909 N. Hayden Island Dr., Portland, OR 97217. ☎ **800/222-TREE** or 503/283-4466. Fax 503/283-4743. 320 rms, 24 suites. A/C TV TEL. $119–$190 double ($85–$99 weekends); $195–$350 suite. AE, CB, DC, DISC, ER, JCB, MC, V. Free parking.

With a design calculated to conjure up images of old Columbia River docks, this is the more resortlike of Doubletree's two Jantzen Beach convention hotels. Arranged in wings around two garden courtyards, one of which has a swimming pool and two tennis courts, the rooms are as large as you're likely to find in any Portland hotel. Most have balconies and many have excellent views of the river and sometimes Mount St. Helens. Bathrooms are equally spacious.

Dining/Entertainment: Elegant dining in plush surroundings with great river views can be found in **Maxi's Restaurant,** which specializes in seafood. For much more casual dining there's the **Coffee Garden** in the lobby. Tuesday through Saturday nights come alive to the sound of live rock 'n' roll bands at **Maxi's Lounge,** which has an art nouveau decor.

Services: Room service, complimentary airport shuttle, valet/laundry service.

Facilities: Heated outdoor pool, whirlpool, tennis courts, gift shop.

INEXPENSIVE

John Palmer House. 4314 N. Mississippi Ave., Portland, OR 97217. ☎ **800/518-5893** or 503/284-5893. 3 rms (1 with private bath). $60–$75 double. Two-night minimum. Rates include expanded continental breakfast. AE, DISC, MC, V.

Although this hotel is not in a very good neighborhood, it is such an elaborate Victorian home that it remains one of my favorite Portland B&Bs. The interior has been done with all the flair for which the Victorian era was known. Dozens of different wallpapers turn the walls into a coordinated riot of colors and patterns. Each room is decorated with massive period furnishings, and stained-glass windows throughout the house filter the sunlight into magical hues. There is also a whirlpool in a gazebo out back. There are claw-foot tubs in both the room with the private bath and in the shared bathroom.

5 The Rose Quarter & Northeast Portland

EXPENSIVE

Doubletree Hotel Portland Lloyd Center. 1000 NE Multnomah St., Portland, OR 97232. ☎ **800/222-TREE** or 503/281-6111. Fax 503/284-8553. 476 rooms, 10 suites. A/C TV TEL. $139–$175 double ($99–$124 weekends); $269–$575 suite. AE, CB, DC, DISC, ER, JCB, MC, V. Parking $9.

Located across the street from the Lloyd Center shopping mall, a large, shady park, and a light-rail station, this convention hotel is a very convenient choice if you don't want to be (or can't get a room) right in downtown. Although the hotel is almost always packed, there are plenty of restaurant choices and a very pleasant pool in a Northwest garden setting.

Most rooms are quite spacious, and some have balconies. The views from the higher floors are stunning. On a clear day you can see Mount Hood, Mount St. Helens, and even Mount Rainier. Ask for a room in the south tower, these rooms are larger, have full baths (rather than bathrooms with showers only), and have been more recently renovated than the hotel's other rooms. The south tower also has glass elevators, which are always fun to ride.

Dining/Entertainment: Maxi's Restaurant, with its etched glass walls and chandeliers, is just off the lobby. Local seafood and steaks are the specialties here. If you're more in the mood for Mexican, cross the lobby to **Eduardo's Cantina,** with stucco walls, tile floors, rough-hewn wood beams, and rattan chairs. Family dining is possible in the **Coffee Garden,** which opens directly onto the lobby. For those seeking a quiet place for conversation and a drink, there's the **Quiet Bar,** which sometimes has live piano music.

Services: Room service, concierge, complimentary airport shuttle, valet/laundry service.

Facilities: Heated outdoor swimming pool, exercise room, gift shop.

MODERATE

Holiday Inn Portland—Downtown. 1021 NE Grand Ave., Portland, OR 97232. ☎ **800/ HOLIDAY** or 503/235-2100. Fax 503/238-0132. 166 rms, 6 suites. A/C TV TEL. $94–$120 double; $155–$255 suite. AE, CB, DC, DISC, MC, V. Free parking.

This hotel, located across the street from the Oregon Convention Center, is a popular choice with conventioneers who don't want to spend a lot for a room. Because Portland's MAX light-rail system stops one block from the hotel, this is also a convenient location if you want to go downtown.

Although rooms currently are a bit worn, there are plans to renovate all the rooms. Large tables, writing desks, two phones, and comfortable armchairs allow guests to spread out. Upper floors have good views either west to the city skyline or east to the Cascades and Mount Hood, and the twin peaks of the Convention Center loom just across the street.

Windows, the hotel's aptly named top-floor restaurant, provides good views of the city, and is one of the best reasons to stay here. While the food may not be that great, you can enjoy the view over a drink any time of day. In summer, there's an outdoor terrace (one of the few roof-top terrace restaurants in the city). In addition, the hotel offers room service, valet/laundry service, a sauna, and a fitness center.

✪ The Lion and the Rose. 1810 NE 15th Ave., Portland, OR 97212. ☎ **800/955-1647** or 503/287-9245. Fax 503/287-9247. 6 rms (5 with private bath). TEL. $115–$120 double. AE, MC, V.

This imposing Queen Anne Victorian bed-and-breakfast inn is in the Irvington District one block off Northeast Broadway and is one of the best-located B&Bs in Portland. Within four blocks are half a dozen excellent restaurants and cafes, a number of eclectic boutiques, and a huge shopping mall. Yet, the Lion and Rose itself is in a fairly quiet residential neighborhood. Even if this inn were not so splendidly located, it would still be a gem. The living room and dining room are beautifully decorated with period antiques, including an ornate pump organ and an upright piano. Breakfasts are sumptuous affairs that are meant to be lingered over.

Guest rooms each have a distinctively different decor and feel ranging from the bright colors and turret sitting area of the Lavonna room to the deep greens of the Starina room, which features an imposing Edwardian bed and armoire. The Garden room and the shared bathroom have claw-foot tubs, but some rooms have cramped, though attractive, bathrooms. If you have problems climbing stairs, ask for the Rose room, which has a modern whirlpool tub in the bathroom.

Portland's White House. 1914 NE 22nd Ave., Portland, OR 97212. ☎ **800/272-7131** or 503/287-7131. Fax 503/249-1641. 9 rms (all with private bath). $88–$139 double. Rates include full breakfast. MC, V.

This imposing Greek-revival mansion bears a more than passing resemblance to its namesake in Washington, D.C. Massive columns frame the entrance, which is reached by a short semicircular driveway. In the front garden, a fountain bubbles near a patio where, on sunny days, you can sit at a table and enjoy a picnic lunch. Behind the mahogany front doors, a huge entrance hall with original hand-painted wall murals, is flanked by a parlor, with French windows and a piano, and the formal dining room, where the large breakfast is served amid sparkling crystal chandeliers. A double staircase leads past a large stained-glass window to the second-floor accommodations.

Canopy and brass queen beds, antique furnishings, and bathrooms with claw-foot tubs further the feelings of classic luxury here. Request the balcony room and you can gaze out past the Greek columns and imagine you're the president. There are also three rooms in the restored carriage house. There is free airport pick-up and afternoon tea.

INEXPENSIVE

Howard Johnson Express. 3939 NE Hancock St., Portland OR 97212. ☎ **503/288-6891.** Fax 503/288-1995. 48 rms. A/C TV TEL. $50–$58 double. AE, DC, DISC, MC, V. Free parking.

Located in the Hollywood District of Northeast Portland about half way between the airport and downtown, this economical choice is in a rather unusual spot (tucked away several blocks from the interstate, but worth finding if you need a budget accommodation). Rooms vary in size, so be sure to ask for one of the larger rooms. The neighborhood takes its name from the mission-revival buildings and Craftsman bungalows that are reminiscent of old Hollywood.

6 Southeast Portland

Hosteling International—Portland. 3031 SE Hawthorne Blvd., Portland, OR 97214. ☎ **503/236-3380.** 50 beds. $13 member, $16 nonmember. MC, V. Bus: 14 from downtown or 12 then 14 from airport.

The Hawthorne District is a shopping and dining area popular with students, artists, and musicians, so it makes an ideal location for a youth hostel. Housed in an old house on a busy street, this hostel is small and has primarily dormitory beds. The common room is also small, but a large wraparound porch makes up for the lack of space inside. There is a large kitchen where guests can prepare their own meals, with a grocery store a short walk away. Between May and September, the hostel offers van tours to Mount St. Helens, Mt. Hood, the Columbia River Gorge, the Oregon coast and even microbrewery and wine tours.

7 The Airport Area & Troutdale

Moderately priced hotels have been proliferating in this area over the past few years, which makes this a good place to look for a room if you arrive with no reservation. Hotels in this area generally provide better value than hotels in the Rose Quarter (near the Oregon Convention Center and Rose Garden stadium), which is where you'll find comparably priced accommodations.

EXPENSIVE

Shilo Inn Suites Hotel Portland Airport. 11707 NE Airport Way, Portland, OR 97220-1075. ☎ **800/222-2244** or 503/252-7500. Fax 503/254-0794. 200 suites. A/C TV TEL. $109–$155 double. Rates include continental breakfast. AE, DC, DISC, MC, V.

If you want to stay near the airport and want a spacious room and the facilities of a deluxe hotel, this is one of your best bets. All the rooms here are called suites, and although they don't actually have separate seating and sleeping rooms, they do have plenty of room and lots of other amenities. There are large closets with mirrored doors, lots of bathroom counter space, and three TVs in the rooms (including ones in the bathrooms). Other amenities include hairdryers, VCRs, and double sinks. The main drawback here is that this is a convention hotel and is often very crowded. To find this hotel, head straight out of the airport, drive under the I-205 overpass and watch for the hotel ahead on the left.

Dining/Entertainment: The hotel's dining room is in the convention center wing and serves surprisingly creative dishes amid casual surroundings. There's a cigar room and a piano lounge adjacent to the restaurant. The complimentary breakfast is served in a large TV lounge just off the lobby.

Services: Room service, complimentary airport shuttle, valet service.

Facilities: Indoor swimming pool, whirlpool spa, exercise room.

MODERATE

Courtyard by Marriott. 11550 NE Airport Way, Portland, OR 97220. ☎ **800/321-2211** or 503/252-3200. Fax 503/252-8921. 140 rms, 10 suites. A/C TV TEL. $54–$83 double; $100–$110 suite. AE, DC, DISC, MC, V.

Despite the name, this modern six-story hotel has no courtyard. What it does have, however, is an elegant little lobby featuring lots of marble and modest but comfortable guest rooms with coffeemakers and irons and ironing boards. If you need some extra room, opt for one of the suites, which come with microwave ovens, wet bars, and small refrigerators. Ask for a room away from the road if you're a light sleeper. This is one of the most convenient hotels to the airport; take the complimentary shuttle or, by car, just head straight out of the airport, go under the I-205 overpass and you'll see the hotel ahead on the right. There's a comfortable lounge off the lobby as well as a moderately priced dining room. The hotel also has a tiny outdoor swimming pool, a whirlpool spa, and a fitness room.

✪ **McMenamins Edgefield Bed and Breakfast Resort.** 2126 SW Halsey St., Troutdale, OR 97060. ☎ **800/669-8610** or 503/669-8610. 103 rms (3 with bath), 24 hostel beds. $75–115 double; $18 hostel bed. Rates include full breakfast. AE, DISC, MC, V.

B&Bs don't usually have 100 rooms, but this is no ordinary inn. Located 30 minutes east of downtown Portland and ideally situated for exploring the Columbia Gorge and Mount Hood, this flagship of the McMenamin microbrewery empire is the former county poor farm. Today, after extensive remodeling, the property includes not only tastefully decorated guest rooms with antique furnishings, but a brewery, a pub, a beer garden, a restaurant, a movie theater, a winery, a wine-tasting room, meeting facilities, extensive gardens, and a hostel. With so much in one spot, this makes a great base for exploring the area. The beautiful grounds give this inn the feel of a remote retreat, though you are still within a short drive of everything Portland has to offer.

Quality Inn/Portland Airport. 8247 NE Sandy Blvd., Portland, OR 97220. ☎ **800/246-4649** or 503/256-4111. Fax 503/254-1507. 120 rms, 4 suites. A/C TV TEL. $65–$75 double; $100 suite. Rates include continental breakfast. AE, CB, DC, DISC, ER, JCB, MC, V. Free parking.

Although the rooms here are a bit small and dark (with the exception of those by the pool), they are very comfortable and clean, and the attractively landscaped surroundings more than make up for any inadequacies in the accommodations. If you're willing to spend a bit more, there are suites and rooms with whirlpool baths. The hotel offers complimentary airport shuttle, valet service, complimentary morning newspaper, free local phone calls, a heated outdoor pool, and laundry facilities.

Steamers Restaurant and Lounge specializes in fresh seafood. If you're a fan of the steam era, you'll love this place. There are plenty of old photos on the walls, and bits and pieces rescued from paddle wheelers and steam locomotives.

✪ **Silver Cloud Inn Portland Airport.** 11518 NE Glenn Widing Rd., Portland, OR 97220. ☎ **800/205-7892** or 503/252-2222. Fax 503/257-7008. 102 rms, 8 suites. A/C TV TEL. $89–$99 double; $119–$139 suite. Rates include continental breakfast. AE, DC, DISC, MC, V. Free parking.

Conveniently located right outside the airport, this hotel has the best backyard of any hotel in the Portland area. A lake, lawns, trees, and bird feeders all add up to a tranquil setting despite the proximity of both the airport and a busy nearby road. Rooms are designed primarily for business travelers, and even if you aren't here on business, they offer good value, especially the king rooms with whirlpool tubs, which are only $10 more than regular rooms. There are refrigerators and microwaves in all the rooms, and some suites have gas fireplaces. Best of all, every room has a view of the lake. An indoor pool is another big plus here. You'll also find a whirlpool and exercise room. Other amenities include guest laundry and free local phone calls. To find this hotel, take the complimentary airport shuttle or head straight out of the airport, drive under the I-205 overpass and watch for the hotel ahead on the left.

INEXPENSIVE

The **Super 8 Motel,** 11011 NE Homan St. (☎ **503/257-8988**), just off of Airport Way after you go under the I-205 overpass, is conveniently located but charges a surprisingly high $61 to $73 a night for a double.

8 The West Side (Including Beaverton & Tigard)

EXPENSIVE

Embassy Suites Hotel. 9000 SW Washington Square Rd., Tigard, OR 97223. ☎ **800/ EMBASSY** or 503/644-4000. Fax 503/641-4654. 354 suites. A/C TV TEL. $139 double. Rates include full breakfast. AE, DC, DISC, MC, V. Free parking.

This hotel, in the western suburbs of Portland, is primarily used by business travelers in town on high-tech business, but with its large suites and indoor swimming pool and whirlpool, this nine-story atrium hotel is also a good choice for families. Outside of rush-hour periods, this hotel is convenient to downtown.

As the name implies, every room here is a suite. In the sitting room you'll find a huge stereo console TV, a relaxing couch, a telephone, and a large table. Each suite also has a microwave, refrigerator, wet bar, and iron and ironing board. In the bedroom you'll find another TV, a clock radio, and a second phone.

Dining/Entertainment: The **Crossroads Restaurant** serves straightforward meals and has an adjacent lounge.

Services: Room service, valet/laundry service, nightly manager's reception with complimentary drinks, courtesy transportation to Washington Square Mall, complimentary newspapers.

Facilities: 24-hour indoor pool, whirlpool, sauna, fitness room and privileges at nearby health club.

MODERATE

✪ **Greenwood Inn.** 10700 SW Allen Blvd., Beaverton, OR 97005. ☎ **800/289-1300** or 503/ 643-7444. Fax 503/626-4553. 251 rms; 2 suites. A/C TV TEL. $109–$125 double; $250–$400 suite. AE, CB, DC, DISC, MC, V. Free parking.

With beautifully landscaped grounds that reflect the garden style of the Pacific Northwest, this resortlike, low-rise hotel is the west side's best, and is located only 15 minutes from downtown Portland. A superb restaurant and a very atmospheric lounge make this an all-around good choice. If you're in the area to do business in the "Silicon Forest," the Greenwood is well located. Guest rooms are large and comfortable and most are designed with business travelers in mind. In the bathrooms, you'll find plenty of counter space for toiletries. Executive rooms, which cost about $15 extra, are exceptional, with original artwork on the walls, interesting wicker-and-log chairs, three phones, and a well-lighted desk/work area. Hotel amenities and facilities include access to a nearby athletic club, a morning newspaper, a shopping shuttle, and the use of an exercise room, sauna, outdoor swimming pool, and hot tub.

The **Pavilion Bar and Grill** serves moderate to expensive Northwest cuisine that is among the best available in the Portland area (see "Southwest Portland and the West Side" in chapter 15 for details). There's live or recorded music five nights a week in the hotel's **Wanigan Lounge,** which is done up very stylishly with a sort of contemporary mountain lodge character.

15 Portland Dining

The Northwest restaurant graveyard is crowded with the ghosts of daring restaurants that served imaginative cuisine, garnered rave reviews, and then disappeared as quickly as a luscious crème brûlée. Luckily for the adventurous palates of Portland, the city does have an ever-growing number of excellent restaurants with staying power.

In the past couple of years the Portland restaurant scene has gotten so fired up that the city has developed almost as much of a reputation as Seattle. Ground zero for the Portland restaurant explosion is Northwest 21st Avenue, where you'll find half a dozen excellent restaurants within a few blocks, but all over the city there are excellent restaurants popping up like mushrooms after a spring rain. The Sellwood and Westmoreland neighborhood of Southeast Portland is another of the city's hot restaurant districts, and for good inexpensive food, its hard to beat the many offerings in the Irvington neighborhood of Northeast Portland.

With Oregon wines, especially Pinot Noir and Pinot Gris, continuing to receive widespread acclaim, a dinner out in Portland isn't complete without a local wine. Expect to pay a bit more for an Oregon wine than you would for one from California.

If you're looking for someplace to do brunch on a leisurely Sunday, try the **London Grill** (you'll want to dress up for this one), **Wildwood** (for the trendiest brunch in town), **Fiddleheads** (for Native American-inspired Northwest cuisine), **Indigine** (for an international feast), **The Esplanade** (for a gourmet brunch with a view of the Willamette River), **Avalon Grill** (for upscale riverfront brunch in stylish surroundings), **Newport Bay** (for seafood brunch at a floating restaurant on the Willamette River), **Salty's on the Columbia** (seafood brunch with a view of the Columbia River), and **Bread and Ink Cafe,** (a three-course Yiddish repast; don't feel guilty if you can't finish your meal), **Papa Haydn** (for brunch with an emphasis on dessert), **Hands on Cafe** (for a casual brunch on an art school campus), or **Ron Paul Charcuterie** (for a creative yet casual neighborhood brunch). See below for details.

If you're ravenous at midnight or later in Portland, you don't have a whole lot of decent options. Try **Garbanzo's, Hamburger Mary's,** or **Montage.**

In the following listings, we consider a restaurant **expensive** if a meal without wine or beer would average $35 or more per person. **Moderate** restaurants offer complete dinners in the $20 to $35 range, and **inexpensive** restaurant are those where you can enjoy a complete meal for less than $20.

1 Best Bets

- **Best Spot for a Romantic Dinner:** With dramatic lighting, dark corners, sensuous food, and superb wines, **Assaggio,** 7742 SE 13th Ave. (☎ **503/232-6151**), a neighborhood trattoria in the Sellwood district is a sure bet for a romantic dinner.
- **Best Place to Close a Deal: The London Grill,** 309 SW Broadway (☎ **503/228-2000**), at the Benson Hotel, a hotel favored by presidents and other power lunchers, is an unparalleled place for conducting business.
- **Best Spot for a Celebration:** With a decor that harkens back to the days of fin de siècle Paris, **Brasserie Montmartre,** 626 SW Park Ave. (☎ **503/224-5552**), has live jazz and a performing magician several nights a week. Plus, your entire party can color all over the (paper) tablecloths with crayons.
- **Best Decor:** If contemporary decor appeals to you, **Wildwood,** 1221 NW 21st Ave. (☎ **503/248-WOOD**), one of the anchors of Northwest 21st Avenue's Restaurant Row, is the place. The hard-edged interior is straight out of *Architectural Digest.*
- **Best View:** On the 30th floor of the U.S. Bancorp Tower, **Atwater's,** U.S. Bancorp Tower, 111 SW Fifth Ave. (☎ **503/275-3600**), offers elegant opulence, spectacular views of Portland and Mount Hood, and Northwest cuisine. It's open for dinner only.
- **Best Wine List:** You can sit at the wine bar at **Caprial's Bistro and Wines,** 7015 SE Milwaukee Ave. (☎ **503/236-6457**), and sample some of the best wines around. The food here is award-winning Northwest cuisine.
- **Best Value:** Beer and pizza are a classic combination and nowhere in town are they better represented than at **B. Moloch/Heathman Bakery and Pub,** 901 SW Salmon St. (☎ **503/227-5700**), where the brews come from the microbrewery in the building and the pizzas come from a wood-burning oven.
- **Best for Kids: The Old Spaghetti Factory,** 0715 SW Bancroft St. (☎ **503/222-5375**), may not serve the best Italian food in town, but it certainly is some of the cheapest, and the waterfront location and eclectic decor is a hit with kids and parents alike.
- **Best French: Couvron,** 1126 SW 18th Ave. (☎ **503/225-1844**), a tiny cottage French restaurant not far from downtown, serves the most eclectic and creative French and French-influenced meals in the city.
- **Best Italian:** At **Genoa,** 2832 SE Belmont St. (☎ **503/238-1464**), which has fewer than a dozen tables, meals are either four-course or seven-course fixed-price extravaganzas that are as far from spaghetti and meatballs as you can get and still be called Italian. This is also a great spot for a special, romantic dinner.
- **Best Northwest:** The **Heathman Restaurant,** SW Broadway at Salmon St. (☎ **503/241-4100**), at the elegant Heathman Hotel features the very best Northwest meat, seafood, wild game, and produce, all with a French accent thanks to chef Philippe Boulot.
- **Best Mediterranean:** A perennial Portland favorite, **Zefiro,** 500 NW 21st Ave. (☎ **503/226-3394**), is usually busy serving its loyal clientele imaginative Mediterranean dishes highly influenced by French, Italian, Moroccan, Greek, and Spanish cuisine.
- **Best Mexican:** With an outpost on either side of the river, **Chez José,** 2200 NE Broadway (☎ **503/280-9888**), serves the most creative and unusual Mexican food in the city. No, it's not exactly traditional, which is exactly what makes it so good.

- **Best Seafood:** Get 'em while they're hot at **Jake's Famous Crawfish,** 401 SW 12th Ave. (☎ **503/226-1419**). They've been serving up these miniature lobsters for years.
- **Best Burger:** Burgers are a very subjective subject, but the best we've found in Portland are at **Dots,** 2521 SE Clinton St. (☎ **503/235-0203**), a neighborhood place that serves juicy, two-fisted burgers in kitschy surroundings.
- **Best Pizza:** Portland's best pizza (crispy crusts and creative ingredients) can be found at the numerous **Pizzicato Gourmet Pizza** restaurants around the city. The downtown outpost is at 705 SW Alder St. (☎ **503/226-1007**).
- **Best Desserts: Papa Haydn,** 701 NW 23rd Ave. (☎ **503/228-7317**), offers a symphony that includes lemon chiffon torte, raspberry gâteau, and Georgian peanut butter mousse, to name but a few. There's usually a waiting line at the door, but don't let that deter you.
- **Best Brunch:** The most lavish brunch in Portland is served at the Benson Hotel's **London Grill,** 309 SW Broadway (☎ **503/228-2000**), located downstairs from the marble-floored lobby.

2 Restaurants by Cuisine

AFTERNOON TEA

British Tea Garden (Downtown and Old Town, *I*)

The Heathman Hotel (Downtown and Old Town, *I*)

AMERICAN

American Palate (Nob Hill and Northwest Portland, *M*)

Red Star Tavern and Roast House (Downtown and Old Town, *M*)

Shakers Café (Nob Hill and Northwest Portland, *I*)

Wildwood (Nob Hill and Northwest Portland, *E*)

Zell's (Southeast Portland, *I*)

ASIAN

Saucebox (Downtown and Old Town, *I*)

BAKERIES/DESSERT PLACES

Marsee Baking (Nob Hill and Northwest Portland, *I*)

Papa Haydn (Nob Hill and Northwest Portland, *M*)

BREAKFAST/BRUNCH

Bijou Café (Downtown and Old Town, *I*)

Bread and Ink Café (Southeast Portland, *M*)

The London Grill— Benson Hotel (Downtown and Old Town, *E*)

Salty's (Northeast Portland, *E*)

Wildwood (Nob Hill and Northwest Portland, *E*)

Zell's (Southeast Portland, *I*)

BURGERS

Hamburger Mary's (Downtown and Old Town, *I*)

CAFES

The Brazen Bean (Nob Hill and Northwest Portland, *I*)

Café Lena (Southeast Portland, *I*)

Coffee Time (Nob Hill and Northwest Portland, *I*)

Common Grounds (Southeast Portland, *I*)

Pied Cow (Southeast Portland, *I*)

Rimsky-Korsakoffee House (Southeast Portland, *I*)

Torrefazione Italia (Nob Hill and Northwest Portland, *I*)

CAJUN

Montage (Southeast Portland, *M*)

Key to abbreviations: *E*=Expensive; *I*=Inexpensive; *M*=Moderate; *VE*=Very Expensive

CHINESE

Fong Chong (Downtown and
Old Town, *I*)
Hunan (Downtown and
Old Town, *M*)

CONTINENTAL

Huber's (Downtown and
Old Town, *M*)
The London Grill (Downtown and
Old Town, *E*)
Rene's Fifth Avenue (Downtown and
Old Town, *I*)
Western Culinary Institute
International Dining Room
(Downtown and Old Town, *I*)

DELICATESSEN

Kornblatts (Nob Hill and
Northwest Portland, *I*)
Ron Paul Charcuterie (Northeast
Portland, *M*)

FRENCH

Brasserie Montmartre (Downtown
and Old Town, *M*)
Couvron (Downtown and
Old Town, *E*)
The Heathman Restaurant and Bar
(Downtown and Old Town, *M*)
L'Auberge (Nob Hill and
Northwest Portland, *E*)
Paley's Place (Southwest Portland, *M*)

GREEK

Alexis Restaurant (Downtown and
Old Town, *M*)

GULF COAST

Bima (Nob Hill and
Northwest Portland, *M*)

INDIAN

Indigine (Southeast Portland, *M*)
Plainfield's Mayur Restaurant and
Art Gallery (Downtown and
Old Town, *M*)
Swagat (Southwest Portland and
the West Side, *I*)

INDONESIAN

Satay House (Southwest Portland
& the West Side, *M*)

INTERNATIONAL

Hands on Café (Southwest Portland
and the West Side, *I*)
Indigine (Southeast Portland, *M*)
Old Wives' Tales (Southeast
Portland, *I*)

ITALIAN

Assaggio (Northeast Portland, *M*)
Bastas (Nob Hill and
Northwest Portland, *M*)
Café Mingo (Nob Hill and
Northwest Portland, *M*)
Delfina's Ristorante Italiano
(Nob Hill and Northwest
Portland, *M*)
Genoa (Southeast Portland, *E*)
Il Piatto (Southeast Portland, *M*)
The Old Spaghetti Factory
(Southwest Portland and
the West Side, *I*)
Pazzo Ristorante (Downtown
and Old Town, *M*)
Rustica (Northeast Portland, *I*)

JAPANESE

Bush Garden (Downtown and
Old Town, *M*)
Saburo's Sushi House (Southeast
Portland, *I*)

LATE NIGHT DINING

Garbanzo's (Nob Hill and
Northwest Portland, *M*)
Hamburger Mary's (Downtown and
Old Town, *I*)
Montage (Southeast Portland, *M*)

LEBANESE

Nicholas (Southeast Portland, *I*)

MEDITERRANEAN

Higgins (Downtown and
Old Town, *M*)
Ron Paul Charcuterie (Northeast
Portland, *M*)
Toulouse Restaurant and Bar 71
(Downtown and Old Town, *M*)
Wildwood (Nob Hill and
Northwest Portland, *E*)
Zefiro Restaurant and Bar
(Nob Hill and Northwest
Portland, *M*)

MEXICAN

Aztec Willie, Joey Rose Taqueria (Northeast Portland, *I*)

Chez José East (Northeast Portland, *I*)

Mayas Tacqueria (Downtown and Old Town, *I*)

Pollo Rey (Northeast Portland, *I*)

MEXICAN/SALVADORAN

El Palenque (Downtown and Old Town, *I*)

MIDDLE EASTERN

Garbanzo's (Nob Hill and Northwest Portland, *M*)

NATIVE AMERICAN

Fiddleheads (Southeast Portland, *M*)

NATURAL FOODS

Bijou Café (Downtown and Old Town, *I*)

NORTHWEST

Atwater's (Downtown and Old Town, *E*)

Avalon Grill (Southwest Portland and the West Side, *M*)

B. Moloch/Heathman Bakery and Pub (Downtown and Old Town, *M*)

Brasserie Montmartre (Downtown and Old Town, *M*)

Bread and Ink Cafe (Southeast Portland, *M*)

Briggs and Crampton Table for Two (Nob Hill and Northwest Portland, *E*)

Caprial's Bistro and Wines (Southeast Portland, *M*)

Esplanade Restaurant (Downtown and Old Town, *E*)

The Heathman Restaurant and Bar (Downtown and Old Town, *M*)

Higgins (Downtown and Old Town, *M*)

L'Auberge (Nob Hill and Northwest Portland, *E*)

The London Grill (Downtown and Old Town, *E*)

Paley's Place (Southwest Portland, *M*)

Pavilion Bar and Grill (Southwest Portland & the West Side, *M*)

PIZZA/PASTA

Caswell (Southeast Portland, *I*)

QUICK BITES

Dots (Southeast Portland, *I*)

Good Dog/Bad Dog (Downtown and Old Town, *I*)

Kitchen Table Cafe (Southeast Portland, *I*)

Pizzicato Gourmet Pizza (Several locations, *I*)

Ron Paul Express (Downtown and Old Town, *I*)

SEAFOOD

Dan and Louis Oyster Bar (Downtown and Old Town, *I*)

Jake's Famous Crawfish (Downtown and Old Town, *M*)

Jake's Grill (Downtown and Old Town, *M*)

McCormick and Schmick's (Downtown and Old Town, *M*)

McCormick and Schmick's Harborside Restaurant (Downtown and Old Town, *M*)

Newport Bay Restaurant (Downtown and Old Town, *M*)

Salty's on the Columbia (Northeast Portland, *E*)

SOUTHWEST

Chez Grill (Southeast Portland, *I*)

SPANISH

Fernando's Hideaway (Downtown and Old Town, *M*)

STEAK

Ringside West (Nob Hill and Northwest Portland, *M*)

TEX/MEX

Esparza's Tex-Mex Cafe (Southeast Portland, *I*)

THAI

Lamthong on Broadway (Downtown and Old Town, *I*)

Saigon Kitchen (Northeast Portland, *I*)

Typhoon! (Nob Hill and Northwest Portland, *I*)

VEGETARIAN

Old Wives' Tales (Southeast Portland, *I*)

VIETNAMESE

Saigon Kitchen (Northeast Portland, *I*)

3 Downtown & Old Town

EXPENSIVE

Atwater's Restaurant and Bar. U.S. Bancorp Tower, 111 SW Fifth Ave. ☎ **503/275-3600.** Reservations highly recommended. Main dishes $17–$25. Fixed-price 4-course menu without wine $45, with wine $65. AE, CB, DC, MC, V. Mon–Sat 5:30–9pm, Sun 5:30–8:30pm. NORTHWEST.

Atwater's whispers elegance from the moment you step off the elevator on the 30th floor. A rosy light suffuses the hall at sunset; richly colored carpets on a blond hardwood floor and large, dramatic flower arrangements add splashes of color throughout the restaurant. In the middle of the dining room is a glass-enclosed wine room that would put many wine shops to shame. But the primary attractions here are the incredible view—far below unwind the Willamette River and Portland, off in the distance stands Mount Hood—and the Pacific Northwest cuisine. The combinations of regional ingredients are unexpected and delectable in such dishes as beef tenderloin with morel mushrooms, roasted fennel, leeks and Pinot Noir sauce or duck breast with grilled asparagus and strawberry risotto. The adjoining bar is a casually elegant place to have a cocktail and listen to live jazz.

✪ **Couvron.** 1126 SW 18th Ave. ☎ **503/225-1844.** Reservations recommended. Main courses $23–$36; tasting menu $60. AE, DISC, MC, V. Tues–Thurs 11:30am–2pm and 5:30–9pm, Fri 11:30am–2pm and 5:30–10pm, Sat 5:30–10pm. CONTEMPORARY FRENCH.

Located in the Goose Hollow neighborhood at the foot of the West Hills, this small French restaurant is utterly unremarkable looking from the exterior and thoroughly French and unpretentiously sophisticated on the inside. The menu is one of the most extraordinary in the city, combining the finest of ingredients in unusual flavor combinations that almost always hit the mark. A recent menu included an exceedingly complex appetizer of pan-roasted Hudson Valley foie gras served with toasted brioche, crawfish stew and a port wine and lobster sauce. Port wine showed up again in the main courses in a sauce served over a duo of honey-glazed duck breast and confit served with white bean ragout and port-candied turnips. With dishes here being among the most memorable in the city, it is not surprising that many people opt for the six-course tasting menu so that they can sample a wide range of dishes. Serious about desserts? How about a Napoleon of chocolate crème brûlée and raspberries served with bittersweet chocolate-hazelnut sauce?

Esplanade Restaurant. RiverPlace Hotel, 1510 SW Harbor Way. ☎ **503/295-6166.** Reservations recommended. Main dishes $14–$28. AE, DC, JCB, MC, V. Daily 6:30–11am, Mon–Fri 11:30am–2pm, Mon–Sat 5–10pm, Sun 5–9pm, Sun brunch 11am–2pm. NORTHWEST.

The Esplanade, surrounded by the quietly sophisticated European-resort atmosphere of the RiverPlace Hotel, is one of the city's few waterfront restaurants. Understated elegance and views of the marina and the city's bridges combine for an interesting

Portland Dining

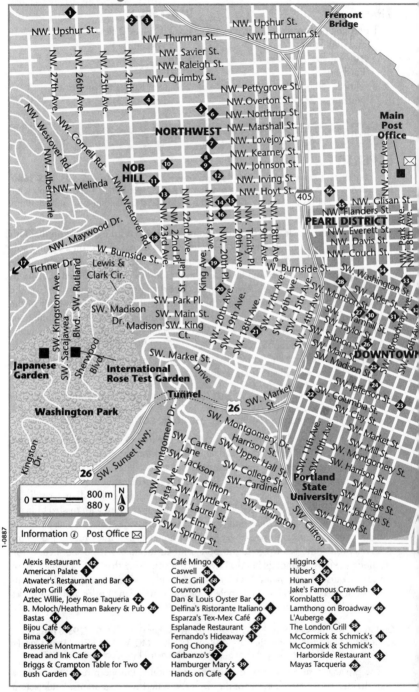

Information ⓘ Post Office ✉

Alexis Restaurant **42**
American Palate **3**
Atwater's Restaurant and Bar **45**
Avalon Grill **55**
Aztec Willie, Joey Rose Taqueria **72**
B. Moloch/Heathman Bakery & Pub **26**
Bastas **16**
Bijou Café **46**
Bima **36**
Brasserie Montmartre **31**
Bread and Ink Cafe **65**
Briggs & Crampton Table for Two **2**
Bush Garden **30**

Café Mingo **9**
Caswell **58**
Chez Grill **68**
Couvron **21**
Dan & Louis Oyster Bar **44**
Delfina's Ristorante Italiano **8**
Esparza's Tex-Mex Café **61**
Esplanade Restaurant **52**
Fernando's Hideaway **51**
Fong Chong **37**
Garbanzo's **7**
Hamburger Mary's **39**
Hands on Cafe **17**

Higgins **24**
Huber's **50**
Hunan **33**
Jake's Famous Crawfish **34**
Kornblatts **13**
Lamthong on Broadway **40**
L'Auberge **1**
The London Grill **38**
McCormick & Schmick's **48**
McCormick & Schmick's
  Harborside Restaurant **53**
Mayas Tacqueria **28**

190

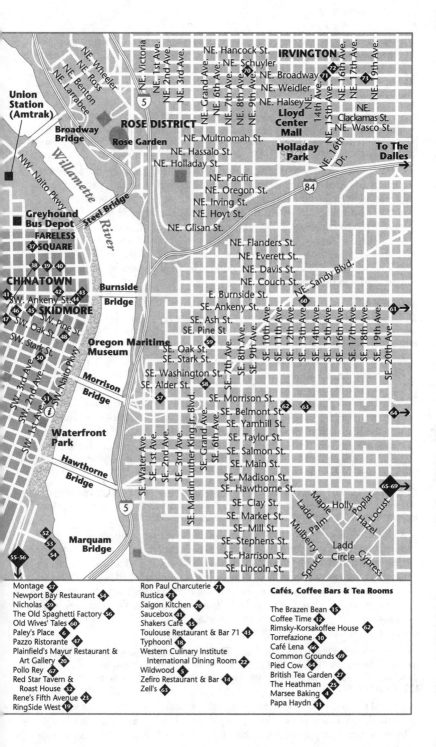

Union Station (Amtrak)

NE. Wheeler
NE. Ross
NE. Benton
NE. Larrabee

Broadway Bridge

NW. Naito Pkwy

Willamette

Greyhound Bus Depot
FARELESS
SQUARE 37

38 39 40

CHINATOWN
41 SW. Ankeny St. 42 43
46 45 **SKIDMORE**
47 SW. Pine St
SW. Oak St. 48
SW. Stark St
50

SW. 3rd Ave.
SW. 2nd Ave.
SW. Naito Pkwy
SW. 1st Ave.
51
(i)

Waterfront Park

Hawthorne Bridge

Marquam Bridge

52
53
54
55–56

NE. Victoria
NE. 1st Ave.
NE. 2nd Ave.
NE. 3rd Ave.

5

ROSE DISTRICT

Rose Garden

Steel Bridge

River

Burnside Bridge

Oregon Maritime Museum

Morrison Bridge

SE. Water Ave.
SE. 2nd Ave.
SE. 3rd Ave.
SE. Martin Luther King Jr. Blvd.
SE. Grand Ave.
SE. 6th Ave.

5

NE. Hancock St.
NE. Schuyler
NE. Broadway 71 72
NE. Weidler 73
NE. Halsey
NE. Grand Ave.
NE. 6th Ave.
NE. 7th Ave.
NE. 8th Ave.
NE. 9th Ave.
70

IRVINGTON

NE. 14th Ave.
NE. 15th Ave.
NE. 16th Ave.
NE. 17th Ave.
NE. 19th Ave.

NE. Clackamas St.
NE. Wasco St.

Lloyd Center Mall

NE. Multnomah St.
NE. Hassalo St.
NE. Holladay St.
NE. Pacific
NE. Oregon St.
NE. Irving St.
NE. Hoyt St.
NE. Glisan St.

Holladay Park

NE. 16th Dr.

To The Dalles

84

NE. Flanders St.
NE. Everett St.
NE. Davis St.
NE. Couch St.

NE. Sandy Blvd.

E. Burnside St.
SE. Ankeny St. 60
SE. Ash St.
SE. Pine St
SE. Oak St. 59
SE. Stark St.
SE. Washington St.
SE. Alder St. 58
SE. Morrison St.
SE. Belmont St. 62 63
SE. Yamhill St.
SE. Taylor St.
SE. Salmon St.
SE. Main St.
SE. Madison St.
SE. Hawthorne St.
SE. Clay St.
SE. Market St.
SE. Mill St.
SE. Stephens St.
SE. Harrison St.
SE. Lincoln St.

57

SE. 7th Ave.
SE. 8th Ave.
SE. 9th Ave.
SE. 10th Ave.
SE. 11th Ave.
SE. 12th Ave.
SE. 13th Ave.
SE. 14th Ave.
SE. 15th Ave.
SE. 16th Ave.
SE. 17th Ave.
SE. 18th Ave.
SE. 19th Ave.
SE. 20th Ave.

61

64

65–69

Maple
Holly
Poplar
Hazel
Locust
Ladd
Palm
Mulberry
Spruce
Cypress
Ladd Circle

Montage 57
Newport Bay Restaurant 54
Nicholas 59
The Old Spaghetti Factory 56
Old Wives' Tales 60
Paley's Place 6
Pazzo Ristorante 47
Plainfield's Mayur Restaurant & Art Gallery 20
Pollo Rey 67
Red Star Tavern & Roast House 32
Rene's Fifth Avenue 23
RingSide West 19

Ron Paul Charcuterie 71
Rustica 73
Saigon Kitchen 70
Saucebox 41
Shakers Café 45
Toulouse Restaurant & Bar 71 43
Typhoon! 18
Western Culinary Institute International Dining Room 22
Wildwood 5
Zefiro Restaurant & Bar 14
Zell's 63

Cafés, Coffee Bars & Tea Rooms

The Brazen Bean 15
Coffee Time 12
Rimsky-Korsakoffee House 62
Torrefazione 10
Café Lena 66
Common Grounds 69
Pied Cow 64
British Tea Garden 27
The Heathman 25
Marsee Baking 4
Papa Haydn 11

setting, and even on the grayest day of Portland's long winter, the warm colors and contemporary art will cheer you up. However, it's the superb cuisine that is truly calculated to brighten your day. Imaginative combinations of fresh seasonal ingredients, such as grilled steelhead with Oregon chanterelles, capture the spirit of the Northwest.

The London Grill. The Benson Hotel, 309 SW Broadway. ☎ **503/228-2000.** Reservations highly recommended. Main dishes $19–$25; Sun brunch $17.50. AE, CB, DC, DISC, ER, JCB, MC, V. Sunday champagne brunch 9:30am–2pm, Mon–Sat 6:30–11am; Mon–Sat 11:30am–2pm; Sun–Thurs 5–10pm, Fri–Sat 5–11pm. NORTHWEST/CONTINENTAL.

Down in the basement of the luxurious Benson Hotel is one of Portland's top restaurants. Modeled after the original London Grill, which was a favorite with Queen Elizabeth I, it has a vaulted ceiling that enhances the wine-cellar feel of the room and mahogany paneling that reflects the glowing chandeliers. Service by tuxedo-shirted waiters is impeccable, and both breakfast and lunch are popular with business executives. The chef uses many of the Northwest's finest fresh fruits and vegetables in dishes such as stuffed quail and a venison chop with wild mushrooms, and yellow-fin tuna with sweet peppers and fried ginger. The Sunday champagne brunch is the most elegant in the city.

MODERATE

Alexis Restaurant. 215 W. Burnside St. ☎ **503/224-8577.** Reservations recommended. Main dishes $9–$14. AE, DC, DISC, MC, V. Mon–Fri 11:30am–2pm; Mon–Thurs 5–10pm, Fri and Sat 5–11pm, Sun 4:30–9pm. GREEK.

Alexis is a classic Greek taverna, and the crowds keep it packed as much for the great food as for the fun atmosphere. On weekends there's belly dancing, and if you happen to be in town on March 25, you can help Alexis celebrate Greek Independence Day with a rousing big party. The menu has all your Greek favorites. The main dishes are good, but the appetizers are out of this world. The not-to-be-missed list includes saganaki (panfried cheese flamed with ouzo), kalamarakia (perfectly fried squid), octopus, and the tart and creamy avgolemono soup. Accompany these with Alexis's own fresh bread, and wash it all down with a bottle of Demestica wine for a meal beyond compare.

✪ **B. Moloch/Heathman Bakery and Pub.** 901 SW Salmon St. ☎ **503/227-5700.** Reservations not accepted. Main courses $7–$13. AE, DC, DISC, MC, V. Mon–Thurs 7am–10pm, Fri 7am–11:30pm, Sat 8am–11:30pm, Sun 8am–10:30pm. NORTHWEST.

At B. Moloch, corporate climbers and bicycle messengers rub shoulders, quaff microbrews, and chow down on creative pizzas. Ostensibly, this is the bakery for the Heathman Hotel dining room a block away, and to that end a cavernous wood-burning brick oven was installed. Nouvelle pizzas from the wood-burning oven are the mainstay of the menu, but if you're not in the mood for pizza, there are sandwiches, pasta dishes, great soups and salads, and daily specials. The restaurant is also a brewpub, and you can sit in the bar and watch the brewers at work while sipping one of their beers.

Brasserie Montmartre. 626 SW Park Ave. ☎ **503/224-5552.** Reservations highly recommended. Main dishes $10–$18. AE, CB, DC, MC, V. Mon–Thurs 11:30am–2am, Fri 11:30am–3am, Sat 10am–3am, Sun 10am–2am; bistro menu available daily from 2pm–closing. NORTHWEST/FRENCH.

Though the menu lacks the creativity of other Northwest and French restaurants in Portland, and dishes are sometimes disappointing, The Bra (as it's known) is popular for its fun atmosphere. There is live jazz nightly, and Tuesday through Saturday nights, a magician performs amazing feats of digital dexterity. On every table you'll find a paper tablecloth and a container of crayons, so let your artistic ambitions run wild. This playfulness is balanced out by dark, formal dining rooms, with massive white pillars, black and white tile floors, velvet banquettes, and silk lamp shades that lend an air of *fin de siècle* Paris. You might start your meal with a ménage à trois of pâtés, then have a cup of onion soup with three cheeses, move on to salmon with lingonberry-and-ginger butter, and finish off with one of the divinely decadent pastries. The wine list is extensive but not expensive.

Bush Garden. 900 SW Morrison St. ☎ **503/226-7181.** Reservations recommended. Main dishes $12–$23; lunches $7–$11. AE, CB, DC, DISC, JCB, MC, V. Mon–Fri 11:30am–1:45pm; Mon–Sat 5–9:45pm, Sun 5–8:45pm. JAPANESE.

The moment you step through the door here, enticing aromas greet you—the scent of salmon teriyaki, perhaps, or the delicate aroma of tempura. The fact that this restaurant is popular with Japanese businessmen is recommendation enough for Bush Gardens. Groups, and anyone seeking privacy and a special experience, can dine in one of the tatami rooms with the shoji rice-paper-screen walls. If you can't sit cross-legged through dinner, don't worry, beneath the low tables are wells that allow you to sit as you are accustomed. If there are two or more of you, you should definitely opt for one of the special dinners. Shabu-shabu is our favorite; you get to do the cooking yourself. For the ultimate Japanese banquet, order the kaiseki dinner, which includes two appetizers, sushi or sashimi, tempura, fish, beef, and dessert.

✪ **Fernando's Hideaway.** 824 SW First Ave. ☎ **503/248-4709.** Reservations recommended. Main courses $13–$20. AE, DC, MC, V. Mon–Thurs 5–10pm, Fri–Sat 5–11pm, Sun noon–9pm. SPANISH.

Excellent tapas, such as spicy oysters and stuffed calamari, have made Fernando's enormously popular, but the Spanish entrees are also a delight. A roasted chicken with an apricot and nut sauce arrived beautifully arranged with wedges of potato and dollops of spinach. Salads, such as eggplant or fruit and cheese combinations, are equally delicious. There are good Spanish wines on the menu and service is professional, without the attitude you might expect at a trendy place such as this. For dessert the flan with mocha sauce is excellent.

✪ **The Heathman Restaurant and Bar.** The Heathman Hotel, SW Broadway at Salmon St. ☎ **503/241-4100.** Reservations highly recommended. Main courses $12–$25. AE, CB, DC, MC, V. Breakfast Mon–Fri 6:30–11am, Sat–Sun 6:30am–2pm; lunch Mon–Fri 11am–2pm; dinner daily 5–11pm. NORTHWEST/FRENCH.

The menu in this elegant hotel dining room changes seasonally, but one thing remains constant: Ingredients used are the very freshest of Oregon and Northwest seafood, meat, wild game, and produce with a French accent. Small and bright, the restaurant exudes a bistro atmosphere. On the walls are Andy Warhol's Endangered Species—a rhino, zebra, lion, panda, and others—part of the Heathman's extensive collection of classic and contemporary art. A recent winter menu offered pheasant with wild mushrooms and cabbage, ravioli with smoked salmon cream, leeks, and shiitake mushrooms, and mahimahi with sun-dried tomato and fennel risotto. Local fruit appears in many of the rich desserts. In the bar, there are Northwest microbrewery beers on tap, while an extensive wine list spotlights Oregon.

✪ **Higgins.** 1239 SW Broadway. ☎ **503/222-9070.** Reservations highly recommended. Main courses lunch $7–$13, dinner $15–$21. AE, DC, MC, V. Mon–Fri 11:30am–2pm; daily 5–10:30pm; bistro menu served daily 2pm–midnight. NORTHWEST/MEDITERRANEAN.

Higgins, located just up Broadway from the Heathman Hotel, where chef Greg Higgins first made a name for himself in Portland, strikes a balance between contemporary and classic in both its decor and its cuisine. The menu, which changes frequently, explores contemporary culinary horizons, while the decor in the trilevel dining room opts for wood-paneling and elegant place settings. In the open kitchen, copper pots hang on the wall. Adding a dash more of classic ambience are waiters in long white aprons. Both subtle and earthy flavors abound here. Manila clams steamed in amber ale with ancho chiles and onions was a heavenly way to begin, and garlic-roasted chicken with a sauce of walnuts and Pinot Noir with buttermilk whipped potatoes was inventive enough to be interesting, yet homey and satisfying. Be sure to leave room for a dessert.

Huber's. 411 SW Third Ave. ☎ **503/228-5686.** Reservations recommended, but not accepted Friday or Saturday evenings. Main dishes $5–$19. AE, DISC, MC, V. Mon–Fri 11:30am–4pm; Mon–Thurs 4–10pm, Fri–Sat 4–11pm. CONTINENTAL.

Portland's oldest restaurant first opened its doors to the public in 1879, though it didn't move to its present location until 1911. You'll find this very traditional establishment tucked inside the Oregon Pioneer Building. Down a quiet hallway you'll come to a surprising little room with vaulted stained-glass ceiling, Philippine mahogany paneling, and the original brass cash register. The house specialty has been turkey since the day the first Huber's opened, so there really isn't any question of what to order. You can gobble turkey sandwiches, turkey Delmonico, turkey nouvelle, or turkey mushroom pie. The menu even has wine recommendations to accompany the different turkey dishes. Lunch prices are much lower, with the turkey sandwich the star of the hour.

Hunan. 515 SW Broadway, at Morgan's Alley. ☎ **503/224-8063.** Reservations recommended for 5 or more. Main dishes $7–$22; lunch main dishes $5–$6. MC, V. Mon–Thurs 11am–8:45pm, Fri 11am–9:45pm, Sat noon–9:45pm, Sun 5–8:45pm. CHINESE.

Located at the end of Morgan's Alley, a small indoor mall, is one of Portland's most reliable Chinese restaurants. Although the menu lists such appetizing main dishes as champagne chicken and Peking duck, there are two items that should absolutely not be missed. General Tso's chicken is both crispy and chewy and is smothered with a succulent, fiery sauce. Lover's eggplant, which is "dedicated to those of our guests with romantic inclinations as well as to all genuine lovers of eggplant," consists of beautifully presented and prepared chunks of creamy eggplant that are truly an eggplant lover's dream come true.

✪ **Jake's Famous Crawfish.** 401 SW 12th Ave. ☎ **503/226-1419.** Reservations recommended. Main dishes $9–$29. AE, DC, DISC, MC, V. Mon–Thurs 11:30am–midnight; Fri 11:30am–1am, Sat 4pm–1am, Sun 4:30–11pm. SEAFOOD.

Jake's has been serving up crawfish (crayfish) since 1909 at an address that has housed a restaurant or bar since 1892. The back bar came all the way around Cape Horn in 1880, and much of the rest of the restaurant's decor looks just as old and well worn. The noise level after work, when local businesspeople pack the bar, can be high, and the wait for a table can be long if you don't make a reservation. However, don't let these obstacles dissuade you from visiting this Portland institution. There's a daily fresh sheet listing 12 to 15 specials, but there's really no question about what to eat at Jake's: crawfish, which are always on the menu and are served several different ways. During happy hour and after 9:30pm, bar appetizers are only $1.95.

✪ **McCormick and Schmick's.** 235 SW First Ave. ☎ **503/224-7522.** Reservations highly recommended. Main dishes $13–$20; bar meals $1.95; lunches $6–$12. AE, DC, MC, V.

Mon–Fri 11:30am–4:30pm; Sun–Thurs 5–10pm, Fri–Sat 5–11pm; bar meals daily 1:30–6:30pm and 9:30pm–close. SEAFOOD.

Patterned after traditional seafood establishments, this restaurant is noted for the freshness of its ingredients. The daily fresh sheet begins with a listing of what's available that day and might list 25 different types of seafood. Whether it's king salmon or Dungeness crab, seafood is king here, and the oysters go by their first names: Olympia, Royal Miyagi, and Quilcene. If you aren't interested in live oysters as an appetizer, there is plenty of cooked seafood to start you out. The extensive wine list features excellent Oregon wines, and while you're waiting for a table, you might want to try one of the more than 30 single-malt scotches available. Both the up-and-coming and the already-there keep this place bustling.

McCormick and Schmick's Harborside Restaurant. 0309 SW Montgomery St. ☎ **503/ 220-1865.** Reservations recommended. Main dishes lunch $5–$12, dinner $10–$20. AE, CB, DC, DISC, MC, V. Mon–Sat 11:30am–2pm; Sun–Thurs 5–10pm, Fri–Sat 5–11pm. SEAFOOD.

Anchoring the opposite end of RiverPlace Esplanade from the RiverPlace Hotel, this large and glitzy seafood restaurant offers a view of the Willamette to go with its excellent seafood. Four dining levels assure everyone a view of the river and marina below, and in summer, customers head out to tables on the Esplanade. Because it's so popular, the place tends to be noisy and the help seems a bit harried; however, don't let this detract from the fine food. Although seafood (such as crab-stuffed salmon, razor clams with rémoulade sauce, and grilled sea scallop fettuccine) is the main attraction here, the menu is quite extensive. The clientele is mostly upscale, especially at lunch and in the après-work hours.

Newport Bay Restaurant. 0425 SW Montgomery St. ☎ **503/227-3474.** Reservations recommended. Main dishes $11–$19; lunches and light main dishes $6–$10. AE, CB, DC, DISC, MC, V. Winter hours Sun–Thurs 11am–10pm, Fri–Sat 11am–11pm, Sun brunch 10am–3pm. Closes 1 hour later in summer. SEAFOOD.

Though there are Newport Bay restaurants all over Portland, this one has the best location—floating on the Willamette River. Located in the marina at Portland's beautiful RiverPlace shopping-and-dining complex, the Newport Bay provides excellent views of the river and the city skyline, especially from the deck. Popular with young couples, families and boaters, this place exudes a cheery atmosphere and service is efficient. Nearly everything on the menu has some sort of seafood in it, even the quiche, salads, and pastas. Entrees are mostly straightforward and well prepared—nothing too fancy. The wine list has mostly West Coast wines at reasonable prices.

✪ **Pazzo Ristorante.** Hotel Vintage Plaza, 627 SW Washington St. (at Broadway). ☎ **503/ 228-1515.** Reservations highly recommended. Main courses $13–$18; lunch $7–$15. AE, CB, DC, DISC, MC, V. Breakfast Mon–Fri 7–10:30am, Sat 8–10:30am, Sun 8–11am; lunch Mon–Sat 11:30am–2:30pm; dinner Mon–Thurs 5–10pm, Fri–Sat 5–11pm, Sun noon–10pm. NORTHERN ITALIAN.

The atmosphere in Pazzo is not nearly as rarefied as in the adjacent hotel lobby, and, in fact, if you take a seat at Pazzo's bar, you'll practically be ducking hanging hams, sausages, and garlic braids. The food here on the whole is creative and tends toward the rich side. We started with *radicchio e pancetta alla griglia,* a wild, highly flavored dish of bitter grilled radicchio and a sauce of creamy goat cheese. This dish was so intense and rich, it was best shared. *Fritto misto,* fried calamari with rock shrimp, fennel, sautéed green beans, was enhanced by a sweet red pepper sauce. In fact, we recommend anything with this sauce. Linguine with clams, roasted fennel and saffron broth was more simple, and satisfying. Dessert here is a must. I like the tiramisu, but wouldn't refuse a *canolli al Pazzo,* almond cookie shells filled with ricotta and mascarpone cheese, toasted pistachios, and drizzled with chocolate sauce.

Red Star Tavern and Roast House. 503 SW Alder St. ☎ **503/222-0005.** Reservations recommended. Main courses $10–$18. AE, DISC, MC, V. Mon–Thurs 6:30–10:30am, 11:30am–2:30pm, and 5–10pm; Fri 6:30–10:30am, 11:30am–2:30pm, and 5–11pm; Sat 8–11am, noon–3pm, and 5–11pm, Sun 8am–2pm and 5–10pm. AMERICAN.

Big and always busy, the Roast House was an instant hit when it opened. Obviously this American bistro provides something that Portlanders crave: big portions of well-prepared and upscale down-home comfort food. With a wood oven, rotisseries, and a smoker, roasted meats are the specialty here, with the spit-roasted pork loin a particular favorite. However, you can also get risotto, oak-roasted vegetables, and goat cheese and roasted garlic ravioli. Side dishes include buttermilk mashed potatoes, brick-oven baked beans, and sweet potato hash. Decor in the large, open restaurant is a comfortable mix of old and new styling, with interesting murals on the walls.

Toulouse Restaurant and Bar 71. 71 SW Second Ave. ☎ **503/241-4343.** Reservations recommended. Main courses $12–$22. Tues–Thurs 11:30am–9:30pm, Fri–Sat 11:30am–10:30pm. AE, MC, V. MEDITERRANEAN.

Located in one of the prettiest spaces in the Old Town neighborhood, this spacious restaurant has a contemporary, yet comfortable feel. The space is equally divided between the restaurant and the bar, and you'll frequently find as many people dining in the bar (a simpler menu) as in the restaurant. There are also a few tables out on the sidewalk. What attracts the crowds here is mostly the selection of offerings from the wood-fired grill and rotisserie, from which emanate such dishes as mesquite-grilled beef tenderloin with artichoke ragout and apple cider sauce. However, it would be easy enough to just make a meal off the appetizers, which include an astounding "grand" aioli that comes with mussels, oysters, a pile of Roquefort cheese, wood-roasted vegetables, fried brie, stuffed grape leaves, and an assortment of olives and cornichons.

INEXPENSIVE

Bijou Café. 132 SW Third Ave. ☎ **503/222-3187.** Reservations not accepted. $3–$8. No credit cards. Daily 7am–3pm. NATURAL FOODS.

The folks who run the Bijou take both food and health seriously. They'll let you know that the eggs are from Chris's Egg Farm in Hubbard, Oregon, and they'll serve you a bowl of steamed brown rice for breakfast. However, the real hits here are the hash browns and the muffins. Don't leave without trying these two. At lunch, there are salads made with organic produce whenever possible. Even the meats are natural.

Dan and Louis Oyster Bar. 208 SW Ankeny St. ☎ **503/227-5906.** Reservations recommended for parties of 5 or more. Main dishes $7–$12. AE, CB, DC, MC, V. Sun–Thurs 11am–10pm, Fri–Sat 11am–11pm. SEAFOOD.

Dan and Louis has been serving up succulent oysters since 1907, and today the oysters come from Dan and Louis's own oyster farm on Yaquina Bay. Half the fun of eating here is enjoying the old-fashioned surroundings. The front counter is stacked high with candies and cigars much as it would have been in the 1920s. The walls are covered with founder Louis Wachsmuth's own collection of old and unusual plates. Beer steins line the shelves, and nautical odds and ends are everywhere. Louis began his restaurant business serving only two items: oyster stew and oyster cocktails. These two are still on the menu, and as good today as they were 85 years ago. Main courses are simple, no-nonsense seafood dishes, mostly fried. The quality can be uneven, but the prices are great.

😊 Family-Friendly Restaurants

Aztec Willie, Joey Rose Taqueria *(see p. 203)*   A huge Mayan-like head oversees a glass-enclosed play area where the kids can amuse themselves while the adults consume Mexican food purchased from a walk-up counter.

Dan and Louis Oyster Bar *(see p. 196)*   You'll think you're eating in the hold of an old sailing ship, and all the fascinating stuff on the walls will keep kids entertained.

Old Wives' Tales *(see p. 207)*   This is just about the best place in Portland to eat if you've got small children. There are children's menus at all meals and in the back of the restaurant, there's a playroom that will keep your kids entertained while you enjoy your meal.

The Old Spaghetti Factory *(see p. 209)*   This chain of inexpensive Italian restaurants got its start here in Portland, and the restaurant here just might have the best location of any in the chain—right on the bank of the Willamette River. Kids and parents both enjoy the atmosphere and low prices.

Fong Chong. 301 NW Fourth Ave. ☎ **503/220-0235.** Reservations not accepted. Main dishes $5–$12; dim sum meals, $2–$5. MC, V. Daily 10:30am–10pm; dim sum 10:30am–3pm daily. CANTONESE.

This popular Chinese restaurant is in a grocery store. Don't worry, you won't be eating between the aisles; the restaurant occupies its own room. Although most of the food here is above average, the dim sum is the best in the city. Flag down a passing cart and point to the most appetizing looking little dishes. We really like the broccoli. Be careful or you might end up with a plate of chicken feet. At the end of the meal, your bill is calculated by the number of plates on your table.

Hamburger Mary's. 239 SW Broadway. ☎ **503/223-0900.** Reservations not accepted. $5–$13. AE, CB, DC, MC, V. Daily 7am–2:30am. BURGERS/LATE NIGHT DINING.

As the name implies, this is a place for burgers—some of the best burgers in Portland, actually. They're thick and juicy, piled high with crisp lettuce and ripe tomatoes, and served on whole-wheat buns. The restaurant looks something like a Goodwill store that was hit by a tornado; there's kitschy junk everywhere—on the tables, floors, walls, and ceiling.

Lamthong on Broadway. 213 SW Broadway. ☎ **503/223-4214.** Reservations recommended for Fri–Sat. Main courses $7–$11. AE, JCB, MC, V. Mon–Fri 11am–2pm; Mon–Thurs 5–9pm; Fri–Sat 5–10pm. THAI.

Lamthong is a dependable Thai restaurant that has been around the Portland area long enough to have branches in the suburbs. The cuisine served here is similar to that at the Saucebox, located across the street, but here you get more for your money. I like to start with the soft spring rolls or spicy calamari salad, and follow up with an entree of sweet basil with chicken, or the rich and spicy *Mussamun* curry with beef, potato, bay leaves and peanuts.

Mayas Tacqueria. 1000 SW Morrison St. ☎ **503/226-1946.** Prices $3–$9. AE, MC, V. Sun–Thurs 10am–10pm, Fri–Sat 10am–11pm. MEXICAN.

Nothing fancy here, just good home-cooked Mexican food, and you can watch the cooks prepare your meal just as in any tacqueria in Mexico. The menu above the counter lists the different meals available, and on a separate list you'll find the choice of meats, which include chicken molé, pork or chicken chile verde, beef or chicken chile Colorado, and carne asada. Look for the Maya-style murals on the walls out front. **Sante Fe Tacqueria** at 831 NW 23rd Ave. (☎ **503/220-0406**) and **Aztec Willie, Joey Rose Taqueria** at 1501 NE Broadway (☎ **503/280-8900**) are run by the same folks and serve equally delicious food.

Rene's Fifth Avenue. 1300 SW Fifth Ave. ☎ **503/241-0712.** Reservations recommended. Lunches $6–$15. MC, V. Mon–Fri 11:30am–2:30pm. CONTINENTAL.

Comfortable and elegant, this 21st-floor lunch spot in the First Interstate Tower is always crowded. Local businesspeople flock here as much for the view as for the food. The menu, though short, is varied and includes daily specials and plenty of seafood. When I last visited, I had a blackened salmon special with lemon sauce, pasta salad, soup, and a splendid view of the Northwest hills, for $8.95. You won't find a view this good at better prices anywhere else in the city.

Saucebox. 214 SW Broadway. ☎ **503/241-3393.** Reservations suggested. Main courses $6–$12. AE, MC, V. Tues–Fri 11:30am–2:30pm, Tues–Sat 6–10pm. Bar menu served 2:30–6pm and 10pm–2am. ASIAN INFLUENCE.

The Saucebox, an offspring of ever-popular Zefiro (see below), was born with a trendy cachet already in place. Popular with the city's scene-makers, the room is a large, dramatically lit dark box and joins the trend toward noisy dining spaces. If you really want to talk, you'd better do it before 10pm, which is when a DJ arrives to turn this place into a dance club. The menu is Asian-inspired, and prices are slightly higher than at a typical Thai restaurant. Potstickers are stuffed with crab and tofu with a wonderful chewy texture. Unfortunately, service can be rather negligent when the restaurant is busy. Because what truly shines here is the dramatic setting and the great cocktails— margaritas, martinis, Singapore slings—I recommend Saucebox most highly as a bar.

Western Culinary Institute International Dining Room. 1316 SW 13th Ave. ☎ **800/ 666-0312** or 503/223-2245. Reservations required. 5-course lunch $7.95; 6-course dinner $10.95; Thurs buffet $15.95. MC, V. Tues–Fri 11am–1pm and 6–8pm. CONTINENTAL.

If you happen to be a frugal gourmet whose palate is more sophisticated than your wallet can afford, you'll want to schedule a meal here. The dining room serves five- to six-course gourmet meals prepared by advanced students at prices even a budget traveler can afford. The dining room decor is modern and unassuming, and the students who wait on you are eager to please. For each course you have a choice among two to five offerings. A sample dinner menu might begin with velouté Andalouse followed by pâté of rabbit, a pear sorbet, grilled chicken breast with blackberry- balsamic sauce, Chinese salad with smoked salmon, and divine chocolate mousse cake. Remember, that's all for less than $11! The four-course lunch for only $7.95 is just as good a deal.

4 Nob Hill & Northwest Portland

EXPENSIVE

Briggs and Crampton Table for Two. 1902 NW 24th Ave. ☎ **503/223-8690.** Reservations several months in advance. Three- or 4-course lunch for 2 people $75. V, MC. Tues–Fri 12:30pm. NORTHWEST.

This personalized dining experience occurs in a screened-off area in the front parlor of an atmospheric old house in Northwest Portland. Lunch starts with an appetizer, followed by a sorbet, breads, the main course with side dishes, dessert and coffee. Dishes are influenced by what is in season, be it a certain type of fish, morel mushrooms, or fresh berries. The person who serves the food also prepares it, so attention is concentrated on your special needs and desires. The wine list has some fine selections. Reservations are taken quarterly, in January, April, July, and October.

L'Auberge. 2601 NW Vaughn St. ☎ **503/223-3302.** Reservations highly recommended. Main dishes $16–$22; 4-course, fixed-price dinner $37. AE, CB, DC, DISC, MC, V. Sun–Thurs 5pm–midnight, Fri–Sat 5pm–1am. NORTHWEST/FRENCH.

Located at the edge of the industrial district, this restaurant offers some of the best French and Northwest cuisine in Portland and is a favorite special-occasion restaurant. A formal atmosphere reigns in the main dining room, but on Sunday nights the French flavor is forsaken in favor of succulent ribs and burgers, and a movie is shown in the bar. The fixed-price dinners feature meals with a French origin but translated with a Northwest accent. Before dining, be sure to stop by the bar to have a look at the delectable morsels on the dessert tray. On the fixed-price menu there are a couple of choices of main dishes, such as rack of lamb with port garlic sauce and seared duck breast with maple-roasted figs and house-made chestnut spaetzle. This is all topped off with a choice from that dessert tray. An à la carte international bistro menu is also available.

✪ Wildwood. 1221 NW 21st Ave. ☎ **503/248-WOOD.** Reservations highly recommended. Main courses $16–$24. AE, MC, V. Mon–Sat 11:30am–2:30pm; Mon–Thurs 5:30–10pm, Fri–Sat 5:30–10:30pm, Sun 5–8:30pm; Sun brunch 10am–2pm. AMERICAN REGIONAL.

With an elegant and spare interior decor straight out of *Architectural Digest* and a menu that changes daily, it isn't surprising that Wildwood is a hit with urban sophisticates. With booths, a meal counter, a bar area, and a patio, the restaurant appeals to celebratory groups, couples, and solo diners. And if you can't get a reservation, it's a great place to have a couple of delicious appetizers at the bar or counter. The menu relies primarily on the subtle flavors of the Mediterranean. Recently, the appetizers list included an unusual prosciutto and mango salad with goat cheese, toasted almonds and curry citrus vinaigrette. Entrees included mesquite-roasted lamb with eggplant and sweet pepper ragout with a rosemary-infused potato cake.

MODERATE

American Palate. 1937 NW 23rd Pl. ☎ **503/223-6994.** Reservations suggested. Main courses $12–$17. AE, DISC, MC, V. Mon–Fri 11am–2:30pm, Mon–Sat 5:30–10pm. CONTEMPORARY AMERICAN.

This small airy space on the far side of fashionable NW 23rd Avenue also has a deck for al fresco dining in warm weather. The young and innovative chefs here start with basic regional ingredients, whatever happens to be fresh in the market, and add familiar yet vivid flavors. We tried roasted stuffed chicken breast with Oregon blue cheese and asparagus, and sea bass with tomato and basil oil, which was mild but nicely grilled. The fish dishes here are very popular and the wine list is short but well-chosen. There are small plates and large plates on the menu, so you can order your meal to suit your appetite. I would save room for bread pudding with whatever local fruit is in season.

Bastas. 410 NW 21st Ave. ☎ **503/274-1572.** Reservations accepted for 5 or more. Main courses $7–$15. AE, MC, V. Mon–Thurs 11:30am–10:30pm, Fri 11:30am–11:30pm, Sat 5–11:30pm, Sun 5–10:30pm. SOUTHERN ITALIAN.

Bastas is located in a renovated Tasti Freez, but there's no way you'd know it except for the peaked roof. Inside, warm Mediterranean colors and candlelight create a spare but relaxing setting in which to enjoy such dishes as pork chops marinated in Provençal herbs or a selection from about a dozen pastas. As an antipasti, the grilled calamari with ricotta and olives we tried was tasty, but the portion was quite small. The sauce on the duck pasta dish was ordinary and almost bland, but we really liked the zingy chile and ginger accented pastas. Fruity sangria is a good accompaniment, as is a selection from the short but well-chosen wine list. Our favorite was dessert—a very superior and utterly creamy crème caramel.

✪ **Bima.** 1338 NW Hoyt St. ☎ **503/241-3465.** Reservations recommended. Main courses $12–$16. AE, MC, V. Mon–Thurs 11:30am–10pm, Fri–Sat 11:30am–11pm. GULF COAST.

A barely noticeable entryway leads into a cavernous converted warehouse, where the space is softened and romanticized with lighting and oversize booths. Sounds of conversation and music blend and bounce around the walls and offers an enticement to join in the atmospheric charm. The food is an unusual combination of Southern and Caribbean styles, a refreshing contrast to other Portland restaurants. We shared an appetizer of tiny kumomoto oysters, and followed that up with large, thick moist slices of corn bread that hinted of crunchy corn. Catfish fillets covered in crushed pecans were served with chipotle-flavored polenta cakes, crispy on the outside and creamy in the middle. Jicama avocado salad with a mango vinaigrette was good, but we all agreed that the jumbalaya was too hot. If anything, the dishes were too consistently fiery.

✪ **Café Mingo.** 807 NW 21st Ave. ☎ **503/226-4646.** Reservations not accepted. Main courses $7–$10. AE, DISC, MC, V. Mon–Wed 5–10pm; Thurs–Sat 5–11pm. ITALIAN.

If there's any problem with this intimate little cafe, which is immensely popular and doesn't take reservations, it's that you almost always have to wait (on the sidewalk) for a table. The solution? Get here as early as possible. The interior is as attractive as that of any other upscale restaurant here on Restaurant Row, but the prices are less expensive. This, I'm sure, is one of the reasons Café Mingo is so popular. Another is the quality of the food. The menu is short, and focuses on painstakingly prepared Italian comfort food. Just about all of the items on the menu are winners, from the *inslata caprese,* a salad with tomato, house-made fresh mozzarella, basil, and extra virgin olive oil, to polenta with mushrooms and fresh Italian sausage. We long to go back here again just for the *panna cotta* dessert: "cooked cream" with poached fruit.

Delfina's Ristorante Italiano. 2112 NW Kearney St. ☎ **503/221-1195.** Reservations highly recommended; required 1 week in advance for Back Kitchen Dinner. Pastas $12.50–$16; main dishes $15–$17. AE, DC, DISC, MC, V. Mon–Fri 11:30am–2:30pm; daily 5–11pm. ITALIAN.

Long a Nob Hill mainstay, Delfina's offers excellent Italian food in a casual neighborhood-bistro atmosphere. The tile floors, exposed brick walls, and cafe curtains on the windows all contribute to a comfortable feeling, while smiling, friendly service makes you feel right at home. Be sure to notice the colander lamps hung from the ceiling. Northern Italian fare predominates here, but southern Italian and even Pacific Northwest manage to sneak onto the menu. You might want to try the roasted New Zealand rack of lamb with red wine, garlic, and rosemary or Dungeness crab with dill, spinach, a lemon cream sauce and homemade fettuccine.

Delfina's most unusual meal is the Back Kitchen Dinner for parties of 8 to 14 people, for $60 to $100 per person with wine. You get to dine in the bustling kitchen, where the chef surprises you with a multicourse menu that your Italian mother-in-law would envy.

✪ **Paley's Place.** 1204 NW 21st Ave. ☎ **503/243-2403.** Reservations highly recommended. Main courses $14–$18. AE, MC, V. Tues–Thurs 5:30–10pm, Fri–Sat 5:30–10:30pm. NORTHWEST/FRENCH.

Paley's is located in a turn-of-the-century Victorian house, and in good weather, the front porch is the preferred place to dine. This porch also doubles as an open-air storage area for some of the restaurant's fresh produce, which lends a traditional

European flavor to the surroundings. Inside, comforting soft pastel colors and tables placed close together give the small dining room a homey and casual feel. Chef Vitaly Paley combines the best of Northwest produce with other ingredients to make such vibrantly flavorful dishes as a salad of roasted beets with pears, blue cheese, organic greens, and toasted hazelnuts. Choices for entrees might include pasta with roasted garlic, pecorino cheese, and chanterelle mushrooms from the porch display, or sautéed sweetbreads with leek-potato gratin and pomegranate sauce. Wines on the list include Northwest and French wines, and for dessert, we can't pass up the crème brûlée and pear-walnut tart with honey.

Plainfield's Mayur Restaurant and Art Gallery. 852 SW 21st Ave. ☎ **503/223-2995.** Reservations recommended. Main dishes $9–$17. AE, DISC, MC, V. Daily 5:30–10pm. INDIAN.

In the words of a friend, "With an Indian restaurant like Mayur's, who needs anything else?" Located in an elegant old Portland home, this the city's premier Indian restaurant (and includes an art gallery). The atmosphere is refined, with bone china and European crystal, and the service is informative and gracious. In addition to the two floors of dining rooms inside, there is a patio out back, and you can watch the cooks bake bread and tandoori chicken in the tandoor show kitchen. Every dish on the menu is perfectly spiced so that the complex flavors and aromas of Indian cuisine shine through. A tray of flavorful condiments accompanies each meal. The dessert list is also an unexpected and pleasant surprise. Save room! The wine list here is one of the finest in the city.

RingSide West. 2165 W. Burnside St. ☎ **503/223-1513.** Reservations highly recommended. Steaks $14–$22; seafood main dishes $17–$38. AE, DC, DISC, MC, V. Mon–Sat 5pm–midnight, Sun 4–11:30pm. STEAK.

RingSide has long been a favorite Portland steakhouse. Though boxing is the main theme of the restaurant, the name is a two-fisted pun as well, referring to the incomparable onion rings that should be an integral part of any meal here. Have your rings with a side order of one of their perfectly cooked steaks for a real knockout meal. There is also a RingSide East at 14021 Northeast Glisan St. (☎ **503/255-0750**), on Portland's east side, with basically the same menu but not as much atmosphere. It's open for lunch Monday through Friday from 11:30am to 2:30pm.

✪ **Zefiro Restaurant and Bar.** 500 NW 21st Ave. ☎ **503/226-3394.** Reservations highly recommended. Main courses $14–$18. AE, DC, MC, V. Mon–Fri 11:30am–2:30pm; Mon–Thurs 5:30–10pm, Fri–Sat 5:30–10:30pm. MEDITERRANEAN.

An initiator of the explosion of upscale restaurants on Northwest 21st Avenue, Zefiro has for many years now been considered the best restaurant in Portland. While old-style French and Italian dishes predominate on the menu, Moroccan, Greek, Spanish, and even Asian influences creep in. For a starter, be sure to try the fragrant bowl of mussels steamed with leeks, white wine, saffron, cream, and thyme if it happens to be on the menu. Roasted mahimahi with an herb salsa verde made from tarragon, parsley, thyme, oregano, capers, garlic, lemon, and olive oil was a recent entree that captured all the fragrances of a Mediterranean herb garden in one dish. Order anything lemony, such as a lemon tartlet or lemon sorbet or lemon ice cream, for dessert and you won't go wrong. The restaurant's chic minimalist decor allows the outstanding creativity of the kitchen to take the fore and service is always outstanding.

INEXPENSIVE

Garbanzo's. NW 21st Ave. and NW Lovejoy St. ☎ **503/227-4196.** Reservations not accepted. Salads $3–$5; sandwiches $4–$5; dinners $7–$9. AE, DISC, MC, V. Sun–Thurs 11:30am–1:30am, Fri–Sat 11:30am–3am (close 1 hour earlier in winter). MIDDLE EASTERN/LATE NIGHT DINING.

This casual little place that calls itself a falafel bar has become very popular, especially late at night. The menu includes all the usual Middle Eastern offerings, most of which also happen to be American Heart Association approved. You can eat at one of the tiny cafe tables or get your order to go. They even serve beer and wine. Another Garbanzo's is at 3433 SE Hawthorne Blvd. (☎ **503/239-6087**).

Kornblatts. 623 NW 23rd Ave. ☎ **503/242-0055.** Reservations not accepted. Sandwiches $5–$9; dinner $9–$12. MC, V. Sun–Wed 7am–9pm, Thurs–Sat 7am–10pm. DELICATESSEN.

In the heart of NW 23rd Avenue, a dozen tables and a take-out corner are the setting for some really satisfying Jewish soul food. The corned beef and pastrami come directly from Brooklyn and there are pickles on the tables to nosh. If you're unfamiliar with the likes of Nova lox, smoked sturgeon, sable, knishes, potato latkes, or blintzes, there's a glossary on the menu for explanation. If the above choices don't tempt you, how about a selection of five different kinds of cheesecake?

Shakers Café. 1212 NW Glisan St. ☎ **503/221-0011.** Reservations not accepted. Breakfast $3–$7, lunch $5–$7. No credit cards. Mon–Fri 7am–3:30pm, Sat 7:30am–3:30pm, Sun 7:30am–2pm. AMERICAN.

I seem to have a penchant for lunch counters—they're casual, fast, and these days, the food you find there is pretty good. Take Shakers Café in the Pearl District, for example. Between 250 and 300 salt and pepper shakers are on display and give the cafe its name. For breakfast it offers homemade scones and blue corncakes. Lunch includes typical and not-so-typical diner fare such as marinated chicken breast sandwiches, veggie or turkey burgers, grilled tuna fish sandwiches, homemade soups, and root beer floats. Service at the tables can be slow, but it's quicker at the counter.

Typhoon! 2310 NW Everett St. ☎ **503/243-7557.** Reservations recommended. Main courses $8–$14. AE, DC, DISC, MC, V. Mon–Thurs 11:30am–2:30pm and 5–9pm, Fri–Sat 11:30am–2:30pm and 5–10pm, Sun 5–9pm. THAI.

Located just off NW 23rd Avenue, this trendy Thai restaurant is a bit pricey (for Thai food), but the unusual menu offerings generally aren't available at other Portland Thai restaurants. Be sure to start a meal with the *miang kum,* which consists of dried shrimp, tiny chiles, ginger, lime, peanuts, shallots, and toasted coconut drizzled with a sweet-and-sour sauce and wrapped up in a spinach leaf. The eruption of flavors that takes place on your taste buds is absolutely astounding (we first had this in Thailand and waited years to get it here in the United States). Also not to be missed is the *hor mok,* a sort of shrimp and coconut pudding appetizer. The whole front wall of the restaurant slides away for Thai-style open-air dining in the summer.

5 Northeast Portland

EXPENSIVE

Salty's on the Columbia. 3839 NE Marine Dr. ☎ **503/288-4444.** Reservations highly recommended. Main dishes $9.50–$32. AE, CB, DC, DISC, MC, V. Mon–Sat 11:15am–3pm, Sun brunch 9:30am–2pm; Mon–Thurs 5–9:30pm, Fri–Sat 5–10pm, Sun 5–9pm. SEAFOOD.

While it's a ways out from downtown, Salty's is one of Portland's best waterfront restaurants. Located out on the Columbia River near the airport, this sprawling restaurant offers views that take in the river, mountains, and forests. Preparations here are creative, especially on the daily specials menu, and portions are large. Salmon is particularly popular. Try it smoked over alder wood, which is a traditional Northwest preparation. A few choice offerings of steak and chicken dishes offer options to those who don't care for seafood. A warning: Though the decks look appealing, the noise from the airport can be distracting.

MODERATE

✪ Ron Paul Charcuterie. 1441 NE Broadway. ☎ **503/284-5347.** Also at 6141 SW Macadam Ave. (☎ 503/977-0313) and 8838 SW Hall Blvd., Beaverton (☎ 503/646-3869). Reservations not accepted. Sandwiches $6–$8; main courses $10–$14. AE, MC, V. Mon–Thurs 8am–10:30pm, Fri 8am–midnight, Sat 9am–midnight, Sun 9am–4pm. Beaverton location closed on Sun. MEDITERRANEAN/DELI.

Chef Ron Paul has become a Portland institution over the years. He started out with a catering business that became so popular that clients demanded he open a restaurant. This is a casual deli-style place in an upwardly mobile neighborhood in northeast Portland. Light streams through the walls of glass illuminating long cases full of tempting pasta-and-vegetable salads, cheeses, quiches, pizzas, sandwich fixings, and, most tempting of all, decadent desserts. My most recent foray here brought a basil pesto stuffed chicken breast overflowing with portobello mushrooms that came with a chickpea salad accented with rosemary and sage—delicious combinations. Both the Broadway and Macadam locations serve brunch on Saturday and Sunday, and the Beaverton location on Saturday only. All have extensive selections of Northwest wines.

INEXPENSIVE

Aztec Willie, Joey Rose Taqueria. 1501 NE Broadway. ☎ **503/280-8900.** Reservations not accepted. Main dishes $5–$10. AE, DISC, MC, V. Sun–Thurs 11am–9pm, Fri–Sat 11am–10pm. MEXICAN.

Aztec Willie is another member of the Mayas Tacqueria family and serves similarly delicious food, which you order at the walk-up counter. This place is cavernous with space-age tables and chairs. For adults there's a bar, and for kids, a glass-enclosed (so you can keep an eye on them) play area overseen by a huge Mayan-like head.

✪ Chez José East. 2200 NE Broadway. ☎ **503/280-9888.** Also Chez José West, 8502 SW Terwilliger Blvd. ☎ 503/244-0007. Reservations not accepted. Main courses $5–$10. MC, V. Mon–Thurs 11:30am–10pm, Fri–Sat 11:30am–11pm, Sun 4–9pm (The bar serves food until 1 hour later each night). MEXICAN.

It's immediately obvious on perusing the menu here that this isn't the kind of Mexican food you get at Taco Bell. While a squash enchilada with peanut sauce (spicy and sweet with mushrooms, apples, jicama, and sunflower seeds) sounds weird, it actually tastes great. But don't worry, there's plenty of traditional fare on the menu too (and at traditional cheap prices, too). Because the restaurant doesn't take reservations, it's a good idea to get here early, before the line starts snaking out the door. This is a family friendly place, so don't hesitate to bring the kids.

Rustica. 1700 NE Broadway. ☎ **503/288-0990.** Reservations recommended. Main dishes $8–$15. AE, DC, MC, V. Mon–Thurs 11:30am–2:30pm and 5–9:30pm, Fri 11:30am–2:30pm and 5–10:30pm, Sat 5–10:30pm, Sun 5–9pm. ITALIAN.

If you're looking for good, inexpensive Italian food in Northeast Portland, look no further than Rustica. The menu is long, portions are large, and prices are cheap. What more could you ask for, right? Luckily, the atmosphere is fun also, with a mural of an Italian street scene on the walls. There is also a small pizzeria adjacent to the main restaurant. Among our favorite dishes here are the al ceppo pasta with grilled prawns wrapped in pancetta and the lasagna rustica made with rock shrimp, bay scallops, and Dungeness crab.

Saigon Kitchen. 835 NE Broadway. ☎ **503/281-3669.** Reservations necessary Fri–Sat only. Main dishes $6–$16. AE, MC, V. Mon–Sat 11am–10pm, Sun noon–10pm. VIETNAMESE/THAI.

A spate of Vietnamese restaurants have been opening around Portland's east side. They are generally quite inexpensive, offer amazing variety, and provide some of the most interesting flavor combinations this side of Thailand. Saigon Kitchen is among the best of these restaurants. Don't expect a fancy atmosphere inside this pink stucco building, just good home cooking, Vietnamese style. If the menu proves too bewildering, try a combination dinner and let the kitchen make the decisions. The spring rolls (chazio rolls on the menu) shouldn't be missed, however, nor should the curried chicken. The salads, such as shrimp and barbecued pork, are tangy and spicy. There is even a menu of Thai dishes for those who prefer this similar cuisine. Another Saigon Kitchen is at 3829 SE Division St. (☎ **503/236-2312**).

6 Southeast Portland

EXPENSIVE

✪ **Genoa.** 2832 SE Belmont St. ☎ **503/238-1464.** Reservations required. Fixed-price 4-course dinner $40; 7-course dinner $50. AE, CB, DC, DISC, MC, V. Mon–Sat 5:30–11:30pm; (4-course on Fri–Sat limited to 5:30 and 6pm only). ITALIAN.

This is one of the best Italian restaurants in Portland, and with only 10 tables, it's also one of the smallest. The dining room is small, furnished in dark classic elegance, with a sitting room in back where you can sip an aperitif while you wait for your table. Everything is made fresh in the kitchen, from the breads to the luscious desserts that are temptingly displayed on a maple burl table just inside the front door. This is an ideal setting for a romantic dinner, and service is attentive—the waiter explains dishes in detail as they are served, and dishes are magically whisked away as they are finished.

The fixed-price menu changes every couple of weeks, but a typical dinner might start with small and spicy pimentos stuffed with salt cod and baked with puréed vegetables and garlic, followed by a creamy wild mushroom soup. The pasta course could be a classic lasagne, with a meat sauce of tomatoes, ham, chicken livers, beef, and pork, layered with a béchamel sauce and Parmesan cheese. This might then be followed by a salad of Belgian endive, roasted walnuts, and Gorgonzola. There is always a choice of main courses such as fresh sturgeon braised in red wine with bacon and shallots or Oregon quail stuffed with wild and cultivated mushrooms and served with creamy polenta and watercress.

Desserts are a standout. We had a lusciously intense mango-almond glacé and a rich and mouth-puckering lemon tart, tempered by raspberry sauce and the mellow flavor of crème fraîche.

MODERATE

✪ **Assaggio.** 7742 SE 13th Ave. ☎ **503/232-6151.** Reservations accepted only for parties of 6 or more. Main courses $9–$14. MC, V. Tues–Thurs 5–10pm, Fri–Sat 5–10:30pm. ITALIAN.

This trattoria in the Sellwood neighborhood focuses its attentions on pastas and wines and to that end, the menu lists 15 pastas and the wine list includes more than 100 wines, almost all of which are from Italy. The atmosphere of this tiny place is extremely theatrical, with indirect lighting, dark walls, and Mario Lanza playing in the background. While pastas are the main attraction, this does not mean the flavors are not robust. Don't be surprised if after taking your first bite, you suddenly hear a Verdi aria. *Assaggio* means a sampling or a taste, and that is exactly what you get if you order salad, bruschetta, or pasta Assaggio style—a sampling of several dishes all served family style. This is especially fun if you're here with a group.

Bread and Ink Cafe. 3610 SE Hawthorne Blvd. ☎ **503/239-4756.** Reservations recommended. Main dishes $12.50–$18.50; Sun brunch $11.50. AE, DISC, MC, V. Mon–Thurs 7am–9pm, Fri 7am–10pm, Sat 8am–10pm, Sun 9am–2pm; and 5–9pm. NORTHWEST.

This is funky Hawthorne Boulevard's most upscale restaurant, yet is still more of a casual neighborhood cafe. Every meal here is carefully and imaginatively prepared using fresh Northwest ingredients, and consequently, flavors change considerably with the seasons. A recent spring menu included fennel-roasted pork loin with rhubarb chutney and cold-smoked steelhead in a ginger infused broth with buckwheat noodles. Desserts are a mainstay of Bread and Ink's loyal patrons, so don't pass them by. The Yiddish Sunday brunch is one of the most filling in the city.

✪ **Caprial's Bistro And Wine.** 7015 SE Milwaukee Ave. ☎ **503/236-6457.** Reservations highly recommended. Main courses $14–$19. MC, V. Tues–Fri 11am–3:30pm, Sat 11:30–3:30pm; Wed–Thurs 5–9pm, Fri–Sat 5–9:30pm. NORTHWEST.

Caprial's Bistro and Wines is easy to miss. It's small, it's nondescript, and it's located in a neighborhood that, though attractive, is not one of the city's busiest. Caprial Pence, who helped put the Northwest on the national restaurant map, is the chef here, and even though this is a strong contender for best restaurant in Portland, it is a very casual place with only about 12 tables. There's no need to dress up, but you do need to make reservations well in advance (at least a week ahead for Friday or Saturday night). About half the restaurant is given over to a superb selection of wine and a wine bar; you may buy a bottle of wine from the wine shop and open it at your table for a small additional charge. This eliminates the markup that most restaurants charge for a bottle of wine. The menu changes monthly and is limited to four or five main dishes and as many appetizers. Entrees combine perfectly cooked meats and fishes such as roast pork loin or lightly breaded oysters, with vibrant sauces such as cranberry-shallot compote or sweet red-pepper pesto. Desserts, such as chocolate-almond-ricotta cake, are rich without being overly sweet. You'll get a large piece of whatever you order, so save room.

✪ **Fiddleheads.** 6716 SE Milwaukee Ave. ☎ **503/233-1547.** Reservations recommended. Main courses $14–$19.75. AE, DISC, MC, V. Mon–Fri 11:30am–10pm, Sat 10am–11pm, Sun 10am–9pm. NATIVE AMERICAN DERIVATIVE.

The setting is handsome: open, yet with cozy tones inspired by Native American designs. Likewise, the menu here draws on traditional Native American fare inspiration. Fiddleheads' Calapooya salad makes a good starter, but the crispy fried oyster tacos, accented by a savory guacamole and tiny serrano peppers are just too good to pass up. The hunter's style pasta is tossed with firm dark pheasant meat, boar bacon, and wild mushrooms in a smooth and flavorful Madeira sauce, while the *tatonka* is an Oregon buffalo stew with corn dumplings, vegetables, and roasted chiles. Entrees are likely to leave you fulfilled but not stuffed, and eager to try dessert. Chocolate Marquis, one of several house-made desserts and nearly a meal in itself, is a delicious flourless chocolate cake that arrives on a large plate garnished with blackberry sauce, cookies, and mint. Wine choices are many, and the prices are moderate. Half a dozen vegetarian dishes appear on the menu, and brunch is served on Saturday and Sunday. Service is some of the best in town.

Il Piatto. 2348 SE Ankeny St. ☎ **503/236-4997.** Reservations highly recommended Thurs–Sat. Main courses $9–$16; lunch main courses $8.50–$11. MC, V. Tues–Fri 11:30am–2:30pm; Sun–Thurs 5:30pm–10pm, Fri–Sat 5:30pm–11pm. NORTHERN ITALIAN.

Il Piatto is a small neighborhood restaurant with a romantic atmosphere. Antiqued walls, dried flowers, and overstuffed chairs in the lounge area provide a comfortable place for sipping coffee or waiting for your table. Start your meal with oven-dried tomato pesto that you spread on crusty bread. The pastas are wonderful. I chose risotto de Gamberi, which is arborio rice with sautéed prawns, mussels, and leeks, with a low-key taste of saffron that was intriguing. The marinated rabbit has also gotten rave reviews. Italian desserts such as tiramisu made with cornmeal cake are all made here in the kitchen by the pastry chef.

Indigine. 3725 SE Division St. ☎ **503/238-1470.** Reservations recommended. Main dishes $10–$15; Saturday night Indian feast $26. MC, V. Tues–Thurs 5:30–9:30pm, Fri–Sat 5:30–10pm, Sun 9–2pm. INDIAN/INTERNATIONAL.

When you step through the front door of this restaurant, you're halfway into the kitchen, but don't worry, this is indeed the front door. Indigine is a very casual place with the feel of a college vegetarian restaurant but a far more interesting menu. At Indigine your taste buds dance through tantalizing flavors the likes of which you may never have encountered before. The menu here is eclectic, with Indian, Mexican, French, and American offerings during the week and an extravagant Indian feast on Saturday evenings. During the week you can sample some of Indigine's flavorful Indian cuisine by ordering the vegetarian sampler. But before it's too late, stop and save room for one of the luscious desserts. Sunday brunch is eclectic and economical.

Montage. 301 SE Morrison St. ☎ **503/234-1324.** Reservations not accepted. Main courses $5–$16. No credit cards. Sun–Thurs 6pm–2am, Fri–Sat 6pm–4am. CAJUN/LATE-NIGHT DINING.

A cacophony of voices and throbbing music punctuated by waiters bellowing out orders for oyster shooters slams you in the face as you step through the door of this in spot *under* the Morrison Bridge. They've definitely got the right idea here— Cajun dishes such as blackened catfish, crawfish étouffée, jambalaya, frogs legs, and alligator salad (and all at surprisingly low prices). A lengthy wine menu promises you'll find something to your liking. If you hate noisy places, don't even think of eating here—otherwise, it's great fun.

INEXPENSIVE

Caswell. 533 SE Grand St. (at Washington Street) ☎ **503/232-6512.** Reservations not usually accepted. Main courses $5–$9.50. MC, V. Mon–Sat 5pm–midnight. PIZZA/PASTA.

Located in a former Starbucks space, Caswell is proof that a good plate of pasta doesn't have to be expensive. The pasta carbonara, with sautéed pancetta and a smoky prosciutto in garlic cream sauce, was strong-flavored and appealing, as was the ravioli, a complexly flavored pillow stuffed with cheeses and wood oven baked vegetables. For an appetizer, we loved the crostini accompanied by a casserole of creamy spinach and artichoke hearts. Pizzas and salads round out the menu. The bar, an important component of the restaurant, serves single malt Scotch and micro brewed beers. To sum up: the food is tasty, and one should have an appreciation for contemporary rock 'n' roll music.

Chez Grill. 2229 SE Hawthorne Blvd. ☎ **503/239-4002.** Reservations for 7 or more only. Main courses $11–$15. MC, V. Mon–Thurs 11:30am–10pm, Fri–Sat 11:30am–11pm, Sun 5–10pm. SOUTHWEST.

Brought to you by the owners of Chez José, this southwestern restaurant on the edge of the Hawthorne district looks as if it could have been transported straight from Tucson or Santa Fe. The menu here, which includes small plates, large plates, and side plates is more grill-oriented than at Chez José and is definitely meant for mixing and matching. There are grilled scallops marinated in serrano chiles and lime, red chile onion rings, and game hen marinated in spicy adobo sauce (served with banana-pepper chutney and grilled banana).

El Palenque. 8324 SE 17th Ave. ☎ **503/231-5140.** Main courses $5–$12. MC, V. Daily 11am–9:30pm. MEXICAN/SALVADORAN.

Though El Palenque bills itself as a Mexican restaurant, the Salvadoran dishes are the real reason for a visit. If you've never had a pupusa, this is your opportunity. A pupusa is basically an extrathick corn tortilla with a meat or cheese filling inside, accompanied by spicy shredded cabbage. Instead of adding the filling after the tortilla is cooked, the filling goes in beforehand. What you end up with is a sort of griddle-cooked turnover. Accompany your pupusa with some fried plantains and a glass of horchata (sweet and spicy rice drink) for a typically Salvadoran meal.

✪ **Esparza's Tex-Mex Café.** 2725 SE Ankeny St. ☎ **503/234-7909.** Reservations not accepted. Main courses $5–$11. MC, V. Tues–Sat 11:30am–10pm (in summer, Fri–Sat until 10:30pm). TEX-MEX.

With red-eyed cow skulls on the walls and marionettes, model planes, and stuffed iguanas and armadillos hanging from the ceiling, the decor here can only be described as Tex-eclectic, an epithet that is equally appropriate when applied to the menu. Sure there are enchiladas and tamales and tacos, but they might be filled with buffalo meat or smoked salmon. Rest assured you can also get standard ingredients such as chicken and beef. Main courses come with some of the best rice and beans I've ever had, and if you want your meal hotter, they'll toss you a couple of jalapeño peppers. The *nopalitos* (fried cactus) are worth a try, and the margaritas just might be the best in Portland. While you're waiting for a seat (there's almost always a wait), check out the vintage tunes on the jukebox.

✪ **Nicholas.** 318 SE Grand St. (between Pine and Oak sts.) ☎ **503/235-5123.** Reservations not accepted. Main courses $2–$8. No credit cards. Mon–Sat 10am–9pm. LEBANESE.

This little hole-in-the-wall is usually crowded at mealtime because the food is delicious and the prices are, well, cheap. In spite of the heat from the pizza oven and the crowded conditions, the customers and wait staff still manage to be friendly. Our favorite dish is the *Manakishe,* Mediterranean pizza with thyme, oregano, sesame seeds, olive oil, and lemony-flavored sumac. Also available are a creamy *humous, baba ghanouj,* kabobs, and *falafel* and *gyros* sandwiches.

Old Wives' Tales. 1300 E Burnside St. ☎ **503/238-0470.** Reservations recommended for dinner. Breakfasts $4–$8; lunch and dinner main dishes $5–$15. AE, DISC, MC, V. Sun–Thurs 8am–9pm, Fri–Sat 8am–10pm. INTERNATIONAL/VEGETARIAN.

Old Wives' Tales is a sort of Portland countercultural institution. The menu is mostly vegetarian, with multiethnic dishes such as spanakopita and burritos, with a smattering of chicken and seafood dishes. Breakfast here is a popular meal and is served until 2pm daily. Old Wives' Tales's other claim to fame these days is as the city's best place to eat out with kids if you aren't into the fast food scene. There are children's menus and a play room.

Pollo Rey. 3832 SE Hawthorne Blvd. ☎ **503/236-5000.** Also at 914 NW 23rd Ave. ☎ **503/226-9600.** Reservations not accepted. Main courses $3–$6. AE, MC, V. Sun–Thurs 11am–10pm, Fri–Sat 11am–11pm. MEXICAN.

Pollo Rey is a California import restaurant with a folksy, bright interior where you order from a walkup counter and then wait for them to call your number. The star here is rotisseried chicken, served by itself with salsa and tortillas, or in tortilla soup, or in a huge Caesar salad. Burritos and quesadillas and tacos also come with the rotisseried chicken, and with steak, or just *frijoles.* Small orders are a little skimpy, so if you're hungry, go for the large. They even have *horchata,* a creamy rice drink that is sweet and filling on a hot day.

Saburo's Sushi House. 1667 SE Bybee Blvd. ☎ **503/236-4237.** Reservations not accepted. Main courses $7.50–$15, sushi $2.50–$7. MC, V. Tues–Sun 4:30–9:30pm. JAPANESE.

Located in Sellwood, as is El Palenque, above, this sushi restaurant is so enormously popular that patrons most frequently have to wait. But when your sushi finally arrives, you'll know it was worth it. Our favorite is the *sabu* roll with lots of fish, and the *maguro* tuna sushi with generous slabs of tuna. Most Westerners don't care for the sea urchin, but you can try it if you're brave.

Zell's. 1300 SE Morrison St. ☎ **503/239-0196.** Reservations not accepted. Breakfast $4–$8.25; lunch $4.75–$7. AE, MC, V. Mon–Fri 7am–2pm, Sat 8am–2pm, Sun 8am–3pm. AMERICAN/BREAKFASTS.

Once a pharmacy and now famed for delicious breakfasts such as clam cakes, German apple pancakes, and real corned beef hash, Zell's has for years been one of Portland's favorite breakfast spots. Come early if you want to try the cinnamon rolls, but if those are gone, you can content yourself with other bakery treats such as dark gingery bread or light and airy scones. The service is great, children are welcomed— and if the restaurant isn't crowded, you can sit as long as you like and the waiter will keep refilling your coffee cup.

7 Southwest Portland & the West Side (Including Beaverton and Tigard)

MODERATE

Avalon Grill. 4630 SW Macadam Ave. ☎ **503/227-4630.** Reservations recommended for weekend evenings. Main courses $15–$22; light entrees $8–$16; Sun brunch $15.95. AE, MC, V. Mon–Sat 11:30am–1am, Sun 10am–midnight; lower level restaurant closes at 9pm Sun–Thurs and 10pm Fri–Sat. NORTHWEST.

Modern decor highlights this triple-story glass-walled restaurant on the Willamette River, creating a glamorous ambience with outstanding views of the river. In the cafe areas, there are granite-topped bars beautified by backlit panels of amber onyx that create a dramatic glow at night. This is a great place to come for a drink and a light meal. A mushroom and spinach lasagna constructed of very thin layers of sweet potato was a tasty assortment of flavors, and goat cheese ravioli with Dungeness crab had a spicy tomato sauce reminiscent of bouillabaisse, but entrees are a little pricey for what you get. What you're paying for is the ambience and the riverside setting. Monday through Friday from 3:30 to 6:30pm, there's an inexpensive happy hour menu, and in the evenings there is frequently live jazz.

✪ **Pavilion Bar and Grill.** Greenwood Inn, 10700 SW Allen Blvd., Beaverton ☎ **503/626-4550.** Reservations recommended. Main dishes $14–$22.50. AE, DC, DISC, MC, V. Mon–Thurs 6:30am–10pm, Fri 6:30am–11pm, Sat 7am–11pm, Sun 7am–2pm and 4–10pm. NORTHWEST.

Portlanders are unaccustomed to heading to the suburbs for dinner, so when Pavillion, located in a hotel no less, began garnering excellent reviews, the city was taken aback. However, there is no denying the superb quality of the meals served at this quintessentially northwestern restaurant. The dining room looks like a gazebo, and in the center of the room, three large columns of basalt have been turned into a bubbling water fountain. In summer the garden patio is the place to dine. The menu is varied and always creative, with the likes of wood-grilled brochettes of lamb and vanilla prawns showing up on a recent appetizer list. Coriander crusted ahi tuna with a lemon-roasted chili butter was a lively combination of flavors. The menu changes seasonally, and the restaurant is well worth the short drive out from downtown; just try to make a reservation for after rush hour.

Satay House. 8601 SW Terwilliger Blvd. (Burlingame). ☎ **503/452-3636.** Reservations accepted. Main courses $14–$26. AE, MC, V. Daily 5–10pm. INDONESIAN.

The owners of the Satay House formerly had a restaurant in Holland, and now bring the exotic flavors of Indonesia to Portland in a small and elegant setting with white linen, candlelight, and roses. If you want the full presentation that turns dinner into an event, order the *rijsttafel,* or rice table, a feast of many Indonesian dishes. For a slightly less bounteous spread, try the *Nassi Ramas* special. Of the entrees on the menu, a few can be quite spicy, as is the chili mackerel, while the chicken satay, tender cubes of chicken on a skewer with a smoky sauce, is simply excellent. For dessert, durian, mango, and jackfruit ice cream with bits of tropical fruits are luscious and exotic.

INEXPENSIVE

Hands on Café. 8245 SW Barnes Rd. ☎ **503/297-1480.** Reservations not accepted. $3–$6. Credit cards not accepted. Mon–Fri 11:30am–2pm; Mon–Thurs 5:30–7:30pm; brunch Sun 9:30am–1:30pm. INTERNATIONAL.

What's special about this cafe is that it's located at the Oregon School of Arts and Crafts, west of downtown Portland. You can enjoy healthy and light foods such as polenta tamale pie, homemade soups, salads, breads, and muffins, and soak up the ambience of an art school. There are artworks by students on the walls, and you can visit the craft shop and gallery if they're open. An outside patio is enjoyable in the warm weather.

The Old Spaghetti Factory. 0715 SW Bancroft St. ☎ **503/222-5375.** Reservations not accepted. Main courses $4.60–$8.40. CB, DC, DISC, MC, V. Mon–Thurs 11:30am–2pm and 5–10pm, Fri 11:30am–2pm and 5–11pm, Sat 1–11pm, Sun noon–10pm. ITALIAN.

Sure this is a chain restaurant, but incredibly low prices, great decor, a fabulous waterfront location on the bank of the Willamette River, and the fact that the chain had its start right here in Portland are reason enough to give this place a chance. This is the best waterfront restaurant in town for kids, and is a lot of fun for adults, too. Sort of a cross between a church, a trolley depot, and a Victorian brothel, this restaurant will keep you entertained and won't cost much more than McDonald's. To find it, watch for the big building with the blue tile roof.

✪ **Swagat.** 4325 SW 109th Ave., Beaverton. ☎ **503/626-3000.** Reservations not accepted. Main courses $7–$13. AE, DISC, MC, V. Daily 11:30am–2:30pm and 5–10pm. INDIAN.

Tucked away in a ranch house in suburban Beaverton, Swagat is a culinary oasis for those who live and work in the area. The *dosas,* crepes made of lentil flour, stuffed with vegetable curry, and served with a variety of sauces, are deliciously savory. We like to begin with vegetable *samosas,* crisp turnovers stuffed with potatoes and peas, and follow up with the *thali* dinner, a multicourse meal available in vegetarian or nonvegetarian. Don't forget to order some of the puffy *nan* (Indian bread).

8 Cafes, Coffee Bars & Tea Rooms

CAFES

If you'd like to sample some cafes around Portland that serve not only the full range of coffee drinks, but also have atmosphere, I recommend the following:

- **The Brazen Bean,** 2075 NW Glisan St. (☎ **503/294-0636**), is open evenings until late, which suits its opulent Victorian theme. There are board games to play, and there is a smoking room.

- **Café Lena,** 2239 SE Hawthorne Blvd. (☎ **503/238-7087**), located in the funky SE Hawthorne neighborhood, has live music and tasty food but is best known for its poetry nights.
- **Coffee Time,** 710 NW 21st Ave. (☎ **503/497-1090**), is a favorite Northwest neighborhood hangout with tables outside, and a variety of atmospheres inside—a cafe with big wooden booths, a lounge with cracked leather chairs and a fake fireplace, and a dark Victorian drawing room. Take your pick.
- **Common Grounds,** 4321 SE Hawthorne Blvd. (☎ **503/236-4835**). Located out beyond Hawthorne Boulevard's main shopping district is this counter-cultural hangout where the magazine rack is filled with literary reviews, small press journals, and other left-wing literature and the crowd of coffee drinkers tends to be tattooed and pierced.
- **Pied Cow,** 3244 SE Belmont St. (☎ **503/230-4866**), is in a Victorian house decorated in Bohemian chic, where there are couches on which to lounge and an outdoor garden. Sandwiches and soups are served, too.
- **Rimsky-Korsakoffee House,** 707 SE 12th Ave. (☎ **503/232-2640**), legendary for the rudeness of its wait staff, has been Portland's favorite coffeehouse for more than a decade. Live classical music and a very skewed sense of humor keep patrons loyal. Oh, there's no sign on the old house to let you know this is the place, but you'll know once you open the door. Open after 7pm. Great desserts.
- **Torrefazione Italia,** 838 NW 23rd Ave. (☎ **503/228-2528**), serves its classic brew in hand-painted Italian crockery, and has a good selection of pastries to go with your drink.

BAKERIES/DESSERT PLACES

Marsee Baking. 1323 NW 23rd Ave. ☎ **503/295-4000.** Reservations not accepted. Sweets $1–$5; sandwiches $5. Mon–Thurs 7:30am–9pm, Fri–Sat 7:30am–10pm, Sun 8am–8pm. BAKERY.

When you've just got to have something gooey and rich, there's no better place to get it than at this little bakery on trendy 23rd Avenue. The cases are crammed to overflow-ing with cakes, pies, and tarts as well as less ostentatious pastries, bagels, focaccia, baguettes, and other breads. There are also panini (Italian sandwiches) and bagels with various fillings. Also at 845 SW Fourth Ave., near Pioneer Place shopping center (☎ 503/226-9000) and at the Portland International Airport shopping mall.

Papa Haydn. 701 NW 23rd Ave. ☎ **503/228-7317.** Reservations not accepted except for Sun brunch. Main dishes $16–$24; desserts $4–$6. AE, MC, V. Tues–Thurs 11:30am–11pm, Fri–Sat 11:30am–midnight, Sun brunch 10am–3pm. ITALIAN.

Say the words *Papa Haydn* to a Portlander and you'll see eyes glaze over, a blissful smile will appear, and then praises will spill forth. What is it about this little bistro that sends locals into accolades of superlatives? Just desserts. That's right, though Papa Haydn is a respectable Italian restaurant, it is legendary for dessert. Lemon chiffon torte, raspberry gâteau, black velvet, Georgian peanut butter mousse torte, tiramisu, boccone dolce. These are just some of the names that stimulate a Pavlovian response in locals. Expect a line at the door (that's the real price you pay for a Papa Haydn symphony). Also at 5829 SE Milwaukee Ave. (☎ 503/232-9440).

AFTERNOON TEA

British Tea Garden. 725 SW Tenth Ave. ☎ **503/221-7817.** Reservations not necessary. Set teas and lunches $6.50–$8.25. AE, DISC, MC, V. Mon and Sat 10am–5pm, Tues–Fri 10am–6pm, Sun noon–4pm. TEA/BRITISH.

Though Portland is a city of java junkies, tea is making a strong showing these days as well. You can get all manner of exotic teas at coffeehouses, but for the genuine

British tea experience, you need to take time out at the British Tea Garden. Not only can you get clotted Devonshire cream and crumpets here, but you can also get Cornish pasties, bangers, shepherd's pie, and finger sandwiches. Don't worry if you're not dressed for tea; it's a casual place.

The Heathman Hotel. 1001 SW Broadway at Salmon St. ☎ **503/241-4100.** Reservations recommended. $6–$14. AE, CB, DC, DISC, MC, V. Daily 2–4:30pm. TEA.

In the Heathman Hotel's lobby lounge, tea hostesses in lace aprons serve finger sandwiches, scones, pastries, and of course excellent tea (blended especially for the hotel). The service is on Royal Doulton bone china at marble-topped tables, and on chilly afternoons a fire crackles in the fireplace. An elegant affair, tea at the Heathman is a welcome respite from shopping or business meetings.

9 Quick Bites

If you're just looking for something quick, cheap, and good to eat, there are lots of great options around the city. Downtown, at **Good Dog/Bad Dog,** 708 SW Alder St. (☎ **503/222-3410**), you'll find handmade sausages. The kosher frank with kraut and onions is a good deal. For more upscale meals, duck into the **Ron Paul Express,** 507 SW Broadway (☎ **503/221-0052**), which is an outpost of a local chain of excellent and reasonably priced restaurants. Salads and sandwiches are good, but the cakes and pastries here are to die for.

Designer pizzas topped with anything from artichoke hearts to bacon to peanut sauce and teriyaki chicken can be had at **Pizzicato Gourmet Pizza.** Find them downtown at 705 SW Alder St. ☎ **503/226-1007;** in Northwest at 505 NW 23rd Ave. ☎ **503/242-0023;** and in Southeast at 2811 E. Burnside ☎ **503/236-6045.**

Over in southeast Portland, you can't miss the **Kitchen Table Café** (400 SE 12th Ave.; ☎ **503/230-6977**) in the yellow and purple building on the corner of SE Oak and SE 12th streets. This is a great place for homemade pies and soups, salads, and breads. If you're in the mood for a great burger, head to **Dots,** 2521 SE Clinton St. (☎ **503/235-0203**), which serves big, fat, juicy burgers in a setting that abounds in 1950s kitsch.

16 What to See & Do in Portland

Portland is a low-key city. What to see and do in the city is not so much about visiting museums as it is about just soaking up atmosphere. More than anything else, Portland is proud of its parks and public art and it is these features that local citizens most like to show off. There just aren't many museums here, and what few there are all fairly small. This isn't to say that Portland is a boring city or that there isn't much for visitors to see or do. However, you can easily visit all of Portland's main tourist attractions in a day or two.

If, however, you happen to be a gardener, you might want to leave a bit more time in your schedule. Gardening is a Portland obsession, and consequently there are numerous world-class public gardens and parks within the city. If you know a daisy from a dianthus, then you'll want to take plenty of time to visit the city's public gardens.

Once you've seen the biggies, it's time to start learning why it is that everyone loves living here so much. Portlanders for the most part are active types, and they enjoy snow skiing on Mount Hood and hiking in the Columbia Gorge just as much as they enjoy going to art museums. Consequently, no visit to Portland would be complete without venturing out into the Oregon countryside. This is the city's real attraction. Within $1^{1}/_{2}$ hours you can be skiing on Mount Hood or walking beside the chilly waters of the Pacific Ocean. However, for those who prefer urban activities, the museums and parks listed below should satisfy.

SUGGESTED ITINERARIES

If You Have 1 Day

Day 1   Start your day with an espresso at Pioneer Courthouse Square, a brick-paved plaza that is considered Portland's living room. From here, walk over to the Oregon History Center museum to get a background in the history of the city and state. Afterwards, cross the park to the Portland Art Museum, which mounts large special exhibits throughout the year. Later in the day, head up to the International Rose Test Garden and the Japanese Garden. If it happens to be a Saturday or Sunday, be sure to visit the Saturday Market.

If You Have 2 Days

Day 1   Follow the outline above for your first day in town.
Day 2   On your second day in town, take a walk through Tom McCall Waterfront Park, explore some of the historic blocks in the

Old Town neighborhood, and visit the American Advertising Museum. Later, take a cruise on the river on one of the many boats that offer trips.

If You Have 3 Days

Days 1–2   Follow the 2-day strategy as outlined above.
Day 3   On your third day, do the Mount Hood Loop, as described in chapter 20.

If You Have 5 Days or More

Days 1–3   Follow the 3-day strategy as outlined above.
Day 4   In the morning, visit Pittock Mansion and perhaps stroll through Hoyt Arboretum or Forest Park. In the afternoon, visit Fort Vancouver across the Columbia River in Washington State (see chapter 20).
Day 5   Drive to the coast or tour through the wine country (see chapter 20).

1 The Top Attractions

✪ **International Rose Test Garden.** 400 SW Kingston Ave., Washington Park. ☎ **503/823-3636.** Free admission. Daily, dawn to dusk. Bus: 63.

Covering 4¹/₂ acres of hillside in the West Hills above downtown Portland, these are the largest and oldest rose test gardens in the United States. They were established in 1917 by the American Rose Society, itself founded in Portland. Though you will likely see some familiar roses in the Gold Medal Garden, most of the 400 varieties on display here are new hybrids being tested before marketing. Among the roses in bloom from late spring to early winter, you'll find a separate garden of miniature roses. There is also a Shakespearean Garden that includes flowers mentioned in the works of William Shakespeare. After seeing these acres of roses, you will certainly understand why Portland is known as the City of Roses and why the Rose Festival in June is the city's biggest annual celebration.

✪ **Japanese Garden.** Off Kingston Ave. in Washington Park. ☎ **503/223-1321.** Admission $5 adults, $2.50 students and seniors, under age 6 free. Apr 1–May 31 and Sept 1–Sept 30, daily 10am–6pm; June 1–Aug 31, daily 9am–8pm; Oct 1–Mar 31, daily 10am–4pm. Closed Thanksgiving, Christmas, and New Year's Day. Bus: 63.

I have always loved Japanese gardens and have visited them all over the world. Outside of those in Japan, this is still my favorite. What makes it so special is not only the design, plantings, and tranquillity, but the view. From the Japanese-style wooden house in the center of the garden, you can gaze over Portland to Mount Hood on a clear day. This perfectly shaped volcanic peak is so reminiscent of Mount Fuji that it seems almost as if it were placed there for the sake of this garden.

✪ **Portland Saturday Market.** Underneath Burnside Bridge between SW First Ave. and SW Ankeny St. ☎ **503/222-6072.** Free admission. 1st weekend in Mar–Christmas Eve, Sat 10am–5pm and Sun 11am–4:30pm. Bus: 12, 19, 20. MAX: Skidmore Fountain Station.

Portland Saturday Market (held on both Saturday and Sunday) is arguably the city's single most important and best-loved event. For years the Northwest has attracted artists and craftspeople, and every Saturday and Sunday nearly 300 of them can be found selling their exquisite creations here. In addition to the dozens of crafts stalls, you'll find flowers, fresh produce, ethnic and unusual foods, and lots of free entertainment. This is the single best place in Portland to shop for one-of-a-kind gifts. The atmosphere is always cheerful and the crowds colorful. At the heart of the Skidmore District, Portland Saturday Market makes an excellent starting or finishing point for a walk around Portland's most historic neighborhood. Don't miss this unique market. On Sunday, on-street parking is free.

Portland Attractions

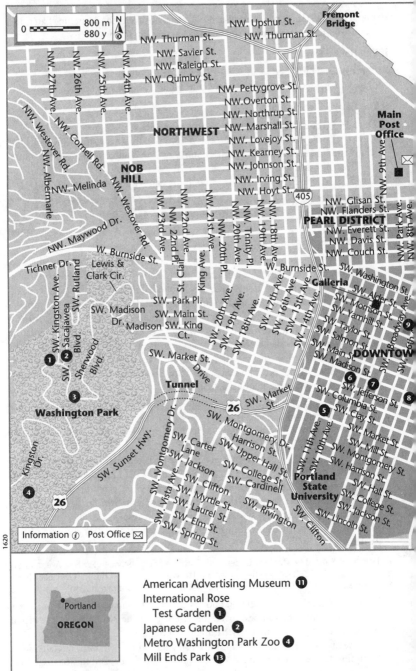

American Advertising Museum ⑪
International Rose
  Test Garden ①
Japanese Garden ②
Metro Washington Park Zoo ④
Mill Ends Park ⑬

Information ⓘ Post Office ✉

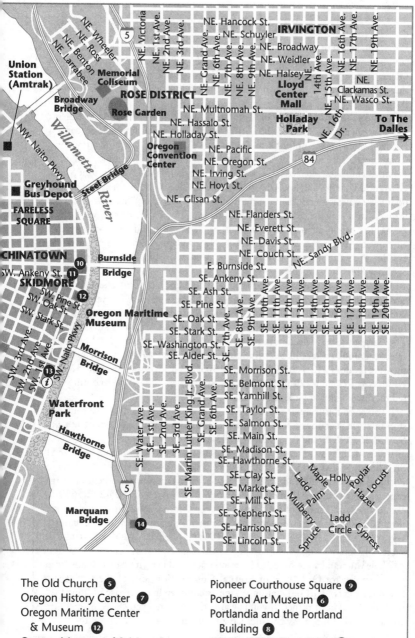

The Old Church **5**
Oregon History Center **7**
Oregon Maritime Center
   & Museum **12**
Oregon Museum of Science
   and Industry **14**

Pioneer Courthouse Square **9**
Portland Art Museum **6**
Portlandia and the Portland
   Building **8**
Portland Saturday Market **10**
Washington Park **3**

Kitsch'n Around Portland

Either you love it or you hate it, but there's no denying that kitsch is in, and Portland is thriving on it. Retro furniture stores sell 1950s chairs and tables at 1990s prices, vintage clothing stores sell platform shoes and bell bottoms, and Elvis worship is raised to an art form. If this is your shtick, then let's go "kitsch'n" around Portland.

Where's the Art? (A Gallery of Art for the Smart; formerly the Church of Elvis), 720 SW Ankeny St. (☎ **503/226-3671** or online at www.churchofelvis.com) is Portland's longtime temple of kitsch and one of the city's most bizarre attractions. Coin-operated art, a video psychic, cheap (though not legal) weddings, and other absurd assemblages, interactive displays, and kitschy contraptions (such as the Vend-O-Matic Mystery Machine with whirling dolls heads) cram this second-floor oddity. As celebrity-spokesmodel/minister S. G. Pierce says, "the tour IS the art form." If you pass the customer test you can even buy a Church of Elvis T-shirt. Great fun if you're a fan of Elvis, tabloids, or the unusual, and if you've seen Elvis anytime in the past decade, a visit is absolutely mandatory. Guided tours of World Headquarters are usually available daily between noon and 5pm and Friday and Saturday 8pm to midnight.

A few blocks away from Where's the Art?, you'll find a concentration of vintage clothing and furniture stores. The biggest and best of these is **Habromania,** 203 SW Ninth Ave. (☎ **503/223-0767**), which has two floors of vintage collectibles from the 1930s through the 1960s. Need a chrome and Formica kitchen table? They've got the best selection in town. Right next door is the smaller, but no less eclectic, **Palookaville,** 211 SW Ninth Ave. (☎ **503/241-4751**). Across the street, there are **Avalon,** 318 SW Ninth Ave. (☎ **503/224-7156**), and **Magpie,** 324 SW Ninth Ave. (☎ **503/220-0920**), which are the places in Portland to outfit yourself for disco nights at local dance clubs.

If you're doubtful about the collectibility of some of the goods at Habromania, stop in at the **Vacuum Cleaner Museum** at Stark's Vacuum Cleaner Sales and Service, 107 NE Grand Ave. (☎ **503/232-4101**).

If after all this you're ready for some refreshment, head over to **Dots Cafe,** 2521 SE Clinton St. (☎ **503/235-0203**) where you can nosh on the best burgers in Portland while oohing and ahhing over the vintage decor. For a genuine retro experience, try **Fuller's Restaurant,** 136 NW Ninth Ave. (☎ **503/222-5608**), a classic diner straight out of an Edward Hopper painting. This one is in the same neighborhood as the above-mentioned shops and museums. In the evening, try **Gypsy,** 625 NW 21st Ave. (☎ **503/796-1859**), a popular bar and restaurant that sports a Jetsons decor.

While you wander the streets of Portland tracking down kitsch of all kinds, keep your eyes out for **Our Lady of Eternal Combustion,** one of the city's most famous art cars. This old station wagon is completely covered with glued-on trinkets. A real head-turner. If you pay attention, you're likely to see many other art cars as well. One of my favorites has a miniature La Brea tar pits on the roof.

✪ **Pioneer Courthouse Square.** Bounded by Broadway, Sixth Ave., Yamhill St., and Morrison St. Any downtown bus. MAX: Pioneer Courthouse Square Station.

Today this is the heart of downtown Portland and acts as an outdoor stage for everything from flower displays to concerts to protest rallies, but not too many years ago this beautiful brick-paved square was nothing but a parking lot. The parking lot itself had been created by the controversial razing in 1951 of the Portland Hotel, an architectural gem of a Queen Anne–style château. Today the square, with its tumbling waterfall fountain and free-standing columns, is Portland's favorite gathering spot, especially at noon, when the Weather Machine, a mechanical sculpture, forecasts the upcoming 24 hours. Amid a fanfare of music and flashing lights, the Weather Machine sends up clouds of mist and then raises either a sun (clear weather), a dragon (stormy weather), or a blue heron (clouds and drizzle). Keep your eyes on the square's brick pavement. Every brick contains a name (or names) or statement, and some are rather curious.

Portland Art Museum. 1219 SW Park Ave. ☎ **503/226-2811.** Admission $6 adults; $4.50 seniors and students, $2.50 ages 6–15, under 5 free, seniors half price every Thurs. Half price 4–9pm on the first Thurs of each month. Tues–Sun 10am–5pm; first Thurs of each month 10am–9pm. Bus: 6. MAX: Library Station.

This small museum has a respectable collection of European, Asian, and American art, but the major emphasis is on visiting exhibitions that feature a range of artistic expression from ancient to avant-garde. Recent exhibitions included a collection of Rodin's bronze sculptures, the Ancient Tombs of China show, Andrew Wyeth's Helga Pictures, and glass sculptures by Dale Chihuly, all of which attracted large crowds. The smaller galleries often feature photography exhibits and video installations. On Wednesday nights (except in summer), the Museum After Hours program presents live music. The adjacent Northwest film Center is affiliated with the Art Museum and shows an eclectic mix of films.

✪ **Metro Washington Park Zoo.** 4001 SW Canyon Rd., Washington Park. ☎ **503/226-1561.** Admission $5.50 adults, $4 seniors, $3.50 children ages 3–11, under age 2 free; free second Tues of each month from 3pm to closing. Memorial Day to Labor Day, daily 9:30am–6pm; Labor Day to Memorial Day, daily 9:30am–4pm. Bus: 63.

This zoo has been successfully breeding elephants for many years and has the largest breeding herd of elephants in captivity; it also has one of the largest chimpanzee exhibits in the United States. The Africa exhibit, which includes a very lifelike rain forest, displays zebras, rhinos, giraffes, hippos and other animals, is one of the most lifelike habitats I have ever seen in a zoo—and it's giving the elephants a lot of competition. Equally impressive is the Alaskan tundra exhibit, with grizzly bears, wolves, and musk oxen. The Cascade Exhibit includes otters and beavers, and other Northwest natives. For the younger set, there's a children's petting zoo filled with farm animals.

The Washington Park and Zoo Railway travels between the zoo and the International Rose Test and Japanese gardens. Tickets for the miniature railway are $2.75 for adults, $2 for senior citizens and children 3 to 11. In the summer, there are jazz concerts on Wednesday nights and rhythm and blues type concerts on Thursday nights from 7 to 9pm. Concerts are free with zoo admission.

Oregon Museum of Science and Industry (OMSI). 1945 SE Water Ave. ☎ **800/955-6674** or 503/797-4000. Admission: $6 adults, $4.50 seniors and children 4–13, OMNIMAX and light shows cost extra, although discounted combination tickets are available. Thurs 3pm until closing all tickets are 2-for-1. Tues–Sat 9:30am–5:30pm (until 7pm in summer), Thurs 9:30am–8pm. Closed Dec 25. Bus: 63.

The impressive OMSI building on the east bank of the Willamette River has six huge halls, and kids and adults find the exhibits fun and fascinating. Two of the most exciting exhibits allow visitors to touch a tornado or ride an earthquake. This is a hands-on museum and everyone is urged to get involved with displays, from a discovery space for toddlers to physics and chemistry labs for older children. There's plenty of pure entertainment at an OMNIMAX theater and the Murdock Sky Theater, which features laser-light shows and astronomy presentations. The USS *Blueback* submarine (used in the film *The Hunt for Red October*) is docked here and tours are given daily. An open-air train departs from OMSI to Oaks Amusement Park May through October; call ☎ **503/659-5452** for the schedule.

2 Other Museums

⭘ **American Advertising Museum.** 50 SW Second Ave. ☎ **503/226-0000.** Admission $3 adults; $1.50 seniors and children 12 and under. Wed–Sat 11am–5pm, Sun noon–5pm. Bus: 12, 19, 20. MAX: Skidmore Fountain Stop.

I long ago gave up watching television and listening to commercial radio because I have no tolerance for advertising. That this is my favorite Portland museum should tell you something about the exhibits. You'll learn (and perhaps reminisce) about historic advertisements, celebrities, and jingles from the 1700s to now. Special shows in the past have included a retrospective of Portland's Homer Groening (father of Matt Groening, creator of *The Simpsons*), including his cartoons, films, and advertising.

Oregon History Center. 1200 SW Park Ave. ☎ **503/222-1741.** Admission $6 adults and seniors, $3 students, $1.50 children 6–12, Thurs free to seniors. Tues–Sat 10am–5pm, Sun noon–5pm. Bus: Any downtown bus. Bus: 6. MAX: Library Station.

Oregon Territory was a land of promise and plenty. Thousands of hardy individuals set out along the Oregon Trail, crossing a vast and rugged country to reach the fertile valleys of Oregon's rivers. Others came by ship around the Horn. Today the state of Oregon is still luring immigrants with its bountiful natural resources, and those who wish to learn about the people who discovered Oregon before them should visit this well-designed museum. Oregon history from before the arrival of the first Europeans to well into this century is chronicled in educational and fascinating exhibits. The displays incorporate parts of old buildings; objects such as snow skis, dolls, and bicycles; fashions; Native American artifacts; nautical and surveying instruments; even a covered wagon. Museum docents, with roots stretching back to the days of the Oregon Trail, are often on hand to answer questions. There is also a research library that includes many journals from early pioneers. You can't miss this complex—stretching across the front is an eight story high trompe l'oeil mural.

Oregon Maritime Center and Museum. 113 SW Naito Pkwy. ☎ **503/224-7724.** Admission $4 adults $3 senior citizens, $2 students, free for children under age 8. Summer, Wed–Sun 11am–4pm; winter, Fri–Sun 11am–4pm. Bus: 12, 19, 20. MAX: Skidmore Fountain Station.

Inside the museum, you'll find models of ships that once plied the Columbia and Willamette. Also on display are early navigation instruments, artifacts from the battleship Oregon, old ship hardware, and other maritime memorabilia. The historic sternwheeler *Portland*, moored across Waterfront Park from the museum, is also open to the public. Inside this old vessel, you'll hear explanations and displays of maritime history.

World Forestry Center. 4033 SW Canyon Rd. ☎ **503/228-1367.** Admission $3 adults, $2 seniors and children 6–18, under age 6 free. Daily 9am–5pm (10am–5pm in winter). Closed Christmas Day. Bus: 63.

Although with each passing year Oregon depends less and less on the timber industry, the World Forestry Center is still busy educating visitors about the importance of our forest resources. Step inside the huge wooden main hall and you come face to bark with a very large and very lifelike tree. Press a button at its base and it will tell you the story of how trees live and grow. In other rooms you can see exhibits on

---

Sweet Dreams Are Made of These

In addition to all the other attractions we list, Portland has one sight that is uncategorizable—a chocolate waterfall! Located in a chocolate shop called **The Candy Basket,** 1924 NE 181st Ave. (☎ **800/864-1924** or 503/666-2000), this amazing cascade is 21 feet tall and uses 2,800 pounds of melted chocolate. You simply have to see it to believe it. This is Willy Wonka come to life! The store is 1 block south of I-84 at exit 13.

---

forests of the world, old-growth trees, a petrified wood exhibit, and a rain forest exhibit from the Smithsonian.

3 Architectural Attractions & Outdoor Art

✪ **Portlandia and the Portland Building.** 1120 SW Fifth Ave. Any downtown bus.

Portlandia is the symbol of the city, and this hammered bronze statue of her is the second-largest such statue in the country. The largest, of course, is New York City's Statue of Liberty. The massive kneeling figure holds a trident in one hand and with the other reaches toward the street. Strangely enough, this classically designed figure reminiscent of a Greek goddess perches above the entrance to Portland's most controversial building: the Portland Building, considered the first postmodern structure in the country. Today anyone familiar with the bizarre constructions of Los Angeles architect Frank Gehry would find it difficult to understand how such an innocuous and attractive building could have ever raised such a fuss, but it did.

Oregon Convention Center. 777 NE Martin Luther King Jr. Blvd. ☎ **503/235-7575.** Free admission for self-guided tours. Mon–Fri 8am–5pm. Bus: 63. MAX: Convention Center Station.

As you approach downtown Portland from the direction of the airport, it is impossible to miss this unusual architectural bauble on the city skyline. Christened "Twin Peaks" even before it opened in the summer of 1990, the center is worth a visit even if you don't happen to be in town for a convention. Its "twin peaks" are two tapering glass towers that channel light into the center of this huge complex. Outside the main entrance are two Asian temple bells, and an old-growth nurse log with a plaque explaining the display. Inside are paintings on a scale to match the building, a dragon boat hanging from the ceiling, and a brass pendulum swinging slowly through the hours. Small plaques on the outside wall of the main lobby spotlight telling quotes about life in Oregon.

4 Historical Buildings

The Old Church. 1422 SW 11th Ave. ☎ **503/222-2031.** Free admission. Mon–Fri 11am–3pm. Bus: 6. MAX: Library Station.

Built in 1883, this wooden Carpenter Gothic church is a Portland landmark. It incorporates a grand traditional design, but was constructed with spare ornamentation. An active church until 1967, the deteriorating building was to be torn down; however, preservationists stepped in to save it. Today it's a community facility, and every Wednesday it hosts a free lunchtime classical music concert.

Pittock Mansion. 3229 NW Pittock Dr. ☎ **503/823-3624.** Admission $4.25 adults; $3.75 seniors; $2 ages 6–18. Daily noon–4pm. Closed 3 days in late Nov, most major holidays, and the first 3 weeks of Jan. Bus: 20 to Burnside and Barnes. Half-mile walk.

At nearly the highest point in the West Hills, 1,000 feet above sea level, stands the most impressive mansion in Portland. Once slated to be torn down to make way for new housing, this grand château built by the founder of Portland's *Oregonian* newspaper has been fully restored and is open to the public. Built in 1914 in a French Renaissance style, the mansion featured many innovations, including a built-in vacuum system and amazing multiple showerheads in the baths. Today it is furnished with 18th- and 19th-century antiques, much as it might have been at the time the Pittocks occupied the building. Lunch and afternoon tea are available in the **Gate Lodge,** the former caretaker's cottage (☎ **503/823-3627**). Reservations are recommended.

5 Parks & Public Gardens

PARKS

With 4,800 acres of wilderness, **Forest Park** (☎ **503/823-4492**), bounded by West Burnside Street, Newberry Road, St. Helens Road, and Skyline Road, is the largest forested city park in the United States. There are 50 miles of trails and old fire roads for hiking, jogging, and mountain biking. More than 100 species of birds call these forests home, making this park a bird-watcher's paradise. Along the forest trails, you can see huge old trees and quiet picnic spots tucked away in the woods.

Adjacent to this park, you'll also find the **Portland Audubon Society,** 5151 NW Cornell Rd. (☎ **503/292-6855**), which has 4 miles of hiking trails on its forested property. In keeping with its mission to promote enjoyment, understanding, and protection of the natural world, these nature trails are open to the public. You can also visit the Nature Center or wildlife care center here.

Right in downtown, **Tom McCall Waterfront Park** serves as the city's festival locale and premier Willamette River access point. There are acres of lawns, shade trees, sculptures, and fountains. The paved path through the park is popular with in-line skaters and joggers. Also in this park are the Waterfront Story Garden, dedicated to storytellers, and the Japanese-American Historical Plaza, dedicated to Japanese Americans who were sent to internment camps during World War II.

South of downtown, you'll find **Tryon Creek State Park** on Terwilliger Road. This park is similar to Forest Park and is best known for its displays of trillium flowers in the spring. A bike path to downtown Portland starts here and there are also several miles of walking trails within the park.

The World's Smallest Park

Pay attention as you cross the median strip on Naito Parkway at the corner of Southwest Taylor Street or you might just walk right past **Mill Ends Park,** which is the smallest public park in the world. Covering a whopping 452.16 square inches of land, this park was the whimsical creation of local journalist Dick Fagen. After a telephone pole was removed from the middle of Naito Parkway (then known as Front Avenue), Fagen dubbed the phone pole hole Mill Ends Park (Mill Ends, a lumber mill term, was the name of Fagen's newspaper column). The columnist, whose office looked down on the hole in the middle of Front Avenue, peopled the imaginary park with leprechauns and would often write of the park's goings on in his column. On St. Patrick's Day 1976, it was officially designated a Portland city park. Rumor has it that despite the diminutive size of the park, it has been the site of several weddings (although the parks department has never issued a wedding permit for the park).

PUBLIC GARDENS

For Portland's two best-loved public gardens, the **International Rose Test Garden** and the **Japanese Garden,** see "The Top Attractions," earlier in this chapter.

The Berry Botanic Garden. 11505 SW Summerville Ave. ☎ **503/636-4112.** Adults $5. Open daylight hours by appointment. Bus: 35, 36.

Originally founded as a private garden, the Berry Botanic Garden now is working to save endangered plants of the Pacific Northwest. There are so many rhododendron shrubs here that they create a forest. A native plant trail, a fern garden, and rock gardens with unusual plants are all there to enjoy, but you must call ahead to make a reservation before arriving.

Crystal Springs Rhododendron Garden. SE 28th Ave. ☎ **503/777-1734** or 503/771-8386. Admission $2 from Mar 1 to Labor Day, Thurs–Mon 10am–6pm, free at other times. Open year-round daily dawn to dusk. Bus: 19.

Eight months out of the year this is a tranquil garden, with a waterfall and ducks to feed. But when the rhododendrons and azaleas bloom from March to June, it becomes a spectacular mass of blazing color. The Rhododendron Show and Plant Sale is held here on Mother's Day weekend.

The Grotto—National Sanctuary of Our Sorrowful Mother. NE 85th Ave. and Sandy Blvd. ☎ **503/254-7371.** Admission free; elevator $1.50. Open daily summer 9am–8pm, winter 9am–5:30pm. Closed Christmas and Thanksgiving. Bus: 12.

One of the main features at this forested 62-acre sanctuary is a shallow rock cave carved into the foot of a cliff which contains a marble replica of Michelangelo's *Pietà*. Although The Grotto is Catholic, it is open to visitors of all faiths. An elevator ride to the top of the bluff offers panoramic views of the Cascade Mountains, the Columbia River Valley, and Mt. St. Helens. This retreat is at its best in the summertime and during the Christmas season when the grounds are decorated with thousands of lights and a choral festival is held. There are also a couple of chapels on the grounds, a nice gift shop, and a coffee shop.

Hoyt Arboretum. 4033 SW Canyon Rd. ☎ **503/823-3654.** Admission free. Open daily 6am–10pm year-round. Bus: 63.

Only about 10 minutes from downtown Portland, this 175-acre arboretum has 850 species of trees from temperate regions around the world and 10 miles of hiking trails. At the south end of the arboretum is the Vietnam Veterans Living Memorial. To reach the Arboretum, take West Burnside Street 1.5 miles west of the Northwest shopping district and look for the sign; or take the Zoo exit from Hwy. 26.

Leach Botanical Garden. 6704 SE 122nd Ave. ☎ **503/761-9503.** Free admission. Tues–Sat 10am–4pm, Sun 1–4pm. Bus: 71.

In the 1920s and '30s, Lilla Leach was a noted Northwest botanist. She and her husband John Leach lovingly built this garden together, and in the late 1970s they donated it to the city of Portland. Diverse types of garden displays include a bog garden, rock gardens, Northwest woodland and a southeastern azalea garden. The Manor House is the visitor center, featuring beautiful woodwork.

6 Especially for Kids

The **Oregon Museum of Science and Industry** is geared primarily for kids, with lots of hands-on exhibits, including a NASA training room, a full computer lab, a chicken hatchery, and laser shows in its planetarium, which is free with museum admission.

At the **World Forestry Center,** there is a carousel operating during the summer months.

The **Metro Washington Park Zoo** is one of the best in the country, and is particularly well known for its elephant-breeding program. From inside the zoo, it's possible to take a small train through Washington Park to the International Rose Test Garden. In addition to these attractions, described earlier in this chapter, there are two other attractions in Portland of particular interest to kids:

Portland Children's Museum. 3037 SW Second Ave. ☎ **503/823-2227.** Admission $3.50 adults and children, under 1 year free. Daily 9am–5pm. Closed some national holidays. Bus: 1, 5, 12, 40, 43, or 45.

Although this museum is small, it's loads of fun. Visitors can shop in a kid-size grocery store, play waiter or diner in a restaurant, or pretend to be a doctor in a medical center. Clayshop is usually open for families who want to build with clay. In H2 Oh! kids can blow giant bubbles and pump water. The Children's Cultural Center presents a child's view of such environments as an African or Native American village complete with artifacts and hands-on activities. Listening to seashells, sculpting clay, blowing bubbles—there's plenty to entertain kids at this big little museum.

Oaks Park. East end of the Sellwood Bridge. ☎ **503/233-5777.** Free (all activities are on individual tickets). May–Oct Mon–Fri noon–5pm, Sat noon–10pm, Sun noon–9pm; longer hours during the summer. Bus: 40.

What would summer be without the screams of happy thrill-seekers risking their lives on a roller coaster? Pretty boring, right? Just ask the kids. They'll tell you that the real Portland excitement is at Oaks Park. Covering more than 44 acres, this amusement park first opened in 1905 to coincide with the Lewis and Clark Exposition. Beneath the shady oaks for which the park is named, you'll find waterfront picnic sites, miniature golf, music, and plenty of thrilling rides. The largest roller-skating rink in the Northwest is also here. The Samtrak Excursion train runs along the Willamette River from Oaks Park to OMSI (Oregon Museum of Science and Industry) May through October; call ☎ **503/659-5452** for schedule.

7 Organized Tours

WALKING TOURS

If you'd like to learn more about downtown Portland, contact **Apple Tours** (☎ **800/ 939-6326** or 503/638-4076) for a foot tour of the area. You'll learn about Portland's architecture and art, its history and the colorful characters who peopled it. Tours cost $15 for adults, $13 for seniors, and $5 for children.

Peter's Downtown Tour (☎ **503/665-2558** or 503/816-1060) is another good way to learn more about Portland. This walking tour of downtown takes about 2 hours, covers 2 miles, and is led by university instructor Peter Chausse. The tour includes visits to the fountains, parks, historic places, art, and architecture that make Portland the energetic city that it is. Tours are in the afternoon (call for reservations) and cost $10 for adults and $5 for children.

Two to three times a season, Sharon Wood, author of *The Portland Bridge Book,* offers a **Bridge Tour and Urban Adventure** that explores several Portland bridges. These tours are offered through **Portland Parks and Outdoor Recreation** (☎ **503/ 823-5132**). Tickets are $16 for adults and $10 for children 14 and under.

BUS TOURS

If you want to get a general overview of Portland, **Gray Line** (☎ **800/422-7042** or 503/285-9845) offers several half-day and full-day tours. One tour visits the

International Rose Test Garden and the grounds of Pittock Mansion, another stops at the Japanese Gardens and the World Forestry Center. The trip I most recommend is the full-day Mt. Hood loop—if you aren't doing the driving, you can enjoy the scenery more. Other tours offered are an excursion to the Columbia Gorge that includes a ride on a sternwheeler, and a northern Oregon coast tour. Tour prices range from $22 to $42 for adults, and from $11 to $21 for children.

BOAT TOURS

If you're interested in seeing Portland from the water, you've got lots of options. Traditionalists will want to book a tour with **Cascade Stern-Wheelers** (☎ 503/223-3928), which offers stern-wheeler cruises on the Columbia River in the Columbia Gorge (summer only) and the Willamette River through downtown Portland (year-round). A trip up the Columbia River, with its towering cliffs, is a spectacular and memorable excursion. Two-hour cruises are $12.95 for adults and $7.95 for children. Call for information on brunch, dinner, and dance cruises.

Alternatively, you can do a cruise on the **Rose Stern-Wheeler** (☎ 503/286-7673), a small stern-wheeler offering Portland harbor tours. Prices range from $10 to $35 for adults.

If a modern yacht is more your speed, try the **Portland Spirit** (☎ 800/224-3901 or 503/224-3900). This 75-foot custom built yacht seats more than 300 people on two decks, and offers views of downtown Portland on lunch, brunch, and dinner cruises featuring Northwest cuisine. Saturday night it becomes a floating nightclub with live bands or a DJ. Call for reservations and schedule. Prices range from $10 to $46 for adults and $14 to $18 for children.

Rose City Riverboat Cruises (☎ 503/234-6665) offers another alternative—a modern catamaran power yacht that cruises the Willamette River between mid-April and October. Dinner, moonlight, Sunday brunch, Portland harbor, and historical river tours are offered. Prices range from $9 to $30, with lower fares for children and seniors.

For high-speed tours up the Willamette River, there are the **Willamette Falls Jetboats** (☎ 503/231-1532 or 888/JETBOAT). The high-powered open-air boats blast their way from downtown Portland to the impressive Willamette Falls at Oregon City. The 2-hour tours, which start at OMSI, are $22 for adults and $14 for children.

SCENIC FLIGHTS

If you want to see some of the region from the air, contact **Hillsboro Aviation** (☎ 503/648-2831), which operates out of the Hillsboro Airport 15 miles west of Portland, and offers airplane and helicopter tours of the Columbia Gorge, the Oregon Coast, and Mount St. Helens. They even offer helicopter dinner flights to two Portland restaurants. Scenic tours run $25 to $60 and specialty tours run $150 to $320.

A TROLLEY EXCURSION

While Portland is busily trying to revive trolleys as a viable mass transit option, the **Willamette Shore Trolley** (☎ 503/222-2226) is offering scenic excursions along the Willamette River. The trolley runs 7 miles along the scenic west side of the river between Portland and the prestigious suburb of Lake Oswego, using historic trolley cars from the early part of this century. The trip takes about 45 minutes each way. In Lake Oswego, the trolley station is on State Street, between "A" Avenue and Foothills Road. In downtown Portland, the station is just south of the RiverPlace Athletic Club on Harbor Way (off Naito Parkway at the south end of Tom McCall Waterfront Park). The round-trip fare is $5 for adults and $3 for children age 3 to 12. Call for a schedule.

WINERY & BREWERY TOURS

If you're interested in learning more about Oregon wines and want to tour the nearby wine country, contact **Grape Escape** (☎ 503/282-4262), which offers an in-depth winery tour of the Willamette Valley. An all-day tour includes stops at several wineries, an elegant picnic lunch, and pick-up and drop-off at your hotel. Tours are $65.

If craft beers and ales are more to your tastes, consider the **Portland Brew Bus** (☎ 888/BIG-BREW). The Brew Bus, a Gray Line motorcoach, takes you on a 4-hour tour of three breweries and brewpubs, where you'll get 2- to 3-ounce samples of about 20 brews—and, you don't have to be concerned about driving yourself around. This isn't a pub crawl, but a way to learn a lot about the process of craft brewing. Tours are $39.95.

OTHER TOURS

The **John Palmer House** (☎ 503/284-5893), a restored Victorian bed-and-breakfast, offers tours of the city by horse-drawn carriage on Friday, Saturday, and Sunday throughout the year. They will pick up passengers at any major hotel, the waterfront, or Pioneer Courthouse Square. The tour can even be pleasant in a drizzle, as the carriage has a bonnet that can be drawn up to protect passengers from the rain. Tours cost $75 for a carriage that can carry four people.

Ecotours of Oregon (☎ 503/245-1428) offers a variety of tours and hikes. They travel to the Columbia River Gorge, Mount Hood, Mount St. Helens, the Oregon coast, ancient forests, and places to whale-watch or experience Native American culture. Visits to wineries, microbreweries, and custom tours can all be arranged. Tour prices range from $38 to $60.

8 Outdoor Activities

If you're planning ahead for a visit to Portland, contact **Metro Regional Parks and Greenspaces,** 600 NE Grand Ave., Portland, OR 97232-2736 (☎ 503/797-1850; Web site www.multnomah.lib.or.us/metro) for its *Metro Green Scene* publication that lists tours, hikes, classes, and other outdoor activities and events being held in the Portland metro area.

BEACHES

The nearest ocean beach to Portland is **Cannon Beach,** about 90 miles to the west. See "The Oregon Coast" in chapter 20 for more information.

There are a couple of freshwater beaches on the Columbia River within 45 minutes of Portland. **Rooster Rock State Park,** just off I-84 east of Portland, includes several miles of sandy beach as does **Sauvie Island,** off Oregon Hwy. 30 northwest of Portland. You'll need to obtain a parking permit for Sauvie Island; it's available at the convenience store located just after you cross the bridge onto the island. Both beaches include clothing optional sections.

BICYCLING

You'll notice many bicyclists on Portland streets. If you want to get rolling with everyone else, head over to **Fat Tire Farm,** 2714 NW Thurman St. (☎ 503/222-3276), to rent a mountain bike for $30 a day. In nearby Forest Park, the **Leif Erikson Trail** is a car-less stretch of dirt road that goes on for miles and is popular with bicyclists and runners. Or rent a bike downtown at **Bike Central,** 835 SW Second Ave. and Taylor Street (☎ 503/227-4439), where rental fees are about $20-$30 per day, or, at **The Bike Gallery,** 821 SW 11th Ave. (☎ 503/222-3821), where a bike rents for $40 per day. Once you have your bike, you can head for **Waterfront**

Park, where there's a 2-mile bike path. The **Terwilliger Path** starts at the south end of Portland State University and travels for 10 miles up into the hills to Tryon Creek State Park. The views from the top are breathtaking. Stop by a bike shop to pick up a bicycling map for the Portland metro area.

BOARDSAILING

Serious enthusiasts already know about the boardsailing mecca at the town of **Hood River** on the Columbia River. The winds come howling down the gorge with enough force to send sailboards airborne. Several shops in Hood River rent boardsailing equipment. Right in Portland, you can rent boards at **Gorge Performance Windsurfing,** 7400 SW Macadam Blvd. (☎ **503/246-6646**), which happens to be conveniently close to **Willamette Park,** which is on the Willamette River and is the city's best boardsailing spot. You'll find this park at the corner of Southwest Macadam Boulevard and Southwest Nebraska Street. Another good spot for experienced sailors is on **Sauvie Island,** where you'll find many miles of sandy beaches. The easiest spot around for beginners is across the Columbia River in Vancouver, Washington, at **Vancouver Lake State Park.**

FISHING

The Portland area is salmon, steelhead, sturgeon, and trout country. You can find out about licenses and seasons from the **Oregon Department of Fish and Wildlife,** P.O. Box 59, Portland, OR 97207 (☎ **503/229-5403**). If you prefer to have a guide take you where the big ones are biting, contact the **Oregon Outdoor Association,** P.O. Box 9486, Bend, OR 97708 (☎ **541/683-9552**), for a copy of its directory. A day of fishing will cost you between $100 and $170 per person. **Page's Northwest Guide Service** (☎ **503/760-3373**) will take you out fishing for salmon, steelhead, walleye, and sturgeon on the Columbia or Willamette rivers, Portland area streams, or Tillamook Bay (all gear is included). **Reel Adventures** (☎ **503/622-5372** or 503/ 789-6860), located in Sandy, Oregon, offers a similar fishing guide service.

GOLF

If you're a golfer, don't forget to bring your clubs along on a trip to Portland. There are plenty of public courses around the area, and greens fees at municipal courses are as low as $18 for 18 holes on a weekday and $20 on weekends and holidays. Municipal golf courses operated by the Portland Bureau of Parks and Recreation include **Eastmoreland Golf Course,** 2425 SE Bybee Blvd. (☎ **503/775-2900**); **Heron Lakes Golf Course,** 3500 N. Victory Blvd. (☎ **503/289-1818**); and **Rose City Golf Course,** 2200 NE 71st Ave. (☎ **503/253-4744**). However, if you want to play where the pros play, head west from Portland 20 miles to **Pumpkin Ridge Golf Club,** 12930 NW Old Pumpkin Ridge Rd. (☎ **503/647-4747**), which has hosted the U.S. Women's Open and Tiger Wood's last amateur tournament. Green fees are $75 Monday through Thursday and $90 Friday through Sunday.

HIKING

Hiking opportunities in the Portland area are almost unlimited. For shorter hikes, you need not leave the city. Bordered by West Burnside Street on the south, Newberry Road on the north, St. Helens Road on the east, and Skyline Road on the west, **Forest Park** is the largest forested city park in the country. You'll find more than 50 miles of trails through this urban wilderness.

However, if you head over to Mount Hood National Forest (less than an hour away), you can get on the **Pacific Crest Trail** and hike all the way to Mexico. Of course, there are also plenty of other shorter hikes in this region. For information on hiking trails on Mount Hood, contact the **Mount Hood Information Center** (☎ **503/622-7674**) or the **U.S. Forest Service,** 70220 E. Hwy. 26, Zig Zag, OR 97049 (☎ **503/666-0704** or 503/622-3191).

If you're interested in a more strenuous mountain experience, Mount Hood offers plenty of mountain- and rock-climbing opportunities. **Timberline Mountain Guides,** P.O. Box 340, Gov't Camp, OR 97028 (☎ **800/464-7704;** fax 503/272-3677), leads summit climbs on Mount Hood. They also offer snow, ice, and rock climbing courses. A 2-day Mount Hood mountaineering course with summit climb costs $245.

You can buy or rent camping and climbing equipment from **REI Co-op,** 1798 Jantzen Beach Center (☎ **503/283-1300**), or 7410 SW Bridgeport Rd., Tualatin (☎ **503/624-8600**). This huge outdoor recreation supply store also sells books on hiking in the area.

If you have been keeping up with the controversy over saving the remaining old-growth forests of the Northwest, you might want to go see an ancient forest for yourself. Though there isn't much publicly accessible ancient forest right in Portland, you can find plenty within 1 1/2 hours' drive. Along the coast, Ecola State Park, Oswald West State Park, Cape Meares State Park, and Cape Lookout State Park all have trails through stands of old-growth trees. If you are heading to Mount Hood, you can detour to Oxbow Park in Sandy to see a small grove of old-growth trees.

IN-LINE SKATING

Waterfront Park is a popular and fairly level place for skating. In-line skates can be rented at the nearby **Sports Works,** 421 SW Second Ave. (☎ **503/227-5323**), for $20 a day, which includes all safety gear.

PARKS

See "Parks & Public Gardens," earlier in this chapter.

SKIING

Portland has several ski resorts, all within about an hour's drive, on the slopes of Mount Hood. One of them even boasts skiing all summer. If you'd like to go to the mountain, but you don't want the hassle of driving yourself, consider **Bus/Lift** (☎ **503/287-5438**), which departs from downtown Portland and goes to Mount Hood Meadows and back for about $49. Purchase tickets at G.I. Joe Ticketmaster outlets (☎ **503/790-2787**).

Timberline Ski Area (☎ **503/231-7979** in Portland, or 503/272-3311 outside Portland; 503/222-2211 for snow report) is the highest ski area on Mount Hood and has one slope that is open all the way through summer. This is the site of the historic Timberline Lodge, which was built during the Depression by the WPA. Adult lift ticket prices range from $11 for night skiing to $32 for a weekend all-day pass. Call for hours of operation.

Mount Hood Meadows (☎ **503/337-2222;** 503/227-7669 for snow report) is the largest ski resort on Mount Hood, with more than 2,000 skiable acres, 2,777 vertical feet, and a wide variety of terrain. Lift ticket prices range from $17 for night skiing to $35 for a weekend all-day pass. Call for hours of operation.

Mt. Hood SkiBowl (☎ **503/272-3206;** 503/222-2695 for snow report) is the closest ski area to Portland and with 1,500 vertical feet, has more expert slopes than any other ski area on the mountain. SkiBowl also claims to be the largest lighted ski area in the United States. Adult lift ticket prices range from $14 for midweek night skiing to $25 for a weekend all-day pass. Call for hours of operation.

TENNIS

Portland Parks and Recreation operates more than 120 tennis courts, both indoor and out, all over the city. Outdoor courts are generally free and available on a first-come, first-served basis. My personal favorites are those in Washington Park just behind the International Rose Test Garden. Some of these courts can be reserved by contacting the **Portland Tennis Center,** 324 NE 12th Ave. (☎ **503/823-3189**). If the weather isn't cooperating, head for the Portland Tennis Center itself. They have indoor courts and charge $6 to $6.75 per hour per person for singles matches and $3.75 to $4.25 per hour per person for doubles. The hours here are 6:30am to 10pm during the week, closing later on the weekend.

WHITE-WATER RAFTING

The Cascade Range produces some of the best white-water rafting in the country and Deschutes River, White Salmon River, and Clackamas River offer plenty of opportunities to shoot the rapids from early spring to early fall. **River Drifters,** 13570 NW Lakeview Dr., Portland, OR 97229 (☎ **800/972-0430** or 503/645-6264), leads trips on these rivers for $65 (with lunch included). **Phil's White Water Adventure,** 38 Northwestern Lake, White Salmon, WA 98672 (☎ **800/366-2004** or 509/493-2641), offers trips on the White Salmon and Klickitat Rivers for $45 to $90.

9 Spectator Sports

In addition to the phone numbers listed below, **Ticketmaster** (☎ **503/224-4400**) is an alternative source of tickets for the Trail Blazers, the Portland Winter Hawks, Portland Power, and the Portland Rockies Baseball Club, and certain other sporting events.

The **Rose Garden** arena (☎ **503/797-9617** for tickets; 503/321-3211 event information hotline) is home to the Trail Blazers and the Portland Winter Hawks, and also hosts a variety of other athletic events and concerts. This relatively new arena is the main focal point of what has become known as the **Rose Quarter.** This sports and entertainment oriented neighborhood is still more an idea than a reality, but it does include the Rose Garden, Memorial Coliseum, and several restaurants and bars. To reach the Rose Garden or Memorial Coliseum, take the Rose Quarter exit off I-5. Parking is expensive, so you might want to consider taking the MAX light-rail line from downtown Portland.

AUTO RACING

Portland International Raceway, 1940 N. Victory Blvd. (☎ **503/285-6635**), operated by the Portland Bureau of Parks and Recreation, is home to road races, drag races, motocross and other motorcycle races, go-kart races, and even vintage-car races. February to October are the busiest months here. Admission is $6 to $75.

BASEBALL

The **Portland Rockies Baseball Club** (☎ 503/223-2837) plays class-A minor-league ball at Civic Stadium, SW 20th Avenue and Morrison Street. The box office is open Monday through Friday from 9am to 5pm and from 9am the day of the game. Tickets are $2.50 to $6.50 for adults, $1 to $4.50 for ages 14 and under.

BASKETBALL

The NBA's **Portland Trail Blazers** (☎ 503/231-8000) pound the boards at the Rose Garden. Call for current schedule and ticket information. Tickets are $15 to $73. Depending on the teams record, tickets can be hard to come by.

Portland Power (☎ 503/236-HOOP), of the newly formed American Basketball League, plays professional women's basketball at Memorial Coliseum. Tickets are $11 to $43.

GREYHOUND RACING

The race season at the **Multnomah Greyhound Track,** NE 223rd Avenue, Wood Village (☎ 503/667-7700), runs from May to September. Post time is 7pm Wednesday through Saturday, with Sunday matinees at 1pm. You must be 18 to bet on the greyhounds, and if you've never bet on dog races before, they'll gladly give you a quick course. To reach the track, take I-84 east to the 181st Street exit south and then turn left on Glisan Street. It's also easy to reach the park by public transit. Take the MAX light-rail system to the Gresham City Hall or Central Station and transfer to bus no. 81, which goes directly to the racetrack. Admission is $1.25 to $3.50.

HORSE RACING

Portland Meadows, 1001 N. Schmeer Rd. (☎ 503/285-9144), is the place to go if you want a little horse-racing action. The race season runs from October to April, with post time at 6:30pm on Friday and 12:30pm on Saturday and Sunday. By car, take I-5 north to the Delta Park exit. Admission is $2 to $3.

ICE HOCKEY

The **Portland Winter Hawks** (☎ 503/238-6366), a junior-league hockey team, carve up the ice at Memorial Coliseum and the Rose Garden from October to March. Call for schedule and ticket information. Tickets are $10 to $14.

MARATHON

The Oregon Road Runners Club **Portland Marathon** is held sometime in late September to early October. The 26.2-mile run is supplemented by shorter runs such as the mayor's walk and the kid's run. For further information, call ☎ 503/226-1111.

10 Day Spas

If you'd rather opt for a massage than a hike in the woods, consider spending a few hours at a day spa. These facilities typically offer massages, facials, seaweed wraps, and the like. Portland day spas include **Aveda Lifestyle Store and Spa,** 5th Avenue Suites Hotel, 500 Washington St. (☎ 503/248-0615); **Boutique Alternáre,** 1444 NE Broadway (☎ 503/282-8200); and **A New Dawn Salon and Spa,** 5512 SW Kelly St. (☎ 503/244-3437). Expect to pay $45 to $65 for a 1-hour massage and $155 to $285 for a full day of pampering.

Strolling Around Portland

Portland's compactness makes it an ideal city to explore on foot. In fact, the local government is doing all it can to convince Portland's citizens to leave their cars behind when they come downtown. There's no better way to gain a feel for this city than to stroll through the Skidmore Historic District, down along Tom McCall Waterfront Park and through Pioneer Courthouse Square. If it happens to be a weekend, you'll also be able to visit the Portland Saturday Market.

You're never far from an outdoor sculpture or fountain in downtown Portland, and these public works of art are as much a part of the local art scene as anything in a gallery or museum. My second walking tour outlines a route that will take you past some of the best outdoor art the city has to offer. Keep your eyes peeled for other works of art not mentioned in this walking tour.

For additional information on several stops in these two strolls, see chapter 16.

WALKING TOUR 1
Old Town & Downtown

Start: Skidmore Fountain.
Finish: Skidmore Fountain.
Time: Allow approximately 3 to 4 hours, including museum visits, breaks, and shopping stops.
Best Times: Saturday and Sunday between March and December, when the Portland Saturday Market is open.
Worst Times: After dark, when the Skidmore neighborhood is not as safe as in daylight.

Although Portland was founded in 1843, most of the buildings in Old Town date only from the 1880s. A fire in 1872 razed much of the town, which afterward was rebuilt with new vigor. Ornate pilasters, pediments, and cornices grace these brick buildings, one of the largest collections of such structures in the country. However, their most notable features are their cast-iron facades.

Begin your exploration of this 20-block historic neighborhood at the corner of SW First Avenue and Ankeny Street at:

1. **Skidmore Fountain,** the heart of Old Town. Erected in 1888, the fountain was intended to provide refreshment for "horses, men,

and dogs," and it did that for many years. Today, however, the bronze and granite fountain is purely decorative. Across SW First Avenue is the:

2. **New Market Block,** constructed in 1872 to house the unlikely combination of a produce market and a theater. The New Market Block is now home to the American Advertising Museum (see "Other Museums" in chapter 16) and also contains some unusual shops and budget restaurants, as do many of the restored historic buildings in this area. The freestanding wall of archways extending out from the New Market Building was salvaged from an Old Town structure that didn't survive the urban renewal craze of the 1960s. Two blocks south is the:

3. **Failing Building,** 235 SW First Ave. Built in 1886, this attractive structure integrates French and Italian influences. (This building houses McCormick and Schmick's seafood restaurant, a good place for lunch if the Saturday Market is closed.) Turn left on SW Oak Street and you'll pass by the:

4. **Dielschneider Building,** 71 SW Oak St., originally a foundry. Built in 1859, it's the third oldest commercial building in Portland. The casting initials of one of the first tenants, O/W (Oregon Ironworks), can be seen on the building's threshold plates. Take a left on SW Naito Parkway (Front Avenue) where you'll find:

5. **Smith's Block,** 111–117 SW Naito Parkway, containing some of the most beautifully restored buildings in Old Town. At one time this whole district was filled with elegant structures such as these. The cast-iron filigree appears both solid and airy at the same time. Here you'll find the:

6. **Oregon Maritime Center and Museum,** 113 SW Naito Pkwy. (☎ **503/ 224-7724**), which is dedicated to Oregon's shipping history. (See "Other Museums" in chapter 16 for details.)

Continue along SW Naito Parkway to SW Ankeny, where you will see the:

7. **Jeff Morris Memorial Fire Museum,** housing Portland's historic horse-drawn steamers from the early part of this century.

If it's a Saturday or Sunday from March through December, you will no doubt have noticed the crowds under the Burnside bridge ahead of you. This is the:

8. **Portland Saturday Market,** where you'll find the best of Northwest crafts being sold by their makers. There typically are more than 250 booths plus entertainers and food vendors.

☕ **TAKE A BREAK**   Portland Saturday Market makes an excellent refueling stop in this neighborhood. In the market's food court you can get all manner of delicious, healthful, and fun foods. Stalls sell everything from "dragon toast" to overstuffed fajitas to pad Thai to barbecued ribs.

After you've visited the market, walk north on the east side of NW First Avenue to the corner of NW Couch (pronounced *Kooch*) Street, where you'll find the:

9. **Blagen Block,** another excellent example of the ornate cast-iron facades that appeared on nearly all the buildings in this area at one time. Note the cast-iron figures of women wearing spiked crowns. They are reminiscent of the Statue of Liberty, which was erected 2 years before this building opened in 1888. Across First Avenue, you will see the covered sidewalk of the:

10. **Norton House.** Though this is not the original covered sidewalk, it is characteristic of Portland buildings 100 years ago. The building has for many years housed a popular rock club. Walk west to Second Avenue, where at the southwest corner you'll see:

Walking Tour 1—Old Town & Downtown

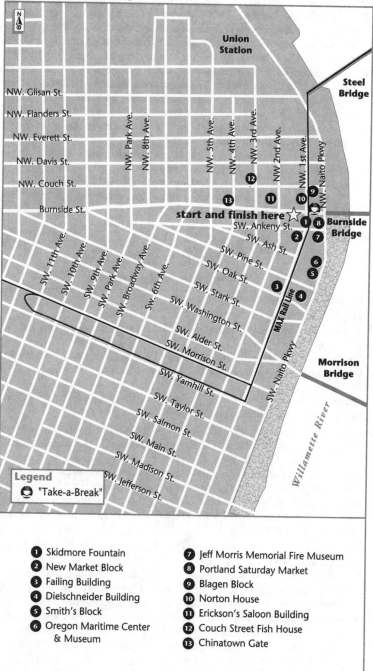

NW. Glisan St.

NW. Flanders St.

NW. Everett St.

NW. Davis St.

NW. Couch St.

Burnside St.

Union Station

Steel Bridge

start and finish here ☆

SW. Ankeny St.

SW. Ash St.

SW. Pine St.

SW. Oak St.

SW. Stark St.

SW. Washington St.

SW. Alder St.

SW. Morrison St.

SW. Yamhill St.

SW. Taylor St.

SW. Salmon St.

SW. Main St.

SW. Madison St.

SW. Jefferson St.

NW. Park Ave.

NW. 8th Ave.

NW. 5th Ave.

NW. 4th Ave.

NW. 3rd Ave.

NW. 2nd Ave.

NW. 1st Ave.

NW. Naito Pkwy

SW. 11th Ave.

SW. 10th Ave.

SW. 9th Ave.

SW. Park Ave.

SW. Broadway Ave.

SW. 6th Ave.

MAX Rail Line

SW. Naito Pkwy

Burnside Bridge

Morrison Bridge

Willamette River

Legend

🍵 "Take-a-Break"

❶ Skidmore Fountain
❷ New Market Block
❸ Failing Building
❹ Dielschneider Building
❺ Smith's Block
❻ Oregon Maritime Center & Museum

❼ Jeff Morris Memorial Fire Museum
❽ Portland Saturday Market
❾ Blagen Block
❿ Norton House
⓫ Erickson's Saloon Building
⓬ Couch Street Fish House
⓭ Chinatown Gate

1-0891

231

11. **Erickson's Saloon Building,** 9 NW Second Ave. Back in the late 1800s this building housed the very popular Erickson's Saloon, with a 684-foot-long bar, card rooms, and a brothel. If you return to NW Couch Street and continue to the corner of NW Third Avenue, you will see on the northwest corner:

12. **Couch Street Fish House,** an excellent example of the innovative methods that have been used to renovate Old Town. This restaurant incorporates two historic structures into its design. One houses the restaurant itself, the inside of which is very modern. The other is merely an ornate brick facade behind which you'll find the restaurant's parking lot. Continue up NW Couch Street to Fourth Avenue and turn left. Directly ahead of you is:

13. **Chinatown Gate.** Since you are already in Chinatown, you will have to cross to the opposite side of the brightly painted three-tiered gateway to appreciate its ornateness, including two huge flanking bronze Chinese lions.

   From here, cross W. Burnside Street, turn left on Ankeny, and walk 3 blocks back to the Skidmore Fountain to end the tour.

WALKING TOUR 2
Fountains & Public Art

Start: Pioneer Courthouse Square.
Finish: Pioneer Courthouse Square.
Time: Allow approximately 2 hours, not including museum visits, breaks, and shopping stops.
Best Times: Saturday and Sunday between March and December, when the Portland Saturday Market is open. The best starting time is noon, when you can see the *Weather Machine* in action.
Worst Times: After dark, when the Skidmore neighborhood is not as safe as in daylight and the artworks aren't as easy to see.

Portland is proud of its public art, and by law, 1% of the cost of every new building must be spent on public art. The **Regional Arts and Culture Council,** 309 SW Sixth Ave., Suite 100 (☎ **503/823-5111**), has put together a booklet outlining several walking tours in the Portland downtown area in which you can discover many of these art and architectural works. You can get a free copy by stopping by their office, the main lobby of the Portland Building (which has the *Portlandia* statue in front of it) between SW Main Street and SW Madison Street, or the Portland Art Museum, 1219 SW Park Ave.

   Start your art and fountain tour at the stroke of noon, if at all possible, by grabbing a latte and parking yourself on a terrace at:

1. **Pioneer Courthouse Square,** which is bordered by Yamhill, Morrison, Sixth Avenue, and Broadway. Known as Portland's living room, this brick plaza has several sculptures, a waterfall fountain (currently under restoration), a Starbucks, and Powell's Travel Store. The reason to get here at noon is to witness the day's weather forecast by the fabulous *Weather Machine,* a sculpture that displays one of three creatures that represent the current weather—a sun (sunny), a dragon (stormy), or a blue heron (drizzle). A weathervane, thermometer, and puffs of smoke are all part of this unusual weather-oriented sculpture. Other works of art on the square include *Allow Me* (a bronze sculpture of a man carrying an umbrella), and *Running Horses.*
   From the square, walk east on SW Yamhill Street, past Pioneer Courthouse. Along the sidewalk here, you'll see:

Walking Tour 2—Fountains & Public Art

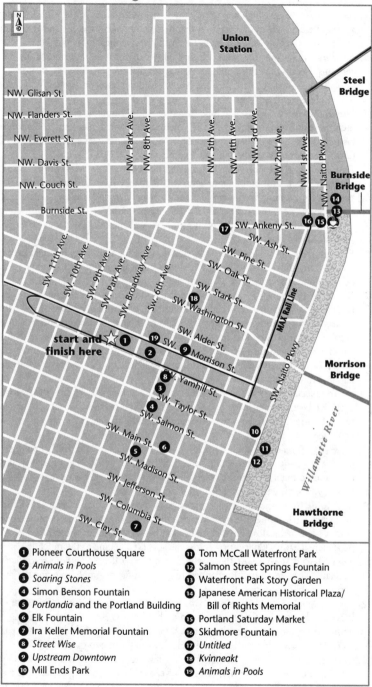

N

Union Station

Steel Bridge

NW. Glisan St.
NW. Flanders St.
NW. Everett St.
NW. Davis St.
NW. Couch St.

Burnside Bridge

Burnside St.

SW. Ankeny St.
SW. Ash St.
SW. Pine St.
SW. Oak St.
SW. Stark St.
SW. Washington St.
SW. Alder St.
SW. Morrison St.
SW. Yamhill St.
SW. Taylor St.
SW. Salmon St.
SW. Main St.
SW. Madison St.
SW. Jefferson St.
SW. Columbia St.
SW. Clay St.

NW. Park Ave.
NW. 8th Ave.
NW. 5th Ave.
NW. 4th Ave.
NW. 3rd Ave.
NW. 2nd Ave.
NW. 1st Ave.
NW. Naito Pkwy

SW. 11th Ave.
SW. 10th Ave.
SW. 9th Ave.
SW. Park Ave.
SW. Broadway Ave.
SW. 6th Ave.

MAX Rail Line

SW. Naito Pkwy

start and finish here

Morrison Bridge

Willamette River

Hawthorne Bridge

1 Pioneer Courthouse Square
2 *Animals in Pools*
3 *Soaring Stones*
4 Simon Benson Fountain
5 *Portlandia* and the Portland Building
6 Elk Fountain
7 Ira Keller Memorial Fountain
8 *Street Wise*
9 *Upstream Downtown*
10 Mill Ends Park
11 Tom McCall Waterfront Park
12 Salmon Street Springs Fountain
13 Waterfront Park Story Garden
14 Japanese American Historical Plaza/ Bill of Rights Memorial
15 Portland Saturday Market
16 Skidmore Fountain
17 *Untitled*
18 *Kvinneakt*
19 *Animals in Pools*

1-0891

233

2. *Animals in Pools,* which are among the best loved statues in the city. Included among these bronze statues are a mother bear with two cubs, a doe and fawn, and two curious river otters. Turn right on SW Fifth Avenue, and you'll see

3. *Soaring Stones,* an unusual sculpture consisting of granite boulders on steel columns. Because the five boulders are staggered above the sidewalk, they appear to be flying. Continue up SW Fifth Avenue to the intersection with SW Salmon Street. Here you'll find one of the:

4. Simon Benson Fountains. These drinking water fountains and many just like them were donated to the city in 1917 by local timber magnate Simon Benson so his mill workers would have something to drink besides beer and whiskey. Continue another block south, and you'll come to:

5. *Portlandia* and the Portland Building, located between SW Main Street and SW Madison Street. This building, designed by Michael Graves, is considered the first postmodern building in the world. Out front is Raymond Kaskey's hammered-copper statue *Portlandia,* the second-tallest beaten-copper statue in the world (second only to the Statue of Liberty). From here, walk east on SW Main Street one and half blocks to the:

6. Elk Fountain. This life-size bronze elk and water fountain were installed here in this park in 1900 and once served as a watering stop for horses. Continue south on SW Fourth Avenue for 4 blocks to the:

7. Ira Keller Memorial Fountain, which is the most amazing fountain in the city. Consisting of a complex waterfall, this fountain, surrounded by a tree-filled park, is meant to conjure up images of waterfalls in the nearby Cascade Range. After lounging around the falls, head back 7 blocks on SW Fourth Avenue to SW Yamhill Street, and turn left to find:

8. *Street Wise,* an installation of granite paving blocks that are engraved with sayings and quotations.

   "You blocks, you stones, you worse than senseless things." (William Shakespeare) and "I've been on a calendar but never on time." (Marilyn Monroe) are just two of our favorites. Looking up from the sidewalk and across the adjacent parking lot, you'll see:

9. *Upstream Downtown,* an installation of large and very colorful fish schooling on the side of a parking garage. From here, head back east to SW Naito Parkway, turn right and go one block to the corner of SW Taylor Street, and here cross Naito Parkway, stopping in the middle of the street to visit:

10. Mill Ends Park, the smallest public park in the world. Once merely a hole left over when a telephone pole was removed, this little circle of flowers became a park after a popular local newspaper columnist began writing of the exploits of the park's leprechauns. Continuing across the street, you come to the much larger:

11. Tom McCall Waterfront Park, where many of Portland's outdoor festivals are held and where you'll find Portlanders biking, skating, or simply enjoying the outdoors. One block south is the:

12. Salmon Street Springs fountain, which amounts to a public sprinkler system for kids (and the occasional adult) to play in on hot summer days. These ever-changing fountains are also fun to just sit and watch. From here walk north through the park on the paved riverside path and in 10 blocks, you'll come to the:

13. Waterfront Park Story Garden. This fascinating installation is a cross between a maze and a board game and consists of carved granite paving stones scattered along a pathway maze of old cobblestones. Carved on the paving stones are images of everything from 1950s board game characters to Northwest Coast Indian images. Other stones ask questions (What is your joy? What is your

failure? What is your secret?). You could easily spend half an hour or more just wandering through this "maze." A few steps away is the:

14. **Japanese American Historical Plaza/Bill of Rights Memorial.** Standing boulders inscribed with poetry are scattered throughout the plaza. In spring, the cherry trees are covered with blossoms. From here, cross NW Naito Parkway, turn left on NW First Avenue, and under the Burnside Bridge, you'll find the:

15. **Portland Saturday Market.** This market is filled with artists from all over the region and has a fascinating assortment of one-of-a-kind art and interesting crafts. This is perhaps Portland's greatest public art treasure.

☕ **TAKE A BREAK** If it is Saturday or Sunday and the market is set up, this is a great place to grab some good, cheap eats. There are all kinds of unusual meals available at market stalls. Other days of the week, you'll find budget eateries in the New Market Block building across SW First Avenue from the market.

Across the market is the:

16. **Skidmore Fountain,** which was erected in 1888 and intended to provide refreshment for "horses, men, and dogs," and it did just that for many years. Today, however, the bronze and granite fountain is purely decorative. From here, walk up SW Ash Street 4 blocks to:

17. *Untitled,* a large sculpture fountain vaguely reminiscent of a giant brass musical instrument. From here, turn left and head south four blocks on SW Fifth Avenue to the corner of SW Washington Street. Here you'll find:

18. *Kvinneakt,* the most notorious piece of public art in Portland. This bronze sculpture of a nude woman was made famous in a poster titled "Expose Yourself to Art," which featured a man in a trench coat flashing the statue. The man in the photo was Bud Clark, local tavern owner and Portland's most colorful former mayor. Continue another 2 blocks on Fifth Avenue, turn right on SW Morrison Street, and you will see the rest of the bronze animals of the:

19. *Animals in Pools* sculpture. On this side of the Pioneer Courthouse you'll see a pair of beavers and a family of seals. Pioneer Courthouse Square, the end point of this stroll, is just across SW Sixth Avenue.

18 Portland Shopping

Perhaps the single most important fact about shopping in Portland, and all of Oregon for that matter, is that there is no sales tax. The price on the tag is the price you pay. If you come from a state with a high sales tax, you might want to save your shopping for your visit to Portland.

1 The Shopping Scene

Over the past few years Portland has managed to preserve and restore a good deal of its historic architecture, and many of these late 19th-century and early 20th-century buildings have been turned into unusual and very attractive shopping centers. **New Market Village** (120 SW Ankeny St.), **Morgan's Alley** (515 SW Broadway), and **Skidmore Fountain Building** (28 SW First Ave.) are all outstanding examples of how Portland has preserved its historic buildings and kept its downtown area filled with happy shoppers.

However, it is the blocks around Pioneer Courthouse Square that are the heartland of upscale shopping in Portland. It is here that you will find Nordstrom, NIKETOWN, Saks Fifth Avenue, Pioneer Place shopping mall, and numerous other upscale boutiques and shops.

Portland's most "happening" area for shopping is the Nob Hill/ Northwest neighborhood along NW 23rd Avenue beginning at West Burnside Street. Here you'll find block after block of unusual boutiques that are, unfortunately, rapidly being replaced by such chains as the Gap, Urban Outfitters, and Pottery Barn. For shops with a more downbeat and funky flavor, head out to the Hawthorne District, which is the city's counterculture shopping area (lots of tie-dye and imports). In the Pearl District, of which NW Glisan Street and NW 10th Avenue is the center, you'll find the city's greatest concentration of art galleries. Northeast Broadway around NE 15th Avenue is home to several interesting interior design and home decor shops.

Hours   Most small stores in Portland are open Monday through Saturday from 9 or 10am to 5 or 6pm. Shopping malls are usually open Monday through Friday from 9 or 10am to 9pm, on Saturday from 9 or 10am to between 6pm and 9pm, and on Sunday from 11am until 6pm. Most art galleries and antique stores are closed on Monday. Department stores stay open on Friday night until 9pm.

ANTIQUES

Old Sellwood Antique Row, at east end of Sellwood Bridge on SE 13th Street. With its old Victorian homes and turn-of-the-century architecture, Sellwood is Portland's main antique district. You'll find 13 blocks with more than 30 antique dealers and restaurants.

ART GALLERIES

If you're in the market for art, try to arrange your visit to coincide with the first Thursday of the month. On these days galleries in downtown Portland schedule coordinated openings in the evening. Stroll from one gallery to the next, meeting artists and perhaps buying an original work of art. As an added bonus, the **Portland Art Museum,** 1219 SW Park Ave. (☎ **503/226-2811**), offers half-price admission from 4 to 9pm on these nights.

An art gallery guide listing almost 60 Portland galleries is available at the **Portland Oregon Visitors Association Information Center,** Two World Trade Center, 25 SW Salmon St. (☎ **800/345-3214** or 503/222-2223; Web site: www.pova.com), or at galleries around Portland.

GENERAL GALLERIES

✪ **Art of the People.** 515 SW Broadway. ☎ **503/221-0569.**

Featured at Art of the People are contemporary paintings and sculpture, and folk and religious art by artists of Latin American descent. Monthly shows sometimes focus on historical and cultural aspects of Latin American art and traditions. The Day of the Dead celebrations here are a bright spot in early November.

✪ **Augen Gallery.** 817 SW Second Ave. ☎ **503/224-8182.**

When it opened 16 years ago, the Augen Gallery focused on internationally recognized artists such as Dine, Warhol, and Hockney, and now has expanded its repertoire to regional contemporary painters and printmakers.

Blackfish Gallery. 420 NW Ninth Ave. ☎ **503/224-2634.**

Artist-owned since 1979, the Blackfish is a large and relaxing space in which you may contemplate cutting-edge and sometimes thought-provoking images.

Butters Gallery Ltd. 223 NW Ninth Ave. ☎ **503/248-9378.**

Along with regional and national painters, Butters specializes in high-quality artworks in metal, natural fibers, and glass.

✪ **The Laura Russo Gallery.** 805 NW 21st Ave. ☎ **503/226-2754.**

The focus here is on Northwest contemporary artists, showcasing talented emerging artists as well as the estates of well-known artists. Laura Russo has been on the Portland art scene for a long time and is highly respected.

Margo Jacobsen Gallery. 1039 NW Glisan St. ☎ **503/224-7287.**

In the heart of the Pearl District, this gallery is where you'll find most of the crowds milling about on First Thursdays. Margo Jacobsen promotes contemporary painters, with a focus on ceramics and glass.

Pulliam Deffenbaugh Gallery. 522 NW 12th Ave. ☎ **503/228-6665.**

Located next to the Quartersaw Gallery (see below), this gallery represents a long list of both talented newcomers and masters from the Northwest.

The City of Books

Though Seattle claims the largest library system in the country, Portland has
✪ **Powell's City of Books,** 1005 W. Burnside St. (☎ **503/228-4651;** on the World
Wide Web at www.powells.com), the bookstore to end all bookstores. Covering
an entire city block three floors deep, Powell's sells more than three million
volumes each year. Though there are arguments over whether the City of Books
is the biggest bookstore in the country, most people agree that Powell's has more
titles on its shelves than any other bookstore in the United States. In any case, there's
no denying Powell's is a contender for the claim to biggest bookstore in the
country.

Powell's has its origins in two used bookstores, one in Chicago and one in Portland, both of which opened in the early 1970s. The Chicago store was opened by
current store owner Michael Powell, while the Portland store was opened by Walter
Powell, Michael's father. In 1979, Michael joined his father in Portland, and
together they began building the store into what it is today.

The City of Books is different from many other bookstores in that it shelves all
its books, new and used, hardback or paperback, together, and with roughly three-
quarters of a million new and used books on the shelves at any given time, the store
had to give up trying to keep a computer inventory of what's in stock. This can be
extremely frustrating if you're looking for an old or out-of-print title, but employees are good about searching the shelves for you, and if they don't have what you're
looking for, they can try tracking down a copy. The upside of not being able to go
straight to the book you're looking for is that you end up browsing.

Browsing is what Powell's is really all about. Once inside you can pick up a store
map that will direct you to color-coded rooms containing different collections of
books. In the Gold Room, you'll find science fiction and children's books; in the

Quartersaw Gallery. 528 NW 12th Ave. ☎ 503/223-2264.

With an emphasis on figurative and expressionistic landscape, Quartersaw is a showcase for progressive Northwest art. Located in the Pearl District.

✪ Quintana Galleries. 501 SW Broadway. ☎ 503/223-1729.

This large bright space is virtually a small museum of Native American art, selling
everything from Northwest Indian masks to contemporary painting and sculpture by
various American Indian artists. The jewelry selection is outstanding. Prices, however,
are not cheap.

Wyland Galleries. 711 SW Tenth Ave. ☎ 503/223-7692.

The Wyland Gallery features the paintings and sculpture of environmental artist
Wyland, as well as other artists whose subjects also are marine mammals, fish, and
the sea.

ART GLASS GALLERIES

Balton Art Glass. 522 SW Yamhill St. ☎ 503/223-2688.

Located across from Pioneer Square, this small shop sells whimsical and exquisite glass
objects from Bohemia, Poland, Germany, Italy, and Egypt in the form of vases,
candle holders, plates, and other pieces.

The Bullseye Connection. 1308 NW Everett St. ☎ 503/227-2797.

Located in the Pearl District, the Bullseye Connection is a large open exhibition and
sales space for glass artists, whose pieces include sculpture and delightful glass

Rose Room, you'll find books on ornithology, civil aviation, Christian theology, and metaphysics among other subjects; in the Orange Room, there are books on art history, antiques, film, drama, and music. Serious book collectors won't want to miss a visit to the Rare Book Room, where you could if you wished buy a copy of a copy of the writings of Cicero published by the Aldine Press in 1570. Of course, you'd need to know how to read Latin. The most expensive book ever sold here was a Fourth Folio Shakespeare with archival repairs for $6,000.

It's so easy to forget the time at Powell's that many customers miss meals and end up in the store's in-house cafe. The Anne Hughes Coffee Room serves espresso and pastries and is always packed with folks perusing books they've pulled from the shelves. This is also where Powell's keeps its extensive magazine rack. So, don't fret if you forgot to pack a lunch for your Powell's outing.

But wait, I forgot to mention that the City of Books outgrew this space and had to open a few satellite stores. There's **Powell's Technical Bookstore,** 33 NW Park St. (☎ **503/228-3906**); **Powell's Books for Cooks and Gardeners,** 3739 SE Hawthorne Blvd. (☎ **503/235-3802**); **Powell's Travel Store,** Pioneer Courthouse Square, SW Sixth Avenue and Yamhill Street (☎ **503/228-1108**); **Powell's Books at Cascade Plaza,** 8775 SW Cascade Ave., Beaverton (☎ **503/643-3131**); **Powell's Books For Health,** Legacy Emanuel Hospital, 501 N. Graham St. (☎ **503/ 413-2988**); **Powell's at PDX,** Portland International Airport (☎ **503/249-1950**); and a couple of others.

One warning: Before stepping through Powell's door, check your watch. If you haven't got at least an hour of free time, you enter at your own risk. Getting lost in the miles of aisles at Powell's has caused many a bibliophile to miss an appointment. Be prepared.

jewelry, paperweights, and marbles. My favorite piece here is the Dale Chihuly chandelier of pink erbium glass, a mass of glowing fruitlike objects. Workshops and lectures related to glass-making are given here.

PHOTOGRAPHY GALLERIES

Blue Sky Gallery. 1231 NW Hoyt St. ☎ **503/225-0210.**

The Blue Sky Gallery is a nonprofit alternative space and the only photography gallery in Portland, founded to exhibit historical and contemporary photography.

Photographic Image Gallery. 240 SW First Ave. ☎ **503/224-3607.**

This large space is full of contemporary landscape, black and white, and nude photographs, and the most extensive selection of photographic posters on the West Coast.

BOOKS

A Children's Place. 1631 NE Broadway. ☎ **503/284-8294.**

If you have a special child in mind, you'll find something for him or her at this small store, which has a wide selection of books, tapes, and CDs.

Annie Bloom's Books. 7834 SW Capitol Hwy. ☎ **503/246-0053.**

It's said in Multnomah Village, where Annie Bloom's is located, that this is a world-class neighborhood bookstore, and as such, it's worth the trip out here. There are easy chairs to sprawl in, two resident cats, free tea and coffee, and they can get any book you want in a very short time. For children, there's a play area and story hour Saturday at 11am.

CRAFTS

For the largest selection of local crafts, visit **Portland Saturday Market** (see "Markets," below). This entertaining outdoor market is a showcase for local crafts.

✪ **Contemporary Crafts Gallery.** 3934 SW Corbett Ave. ☎ **503/223-2654.**

In business since 1937, this is the nation's oldest nonprofit art gallery showing exclusively artwork in clay, glass, fiber, metal, and wood. It's located in a residential neighborhood between downtown and the John's Landing neighborhood, and has a spectacular tree-shaded porch overlooking the Willamette River. The bulk of the gallery is taken up by glass and ceramic pieces, with several cabinets of designer jewelry. Open Tuesday through Saturday 10am to 5pm, Sunday 1 to 5pm.

Graystone Gallery. 3279 SE Hawthorne Blvd. ☎ **503/238-0651.**

This gallery in the SE Hawthorne neighborhood is full of fun and whimsical artwork and home furnishings, including paintings, jewelry, furniture, and greeting cards.

Hoffman Gallery. 8245 SW Barnes Rd. ☎ **503/297-5544.**

The Hoffman Gallery is located on the campus of Oregon College of Art and Craft, which has been one of the nation's foremost crafts education centers since 1906. The gallery hosts installations and group shows by local, national, and international artists. The adjacent gift shop has an outstanding selection of hand-crafted items. The grounds are serene and relaxing, and there is also a cafe open to the public.

✪ **The Real Mother Goose.** 901 SW Yamhill St. ☎ **503/223-9510.**

This is Portland's premier crafts shop. It showcases only the very finest contemporary American crafts, including imaginative ceramics, colorful art glass, intricate jewelry, exquisite wooden furniture, and sculptural works. Hundreds of craftspeople and artists from all over the United States are represented here, and even if you're not buying, you should stop by to see the best of American craftsmanship.

Other locations include Washington Square; Tigard (☎ **503/620-2243**); and Portland International Airport, Main Terminal (☎ **503/284-9929**).

DEPARTMENT STORES

Meier and Frank. 621 SW Fifth Ave. ☎ **503/223-0512.**

Meier and Frank is a Portland institution. They have been doing business here for more than 100 years. Their flagship store on Pioneer Courthouse Square was built in 1898 and, with 10 stories, was at one time the tallest store in the Northwest. Today those 10 stories of consumer goods still attract crowds of shoppers. The store is open daily, with Friday usually the late night. Other locations include 1100 Lloyd Center (☎ **503/281-4797**) and 9300 SW Washington Square Rd. in Tigard (☎ **503/620-3311**).

Nordstrom. 701 SW Broadway. ☎ **503/224-6666.**

Directly across the street from Pioneer Courthouse Square and a block away from Meier and Frank, Nordstrom is a top-of-the-line department store that originated in the Northwest and takes great pride in its personal service and friendliness. This pride is well founded—the store has devoutly loyal customers who would never dream of shopping anywhere else. There is even a pianist playing a baby grand to accompany

shoppers on their rounds. Other Nordstroms in the area are at 1001 Lloyd Center
(☎ **503/287-2444**) and 9700 SW Washington Square Rd. in Tigard (☎ **503/
620-0555**).

FASHION

In addition to the Columbia and Nike outlet stores listed below, Adidas is planning
to open a shoe and apparel outlet store at the corner of NE Martin Luther King Jr.
Boulevard and Alberta Street.

SPORTSWEAR

Columbia Sportswear Company. 911 SW Broadway and Taylor St. ☎ **503/226-6800.**

This new flagship store is surprisingly low key, given that the nearby Nike flagship
store and the new REI in Seattle are designed to knock your socks off. Displays showing the Columbia line of outdoor clothing are rustic, with lots of natural wood. The
most dramatic architectural feature of the store is the entryway, in which a very wide
tree trunk seemingly supports the roof, and a mini-video light show plays upon the
floor.

Columbia Sportswear Company Outlet Store. 8128 SE 13th Ave. ☎ **503/238-0118.**

This outlet store in Sellwood (go over the Sellwood Bridge) sells well-made outdoor
and sports clothing from one of the Northwest's premiere outdoor clothing manu-
facturers. Prices here are much less than in other retail stores.

Hanna Andersson. 327 NW Tenth Ave. (Pearl District). ☎ **800/222-0544** or 503/321-5275.

Based on Swedish designs with comfort and warmth in mind, Hanna's carries 100%
cotton clothing for babies, kids, women, and unisex sizes. Striped Swedish long johns,
snugly baby suits, and girl's dresses are some of the things you'll see here.

Langlitz Leathers. 2443 SE Division St. ☎ **503/235-0959.**

This family run shop produces the Rolls Royce of leather jackets. Even though there
may be a wait for a motorcycle jacket (the shop turns out only six handmade jackets a day), motorcyclists ride their Harleys from the East Coast to be fitted for a gar-
ment. It's rumored that Jay Leno bought a leather jacket here before he became
famous.

✪ NIKETOWN. 930 SW Sixth Ave. ☎ **503/221-6453.**

This superglitzy, ultracontempo showcase for Nike products blasted onto the
Portland shopping scene with all the subtlety of a Super Bowl celebration. Matte
black decor, George Segal–style plaster statues of athletes, and videos everywhere give NIKETOWN the feel of a sports museum or disco. A true shopping
experience.

Nike Factory Outlet. 3044 NE Martin Luther King Jr. Blvd. (³/₄ mile north of Broadway)
☎ **503/281-5901.**

The Nike outlet is one season behind the current season at NIKETOWN, selling
swoosh brand running, aerobic, tennis, golf, basketball, kids, and you name it sports
clothing and accessories at discounted prices.

Norm Thompson. 1805 NW Thurman St. ☎ **503/221-0764.**

Known throughout the rest of the country from its mail-order catalogs, Norm
Thompson is a mainstay of the well-to-do in Portland. Classic styling for men and
women is the name of the game here. A second store is at Portland International
Airport (☎ **503/249-0170**).

NIKETOWN, USA

Despite the controversies surrounding overseas manufacturing, Nike, headquartered in the Portland suburb of Beaverton, has managed to put Portland on the world fashion map. However, long before the famous swoosh ever appeared on a pair of running shoes, Portland was already a center for sportswear manufacturing.

Jantzen, swimwear manufacturer for much of this century, got its start here in Portland, where an entire neighborhood now bears the company's name. Jantzen Beach, located on an island in the Columbia River was once the site of a large public swimming pool, and it was here that Jantzen first made a name for itself. Today Jantzen Beach is the site of a large shopping mall.

If you've ever owned a plaid wool shirt, chances are it was a Pendleton, and though this famous manufacturer of clothing for cool weather is named for the town of Pendleton in eastern Oregon, they also have a mill just outside Portland in Washougal, Washington. Mill tours are given and there's also an outlet shop.

These days people are more likely to be wearing high-tech waterproof materials when they head outdoors, and more and more often, those clothes are turning out to be made by Portland's Columbia Sportswear. This company got its start in ski jackets but has since expanded its lines considerably.

If you happen to be visiting Portland in December, keep an eye out for a neon Rudolph atop a building at the west end of the Burnside Bridge. The sign is an old advertisement for White Stag, a sportswear maker that is no longer headquartered in Portland. However, the white stag (with its Christmastime red nose) is a Portland landmark every bit as important as Nike world headquarters.

The Portland Pendleton Shop. 900 SW Fifth Ave. (entrance is actually on Fourth Ave. between Salmon and Taylor). ☎ **503/242-0037.**

Pendleton wool is as much a part of life in the Northwest as forests and salmon. This company's fine wool fashions for men and women define the country-club look in the Northwest and in many other parts of the country. Pleated skirts and tweed jackets are de rigueur here, as are the colorful blankets that have helped keep generations of northwesterners warm through long chilly winters.

MEN'S CLOTHING

Mario's. 921 SW Morrison St. ☎ **503/227-3477.**

Located inside the Galleria, Mario's sells self-consciously stylish European men's fashions straight off the pages of GQ and M. Prices are as high as you would expect. If you long to be European, but your birth certificate says otherwise, here you can at least adopt the look.

WOMEN'S CLOTHING

Byrkit. 2129 NE Broadway. ☎ **503/282-3773.**

Byrkit specializes in natural fabric clothing of cotton, silk, rayon, and linen for women. The contemporary designs, including dresses, jumpers, and separates, are built for comfort but include a lot of style. There's also a small selection of men's clothes here.

Changes. 927 SW Yamhill St. ☎ **503/223-3737.**

Located next door to The Real Mother Goose gallery, this shop specializes in handmade clothing, including hand-woven scarves, jackets, shawls, hand-painted silks, and other wearable art.

Elizabeth Street. 635 NW 23rd Ave. ☎ **503/243-2456.**

Here you'll find a small and basic selection of casual, comfortable women's fashion, accessories, and jewelry.

✪ **The Eye of Ra.** 5331 SW Macadam Ave. ☎ **503/224-4292.**

Women with sophisticated tastes in ethnic fashions will want to visit this pricey shop in The Water Tower at John's Landing shopping center. Silk and rayon predominate, and there is plenty of ethnic jewelry by creative designers to accompany any ensemble you might put together here. Ethnic furniture and home decor are also for sale.

Mario's for Women. 811 SW Morrison St. ☎ **503/241-8111.**

Flip through the pages of a European edition of *Vogue* magazine and you'll get an idea of the fashions you can find at the women's version of fashionable Mario's. Up-to-the-minute and back-to-the-future European fashions fill the racks.

Mercantile. 735 SW Park St. (across the street from Nordstrom). ☎ **503/223-6649.**

This specialty store for women carries modern classic clothing from blue jeans to black tie. Designers represented are both European and American, from Zannela Italian separates to the whimsical fashions of Nicole Miller. You'll find stylish purses, exquisite formal wear, and cashmere sweaters. The occasional sale yields some good selections at marked-down prices.

M. Sellin Ltd. 3556 SE Hawthorne Blvd. ☎ **503/239-4605.**

Located in the relaxed and low-key Hawthorne district, this shop carries women's clothes of a similar nature, including natural fabrics, comfortable styling, and ethnic designs. There's also a good selection of jewelry at reasonable prices.

FOOD

The Made in Oregon shops offer the best selection of local food products such as hazelnuts, marionberry and raspberry jam, and smoked salmon. See "Gifts & Souvenirs," below, for details.

GIFTS & SOUVENIRS

For unique locally made souvenirs, your best bet is Portland Saturday Market (see "Markets," below, for details).

Made in Oregon. 921 SW Morrison St. (in the Galleria). ☎ **800/828-9673** or 503/241-3630.

This is your one-stop shop for all manner of made-in-Oregon gifts, food products, and clothing. Every product they sell is either grown, caught, or made in Oregon. This is the place to visit for salmon, filberts, jams and jellies, Pendleton woolens, and Oregon wines.

Other Portland area branches can be found in Portland International Airport's Main Terminal (☎ **503/282-7827**); in Lloyd Center, SE Multnomah Street and SE Broadway (☎ **503/282-7636**); in Old Town at 10 NW First Ave. (☎ **503/273-8354**). All branches are open daily, but hours vary from store to store.

HOUSEWARES, HOME FURNISHINGS & GARDEN ACCESSORIES
Blue Pear. 1313 NW Glisan St. ☎ **503/227-0057.**

Located in the Pearl District, this shop offers contemporary and unusual furniture, wall art, linens, cushions, and tabletop pieces such as lamps, iron bowls, glassware, and candlesticks that are both functional and beautiful.

KaBoom. 1115 NW Glisan St. ☎ **503/223-1465.**

Also in the Pearl District, KaBoom sells "clothes for your home"—wildly trendy and colorful furniture and accessories.

Urbino. 521 NW 23rd Ave. ☎ **503/220-0053.**

This store is artistic and lush, selling special things for the home and body. You'll find handmade candles and hand-milled soaps, napkins and scarves, ceramics, jewelry, pillows and picture frames, among other items.

JEWELRY
✪ **Twist.** 30 NW 23rd Place. ☎ **503/224-0334.**

Twist showcases handmade jewelry from artists around the United States, from Thomas Mann techno-romantic jewelry to imaginative charm bracelets to hand-sculpted earrings. Surely you'll find a piece you'll want to wear every day. They also carry furniture, housewares, and pottery. Another store is located in Pioneer Place mall (☎ **503/222-3137**).

MALLS/SHOPPING CENTERS
✪ **The Galleria.** 921 SW Morrison St. ☎ **503/228-2748.**

Located in the heart of downtown Portland, The Galleria is a three-story atrium shopping mall with more than 50 specialty shops and restaurants, including a Made in Oregon store. Before being restored and turned into its present incarnation, this building was one of Portland's earliest department stores. Parking validation is available at an adjacent parking garage.

Jantzen Beach Center. 1405 Jantzen Beach Center. ☎ **503/289-5555.**

This large shopping mall is located on the site of a former amusement park where an old carousel still operates. There are four major department stores and more than 80 other shops. You'll also find the REI co-op recreational-equipment store here. This mall has long been popular with residents of Washington State, who come to shop where there is no sales tax.

Lloyd Center. Bounded by SE Multnomah St., NE Broadway, NE 16th Ave., and NE Ninth Ave. ☎ **503/282-2511.**

Lloyd Center was the largest shopping mall on the West Coast when it opened in 1960. In 1991 an extensive renovation was completed to bring it up to current standards. There are five anchor stores and more than 200 specialty shops here, including a Nordstrom and a Meier and Frank. A food court, ice-skating rink, and eight-screen cinema complete the mall's facilities.

✪ **New Market Village.** 120 SW Ankeny St. ☎ **503/228-2392.**

Housed in a brick building built in 1872, this small shopping center is listed in the National Register of Historic Places. You'll find it directly across the street from the Skidmore Fountain and the Portland Saturday Market. A long row of freestanding archways salvaged from a demolished building creates a courtyard on one side of the New Market Village building.

✪ **Pioneer Place.** 700 SW Fifth Ave. ☎ **503/228-5800.**

Located only a block from Pioneer Courthouse Square, Portland's newest downtown shopping center is also its most upscale. Anchored by a Saks Fifth Avenue, Pioneer Place is where the elite shop for high fashions and expensive gifts. You'll also find Portland's branch of the Nature Company and the city's only Godiva chocolatier here.

The Water Tower at Johns Landing. 5331 SW Macadam Ave. ☎ **503/228-9431.**

As you're driving south from downtown Portland on Macadam Avenue, you can't miss the old wooden water tower for which this unusual shopping mall is named. Standing high above the roof of the mall, it was once used as a storage tank for fire-fighting water. Hardwood floors, huge overhead beams, and a tree-shaded courtyard paved with Belgian cobblestones from Portland's first paved streets give this place plenty of character. There are about 40 specialty shops and restaurants here.

MARKETS

✪ **Portland Saturday Market.** Underneath Burnside Bridge (between SW First Ave. and SW Ankeny St.). ☎ **503/222-6072.**

Portland Saturday Market (held on both Saturday and Sunday) is arguably the city's single most important and best-loved event. For years the Northwest has attracted artists and craftspeople, and every Saturday and Sunday nearly 300 of them can be found selling their exquisite creations here. In addition to the dozens of crafts stalls, you'll find flowers, fresh produce, ethnic and unusual foods, and lots of free enter-tainment. This is the single best place to shop for one-of-a-kind gifts in Portland. The atmosphere is always cheerful and the crowds are always colorful. At the heart of the Skidmore District, Portland Saturday Market makes an excellent starting or finish-ing point for a walk around Portland's most historic neighborhood. Don't miss this unique market. On Sunday, on-street parking is free. Open first weekend in March through Christmas Eve, Saturday 10am to 5pm, Sunday 11am to 4:30pm; closed January and February.

TOYS

✪ **Finnegan's Toys and Gifts.** 922 SW Yamhill St. ☎ **503/221-0306.**

We all harbor a small child within ourselves, and this is the sort of place that has that inner child kicking and screaming in the aisles if you don't buy that silly little toy you never got when you were young. (Kids love this place, too.) It's the largest toy store in downtown Portland.

WINE

Great Wine Buys. 1515 NE Broadway. ☎ **503/287-2897.**

Oenophiles who have developed a taste for Oregon wines will want to stock up here before heading home. One of the best wine shops in Portland, this store has a tast-ing bar where you can sample the wines. The staff is helpful and many of them make wine. Open Monday through Saturday 10:30am to 6:30pm, Sunday noon to 5pm.

Harris Wine Cellars Ltd. 2300 NW Thurman St. ☎ **503/223-2222.**

Located at the northern and less fashionable end of NW 23rd Avenue, Harris Wine Cellars caters to serious wine connoisseurs, and has been doing so for many years. It isn't glamorous, but the folks here know their wine. Hearty lunches are also avail-able. Open Monday through Saturday from 10am to 6pm.

Oregon Wines on Broadway. 515 SW Broadway (in Morgan's Alley). ☎ **503/228-4655.**

This cozy wine bar/shop is located diagonally across from the Hotel Vintage Plaza. Here you can taste Oregon's Pinot Noir, Chardonnay, Gewürztraminer, or other wines, and then buy a bottle or two.

19

Portland After Dark

Portland has become the Northwest's second cultural center. Its symphony orchestra, ballet, and opera are all well regarded, and the many theater companies offer classic and contemporary plays. If you are a jazz fan, you'll feel right at home—there's always a lot of live jazz being played around town. In summer, festivals move the city's cultural activities outdoors.

To find out what's going on during your visit, pick up a copy of *Willamette Week,* Portland's free weekly arts-and-entertainment newspaper. You can also check the Friday arts section and Sunday editions of the *Oregonian,* the city's daily newspaper.

Many theaters and performance halls in Portland offer discounts to students and senior citizens. You can often save money by buying your ticket on the day of a performance or within a half hour of curtain time.

Tickets for many of the venues listed below can be purchased through **GI Joe's/Ticketmaster** (☎ **503/790-2787** or 503/224-4400) or **Fastixx** at Fred Meyer (☎ **503/224-TIXX**).

1 The Performing Arts

For the most part, the Portland performing arts scene revolves around the **Portland Center for the Performing Arts,** 1111 SW Broadway (☎ **503/248-4335**), which is comprised of four theaters in three different buildings. The **Arlene Schnitzer Concert Hall,** Southwest Broadway and Southwest Main Street, known locally as the Schnitz, is an immaculately restored 1920s movie palace that still displays the original Portland theater sign and marquee out front and is home to the Oregon Symphony (☎ **800/228-7343** or 503/228-1353). This hall also hosts popular music bands, lecturers, a travel-film series, and many other special performances. Free tours of the Schnitz are held Wednesday at 11am and Saturday at 11am, noon, and 1pm. Directly across Main Street from the Schnitz, at 1111 SW Broadway, is the sparkling glass jewel box known as the **New Theater Building.** This building houses both the **Intermediate** and **Winningstad** theaters. The Intermediate Theatre is home to **Portland Center Stage** (☎ **503/274-6588**), while the two theaters together host stage productions by local and visiting companies. Free tours of this building are offered Wednesday at 11am and Saturday at 11am, noon, and 1pm. A few blocks away from this concentration of venues is the 3,000-seat **Portland Civic Auditorium,** SW Third

Avenue and SW Clay Street, the largest of the four halls and the home of the **Portland Opera** (☎ **503/241-1802**) and the **Oregon Ballet Theatre** (☎ **503/222-5538**). The Civic was constructed shortly after World War I and completely remodeled in the 1960s. In addition to resident companies mentioned above, these halls together host numerous visiting companies each year, including touring Broadway shows.

When funding for performance art disappeared in Portland, the **Portland Institute for Contemporary Art,** also known as PICA (☎ **503/242-1419**), was created as a resource for exploring and supporting experimental art and new music in this city. Using various venues around the city, PICA presents innovative performances by well-known artists such as Philip Glass, Karen Finley, and Spalding Gray, as well as less established performance artists and musicians. PICA also presents visual exhibitions focusing on contemporary trends in the regional, national, and international art scene. Call for its current schedule. Ticket prices range from $12 to $20.

OPERA & CLASSICAL MUSIC

Founded in 1896, the **Oregon Symphony** (☎ **800/228-7343** or 503/228-1353), which performs at the Arlene Schnitzer Concert Hall, 1111 SW Broadway, is the oldest symphony orchestra on the West Coast, achieving national recognition under the expert baton of conductor James de Preist. Several series, including classical, pops, Sunday matinees, and children's concerts, are held during the September-to-June season. Ticket prices range from $10 to $50 (seniors and students may purchase half-price tickets 1 hour before a classical concert).

Each season, the **Portland Opera** (☎ **503/241-1802**), which performs at the Portland Civic Auditorium at the corner of SW Third Avenue and SW Clay Street, offers five different productions of grand opera and musical theater. The season runs from September to May. Ticket prices range from $21 to $100 (students may attend dress rehearsals for a nominal charge).

Other classical music ensembles of note in Portland include the **Portland Baroque Orchestra** (☎ **503/222-6000**), which performs on period instruments at a couple of different Portland venues, and the **Portland Youth Philharmonic** (☎ **503/223-5939**), which is the oldest youth orchestra in the country and which showcases very talented musicians ages 10 to 23.

Summer is the time for Portland's annual chamber music binge. **Chamber Music Northwest** (☎ **503/223-3202**) is a 5-week-long series that starts in late June and attracts the world's finest chamber musicians. Performances are held at Reed College and Catlin Gable School.

THEATER

Portland Center Stage (☎ **503/274-6588**), which stages performances at the Portland Center for the Performing Arts, 1111 SW Broadway, is Portland's largest professional theater company. They stage a combination of five classic and contemporary plays during their October-to-April season. Ticket prices range from $11 to $35.

Portland's oldest Equity theater, the **Portland Repertory Theater,** World Trade Center, 25 SW Salmon St. (☎ **503/224-4491**), offers consistently excellent productions and is acclaimed for its presentations ranging from off-Broadway hit comedies to world-premier dramas by contemporary American and British playwrights. Ticket prices range from $25 to $27 ($20 previews).

The play's the thing at **Tygres Heart Shakespeare Co.** (☎ **503/222-9220**), which performs at the Dolores Winningstad Theatre, 1111 SW Broadway, and old Will would be proud. Tygres Heart remains true to its name and stages only works by the bard himself. Ticket prices range from $8 to $25.

If it's musicals you want, you've got plenty of options in Portland. At Civic Auditorium, you can catch the latest touring Broadway show thanks to the **Portland's Broadway Theater Season** (☎ **503/241-1407**). Also at the Civic, you can catch more tried and true shows courtesy of the **U.S. Bank Broadway Series** (☎ **503/228-9571**). For other classics from Broadway's past, check the schedule of the **Musical Theatre Company** (☎ **503/224-8730**), a semi-professional company that performs at the Intermediate Theatre.

For more daring theater productions, see what's on tap at the **Artists Repertory Theater,** 1111 SW Tenth Ave. (☎ **503/294-7373**); **Main Street Playhouse,** 904 SW Main St. (☎ **503/282-9303**); the **Stark Raving Theater,** 4319 SE Hawthorne Blvd. (☎ **503/232-7072**); or the **Miracle Theater,** 525 SE Stark St. (☎ **503/236-7253**).

CHILDREN'S THEATER

Oregon Children's Theatre Company (☎ **503/228-9571**) performs plays such as the *Little House on the Prairie* and *Charlie and the Chocolate Factory,* as well as special holiday productions at Civic Auditorium and other venues. Ticket prices range from $14 to $16.

Tears of Joy Theater (☎ **503/248-0557** or 360/695-0477) performs exciting puppet theater for both children and adults. Performances are held in the Winningstad Theatre at the Portland Center for the Performing Arts. Tickets are $12 for adults and $9 for children.

DANCE

Although the **Oregon Ballet Theatre** (☎ **503/222-5538**), which performs at the Portland Civic Auditorium, is best loved for its sold-out performances each December of *The Nutcracker,* this company also stages the annual American Choreographers Showcase. This latter performance often features world premieres. Rounding out the season are performances of classic and contemporary ballets. Ticket prices range from $10 to $65.

Imago, 17 SE Eighth Ave. (☎ **503/231-9581**), uses a variety of unusual masks and outlandish costumes to produce strange and whimsical performance pieces. Each number they do is a cross between vaudeville, carnival, theater, and dance. A national reputation keeps the company on the road much of the year, but devoted fans here at home never miss their outrageous performances when they return. Tickets are $15 for adults, $12 for students and seniors, and $8 for children.

SUMMER CONCERT SERIES

When summer hits, Portlanders like to head outdoors to hear music. Most of this music is popular rock, reggae, jazz, blues, and folk, and most of these series schedule enough variety over the summer that they'll eventually appeal to almost every music listener in the city.

Outdoor music series to check on in the summer include **Champoeg Under the Stars** at Champoeg State Park south of Portland near Wilsonville (in 1997, performers included Lyle Lovett, Ani Difranco, the Allman Brothers Band, and Ziggy Marley); **Live at Sokol Blosser** at the Sokol Blosser Winery southwest of Portland outside Dundee (the 1997 series included Dan Fogelberg, Johnny Mathis, The Manhattan Transfer, and Peter, Paul, and Mary); **Washington Park Rose Garden Concerts** (David Byrne, Soul Coughing, Shawn Colvin, Calobo, and Taj Mahal in 1997); **Music by Blue Lake** at Blue Lake Park east of downtown Portland near the airport (local acts; ☎ **503/797-1850**); and **Rhythm and Zoo Concerts** at Washington Park

Zoo Amphitheater (Richard Thompson, The Bobs, Karla Bonoff, Booker T. Jones, Michele Schocked in 1997; ☎ **503/226-1561**). With the exception of the zoo concerts and Music by Blue Lake, tickets for shows in these series are available either through **Ticketmaster** (☎ **503/224-4400**) or **Fastixx** (☎ **503/224-8499**).

2 The Club & Music Scene

FOLK & ROCK

Aladdin Theater. 3017 SE Milwaukee Ave. ☎ **503/233-1994.** Tickets $10–$20.

This former movie theater now serves as one of Portland's main venues for touring performers from a very diverse musical spectrum that includes blues, rock, ethnic, country, folk, and jazz.

Bar of the Gods. 4801 SE Hawthorne Blvd. ☎ **503/232-2037.** Cover free to $2.

Despite the interesting contemporary facade, this place is just a dark little bar at the foot of Mount Tabor. However, several nights a week there is live rockabilly music, and other nights you can expect interesting recorded swing music to be playing. There's a little, back-alley patio as well.

Berbati's Pan. 231 SW Ankeny St. ☎ **503/248-4579.** Cover $2–$7.

Located in Old Town and affiliated with a popular Greek restaurant, this is currently one of Portland's most popular rock clubs. A wide variety of acts, often those on the verge of breaking into the national limelight, play here.

Crystal Ballroom. 1332 West Burnside St. ☎ **503/225-0047.** Cover free to $10.

The Crystal Ballroom has a long and not-so-illustrious history. It first opened before 1920, and since then has seen performers from the early jazz scene to James Brown, Marvin Gaye, and The Grateful Dead. The McMenamin Brothers (of local brewing fame) have now renovated the Crystal Ballroom and refurbished its dance floor, which, due to its mechanics, actually floats. The ballroom is now host to a variety of performances and special events nearly every night of the week. A brewery and Ringlers Pub round out the complex.

Key Largo. 31 NW First Ave. ☎ **503/223-9919.** Cover $3–$9 (sometimes higher for national acts).

One of Portland's most popular nightclubs, Key Largo has been packing in music fans for more than a decade. A tropical atmosphere prevails at this spacious club, and basic American food is served. Rock, reggae, blues, and jazz performers all find their way to the stage here, with local R&B bands a mainstay. A nationally known act occasionally shows up here. Open nightly.

La Luna. 215 SE Ninth Ave. ☎ **503/241-5862.** Cover $6.50–$18.

The stage at La Luna is in a cavernous room with a ceiling so high that the cigarette smoke doesn't get too bad. Here you can catch a wide range of lesser known national acts for a reasonable price. The club also includes a small cafe where you can get a snack food between the acts, and a lounge with a pool table upstairs.

Laurelthirst. 2958 NE Glisan St. ☎ **503/232-1504.** Cover $2–$3.

Basically just a neighborhood pub, the Laurelthirst is well known in Portland as the city's best place to hear live bluegrass and folk music. With the recent resurgence of interest in bluegrass, this place is more popular than ever. There's free live music at happy hour and then more music later in the evening.

Of Shanghaied Sailors & Floating Brothels

While *polite, clean,* and *livable* are the sort of adjectives that are used to describe Portland these days, there was a time when wild and wicked were far more appropriate.

Back in the late 1800s, Joseph "Bunco" Kelly and "Sweet Mary" summed up the sort of Wild West enterprising spirit that characterized the young Portland. At the time, the city was one of the West Coast's main port towns, and as is the case with such waterfront communities, it attracted a few unsavory characters. Kelly, a local hotelier, was well known by ship's captains who would rely on him to shanghai crew members when a ship was ready to sail and didn't yet have a full complement of sailors. Kelly would get men drunk and then haul them off to a ship about to set sail. As unscrupulous an occupation as shanghaiing was, Kelly outdid himself when he happened upon a group of men who had mistakenly been drinking embalming fluid in a basement mortuary they had stumbled into. With men both dead and dying, Kelly saw a chance to turn a tidy profit and foisted them off to a desperate ship's captain as merely dead drunk. On another occasion he wrapped a cigar store wooden Indian in blankets and convinced a captain that it was a soon to be able-bodied seamen.

As one of the city's most notorious madams, "Sweet Mary" saw to the needs of ship's captains and sailors alike. However, even in the late 19th century, Portland had laws against prostitution. "Sweet Mary" took full advantage of a loophole in the law by setting up shop on a barge that she floated up and down the Willamette River. On the river, she was outside the jurisdiction of the city, and also managed to avoid paying taxes.

Roseland Theater. 8 NW Sixth Ave. ☎ **503/224-2038.** Cover $5–$22.

Roseland Theater is only a couple of blocks from Key Largo, and the same diversity of popular musical styles prevails. A couple of heavy-metal nights each week attract a rougher crowd than you're likely to find at Key Largo, but other nights you might encounter the likes of John Mayall or the latest Seattle grunge band. Open nightly.

JAZZ & BLUES

Brasserie Montmartre. 626 SW Park Ave. ☎ **503/224-5552.** No cover.

There's live jazz nightly from 8:30pm at this French restaurant. Both the food and the music are popular with a primarily middle-aged clientele that likes to dress up. Open Sunday to Thursday until 2am; Friday and Saturday until 3am.

Jazz De Opus. 33 NW Second Ave. ☎ **503/222-6077.** $5 cover on weekends; 50¢ surcharge on drinks other nights.

This restaurant/bar has long been one of Portland's bastions of jazz, with a cozy room and smooth jazz on the stereo. You can also catch live performances nightly by jazz musicians.

The Green Room. 2280 NW Thurman St. ☎ **503/228-6178.** No cover.

Located just around the corner from Northwest 23rd Avenue, this is a classic backstreets blues bar. Little more than a local bar, this nondescript place books the best of the local blues brothers and sisters.

Parchman Farm. 1204 SE Clay St. ☎ **503/235-7831.** Cover $2 Fri–Sat.

If you're into blues, Parchman Farm is a good place to hang out. There's live music nightly Monday through Saturday starting about 9pm, and if you're hungry you can order a gourmet pizza or prime rib from the menu.

COMEDY, CABARET & DINNER THEATER

ComedySportz Arena. 1963 NW Kearney St. ☎ **503/236-8888.** Cover $7.

This is the home of the ever-popular ComedySportz improv comedy troupe. Shows are Friday and Saturday nights, and the nature of the beast is that you never know what to expect. Have fun.

Darcelle's XV. 208 NW Third Ave. ☎ **503/222-5338.** Cover $8. Reservations recommended Fri–Sat.

This is a campy Portland institution with a female-impersonator show that has been a huge hit for years. Shows are Wednesday and Thursday at 8:30pm and Friday and Saturday at 8:30 and 10:30pm.

DANCE CLUBS

In addition to the clubs listed here, there is a dance club several nights a week at Bar 71. See "The Bar Scene" below for details.

Andrea's Cha-Cha Club. 832 SE Grand Ave. ☎ **503/230-1166.** Cover $4.

Located in the Grand Cafe and open on Friday and Saturday nights only, this is Portland's premier dance spot for fans of Latin dancing. Whether it's salsa, macarena, or cha-cha, they'll be doing it here. Lessons are available early in the evening.

Lotus Cardroom and Cafe. 932 SW Third Ave. ☎ **503/227-6185.** Cover $3–$5.

Established in 1924, this place looks as if it could have posed for an Edward Hopper painting. However, at night, a back room off the cafe becomes one of Portland's most popular dance clubs, with a different style of music Wednesday through Sunday night. This place is a real meat market.

Red Sea. 318 SW Third Ave. ☎ **503/241-5450.** Cover $4.

By day this is an Ethiopian restaurant, but by night it's the busiest Afro-Caribbean dance club in Portland. The dance floor is small and the place gets hot, but the music, a mix of Afro-pop, reggae, and calypso is imminently danceable. There's live reggae on Thursday nights.

✪ Rock 'n' Rodeo. 220 SE Spokane St. ☎ **503/235-2417.** Cover $5 after 8:30pm.

If you're a fan of Western line dancing, West Coast swing, or the two-step (or you just want to learn), join the fun at Rock 'n' Rodeo, where a 1-hour lesson will cost only a buck. Lessons start at 7pm nightly. Afterward, this place becomes a swirl of cowboy boots, skirts, and tight jeans, attesting to the enthusiasm for the western dancing sport here.

GAY DANCE CLUBS

Embers. 110 NW Broadway. ☎ **503/222-3082.** Cover Thurs $2, Fri–Sat $3, Sun–Wed free.

Though this is still primarily a gay disco, straights have discovered its great dance music and have started making the scene as well. There'll be lots of flashing lights and sweaty bodies until the early morning. There are drag shows seven nights a week.

Panorama. 341 SW Tenth Ave. ☎ **503/221-7262.** Cover Fri–Sat $4 before 2am, $6 after 2am.

Open only on Friday and Saturday, Panorama is a large dance club playing currently popular dance music. It's connected to The Brig, a smaller dance club, and Boxes, a video club. The admission allows you into all three. With several different environments and a mixed crowd, an evening here can be quite entertaining. The crowd is mostly gay.

3 The Bar Scene

BARS

✪ **Atwater's Restaurant and Bar.** 111 SW Fifth Ave. ☎ **503/275-3600.**

Up on the 30th floor of the pale-pink U.S. Bancorp Tower is one of Portland's most expensive restaurants and certainly the one with the best view. However, if you'd just like to sit back and sip a martini while gazing out at the city lights below, they have a splendid bar, perfect for a romantic nightcap. Thursday through Saturday evenings there is live jazz. The lounge menu is one of the most creative in Portland.

Bar 71. 71 SW Second Ave. ☎ **503/241-0938.** Cover $1–$5 for dance club.

Hands down the most romantic bar in town, this is the perfect place to sip a blue martini while snuggled up on the maroon velvet sofa with the one you love. Attached to a French restaurant, Bar 71 has great bar food, and Thursday through Sunday, there's an open-air dance patio out back.

Champions. Portland Marriott Hotel, 1401 SW Naito Pkwy. ☎ **503/274-2470.**

Portland's premier sports bar boasts "good food, good times, and good sports." If sports are your forte, this is the bar for you. There is also a small dance floor, with dancing Friday through Saturday to Top 40 tunes.

Gypsy. 625 NW 21st Ave. ☎ **503/796-1859.**

This is Portland's premier lounge scene with a classic Sputnik era decor and martinis to match. This is retro—not the real thing—and has been somewhat upgraded for the '90s. The small bar through the velvet-covered door from the restaurant is generally livelier than the main bar.

Jake's Famous Crawfish. 401 SW 12th Ave. ☎ **503/226-1419.**

Although Jake's is best known for its crawfish, the bar is one of the busiest in town when the downtown offices let out. In business since 1892, Jake's has the most historic feel of any bar in town. Definitely a bar not to be missed.

The Lobby Court. The Benson Hotel, 309 SW Broadway. ☎ **503/228-2000.**

If you never knew cigars or martinis ever went out of fashion, this is the bar for you. The Circassian walnut paneling and crystal chandeliers assure you that this is the classiest bar in town. Several nights a week there is live jazz music.

McCormick and Schmick's Pilsner Room. 0309 SW Montgomery St. ☎ **503/220-1865.**

Located at the south end of Tom McCall Waterfront Park overlooking the Willamette River and RiverPlace Marina, the Pilsner Room keeps more than 20 local microbrews on tap, but it also does a brisk cocktail business. The crowd is upscale, and the view is one of the best in town.

Saucebox. 214 SW Broadway. ☎ **503/241-3393.**

Popular with the city's scene-makers, this hybrid restaurant-bar is a large, dramatically lit dark box and joins the trend toward noisy dining spaces. If you really want to talk, you'd better do it before 10pm, which is when a DJ arrives to turn this place into a dance club. They serve great cocktails—look for their margaritas, martinis, and Singapore slings.

Veritable Quandry. 1220 SW First Ave. ☎ **503/227-7342.**

This tiny old brick building sits alone in the shadow of the Hawthorne Bridge and looks like a relic from the past. Inside you'll find a lively bar scene popular with the young cigar and martini crowd.

Who-Song and Larry's. 4850 SW Macadam Ave. ☎ **503/223-8845.**

Sure it's a bar in a Mexican restaurant chain, but the location right on the Willamette River is hard to beat. Grab a table out on the deck and watch the boats drift by.

PUBS

If you're a beer connoisseur, you'll probably find yourself with little time out from your brew tasting to see any other of Portland's sights. This is the heart of the Northwest craft brewing explosion and has more microbreweries and craft breweries (microbreweries are smaller) than any other city in the United States. They're brewing beers up here the likes of which you won't taste anywhere else this side of the Atlantic. Although many of these beers—as well as ales, porters, stouts, and bitters—are available in restaurants, you owe it to yourself to go directly to the source.

Brewpubs are becoming big business in Portland and there are now glitzy upscale pubs as well as funky warehouse-district locals. What this means is that no matter what vision you have of the ideal brewpub, you're likely to find your dream come true here in Portland. Whether you're wearing bike shorts or a three-piece suit, there's a pub in Portland where you can get a hand-crafted beer, a light meal, and a vantage for enjoying the convivial atmosphere that only a pub can provide.

✪ **Bridgeport Brewery and Brew Pub.** 1313 NW Marshall St. ☎ **503/241-7179.**

Portland's oldest microbrewery was founded in 1984 and is housed in the city's oldest industrial building (where workers once produced rope for sailing ships). The brewery has four to seven of its brews on tap on any given night (including several cask-conditioned ales), and live music on the first Thursday of the month. They make great pizza here—the crust is made with wort, a byproduct of the brewing process.

✪ **Cornelius Pass Roadhouse.** Sunset Highway and Cornelius Pass Road, Hillsboro. ☎ **503/640-6174.**

Housed in an old farmhouse and surrounded by lawns and picnic tables, this McMenamin brothers pub is a favorite summertime after-work watering hole for employees of the many area high-tech companies and is also very popular on sunny weekends. The shade trees and old farmhouse setting lend this pub a very Oregon atmosphere. Also on the grounds is a hexagonal barn that is one of the few such structures in the state.

✪ **Edgefield.** 2126 SW Halsey St., Troutdale. ☎ **503/669-8610.**

Located about 20 minutes from downtown Portland just off I-84 at exit 16A, this McMenamin brother's flagship is a sprawling complex that used to be the Multnomah County poor farm. On the beautifully landscaped grounds you'll find not only the brewery and Power Station Pub but the Power Station Theater (a movie pub), the Loading Dock Beer Garden and Grill, the Black Rabbit Restaurant and Bar, the Ice House Sports Bar, a winery and tasting room, a bed-and-breakfast inn, a hostel, craft shops and artists' studios, and our personal favorite, the diminutive Little Red Shed, a tiny cottage pub that sells cocktails and cigars as well as beer.

Hillsdale Brewery and Public House. 1505 SW Sunset Blvd. ☎ **503/246-3938.**

This was the cornerstone of the McMenamin brothers' microbrewery empire, which now includes more than 30 pubs in the greater Portland metropolitan area and beyond. The McMenamins pride themselves in crafting flavorful and unusual ales with bizarre names like Terminator stout and Purple Haze. Some of their other pubs include **Blue Moon Tavern,** 432 NW 21st St. (☎ 503/223-3184), on a fashionable street in northwest Portland; and **The Ram's Head,** 2282 NW Hoyt St. (☎ **503/221-0098**), between 21st and 22nd avenues.

Portland's Brewing Up a Microstorm

Though espresso is the drink that drives Portland, it is to the city's dozens of brewpubs that educated beer drinkers head when they want to relax over a flavorful pint of ale. No other city in America has as great a concentration of brewpubs, and it was here that the craft brewing business got its start in the mid-1980s. Today, brewpubs continue to proliferate with cozy neighborhood pubs vying for business with big, polished establishments.

To fully appreciate what the city's craft brewers are concocting, it helps to have a little beer background. There are four basic ingredients in beer: malt, hops, yeast, and water. The first of these, malt, is made from grains, primarily barley and wheat, which are roasted to convert their carbohydrates into the sugar needed to grow yeast. The amount of roasting the grains receive during the malting process will determine the color and flavor of the final product. The darker the malt, the darker and more flavorful the beer or ale. There is a wide variety of malts, each providing its own characteristic flavor. Yeast in turn converts the malt's sugar into alcohol. There are many different strains of yeast that all lend different characters to beers. The hops are added to give beer its characteristic bitterness. The more "hoppy" the beer or ale, the more bitter it becomes. The Northwest is the nation's only commercial hop-growing region, with 75% grown in Washington and 25% grown in Oregon and Idaho.

Pilsners are the most common beers in America and are made from pale malt with a lot of hops added to give them their characteristic bitter flavor. **Lagers** are made in much the same way as pilsners but are cold-fermented, which gives them a distinctive flavor. **Ales,** which are the most common brews served at microbreweries, are made using a warm fermentation process and usually with more malt and darker malt than is used in lagers and pilsners. **Porters** and **stouts** get their characteristic dark coloring and flavor from the use of dark, even charred, malt.

To these basics, you can then add a few variables. Fruit flavored beers, which some disparage as soda pop beer, are actually an old European tradition and, when considering the preponderance of fresh fruits in the Northwest, are a natural. If you see a sign for nitro beer in a pub, it doesn't mean they've got explosive brews, it means they've got a keg charged with nitrogen instead of carbon dioxide for an extra creamy head. A nitro charge is why Guinness Stout is so distinctive. Cask-conditioned ales, served almost room temperature and with only their own carbon dioxide to create the head, are also gaining in popularity. While some people think these brews are flat, others appreciate them for their unadulterated character. What this all adds up to is a lot of variety in Portland pubs. Cheers!

Lucky Labrador Pub. 915 SE Hawthorne Blvd. ☎ **503/236-3555.**

With a warehouse-size room, industrial feel, and picnic tables on the loading dock out back, this brewpub is a classic southeast Portland local. The crowd is young and dogs are welcome (even ones that aren't Labradors).

Portland Brewing Company's Brewhouse Tap Room and Grill. 2730 NW 31st Ave. ☎ **503/228-5269.**

With huge copper fermenting vats proudly displayed and polished to a high sheen, this is by far the city's most ostentatious, though certainly not its largest, brewpub. We aren't particularly fond of their brews, but decide for yourself.

Ringlers Pub. 1332 West Burnside St. ☎ **503/225-0543.**

Located almost across the street from the huge Weinhard Brewery, this cavernous pub is filled with big old signs and Indonesian antiques. Mosaic pillars frame the bar and there are big booths as well as cozy cafe tables. A block away are two associated pubs, one below street level and with a beer cellar feel and the other in a flat-iron building. Together these three pubs are the most atmospheric ale houses in town.

Rock Bottom Brewery. 206 SW Morrison St. ☎ **503/796-2739.**

Located in downtown Portland, this brewpub is an outpost of a small brewing empire that started in Boulder, Colorado, the west's other brewing capital. This place is a bit corporate, but is popular with the downtown after-work crowd.

Widmer Brewing and Gasthaus. 955 N. Russell St. ☎ **503/281-3333.**

Located in an industrial area just north of the Rose Garden arena, this place has the feel of a classic working man's pub. This is the brewery for Portland's largest craft brewing company, which is best known for its hefeweizen. German food is served in the pub.

IRISH PUBS

Dublin Pub. 6821 Beaverton-Hillsdale Hwy. ☎ **503/297-2889.**

Located west of downtown toward the suburb of Beaverton, this pub plays up the Irish decor a bit too much and otherwise is a bit short on atmosphere. However, the pub's claim to fame is its 102 beer taps, the largest selection in the Northwest, and we're not talking Bud, Bud Lite, Bud Dry, Bud Ice, Bud Dry Ice, or the like; we're talking microbrews and imports.

Kells. 112 SW Second Ave. ☎ **503/227-4057.**

Located in Old Town, Kells is a traditional Irish pub and restaurant. In addition to pulling a good pint of Guinness, the pub has the most extensive Scotch whiskey list on the West Coast. You can hear live music here every night.

GAY BARS

The area around the intersection of SW Stark Street and West Burnside Street has the largest concentration of gay bars in Portland. These include **C. C. Slaughter's,** 1014 SW Stark St. (☎ **503/248-9135**), **Eagle Tavern,** 1300 W. Burnside St. (☎ **503/241-0105**), **Scandal's Tavern,** 1038 SW Stark St. (☎ **503/227-5887**), and **Silverado,** 1217 SW Stark St. (☎ **503/244-4493**). Also in this same area, at the corner of Stark Street and 10th Avenue is **Panorama** (☎ **503/221-RAMA**), a dance club popular with both gays and straights.

4 More Entertainment

MOVIES

Portland brewpub magnates, the McMenamin brothers, have hit upon a novel way to sell their craft ales, in movie pubs. Although it's often hard to concentrate on the movies being screened, it's always a lot of fun to attend a show. The **Bagdad Theater and Pub**, 3702 SE Hawthorne Blvd. (☎ **503/230-0895**), a restored classic Arabian Nights movie palace, shows second-run films and pours more than 20 microbrews at the bar. There's good pizza by the slice to go with your brew and a separate non-theater pub. The **Mission Theater and Pub,** 1624 NW Glisan St. (☎ **503/223-4031**), was the McMenamin brothers' first theater pub. The movies shown are recent releases that have played the main theaters but have not yet made it onto video.

Located in the heart of downtown, the **Koin Center,** Third Avenue and Clay Street (☎ **503/243-3516**), a six-plex, is Portland's main theater for first-run, foreign, and independent films. Buy tickets early—screening rooms here are small and often sell out. **Cinema 21,** 616 NW 21st Ave. (☎ **503/223-4515**), is a reliable art-film house screening more daring films than make it to the Koin Center. This is also where you can catch animation festivals and the occasional revival of an obscure classic. The **Northwest Film Center,** 1219 SW Park Ave. (☎ **503/221-1156**), affiliated with the Portland Art Museum, is a repertory cinema that schedules an eclectic blend of classics, foreign films, daring avant-garde films, documentaries, visiting artist programs, and thematic series. There's no telling what might turn up on a given night.

POOL

Uptown Billiard Club. 120 NW 23rd Ave. ☎ **503/226-6909.**

Elegant and tasteful, this second-floor billiard parlor has high quality tables (and prices to match) and attracts a wide mix of people from the Nob Hill neighborhood along with pool players from around the city.

Excursions from Portland

20

Portland likes to boast about how close it is to both mountains and ocean, and no visit would be complete without a trip or two into the countryside. In 1½ hours you can be walking on a Pacific Ocean beach or skiing in the Cascade Range. In fact, you'll even have this latter choice in the middle of summer, when there is still lift-accessed snow skiing on Mount Hood. A drive through the Columbia River Gorge, a National Scenic Area is an absolute must. If wine is your interest, you can spend a day visiting wineries and driving through the rolling farmland that enticed pioneers to travel the Oregon Trail beginning in the 1840s.

1 Mount Hood Loop

If you have time for only one excursion from Portland, I strongly urge you to do the Mount Hood Loop. This is a long trip, so start your day as early as possible.

To begin your trip, take I-84 east out of Portland. Sixteen miles from downtown, take the second Troutdale exit onto the **Columbia River Scenic Highway** (U.S. 30), which was opened in 1915. The highway is an engineering marvel, but it is dwarfed by the spectacular vistas that present themselves whenever the scenic road emerges from the dark forest. To learn more about the road and how it was built, stop at **Vista House,** 733 feet above the river on **Crown Point.** There are informative displays with old photos and a spectacular view of the gorge, including **Beacon Rock,** an 800-foot-tall monolith on the far side of the river.

Between Troutdale and Ainsworth State Park, 22 miles east, the road passes nine waterfalls and six state parks. Latourelle, Shepherds Dell, Bridal Veil, Wahkeena, Horsetail, Oneonta, Multnomah—the names of the falls evoke the Native American and pioneer heritage of this region. Of all the falls, **Multnomah** is the most famous. At 620 feet from the lip to the pool, it's the tallest waterfall in Oregon.

The next stop on your tour should be the **Bonneville Lock and Dam.** Some of the dam's most important features, and the attractions drawing thousands of visitors each year, are the fish ladders. These ladders allow salmon and other anadromous fish (fish that are spawned in freshwater, mature in saltwater, and return to freshwater to spawn) to migrate upstream. Underwater windows permit visitors to see fish as they pass through the ladders. Visit the adjacent fish hatchery to see how trout, salmon, and sturgeon are raised before they are released into the river. June and September are the best months to observe salmon at Bonneville Dam's fish ladder.

This is the first of many dams on the Columbia River and, along with the other dams, is currently the focus of a heated environmental debate over saving the region's dwindling native wild salmon populations. Despite fish ladders and fish hatcheries, salmon have been fighting a losing upstream battle for survival. Adult salmon heading upstream to spawn have to contend with fish ladders, fishermen (both commercial and sport), and spawning beds that are sometimes destroyed or silted up, often by the common practice of clear-cutting timber from steep mountainsides. Among the perils faced by young salmon heading downstream are slow, warm waters that delay the journey to the Pacific Ocean, electrical turbines in dams (these kill countless numbers of fish), and irrigation culverts that often lead salmon out into farm fields. With many populations now listed as threatened species (a step below endangered species), a plan for salmon survival is being hammered out. It is hoped that the dams that once brought prosperity and cheap electricity to the Northwest won't bring about the demise of the salmon.

Not far past the dam is the **Bridge of the Gods,** which connects Oregon to Washington at the site where an old Indian legend says a natural bridge once stood. Because of the unusual formation of rocks in the river at this site, as well as the frequent volcanic activity here in the past, geologists tend to believe the legend.

On the Washington side of the Columbia River, east of the Bridge of the Gods, is the **Columbia Gorge Interpretive Center,** 990 SW Rock Creek Dr., Stevenson (☎ **509/427-8211**). This modern and architecturally striking museum is the single best introduction to the natural and human history of the Columbia Gorge and has an awesome view (when it's not cloudy). Exhibits focus on the Gorge's early Native American inhabitants and the development of the area by white settlers. A relic here that you can't miss is a 37-foot-high replica of a 19th-century fishwheel, which gives an understanding of how salmon runs have been threatened in the past as well as in the present. Admission is $6 for adults, $5 for seniors and students, $4 for children 6 to 12, and free for children 4 and under. The Center is open daily from 10am to 5pm.

Just beyond Bridge of the Gods on the Oregon side are the **Cascade Locks.** These navigational locks were built to enable river traffic to avoid the treacherous passage through the cascades here. In earlier years, many boats were portaged around the cascades instead of attempting the dangerous trip. When the locks were opened in 1896, they made traveling between the Dalles and Portland much easier. But the completion of the Columbia River Scenic Highway in 1915 made the trip even easier by land. With the construction of the Bonneville Dam, the cascades were flooded and the locks became superfluous.

There are two small museums here at the locks, one of which also holds the ticket office for the stern-wheeler *Columbia Gorge* (☎ **503/223-3928**), which makes regular trips on the river all summer.

Anyone who boardsails has likely heard of the town of **Hood River.** This section of the Columbia River is one of the most popular boardsailing spots in the world because of the strong winds that come rushing down the gorge. Almost every other car in this once-sleepy little town has a sailboard on the roof. If you want to try this thrilling sport yourself, stop by one of the many sailboard shops downtown for rental information.

If you are staying overnight on the loop, you might want to consider getting out of your car and riding the rails. The **Mount Hood Railroad,** 110 Railroad Ave. (☎ **541/386-3556**), operates its Fruit Blossom Special from mid-April to Christmas. The cars that carry you up the Hood River are vintage Pullman coaches, and the

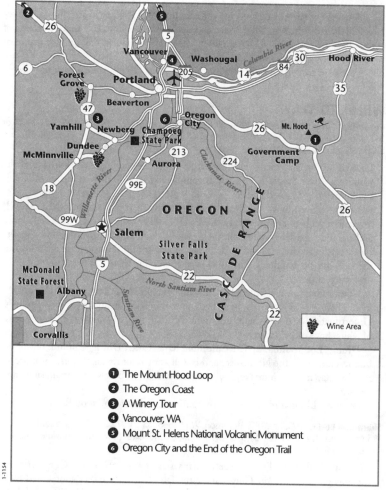

1. The Mount Hood Loop
2. The Oregon Coast
3. A Winery Tour
4. Vancouver, WA
5. Mount St. Helens National Volcanic Monument
6. Oregon City and the End of the Oregon Trail

Mount Hood Railroad Depot is a National Historic Site. Departures are at 10am and 3pm. The trip lasts 4 hours and costs $21.95 for adults, $18.95 for seniors, and $13.95 for children 2 to 12. In summer and early fall, the train runs daily except Monday, and in late spring it runs Wednesday through Sunday, changing to weekends only in the colder months.

From Hood River, turn south on Oregon Hwy. 35, passing through thousands of acres of apple and pear orchards. Every fall, roadside stands in this area sell fresh fruit, butter, and juice. The orchards are especially beautiful in the spring, when the trees are in bloom. No matter what time of year, you will have the snow-covered peak of Mount Hood in view as you drive through the orchards, making them all the more spectacular.

Just after Hwy. 35 merges into U.S. 26, turn right onto the road to **Timberline Lodge.** As the name implies, this is the timberline, and a walk on one of the trails in its vicinity will lead you through wildflower-filled meadows in summer. Surprisingly, you can also ski here all summer on a glacier above the lodge.

Between Government Camp and the community of Zig Zag, watch for the marker beside the road showing the western end of the **Barlow Trail toll road** (a section of the Oregon Trail) around Mount Hood. There is a reproduction of the gate that once stood on this spot, and you can still see the trail itself.

To return to Portland just stay on Oregon Hwy. 26 all the way back to town or follow the signs for I-84.

WHERE TO STAY

Columbia Gorge Hotel. 4000 Westcliff Dr., Hood River, OR 97031. ☎ **800/345-1921** or 541/386-5566. Fax 541/387-5414. 42 rms. TV TEL. $150–$250 double (including five-course breakfast). AE, DC, DISC, MC, V.

Located just west of the town of Hood River off I-84 and opened shortly after the Columbia River Scenic Highway was completed in 1915, this little oasis of luxury was completely restored in 1989 and today offers the same genteel atmosphere that was once enjoyed by the likes of Rudolph Valentino and Clara Bow. With its yellow stucco walls and red-tile roofs, this hotel would be right at home in Beverly Hills, and the hotel gardens could hold their own in Victoria, British Columbia. Despite the attractive furnishings and gardens, it is almost impossible to notice anything but the view out the windows. The hotel is perched more than 200 feet above the river on a steep cliff.

Guest rooms are all a little different, with a mixture of antique and classic furnishings. There are canopy beds, brass beds, and even some hand-carved wooden beds. Unfortunately, many of the rooms are rather cramped, as are the bathrooms, most of which have older fixtures.

Dining/Entertainment: The **Columbia River Court Dining Room** is one of the best restaurants in the Northwest, and is well known for its four-course farm breakfast. Evening meals feature Northwest cuisine with an emphasis on salmon, lamb, and venison.

Services: Limited room service, complimentary shuttle to Hood River.

Skamania Lodge. P.O. Box 189, Stevenson, WA 98648. ☎ **800/221-7117** or 509/427-7700. 195 rms, 6 suites. A/C TV TEL. $1,355–$210 double; $240 suites (lower rates in winter). AE, CB, DC, DISC, MC, V.

Skamania Lodge has the most spectacular vistas of any hotel in the Gorge. It's also the only golf resort in the Gorge, and although golf seems to be the preferred sport around here, the hotel is well situated whether you brought your sailboard, hiking boots, or mountain bike. This is a full-service resort and conference hotel catering almost exclusively to groups and consequently it can feel too crowded for a romantic getaway. The interior decor is classically rustic with lots of rock and natural wood. In the cathedral-ceilinged lobby, huge windows take in the best view on the property. Big wicker chairs are set by the stone fireplace, so you can curl up by the fire on a cold winter night. Throughout the hotel there are Northwest Indian artworks and artifacts on display.

If you should opt for a fireplace room, you won't have to leave your bed to enjoy a fire. The river-view guest rooms are only slightly more expensive than the forest-view rooms, which look out over the huge parking lot as well as the forest.

Dining/Entertainment: Though the wood floors and stone walls can make the lodge's restaurant rather noisy, the casual Northwest cuisine is excellent (and the view of the Gorge amazing). Adjacent to the dining room is a lounge with a large, free-standing stone fireplace.

Services: Room service, concierge.

The Columbia Gorge

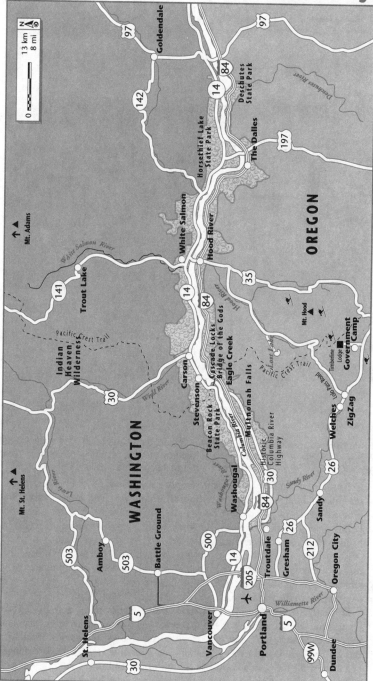

Mount Hood

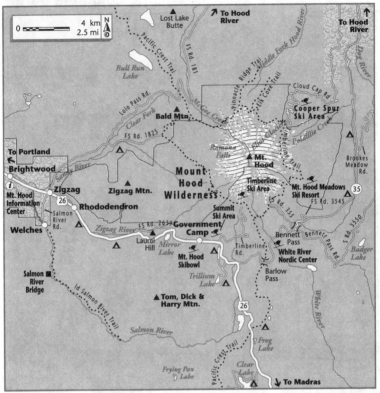

Facilities: 18-hole golf course, tennis courts, swimming pool, whirlpool, exercise facility, nature trails, volleyball court.

Timberline Lodge. Timberline, OR 97028. ☎ **800/547-1406** or 503/231-7979. Fax 503/272-3710. 59 rms (49 with private bath). $65 double without bath; $95–$165 double with bath. AE, DISC, MC, V. Snow-park permit required in winter, but hotel will loan you one.

Constructed during the Great Depression of the 1930s as a WPA project, this classic Alpine ski lodge overflows with craftsmanship. The grand stone fireplace, huge exposed beams, and wide plank floors of the lobby impress every first-time visitor. Details are not overlooked either. Wood carvings, imaginative wrought-iron fixtures, hand-hooked rugs, and handmade furniture complete the rustic picture.

Rooms vary in size considerably, with the smallest rooms lacking private bathrooms. However, no matter which room you stay in, you'll be surrounded by the same rustic furnishings. Unfortunately room windows are not very large, but you can always retire to the Ram's Head lounge for a better view of Mount Hood.

Dining/Entertainment: The **Cascade Dining Room** enjoys a nearly legendary reputation. The tables are rustic and the windows are small (which limits views), but the Northwest-style food is superb, if a bit pricey. There is also a casual snack bar in the Wy'East Day Lodge across the parking lot. The **Blue Ox Bar** is a dark dungeon of a place while the **Ram's Head Bar** is a more open and airy spot.

Services: Fire starters for rooms with fireplaces, guided hotel tours.

Facilities: Ski lifts, ski school and rentals, outdoor swimming pool, hiking trails, gift shop, coin laundry.

2 The Oregon Coast

The spectacular Oregon coast is this state's single largest tourist attraction and favorite summer vacation destination. If you'd like to catch a glimpse of one of the most beautiful coastlines in the United States, you're in luck. The beach is less than two hours away and offers everything from rugged coves to long sandy beaches, artists' communities to classic family beach towns.

The quickest route from Portland to the Oregon coast is via U.S. 26, also called the Sunset Highway. Just before reaching the junction with U.S. 101, watch for a sign marking the **world's largest Sitka spruce tree.** This giant is located in a small park just off the highway. Trees of this size were once common throughout the Coast Range, but almost all have now been cut down. The fight to preserve the remaining big trees is a bitter one that has divided the citizens of Oregon.

If you've got kids with you, turn north at the junction with U.S. 101 and head into **Seaside,** the coast's most traditional beach town (saltwater taffy, arcade games, the works). Otherwise, head south and watch for the turnoff to **Ecola Beach State Park.** Located just north of the town of Cannon Beach, this park provides some of the most spectacular views on the coast. Just offshore is **Haystack Rock,** a massive 235-feet-tall rock island that is the most photographed rock on the coast. Here in the park there are stands of old-growth spruce, hemlock, and Douglas fir, and several trails offer a chance to walk through this lush forest. The park's **Indian Beach** is popular with wetsuit-wearing surfers.

Stretching out to the south of the park is **Cannon Beach,** known as the Provincetown or Carmel of the Northwest, depending on which coast you hail from. The town is named for the cannon of the USS *Shark,* which washed ashore here after the ship sank in 1849. Haystack Rock, only a few feet out from the beach, is popular with beachcombers and tide-pool explorers. In town, there are many art galleries and interesting shops, even a popular little theater (the Coaster Theater). Every summer the **Cannon Beach Sandcastle Contest** attracts sand sculptors and thousands of appreciative viewers. Any time of year, you'll find the winds here ideal for kite flying.

Heading south out of Cannon Beach will bring you to the rugged and remote **Oswald West State Park,** named for the governor who promoted legislation to preserve all Oregon beaches as public property. The beach is in a cove that can only be reached by walking a few hundred yards through dense rain forest; once you're there, all you'll hear is the crashing of the surf. The beach is strewn with huge driftwood logs that give it a wild look. High bluffs rise up at both ends of the cove and it is possible to hike to the top of them. There are plenty of picnic tables and a campground for tent campers only. This is another popular surfing spot.

U.S. 101 continues south from Oswald West State Park and climbs up over **Neahkahnie Mountain.** Legend has it that at the base of this oceanside mountain, the survivors of a wrecked Spanish galleon buried a fortune in gold. Keep your eyes open for elk, which frequently graze in the meadows here.

Just below this windswept mountain is the quiet resort village of **Manzanita.** Tucked under the fir, spruce, and hemlock trees are the summer homes of some of Portland's wealthier residents. There is also a long stretch of sandy beach at the foot of the village.

Tillamook Bay is one of the largest bays on the Oregon coast and at its north end is the small town of Garibaldi, which is a popular sportfishing spot. If you aren't an angler, you can still go for a cruise either around the bay or to look for whales.

Just before reaching the busy town of **Tillamook,** you will come to the **Tillamook Cheese Factory.** This region is one of Oregon's main dairy-farming areas, and much of the milk is turned into cheddar cheese and butter. The first cheese factory opened

The Northern Oregon Coast

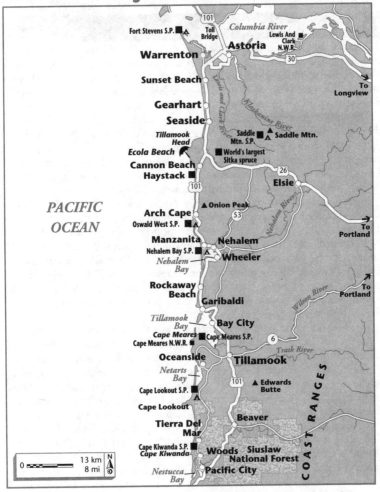

here in 1894. Today you can watch the cheese-making process through large windows. The cheese-factory store is a busy place, but the lines move quickly and you can be on your way to the next picnic area with an assortment of tasty cheeses or some ice cream cones.

From Tillamook the **Three Capes Scenic Route** leads to Cape Meares, Cape Lookout, and Cape Kiwanda, all of which provide stunning vistas of rocky cliffs, misty mountains, and booming surf. As the name implies, this is a very scenic stretch of road, and there are plenty of places to stop and enjoy the views and the beaches.

Cape Meares State Park perches high atop the cape, with the Cape Meares lighthouse just a short walk from the parking lot. This lighthouse, 200 feet above the water, was built in 1890. Today it has been replaced by an automated light a few feet away. Be sure to visit the **octopus tree** here in the park. This Sitka spruce has been twisted and sculpted by harsh weather.

As you come down from the cape, you will come to the village of **Oceanside**, which clings to the steep mountainsides of a small cove. One tavern and one restaurant are the only commercial establishments, and that's the way folks here like it.

South of Oceanside, the road runs along a flat stretch of beach before reaching **Cape Lookout State Park.** Cape Lookout, a steep forested ridge jutting out into the Pacific, is an excellent place for whale watching in the spring. A trail leads from either the main (lower) parking area or the parking area at the top of the ridge out to the end of the point. From the upper parking lot it is a 5-mile round trip to the point.

At Sandlake Junction, about 14 miles south of Oceanside, turn left and you will return to U.S. 101. Head north to **Tillamook,** where Ore. 6 heads east toward Portland. This road is subject to landslides and is sometimes closed, so be sure to ask in Tillamook before heading east. Ore. 6 joins U.S. 26 about 25 miles west of Portland. Allow about 2¹/₂ hours to get back from Tillamook.

3 A Winery Tour

For many years now Oregon wines have been winning awards for their outstanding quality. This isn't surprising when you realize that Oregon is on the same latitude as France's wine-growing regions. The climate is also very similar—cool, wet winters and springs and long, dry summers with warm days and cool nights. These are ideal conditions for growing wine grapes, and local vineyards are making the most of a good situation.

A "Discover Oregon Wineries" brochure describing more than 70 Oregon wineries is available from the **Oregon Winegrowers' Association,** 1200 NW Front Ave., Suite 400, Portland, OR 97209 (☎ **800/242-2363**), or at the **Portland Oregon Visitors Association Information Center,** Two World Trade Center, 25 SW Salmon St. (☎ **800/345-3214** or 503/222-2223; Web site: www.pova.com). A good many wineries are within an hour or two of Portland, and consequently a day of driving from one winery to another makes for a pleasant outing. I suggest picking four or five that sound interesting and then mapping out the best routes among them. A trip through wine country is a chance to see the fertile valleys that lured pioneers across the Oregon Trail. For more information about the Oregon wine scene, including a calendar of winery events, pick up a copy of *Oregon Wine,* a monthly newspaper, in any local wine shop, or contact the **Oregon Wine Press,** 644 SE 20th Ave., Portland, OR 97214 (☎ **503/232-7607**). With summer festivals a big part of the Oregon winery scene, you can enjoy picnics while listening to live music at many vineyards.

The trip outlined below takes in some of the region's best wineries and most beautiful countryside. Allow yourself at least half a day for a winery tour. I recommend taking along a picnic lunch, which you can supplement with a wine purchase. Most wineries have picnic tables, and many of them have lovely views.

To begin your winery tour, head west out of Portland on U.S. 26 (Sunset Highway) and then take Ore. 6 toward Tillamook. After a few miles on this two-lane highway, watch for signs indicating a left turn onto Ore. 8 toward Forest Grove. Heading back east on this road, watch for a sign to **Laurel Ridge Winery,** 46350 NW David Hill Rd. (☎ **503/359-5436**). This is one of the oldest wineries in Oregon. The first grapes were planted here in the late 1800s, but Prohibition interrupted wine production and the vineyard was slow to return to wine making. However, today, Laurel Hill produces excellent Pinot Noir, Gewürztraminer, Semillon, Sylvaner, and Riesling. Laurel Ridge also produces excellent sparkling wine by the *méthode champagnoise.* The winery is open February through December daily from noon to 5pm.

Continue into Forest Grove on Ore. 8 and then turn right onto Ore. 47 toward Yamhill. Just south of town, you'll see signs for **Montinore Vineyards,** 3663 SW Dilley Rd. (☎ **503/359-5012**). This is the largest wine producer in the state and enjoys an enviable location with sweeping views across the Tualatin Valley to the Cascade Range. A tree-lined drive leads up to a Victorian mansion. With more than a dozen wines available and a large tasting room and gift shop, Montinore is popular with tour groups. Landscaped grounds invite a stroll or picnic after tasting a few wines. Pinot Noir, Pinot Gris, Chardonnay, and Riesling are among the more popular wines produced here. The winery is open daily from noon to 5pm.

Back on Ore. 47, continue south to the small town of Yamhill where you turn east on Ore. 240. After a few miles, watch for signs to **Erath Winery,** 9009 NE Worden Hill Rd. (☎ 800/KEW-WINE). Situated on 45 acres above the town of Dundee, this winery has one of the most spectacular settings in the region. The cedar-shingled buildings of the winery are set between forest and vineyard, and the views are stunning. Wines produced here include Pinot Noir, Riesling, Gewürztraminer, Chardonnay, Cabernet Sauvignon, and a brut. The winery is open May 15 to October 15 daily from 10:30am to 5:30pm, and the rest of the year daily from 11am to 5pm.

At the bottom of the Erath driveway, you'll find a shady little park that makes a good picnic spot if you haven't already eaten at one of the wineries.

Head downhill into the valley from Erath and you'll soon see a sign for **Lange Winery,** 18380 NE Buena Vista Rd. (☎ 503/538-6476). This is a tiny winery with only a few acres of its own grapes, and the tasting room is the basement of the owners' home. However, the wines produced here are some of the best in the state. Pinot Noir, Chardonnay, and Pinot Gris are specialties. The winery is open June through November daily from 11am to 6pm, and December through May weekends from noon to 5pm and weekdays by chance or appointment.

Continuing down into the valley again, you will come to the town of Dundee and U.S. Hwy. 99W. Turn right on the highway and a few miles out of town you'll see the sign for **Sokol Blosser Winery,** 5000 NE Sokol Blosser Lane (☎ 800/582-6668 or 503/864-2282), which sits high on a hill overlooking the valley. This is one of the larger wineries in Oregon and maintains a spacious tasting room and gift shop. On any given day, three wines will be available for tasting. These might include Pinot Noir, Chardonnay, Gewürztraminer, Riesling, or Muller-Thurgau. The winery is open May through October daily from 10:30am to 5:30pm, and November through April daily from 11am to 5pm.

Directly across the street from Sokol Blosser's driveway, you'll see **Laube Orchards.** This former roadside fruit stand is now a full-fledged specialty foods shop featuring Oregon products. Stop in and stock up on boysenberry jam or roasted hazelnuts. If it is late in the day, you might want to stop for dinner in Dundee, which has a couple of excellent restaurants. **Tina's,** 760 Hwy. 99W (☎ 503/538-8880), is a tiny place with a menu that is limited to about half a dozen wellprepared dishes. **Red Hills Provincial Dining,** 276 Hwy. 99W (☎ 503/538-8224), in an old house beside the highway, serves a combination of Northwest and Mediterranean cuisine. The dinner menu here changes every 2 weeks, and reservations are highly recommended.

Should you wish to spend the night, there are also quite a few bed-and-breakfast inns in the area. Contact the **McMinnville Chamber of Commerce,** 417 N. Adams St., McMinnville, OR 97128 (☎ 503/472-6196), for a list of area B&Bs. There are also motels in McMinnville and Newberg. To return to Portland, just head east on U.S. Hwy. 99W.

4 Vancouver, Washington

Because Vancouver, Washington, is part of the Portland metropolitan area and because it bears the same name as both a large island and a city in Canada, it is often overlooked by visitors to the Northwest. However, the city has several historic sites and other attractions that make it a good day-long excursion from Portland. The first three attractions listed here are all in the one-square-mile Central Park, which is located just east of I-5 (take the East Mill Plain Boulevard exit just after you cross the bridge into Washington).

It was here in Vancouver that much of the Northwest's important early pioneer history unfolded at the Hudson's Bay Company's (HBC) Fort Vancouver. The HBC, a British company, came to the Northwest in search of furs and, for most of the first half of the 19th century, was the only authority in this remote region. Fur trappers, mountain men, missionaries, explorers, and settlers all made Fort Vancouver their first stop in Oregon. Today the **Fort Vancouver National Historic Site,** 1501 E. Evergreen Blvd. (☎ 360/696-7655), houses several reconstructed buildings that are furnished as they might have been in the middle of the 19th century (open daily 9am to 5pm, until 4pm in the winter; admission $2 in summer, free in winter).

After the British gave up Fort Vancouver, it became the site of the Vancouver Barracks U.S. military post, and stately homes were built for the officers of the post. These buildings are now preserved as the Officers' Row National Historic District. You can stroll along admiring the well-kept homes, and then stop in at the **Grant House Folk Art Center** (☎ 360/694-5252), which is named for Pres. Ulysses S. Grant, who was stationed here as quartermaster in the 1850s. Free and open Tuesday through Sunday from 10am to 5pm, this building was the first commanding officer's quarters. In addition to the art center, there is a cafe that serves good lunches. Further along Officers' Row, you'll find the **George C. Marshall House** (☎ 360/693-3103), which is also free and open to the public. This Victorian-style building replaced the Grant House as the commanding officer's quarters. The Marshall House is open Monday through Friday from 9am to 5pm. You'll find the tree-shaded row of 21 homes just north of Fort Vancouver.

A very different piece of history is preserved at **Pearson Air Museum,** 1115 E. Fifth St. (☎ 360/694-7026), on the far side of Fort Vancouver from Officers' Row. This airfield was established in 1905 and is the oldest operating airfield in the United States. Dozens of vintage aircraft, including several World War I–era biplanes and the plane that made the first transpacific flight, are on display in a large hangar. The museum is open Wednesday through Sunday from noon to 5pm; admission is $4 for adults, $3 for seniors, and $1.50 for students.

In the town of **Washougal,** 16 miles east of Vancouver on Wash. 14, you can visit the **Pendleton Woolen Mills and Outlet Shop,** 2 17th St., Washougal (☎ 360/835-2131), and see how the famous wool blankets and classic wool fashions are made. The store is open Monday through Friday from 8am to 5pm and Saturday from 9am to 5pm, with free mill tours offered Monday through Friday at 9, 10, and 11am, and 1:30pm.

Railroading buffs may want to drive north 10 miles to the town of Battle Ground and take a ride on the diesel-powered **Lewis River Excursion Train,** which has its depot at 1000 E. Main St. in Battle Ground (☎ 360/687-2626). The 2-hour excursions run from Battle Ground to Moulton Falls County Park, where there is a 20-minute stop for passengers to view the falls. There are also dinner train excursions. Call ahead for the days and hours of scheduled trips. Tickets for the regular excursion are $10 for adults and $5 for children.

North of Vancouver 23 miles in the town of Woodland are the **Hulda Klager Lilac Gardens,** 115 S. Pekin Rd., Woodland (☎ 360/225-8996). Between late April and Mother's Day each year, these gardens burst into color and the fragrance of lilacs hangs in the air. The gardens are open daily from dawn to dusk and admission is $1.

Ten miles east of Woodland off NE Cedar Creek Road, you'll find the **Cedar Creek Grist Mill,** Grist Mill Road (☎ **360/225-9552**), the only remaining 19th-century grist mill in Washington. Built in 1876, the mill was restored over a 10-year period, and in 1989, it once again became functional. When the mill is open, volunteers demonstrate how wheat is ground into flour. Hours of operation are Saturday from 1 to 4pm and Sunday from 2 to 4pm. Admission is by donation.

5 Mount St. Helens National Volcanic Monument

Once it was regarded as the most perfect of the Cascade peaks, a snow-covered cone rising above lush forests, but on May 18, 1980, all that changed when Mount St. Helens erupted with a violent explosion. Today the area surrounding the volcano is designated the Mount St. Helens National Volcanic Monument.

The best place to start an exploration of the monument is at the **Mount St. Helens Visitor Center at Silver Lake** (☎ **360/274-2100**), which is located at Silver Lake, 5 miles east of Castle Rock on Wash. 504. The visitor center houses extensive exhibits on the eruption and its effects on the region. Summer hours at the visitor center are daily from 9am to 5pm. Admission is $8 per person, as it is for any developed area within Mount St. Helens National Volcanic Monument. However, once paid, this admission will get you into all the other monument visitor centers. Before even reaching this center, you can stop and watch a 25-minute, 70mm film about the eruption at the **Mount St. Helens Cinedome Theater** (☎ **360/274-8000**), which is located at exit 49 off of I-5 (tickets $5 adults, $4 seniors and children).

Continuing east from the visitor center, you'll come to the **Hoffstadt Bluffs Visitor Center** (☎ **800/752-8439**) at milepost 27 (open daily 9am to 9pm in summer; daily 10am to 4pm in winter), which has a snack bar and is the take-off site for helicopter flights over Mount St. Helens ($69). A few miles farther, just past milepost 33, you'll arrive at the **Forest Learning Center** (☎ **360/414-3439**), which is open May through October daily 10am to 6pm. This is primarily a promotional center for the timber industry but does show a short but fascinating video about the eruption in a theater designed to resemble an ash-covered landscape. There are also displays on how forests destroyed by the blast have been replanted. Outside the center you can look down on a herd of elk that live in the Toutle River valley far below.

The **Coldwater Ridge Visitor Center** (☎ **360/274-2131**), which is at milepost 47 on Wash. 504, only 8 miles from the crater is the second monument visitor center. This center features interpretive displays on the events leading up to the eruption and the subsequent slow regeneration of life around the volcano. Hours are May through September daily 10am to 6pm, and October through April daily 9am to 5pm. Here at Coldwater Ridge, you'll also find a picnic area, interpretive trail, a restaurant, and a boat launch at Coldwater Lake.

The newest visitor center, the **Johnston Ridge Observatory** (☎ **360/274-2140**), is a little bit farther up this same road. Built into the mountainside and designed to blend into the landscape, this observatory houses the equipment that is still used to monitor activity within Mount St. Helens. This view from here is stupendous. The observatory is open daily from 9am to 6pm.

Though these three centers can give you an idea of the power of the explosion that blew off this mountain's top, you need to drive around to the monument's east side for a close-up view of how the eruption effected the surrounding lands. It is here that you will see the forest that was blown down by the eruption. For the best views, take U.S. 12 east from exit 68 off I-5. In Randle, head south on Local Route 25 and then take Local Route 26. The **Woods Creek Information Center,** on Route 25 just

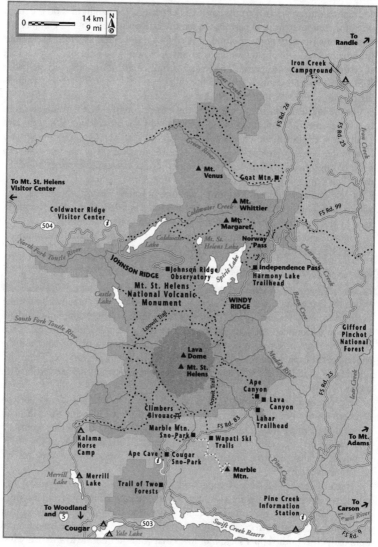

before the junction with Route 26, has information on this part of the monument. Route 26 travels through mile after mile of blown-down trees, and though the sight of the thousands of trees that were felled by a single blast is quite bleak, it reminds one of the awesome power of nature. More than a decade after the eruption, life is slowly returning to this devastated forest. At Meta Lake, Route 26 joins Route 99, which continues to the **Windy Ridge Viewpoint,** where visitors get their closest look at the crater. Below Windy Ridge lies Spirit Lake, which was once one of the most popular summer vacation spots in the Washington Cascades. Today the lake is desolate and lifeless.

If you are an experienced hiker in good physical condition, you may want to consider climbing to the top of Mount St. Helens. It is an 8- to 10-hour, 10-mile hike and can require an ice ax. Permits cost $15 per person. The trailhead is on the south side of the monument, and permits are required between May 15 and October 31. Because this is a very popular climb, it is advisable to request a permit in advance (summer weekends book up months in advance). However, you can also try your luck at getting an unreserved permit on the day of your climb. These are issued at **Jack's Restaurant and Store** on Wash. 503 five miles west of Cougar. To request a climbing permit, phone ☎ **360/247-3900.**

On the south side of the monument, you can explore the **Ape Cave,** a lava tube that was formed 1,900 years ago when lava poured from the volcano. When the lava finally stopped flowing, it left a 2-mile-long cave that is the longest continuous lava tube in the Western Hemisphere. At the Apes Headquarters, you can rent a lantern for exploring the cave on your own, or join a regular ranger-led exploration of the cave. This center is open daily from late May through September.

Hikers who aren't doing the climb to the summit will find many other hiking trails within the monument, some in blast zones and some in forests that were left undamaged by the eruption. Ask at any visitor center for trail information.

For more information, contact **Mount St. Helens National Volcanic Monument,** 42218 NE Yale Bridge Rd., Amboy, WA 98601 (☎ **360/247-3900**).

6 Oregon City & the End of the Oregon Trail

When the first white settlers began crossing the Oregon Trail in the early 1840s, their destination was Oregon City and the fertile Willamette Valley. At the time Portland had yet to be founded and Oregon City, set beside powerful Willamette Falls, was the largest town in Oregon. However, with the development of Portland and the shifting of the capital to Salem, Oregon City began to lose its importance. Today this is primarily an industrial town, though one steeped in Oregon history and well worth a visit.

To get to Oregon City from Portland, you can take I-5 south to I-205 east or you can head south from downtown Portland on SW Riverside Drive and drive through the wealthy suburbs of Lake Oswego and West Linn. Once in Oregon City, your first stop should be just south of town at the **Willamette Falls overlook** on Ore. 99E. Though the falls have been much changed by industry over the years, they are still an impressive sight.

Oregon City is divided into upper and lower sections by a steep bluff. A free municipal elevator connects the two halves of the city and affords a great view from its observation area at the top of the bluff. You'll find the 100-foot-tall elevator at the corner of Seventh Street and Railroad Avenue. Service is available from 6am to 8pm daily. It is in the upper section of town that you will find the town's many historic homes.

Oregon City's most famous citizen was retired Hudson's Bay Company chief factor John McLoughlin, who helped found Oregon City in 1829. By the 1840s, immigrants were pouring into Oregon, and McLoughlin provided food, seeds, and tools to many. Upon retirement in 1846, McLoughlin moved to Oregon City, where he built what was at that time the most luxurious home in Oregon. Today the **McLoughlin House,** 713 Center St. (☎ **503/656-5146**), is a National Historic Site and is open to the public. The house is furnished as it would have been in McLoughlin's days and includes many original pieces. The house is open Tuesday through Saturday from 10am to 5pm (4pm in winter) and on Sunday from 1 to 4pm. Admission is $3 for adults, $2.50 for senior citizens, and $1 for children.

Several other Oregon City historical homes are also open to the public. The **Clackamas County Historical Museum,** 211 Tumwater Dr. (☎ **503/655-5574**), houses collections of historic memorabilia and old photos from this area. The museum is open Monday through Friday from 10am to 4pm and Saturday and Sunday from 1 to 5pm. Admission is $3.50 for adults, $2.50 for senior citizens and $1.50 for children ages 6 to 12. The **Stevens Crawford House,** 603 Sixth St. (☎ **503/655-2866**), is a foursquare-style home and is furnished with late 19th-century antiques. The house is open Tuesday through Sunday from 10am to 4pm (plus Monday from 1 to 4pm in summer). Admission is $3 adults, $2 seniors, and $1.50 children 6 to 12. The **Ermatinger House,** on the corner of Sixth and John Adams streets (☎ **503/557-9199**), is the town's oldest home. The hours are Saturday and Sunday from noon to 4pm. Admission is $2 for adults.

The story of the settlers who traveled the Oregon Trail is told at the **End of the Oregon Trail Interpretive Center,** 1726 Washington St. (☎ **503/657-9336**), which is designed to resemble three giant covered wagons. The center is open Monday through Saturday from 9am to 5pm and Sunday from 11am to 5pm; admission is $4.50 for adults, $2.50 for seniors and children 5 to 12. There are guided tours. During the summer of 1998 and thereafter, the history of the Oregon Trail will come alive at the interpretive center with the staging of the *Oregon Trail Pageant.* Performances are in July and early August.

Another interesting chapter in Oregon pioneer history is preserved 13 miles south of Oregon City in the town of **Aurora,** which was founded in 1855 as a Christian communal society. Similar in many ways to such more famous communal experiments as the Amana Colony and the Shaker communities, the Aurora Colony lasted slightly more than 20 years. Today Aurora is a National Historic District and the large old homes of the community's founders have been restored. Many of the old commercial buildings now house antiques stores, which are the main reason most people visit Aurora. You can learn about the history of Aurora at the **Old Aurora Colony Museum,** Second and Liberty streets (☎ **503/678-5754**). Between March and December, the museum is open Tuesday through Saturday from 10am to 4pm and on Sunday from noon to 4pm. Admission is $3.50 for adults, $3 for seniors, and $1.50 for children under 18.

On your way back to Portland, consider taking the **Canby ferry,** which is one of the last remaining ferries on the Willamette River. To take the ferry, head 4 miles north on Oregon Hwy. 99E to Canby and watch for ferry signs.

Appendix:
For Foreign Visitors

Although American trends have spread across Europe and other parts of the world to the extent that America may seem like familiar territory before your arrival, there are still many peculiarities and uniquely American situations that any foreign visitor will encounter.

1 Preparing for Your Trip

ENTRY REQUIREMENTS

Document Regulations   Citizens of Canada and Bermuda may enter the United States without visas, but they will need to show proof of nationality, the most common and hassle-free form of which is a passport.

The U.S. State Department has a **Visa Waiver Pilot Program** allowing citizens of certain countries to enter the United States without a visa for stays of fewer than 90 days of holiday travel. At press time these included Andorra, Argentina, Australia, Austria, Belgium, Brunei, Denmark, Finland, France, Germany, Iceland, Ireland, Italy, Japan, Liechtenstein, Luxembourg, Monaco, the Netherlands, New Zealand, Norway, San Marino, Spain, Sweden, Switzerland, and the United Kingdom. (The program as applied to the United Kingdom refers to British citizens who have the "unrestricted right of permanent abode in the United Kingdom," that is, citizens from England, Scotland, Wales, Northern Ireland, the Channel Islands, and the Isle of Man; and not, for example, citizens of the British Commonwealth of Pakistan.)

Citizens from these countries need only a valid passport and a round-trip air or cruise ticket in their possession upon arrival. If they first enter the United States, they may then visit Mexico, Canada, Bermuda, and/or the Caribbean islands and return to the United States without needing a visa. Further information is available from any U.S. embassy or consulate.

Citizens of countries other than those specified above, or those traveling to the United States for reasons or length of time outside the restrictions of the Visa Waiver program, or those who require waivers of inadmissibility must have two documents:

- a **valid passport,** with an expiration date at least 6 months later than the scheduled end of the visit to the United States. (Some countries are exceptions to the 6-month validity rule. Contact any U.S. embassy or consulate for complete information.)

- a **tourist visa,** available from the nearest U.S. consulate. To obtain a visa, the traveler must submit a completed application form (either in person or by mail) with a 1¹/₂-inch square photo and the required application fee. There may also be an issuance fee, depending on the type of visa and other factors. Usually you can obtain a visa right away or within 24 hours, but it may take longer during the summer rush period (June to August). If you cannot go in person, contact the nearest U.S. embassy or consulate for directions on applying by mail. Your travel agent or airline office may also be able to provide you with visa applications and instructions. The U.S. consulate or embassy that issues your visa will determine whether you will be issued a multiple- or single-entry visa. The Immigration and Naturalization Service officers at the port of entry in the United States will make an admission decision and determine your length of stay.

Medical Requirements   No inoculations are needed to enter the United States unless you are coming from, or have stopped over in, areas known to be suffering from epidemics, particularly of cholera or yellow fever.

If you have a disease requiring treatment with medications containing narcotics or drugs requiring a syringe, carry a valid signed prescription from your physician to allay any suspicions that you are smuggling drugs.

Customs   Every adult visitor may bring in free of duty: 1 liter of wine or hard liquor; 200 cigarettes or 100 cigars (but no cigars from Cuba) or 3 pounds of smoking tobacco; and $100 worth of gifts. These exemptions are offered to travelers who spend at least 72 hours in the United States and who have not claimed these exemptions within the preceding six months. It is altogether forbidden to bring into the country foodstuff (particularly cheese, fruit, cooked meats, and canned goods) and plants (vegetables, seeds, tropical plants, and so on). Foreign tourists may bring in or take out up to $10,000 in U.S. or foreign currency with no formalities; larger sums must be declared to Customs on entering or leaving.

INSURANCE

There is no national health system in the United States. Because the cost of medical care is extremely high, we strongly advise every traveler to secure health coverage before setting out.

You may want to take out a comprehensive travel policy that covers (for a relatively low premium) sickness or injury cost (medical, surgical, and hospital); loss or theft of your baggage; trip-cancellation costs; guarantee of bail in case you are arrested; costs of accident, repatriation, or death. Such packages (for example, "Europe Assistance" in Europe) are sold by automobile clubs at attractive rates, as well as by insurance companies and travel agencies.

MONEY

Currency & Exchange   The U.S. monetary system has a decimal base: 1 American dollar ($1) = 100 cents (100¢).

Dollar bills commonly come in $1 ("a buck"), $5, $10, $20, $50, and $100 denominations (the last two are not always welcome when paying for small purchases and are not accepted in taxis or subway ticket booths). There are also $2 bills (seldom encountered).

There are six denominations of coins: 1¢ (one cent, or "penny"), 5¢ (five cents, or "a nickel"), 10¢ (ten cents, or "a dime"), 25¢ (twenty-five cents, or "a quarter"), 50¢ (fifty cents, or "a half dollar"), and the rare $1 piece.

Traveler's Checks   Traveler's checks in U.S. dollar denominations are readily accepted at most hotels, motels, restaurants, and large stores.

But the best place to change traveler's checks is at a bank. Do not bring traveler's checks denominated in other currencies, with the possible exception of those in Canadian dollars. Because of the proximity of the Canadian border, many hotels, restaurants, and shops will accept Canadian currency.

Credit Cards   The method of payment most widely used is the credit card: Visa (BarclayCard in Britain), MasterCard (EuroCard in Europe, Access in Britain, Charges in Canada), American Express, Diners Club, Discover Card, and Carte Blanche. You can save yourself trouble by using "plastic money," rather than cash or traveler's checks in most hotels, motels, restaurants, and retail stores (a growing number of food and liquor stores now accept credit cards). You must have a credit card to rent a car. It can also be used as proof of identity (often carrying more weight than a passport), or as a "cash card," enabling you to draw money from banks that accept them.

Note: The "foreign-exchange bureaus" so common in Europe are rare except at airports in the United States and nonexistent outside major cities. Try to avoid having to change foreign money or traveler's checks not denominated in U.S. dollars at a small-town bank, or even a branch in a big city; in fact, leave any currency other than U.S. dollars at home—it may prove to be more of a nuisance to you than it's worth.

SAFETY

General   While tourist areas are generally safe, crime is on the increase everywhere, and U.S. urban areas tend to be less safe than those in Europe or Japan. Visitors should always be alert. This is particularly true of large U.S. cities. It is wise to ask the city's or area's tourist office if you are in doubt about which neighborhoods are safe.

Avoid deserted areas, especially at night. Don't enter a city park at night unless there is an event that attracts crowds—for example, performances in the amphitheater in Volunteer Park in Seattle or summer concerts at the Rose Garden amphitheater in Portland. Generally speaking, you can feel safe in areas where there are many people, and many open establishments.

Avoid carrying valuables with you on the street, and don't display expensive cameras or electronic equipment. Hold on to your pocketbook, and place your billfold in an inside pocket. In restaurants, theaters, and other public places, keep your possessions in sight.

Remember also that hotels are open to the public, and in a large hotel, security personnel may not be able to screen everyone entering. Always lock your room door—don't assume that once inside your hotel you are automatically safe and need no longer be aware of your surroundings.

Driving   Safety while driving is particularly important. Question your car-rental agency about personal safety, or ask for a brochure of traveler safety tips when you pick up your car. Obtain written directions, or a map with the route marked in red, from the agency showing how to reach your destination. And, if possible, arrive and depart during daylight hours.

Recently, more and more crime has involved cars and drivers. If you drive off a highway into a neighborhood that seems threatening, leave the area as quickly as possible. If you have an accident, even on a highway, remain inside your car with the doors locked until you assess the situation, or until the police arrive. If you are bumped from behind on the street or are involved in a minor accident with no injuries and the situation appears to be suspicious, motion to the other driver to follow you. Never get out of your car in such situations.

You can also keep a premade sign in your car that reads: Please follow this vehicle to report the accident. Show the sign to the other driver and go directly to the nearest police precinct, well-lighted service station, or all-night store.

If you see someone on the road who indicates a need for help, do not stop. Take note of the location, drive on to a well-lighted area, and telephone the police by dialing 911.

Park in well-lighted, well-traveled areas if possible. Always keep your car doors locked, whether attended or unattended. Look around you before you get in or out of your car, and never leave packages or valuables in sight. If someone attempts to rob you or steal your car, do not try to resist the thief/carjacker—report the incident to the police department immediately.

2 Getting to & Around the United States

Travelers from overseas can take advantage of **APEX** (advance purchase excursion) fares offered by all major U.S. and European carriers. Aside from these, attractive values are offered by **Icelandair** on flights from Luxembourg to New York and by **Virgin Atlantic Airways** from London to New York/Newark.

From Toronto, there are flights to Seattle and Portland on **Air Canada, American, Delta, Northwest, TWA,** and **United.** There are flights from Vancouver, B.C., to Seattle and Portland on **Air Canada** and **Horizon.**

Airlines traveling from London to Seattle and Portland are **American, Delta, Northwest, TWA,** and **United. British Airways** flies direct to Seattle from London.

From New Zealand and Australia, there are flights to Los Angeles on **Quantas** (☎ **131211** in Australia) and **Air New Zealand** (☎ **0800/737-000** in Auckland, or 3/379-5200 in Christchurch). **United** flies to Seattle from New Zealand and Australia, with a stop in Los Angeles or San Francisco.

Some large airlines (for example, **American, Delta, Northwest, TWA,** and **United**) offer transatlantic and transpacific travelers special discount tickets under the name **Visit USA,** allowing travel between any U.S. destination at minimum rates. These tickets are not on sale in the United States and must therefore be purchased before you leave your foreign point of departure. This system is the best, easiest, and fastest way to see the United States at low cost. You should obtain information well in advance from your travel agent or the office of the airline concerned, since the conditions attached to these discount tickets can be changed without advance notice.

The visitor arriving by air, no matter what the port of entry, should cultivate patience and resignation before setting foot on U.S. soil. Getting through Immigration control may take as long as 2 hours on some days, especially summer weekends. Add the time it takes to clear Customs and you'll see that you should make very generous allowance for delay in planning connections between international and domestic flights—an average of 2 to 3 hours at least.

In contrast, travelers arriving by car, rail, or ferry from Canada will find border-crossing formalities streamlined to the vanishing point. And air travelers from Canada, Bermuda, and some places in the Caribbean can sometimes go through Customs and Immigration at the point of departure, which is much quicker and less painful.

For further information about travel to and around Seattle and Portland, see "Getting There" in chapters 2 and 12, and "Getting Around" in chapters 3 and 13.

International visitors can also buy a **USA Railpass,** good for 15 or 30 days of unlimited nationwide travel on **Amtrak** (☎ **800/872-7245**). The pass is available through many foreign travel agents and at any staffed Amtrak station in the United States. The price at press time for a 15-day peak period pass was $375, and for a

15-day off-peak period pass $260; a 30-day peak period pass cost $480, and a 30-day off-peak period pass was $350. (With a foreign passport, you can also buy passes at major Amtrak offices in the United States, including locations in San Francisco, Los Angeles, Chicago, New York, Miami, Boston, and Washington, D.C.) Reservations are generally required and should be made for each part of your trip as early as possible.

Visitors should also be aware of the limitations of long-distance rail travel in the United States. With a few notable exceptions (for instance, the Northeast Corridor line between Boston and Washington, D.C.), service is rarely up to European standard: delays are common, routes are limited and often infrequently served, and fares are rarely significantly lower than discount airfares. Thus, cross-country train travel should be approached with caution.

The cheapest way to travel the United States is by bus. **Greyhound** (☎ **800/ 231-2222**), the nation's nationwide bus line, offers an **Ameripass** for unlimited travel for seven days (for $179), 15 days (for $289), and 30 days (for $399). Bus travel in the United States can be both slow and uncomfortable, so this option is not for everyone.

FAST FACTS: For the Foreign Traveler

Accommodations   It is always a good idea to make hotel reservations as soon as you know your trip dates. Reservations require a deposit of one night's payment. Seattle and Portland are particularly busy during summer months, and hotels book up in advance, especially on weekends when there is a festival on. If you do not have reservations, it is best to look for a room in the midafternoon. If you wait until evening, you run the risk that hotels will be filled.

In the United States, major downtown hotels, which cater primarily to business travelers, commonly offer weekend discounts of as much as 50% to entice vacationers to fill empty rooms. Note that rates in Seattle and Portland tend to go up in the summer, when there is a greater demand. If you wish to save money and don't mind cloudy or rainy weather, consider visiting sometime other than summer, though these cities really are at their best when the sun is shining.

Automobile Organizations   Auto clubs will supply maps, suggested routes, guidebooks, accident and bail-bond insurance, and emergency road service. The major auto club in the United States, with 955 offices nationwide, is the **American Automobile Association (AAA).** Members of some foreign auto clubs have reciprocal arrangements with the AAA and enjoy its services at no charge. If you belong to an auto club, inquire about AAA reciprocity before you leave. If your driver's license isn't in English, check with your foreign auto club to see if they can provide you with an International Driving Permit validating your foreign license in the United States. You may be able to join the AAA even if you are not a member of a reciprocal club. To inquire, call ☎ **800/AAA-HELP.** In addition, some automobile rental agencies now provide these services, so you should inquire about their availability when you rent your car.

Automobile Rentals   To rent a car you need a major credit card and a valid driver's license. Sometimes a passport or an international driver's license is also required if your driver's license is in a language other than English. You usually need to be at least 25, although some companies do rent to younger people but may add a daily surcharge. Be sure to return your car with the same amount of gasoline you started out with as rental companies charge excessive prices for gas. Keep in mind that a separate motorcycle-driver's license is required in most states. See "Getting Around" in chapters 3 and 13 for specifics on auto rental in Seattle and Portland.

Business Hours   Banks are open weekdays from 9am to 5pm, with later hours on Friday; many banks are now open on Saturday also. There is also 24-hour access to banks through automatic teller machines (ATMs) at most banks and other outlets. Most offices are open weekdays from 9am to 5pm. Most post offices are open weekdays from 8am to 5pm, with shorter hours on Saturday. In general, stores open between 9 and 10am and close between 5 and 6pm, Monday through Saturday; stores in malls generally stay open until 9pm; some department stores stay open till 9pm on Thursday and Friday evening; and many stores are open on Sunday from 11am to 5 or 6pm.

Climate   See "Climate" in section 2 of chapters 2 and 12.

Currency   See "Money" in "Preparing for Your Trip," above.

Currency Exchange   You will find currency exchange services in major airports with international service (including Seattle-Tacoma International Airport). Elsewhere, they may be quite difficult to come by.

To exchange money in Seattle, go to **American Express,** 600 Stewart St. (☎ **206/441-8622**), or **Thomas Cook,** 906 Third Ave. (☎ **206/623-4012**) or Westlake Center (☎ **206/682-4525**). To exchange money in Portland, go to **American Express,** 1100 SW Sixth Ave. (☎ **206/226-2961**), or **Thomas Cook** at Powell's Travel Store, 701 SW Sixth Ave. (☎ **206/222-2665**).

Drinking Laws   The legal drinking age in both Washington and Oregon is 21. The penalties for driving under the influence of alcohol are stiff.

Electricity   The United States uses 110 to 120 volts AC (60 cycles), compared to 220 to 240 volts AC (50 cycles), in most of Europe. In addition to a 110-volt converter, small appliances of non-American manufacture, such as hair dryers or shavers, will require a plug adapter with two flat, parallel pins.

Embassies & Consulates   All embassies are located in the national capital, Washington, D.C. Some consulates are located in major cities, and most nations have a mission to the United Nations in New York City. Listed here are embassies and consulates of some major English-speaking countries. If you are from another country, you can obtain the telephone number of your embassy or consulate by calling **Information** in Washington, D.C. (☎ **202/555-1212**).

- **Australia**   The embassy is at 1601 Massachusetts Ave. NW, Washington, DC 20036 (☎ **202/797-3000**). The nearest consulate is in **San Francisco** at 1 Bush St., San Francisco, CA 94104-4425 (☎ **415/362-6160**).
- **Canada**   The embassy is at 501 Pennsylvania Ave. NW, Washington, DC 20001 (☎ **202/682-1740**). The regional consulate is at 412 Plaza 600 Building, Sixth Ave. and Stewart St., Seattle, WA 98101-1286 (☎ **206/443-1777**).
- **Ireland**   The embassy is at 2234 Massachusetts Ave. NW, Washington, DC 20008 (☎ **202/462-3939**). The nearest consulate is in **San Francisco** at 44 Montgomery St., Suite 3830, San Francisco, CA 94104 (☎ **415/392-4214**).
- **New Zealand**   The embassy is at 37 Observatory Circle NW, Washington, DC 20008 (☎ **202/328-4800**). The nearest consulate is in **Los Angeles** at 12400 Wilshire Blvd., Suite 1150, Los Angeles, CA 90025 (☎ **310/207-1605**).
- **United Kingdom**   The embassy is at 3100 Massachusetts Ave. NW, Washington, DC 20008 (☎ **202/462-1340**). There is a consulate in **Seattle** at 999 Third Ave., Suite 820, Seattle, WA 98104 (☎ **206/622-9255**).

Emergencies　Call **911** to report a fire, call the police, or get an ambulance.

If you encounter traveler's problems, contact the **Traveler's Aid Society** (in Seattle ☎ **206/461-3888**), a nationwide, nonprofit, social-service organization geared to helping travelers in difficult straits. Their services might include reuniting families separated while traveling, providing food and/or shelter to people stranded without cash, or even emotional counseling. If you're in trouble, seek them out.

Gasoline (Petrol)　One U.S. gallon equals 3.75 liters, while 1.2 U.S. gallons equals one Imperial gallon. You'll notice there are several grades (and price levels) of gasoline available at most gas stations. And you'll also notice that their names change from company to company. The unleaded ones with the highest octane are the most expensive (most rental cars take the least expensive "regular" unleaded) and leaded gas is the least expensive, but only older cars can take this any more, so check if you're not sure.

In Oregon you are not allowed to pump your own gasoline, but in Washington "self-service" gas stations are common and usually are less expensive than full-service stations.

Holidays　On the following legal national holidays, banks, government offices, post offices, and many stores, restaurants, and museums are closed: January 1 (New Year's Day); third Monday in January (Martin Luther King Jr. Day); third Monday in February (Presidents' Day, Washington's Birthday); last Monday in May (Memorial Day); July 4 (Independence Day); first Monday in September (Labor Day); second Monday in October (Columbus Day); November 11 (Veterans Day/Armistice Day); fourth Thursday in November (Thanksgiving Day); December 25 (Christmas Day).

The Tuesday following the first Monday in November is Election Day and is a legal holiday in presidential election years.

Languages　Major hotels may have multilingual employees. Unless your language is very obscure, they can usually supply a translator on request.

Legal Aid　If you are stopped for a minor driving infraction (for example, of the highway code, such as speeding), never attempt to pay the fine directly to the police officer; you may wind up arrested on the much more serious charge of attempted bribery. Pay fines by mail, or directly into the hands of the clerk of the court. If accused of a more serious offense, it is wise to say and do nothing before consulting a lawyer. Under U.S. law, an arrested person is allowed one telephone call to a party of his or her choice. Call your embassy or consulate.

Mail　If you want to receive mail on your vacation and you aren't sure of your address, your mail can be sent to you, in your name, c/o General Delivery at the main post office of the city or region where you expect to be. The addressee must pick it up in person and produce proof of identity (driver's license, credit card, passport, etc.).

Generally to be found at intersections, mailboxes are blue with a red-and-white stripe and carry the inscription U.S. mail. If your mail is addressed to a U.S. destination, don't forget to add the five-figure postal code, or ZIP (zone improvement plan) Code, after the two-letter abbreviation of the state to which the mail is addressed (OR for Oregon, WA for Washington, CA for California, and so on).

Newspapers/Magazines　National newspapers include *The New York Times, USA Today,* and the *Wall Street Journal.* National news weeklies include *Newsweek, Time,* and *U.S. News and World Report.* For local news publications, see "Fast Facts" for Seattle and Portland in chapters 3 and 13.

Radio & Television   Radio and TV, with four coast-to-coast networks—ABC, CBS, NBC, and Fox—joined by the Public Broadcasting System (PBS) and the cable network CNN, play a major part in American life. In big cities, viewers have a choice of about a dozen channels (including the UHF channels), most of them transmitting 24 hours a day, without counting the pay-TV channels showing recent movies or sports events. All options are usually indicated on your hotel TV set. You'll also find a wide choice of local radio stations, each broadcasting particular kinds of talk shows and/or music—classical, country, jazz, pop, gospel— punctuated by news broadcasts and frequent commercials.

Safety   See "Safety" in "Preparing for Your Trip," above.

Taxes   In the United States there is no value-added tax (VAT) or other indirect tax at a national level. Every state, and each city in it, can levy a local tax on all purchases, including hotel and restaurant checks, airline tickets, and so on. In Seattle and King County the sales tax rate is 8.6%. In Portland and the rest of Oregon, there is no sales tax.

Telephone, Telegraph, Telex & Fax   The telephone system in the United States is run by private corporations, so rates, especially for long distance service, can vary widely, even on calls made from public telephones. Local calls in the United States usually cost 25¢.

Generally, hotel surcharges on long-distance and local calls are astronomical. You are usually better off using a public pay telephone, which you will find clearly marked in most public buildings and private establishments as well as on the street. Outside metropolitan areas, public telephones are more difficult to find. Stores and gas stations are your best bet.

Most long-distance and international calls can be dialed directly from any phone. For calls to Canada and other parts of the United States, dial 1 followed by the area code and the seven-digit number. For international calls, dial 011 followed by the country code, city code, and the telephone number of the person you wish to call.

For reversed-charge or collect calls, and for person-to-person calls, dial 0 (zero, not the letter "O"), followed by the area code and number you want; an operator will then come on the line, and you should specify that you are calling collect, or person-to-person, or both. If your operator-assisted call is international, ask for the overseas operator.

For local directory assistance ("information"), dial ☎ 555-1212; for long-distance information, dial 1, then the appropriate area code and ☎ 555-1212.

Like the telephone system, telegraph and telex services are provided by private corporations like ITT, MCI, and, above all, **Western Union.** You can bring your telegram to the nearest Western Union office (there are hundreds across the country), or dictate it over the phone (a toll-free call, ☎ **800/325-6000**). You can also telegraph money, or have it telegraphed to you very quickly over the Western Union system.

If you need to send a fax, almost all shops that make photocopies offer fax service as well.

Telephone Directory   There are two kinds of telephone directories available to you. The general directory is the so-called **White Pages,** in which private and business subscribers are listed in alphabetical order.

The inside front cover lists emergency numbers for police, fire, and ambulance, as well as other vital numbers (coast guard, poison control center, crime-victims hot line, and so on). The first few pages are devoted to community-service numbers, including a guide to long-distance and international calling, complete with country codes and area codes.

The second directory, printed on yellow paper (hence its name, **Yellow Pages**), lists local services, businesses, and industries by type, with an index at the back. The listings cover not only such obvious items as automobile repair services by make of car, or drugstores (pharmacies)—often by geographical location—but also restaurants by type of cuisine and geographical location, bookstores by special subject and/or language, places of worship by religious denomination, and other information that the tourist might otherwise not readily find. The Yellow Pages also include city plans or detailed area maps, often showing postal zip codes and public transportation.

Time The United States is divided into four time zones (six, if Alaska and Hawaii are included). From east to west, these are: eastern standard time (EST), central standard time (CST), mountain standard time (MST), Pacific standard time (PST), Alaska standard time (AST), and Hawaii standard time (HST). Always keep changing time zones in mind if you are traveling (or even telephoning) long distance in the United States. For example, noon in Seattle (PT) is 1pm in Denver (MT), 2pm in Chicago (CT), 3pm in New York City (ET), 11am in Anchorage (AT), and 10am in Honolulu (HT). Daylight saving time is in effect from 2am on the last Sunday in April until 2am on the last Sunday in October except in Arizona, Hawaii, part of Indiana, and Puerto Rico. Daylight saving time moves the clock 1 hour ahead of standard time.

Tipping This is part of the American way of life, on the principle that you must expect to pay for any service you get. Here are some rules of thumb:

Bartenders: 10% to 15%.
Bellhops: at least 50¢ per piece; $2 to $3 for a lot of baggage.
Cab drivers: 15% of the fare.
Cafeterias, fast-food restaurants: no tip
Chambermaids: $1 a day.
Checkroom attendants (restaurants, theaters): $1 per garment.
Cinemas, movies, theaters: no tip.
Doormen (hotels or restaurants): not obligatory.
Gas-station attendants: no tip.
Hairdressers: 15% to 20%.
Redcaps (airport and railroad stations): at least 50¢ per piece, $2 to $3 for a lot of baggage.
Restaurants, nightclubs: 15% to 20% of the check.
Sleeping-car porters: $2 to $3 per night to your attendant.
Valet parking attendants: $1.

Toilets Foreign visitors often complain that public toilets (or "restrooms") are hard to find in most U.S. cities. True, there are none on the streets, but the visitor can usually find one in a bar, restaurant, hotel, museum, department store, or service station and it will probably be clean (although the last-mentioned sometimes leaves much to be desired).

Note, however, that some restaurants and bars display a notice that "Toilets Are for the Use of Patrons Only." You can ignore this sign, or better yet, avoid arguments by ordering a cup of coffee or a soft drink, which will qualify you as a patron. The cleanliness of toilets at railroad stations and bus depots may be questionable; some public places are equipped with pay toilets, which require you to insert one or more coins into a slot on the door before it will open.

Index

See also separate Accommodations and Restaurant indexes, below.

SEATTLE ACCOMODATIONS

FROMMER'S COMPLETE TRAVEL GUIDES
*(Comprehensive guides to destinations around the world, with
selections in all price ranges—from deluxe to budget)*

Acapulco, Ixtapa & Zihuatenejo
Alaska
Amsterdam
Arizona
Atlanta
Australia
Austria
Bahamas
Barcelona, Madrid & Seville
Belgium, Holland & Luxembourg
Bermuda
Boston
Budapest & the Best of Hungary
California
Canada
Cancún, Cozumel & the Yucatán
Cape Cod, Nantucket & Martha's Vineyard
Caribbean
Caribbean Cruises & Ports of Call
Caribbean Ports of Call
Carolinas & Georgia
Chicago
Colorado
Costa Rica
Denver, Boulder & Colorado Springs
England
Europe
Florida
France
Germany
Greece
Hawaii
Hong Kong
Honolulu, Waikiki & Oahu
Ireland
Israel
Italy
Jamaica & Barbados
Japan
Las Vegas
London
Los Angeles
Maryland & Delaware
Maui

Mexico
Miami & the Keys
Montana & Wyoming
Montréal & Québec City
Munich & the Bavarian Alps
Nashville & Memphis
Nepal
New England
New Mexico
New Orleans
New York City
Northern New England
Nova Scotia, New Brunswick
   & Prince Edward Island
Paris
Philadelphia & the Amish Country
Portugal
Prague & the Best of the Czech Republic
Provence & the Riviera
Puerto Rico
Rome
San Antonio & Austin
San Diego
San Francisco
Santa Fe, Taos & Albuquerque
Scandinavia
Scotland
Seattle & Portland
South Pacific
Spain
Switzerland
Thailand
Tokyo
Toronto
Tuscany & Umbria
U.S.A.
Utah
Vancouver & Victoria
Vienna & the Danube Valley
Virgin Islands
Virginia
Walt Disney World & Orlando
Washington, D.C.
Washington & Oregon

FROMMER'S DOLLAR-A-DAY BUDGET GUIDES
(The ultimate guides to low-cost travel)

Australia from $50 a Day
Berlin from $50 a Day
California from $60 a Day
Caribbean from $60 a Day
Costa Rica & Belize from $35 a Day
England from $60 a Day
Europe from $50 a Day
Florida from $50 a Day
Greece from $50 a Day
Hawaii from $60 a Day
India from $40 a Day

Ireland from $45 a Day
Israel from $45 a Day
Italy from $50 a Day
London from $60 a Day
Mexico from $35 a Day
New York from $75 a Day
New Zealand from $50 a Day
Paris from $70 a Day
San Francisco from $60 a Day
Washington, D.C., from $50 a Day

FROMMER'S PORTABLE GUIDES
(Pocket-size guides for travelers who want everything in a nutshell)

Charleston & Savannah
Dublin
Las Vegas
Maine Coast
New Orleans

Puerto Vallarta, Manzanillo & Guadalajara
San Francisco
Venice
Washington, D.C.

FROMMER'S IRREVERENT GUIDES
(Wickedly honest guides for sophisticated travelers)

Amsterdam
Chicago
London
Manhattan

Miami
New Orleans
Paris
San Francisco

Santa Fe
U.S. Virgin Islands
Walt Disney World
Washington, D.C.

FROMMER'S AMERICA ON WHEELS
(Everything you need for a successful road trip, including full-color road maps and ratings for every hotel)

California & Nevada
Florida
Great Lakes States & Midwest
Mid-Atlantic
New England & New York

Northwest & Great Plains
South-Central States & Texas
Southeast
Southwest

FROMMER'S BY NIGHT GUIDES
(The series for those who know that life begins after dark)

Amsterdam
Chicago
Las Vegas
London
Los Angeles

Madrid & Barcelona
Manhattan
Miami
New Orleans

Paris
Prague
San Francisco
Washington, D.C.

WHEREVER YOU TRAVEL, *H*ELP IS NEVER FAR AWAY.

From planning your trip to providing travel assistance along the way, American Express® Travel Service Offices are always there to help you do more.

> ## *Seattle/Portland*

American Express Travel Service
Plaza 600 Building
600 Stewart Street
Seattle, WA
206/441-8622

American Express Travel Service
Standard Plaza Building
1100 S.W. Sixth Street
Portland, OR
503/226-2961

do more AMERICAN EXPRESS
Travel

http://www.americanexpress.com/travel

American Express Travel Service Offices are located throughout the United States. For the office nearest you, call 1-800-AXP-3429.